Andrew Marr was born in Glasgow in 1959. He studied English at the University of Cambridge and has since enjoyed a long career in political journalism, working for the *Scotsman*, the *Independent*, the *Daily Express* and the *Observer*. From 2000 to 2005 he was the BBC's Political Editor. He has written and presented TV documentaries on history, science and politics, and presents the weekly *Andrew Marr Show* on Sunday mornings on BBC1 and *Start the Week* on Radio 4. Andrew's two books spanning the history of the twentieth century – *A History of Modern Britain* and *The Making of Modern Britain* – have been huge *Sunday Times* bestsellers. Both books led to eponymous prime time BBC2 documentaries, and Andrew's inimitable way of bringing politics and history to life in series such as these has made him a much-loved household name. Andrew lives in London with his family.

Further praise for **The Making of Modern Britain**

'[Andrew Marr] traces our painful transformation from a tired, sprawling imperial power into a taut modern democracy . . . This is the most exciting book of history I can remember reading, not least because it tells a story I feel I know already. The route is familiar, the scenery startlingly novel . . . Exhilarating'   *Spectator*

'Exciting and enjoyable to read . . . It is the social crazes for things such as smoking, dancing and nudity and the cameo portraits of eccentrics that keep Marr's narrative so lively'   *Daily Mail*

'Both a fabulous history and a good read'   *Irish Times*

'A brainy book by a compelling talker . . . Marr has a keen journalistic eye for the colours as they shifted – for the fug of the Edwardian music hall, the ice of the trenches, and the painted-on beams of newly built homes'   *Daily Telegraph*

Also by Andrew Marr

MY TRADE
A Short History of British Journalism

A HISTORY OF MODERN BRITAIN

Andrew Marr

THE MAKING OF MODERN BRITAIN

From Queen Victoria to VE Day

PAN BOOKS

First published 2009 by Macmillan

First published in paperback 2010 by Pan Books
an imprint of Pan Macmillan, a division of Macmillan Publishers Limited
Pan Macmillan, 20 New Wharf Road, London N1 9RR
Basingstoke and Oxford
Associated companies throughout the world
www.panmacmillan.com

ISBN 978-0-330-51099-8

Typeset by SetSystems Ltd, Saffron Walden, Essex
Printed in the UK by CPI Mackays, Chatham ME8 5TD

Visit www.panmacmillan.com to read more about all our books
and to buy them. You will also find features, author interviews and
news of any author events, and you can sign up for e-newsletters
so that you're always first to hear about our new releases.

For Jackie

Contents

Preface

This new book comes both before and after. I wrote it after my *History of Modern Britain*, which ran from the austerity years at the end of the Second World War to the current time – from Grey to Brown. Here, I describe the near half-century before that. Those forty-five years, short enough, were crammed, almost modern, and tragic. They include the Edwardian age, which was one of the most interesting periods in all British history, both world wars, and the wild roller-coaster ride of the twenties and thirties. This was the time when modern Britain was born. We had been one thing – an empire – and became another – a democracy. At the time few people realized how incompatible the two things are. We moved from living in Britannia, with her king-emperors and grand landed aristocracy, a place where most people could not vote, and found ourselves in Britain, a northern welfare state in the shadow of the United States. On the way, millions of people struggled with the dilemma of how to live a good life. It was a time of new technologies, political uproar and fights about class and sex. It was a time of fools and visionaries and heroes – sometimes, as in the case of Winston Churchill, whose spirit stalks these pages, all of them wrapped up in a single life.

Looking back, we learn to see ourselves more sharply. Our forebears were living on the lip of the future, just as we are. Their illusions about what was to come should make us, right now, a little humble. They were tough, passionate and young, however ancient they seem now. They worried about sleaze, told bad jokes, liked films and fatty foods, and occasionally rose to greatness when tested by terrible times. Inevitably, the two world wars overshadow much of the life around them. In recent years both have been reassessed, quite roughly. For many the Great War was converted from a significant national triumph to an inhuman and pointless disaster. Some say that by paving the way for Lenin, Stalin and Hitler, it was one of the great failures of humankind. The Second World War is now being almost as radically reassessed. Did we really have to fight it? Would Hitler not have softened into a non-genocidal if autocratic leader had Britain done a deal in 1940? Perhaps there would have been no Holocaust, the Empire would have slowly evolved into a federation of democracies and, because the United States would have stayed away, there would have been no Cold War, with its threat of global annihilation, either? Since Britannia's role in the opening stages of both world conflicts was pivotal, these are clearly huge questions about the role of the British in modern times.

No one can be sure about the lost futures that vanished with paths not taken. But the Kaiser's German empire was an expansionist military regime, with little real parliamentary safeguard, which was intent on dominating Europe. It offered an alternative version of modernity, a powerful autocratic one, which came very close to triumphing. The future for Europeans would not have been either peaceful or democratic had the German armies broken through in 1914, or in 1918. Certainly, the fate of the colonized around the world would not have been pleasanter. Had Britain succumbed in 1940 to the Nazi offer – keep your empire and we will keep Europe – then there is no evidence that Hitler would have renounced his obsessive desire to sweep Jewry from Europe. Nor is there much evidence that he would have kept his word. He would have been in a better position to defeat Stalin, it is true; yet a longer, even bloodier conflict would surely have followed, since a total German invasion of European and Asian Russia seems impossible. Atomic weaponary would have become real inside Germany, at least as quickly (probably more quickly) as it did at Los Alamos.

And the British? Linked to a fading imperial past but without the markets or industry to sustain or protect the old glory, we would have crumbled into a vassal state, one act of appeasement followed by another, as Churchill predicted. There would have been no Atlantic alliance and America would have gone her own way, probably forced to accept a world divided into zones of influence – Nazi, Russian, Japanese and so on. For all the horrors of the past century, this does not seem an appetizing alternative. So, for this writer, the wars for the protection of democracy were real conflicts, which could not have been side-stepped and which, once begun, had to be won.

My last book described what I called with only some journalistic flippancy the defeat of politics by shopping. That is, the ideologies were trounced by consumerist materialism. It takes a lot of politics, of course, to set up and maintain a market-dominated and market-mimicking way of life. It was not inevitable; there were other roads not taken. This book describes what happened before the triumph of the market, or 'shopping', when it seemed the world would be shaped by politics. It was no paradise. If these were the decades when modern Britain was born, it was a bloody and painful birth. The people whose blood was spilt and who experienced the pain looked different from us, smelt different and thought differently. But in the majority of cases they were our close relatives. Their idealism, their mistakes, even their hobbies and entertainments, have plenty to teach us still.

Like the previous book, this one accompanies a BBC2 television series. In both cases, I wrote the book first, relying on my own research – and so the mistakes really are mine. Then, working with friends and colleagues, we reshaped the material to form the documentaries. The films and the book are not the same, however. There are many stories, judgements and characters in these pages that do not appear on screen; and there are a few points covered in the TV series that are not described here, usually because they were highlighted by one of the directors or researchers. But this was written as a book, not as something to accompany something else. My only guiding principle is that I have kept in what is most important, and what interested me most. The last few years have been grim ones for patriotic people in Britain, when our politics have seemed embarrassing and we have almost drowned in a dirty puddle of mutual recrimination. The past was not so totally different; what we need most is perspective. My dream is that by returning to our not-so-distant history, I might remind readers why, with all its faults, this is a lucky place to be living in, and one we can be quietly proud of.

Andrew Marr
June 2009

Part One

LIVING IN THE FUTURE

1900–1914

Don't worry, darlin'
No baby, don't you fret
We're livin' in the future,
And none of this has happened yet

Bruce Springsteen,
'Livin' in the Future', 2007

Edwardians: the Shock of the Familiar

They are very far, and strangely near. Almost nobody is still alive who remembers Edwardian Britain. To that extent, it has become proper history. Its rigid class distinctions, its imperial pride, its strange ideas – from theosophy to racial purity – are the vivid coral of a lost world. Few of us would feel at home there for any length of time. Every town had places where the children were literally shoeless and where people were withering (not growing fatter) from malnutrition. The smells of the town included human excrement and unwashed bodies, along with tobacco, beer, coal smoke and the rich reek of horse. Child prostitutes were readily available on busy streets. The largest single group of the employed were not factory workers but domestic servants. Every middle-class household had a maid, or maids, a cook, and often a gardener or groom. Class distinction was not an abstract thing, but present in most houses, standing quietly in the room.

Today we still read one another instantly by clothing. A Barbour jacket means one thing, a hoodie another. Everyone can spot a cheap suit bought for that first job. But in Edwardian Britain the distinctions of dress were sharper and harsher. A shopkeeper's assistant without a tail-coat could not stroll along the seafront promenade on a Sunday. An aristocrat seen wearing a coloured tie with a morning coat was angrily rebuked by his monarch. Respectable women always wore hats and gloves when outdoors. Gaiters, top hats with ribbons, pantaloons, three-inch boiled collars all sent messages, meaning drayman, bishop, suffragist and 'masher'. For the poor there was no state welfare, just charity relief or the threat of the dreaded work-house. Union flags billowed above the buildings. Race destiny was accepted by nearly everyone. We have a state. They had an empire.

The streets were crowded, as they are now, and noisy. But the omnibuses were horse-drawn, the carts and hansom cabs likewise, and the noise was of hooves, neighing, whips and cursing. Bicycling was popular and there were a few cars, regarded with amusement or suspicion as they passed, driven by people dressed, in the words of one observer, like 'a cross between an overgrown goat and a doormat'. The first fatal accident involving a pedestrian and a car is generally reckoned to have happened in the Lower Shoreham Road in Hove, Sussex. The car was doing a dangerous 8 m.p.h. Crime was, by today's standards, remarkably low. Yet anyone could walk into one of numerous shops and buy a revolver. The fashionable Webley-Green could be had blued or in nickel plate, with an ivory or mother-of-pearl handle. Edwardian Britain was an armed country, even after the Pistols Act of 1903 thoughtfully banned sales of handguns to people under eighteen or 'drunken or insane'. In the 'Tottenham Outrage' of 1909, police chasing a gang simply picked up four pistols from passers-by for the pursuit; other armed citizens joined in. Regional accents were much stronger, suspicion of foreigners much more intense. As George Orwell noted later, Chinamen were sinister and funny too; Africans simple-minded; Indians loyal, or alternatively treacherous. There was music everywhere, but it was live and not recorded, tinkling out of pubs or being lustily sung in the open air. Yet the air of the cities, at least, was rarely open. Thick palls hung over industrial Yorkshire, the Clyde and London. When the 1906 Liberal government won its landslide victory and the new cabinet ministers were summoned to see the King, they could not find their way back from Buckingham Palace in the fog and had to feel past rows of horses with their hands.

Yet in so many other ways, Edwardian Britain confronts us with the shock of the entirely familiar. If you walk through most British town centres and look only in front then, yes, the Edwardians and Victorians have gone. The old specialist shops with tradesmen's bicycles outside and the freshly scrubbed steps have been replaced by large glass chain-store frontages and a glut of metal, parked or crawling cars. But raise your gaze by a few degrees and often you find they are still with us. There are the elaborate brickwork upper storeys, fake turrets, old chimneys, faded shop signs, dates, spires and elaborate windows, evidence that these buildings were originally erected by craftsmen before the First World War. When they first went up, on wooden scaffolding ringing to the sound of Irish voices, the people who moved in were, like us, fascinated by celebrity gossip which they devoured in cheap newspapers and the popular magazines. They ate fish and chips and drank quite a lot, even by our standards. Though sex outside marriage and illegitimate children were matters to be ashamed of, there was plenty of sexual tension in the air. The upper classes and working classes behaved in ways that horrified the middle, who followed awful murders, worried about the unruly young and argued about divorce, state pensions, socialism and unemployment much as we do. In the new luxury variety halls and huge theatres, working-class culture had seized the imagination of the middle classes too, with sentimental songs, magicians, dancers, entertainers, infuriatingly hummable tunes and bad jokes – very much as happened when television culture arrived sixty years later. They were also great club-formers, creating endless leagues and associations, including many of today's football and other sporting clubs.

As now, the middle classes looked to science to make life easier, and to save the world from possible calamities ahead. In the first *Illustrated London News* of 1901, various eminent scientists were asked to give their predictions about the new century. Sir Norman Lockyer explains that studying sunspots will enable people to forecast the weather, tackling 'famines in India, and droughts in Australia' long in advance. Sir W. H. Preece, co-inventor of the wireless telegraph, thinks that 'the people of 2000 will smile at our achievements as we smile at those of 1800' but warns that wireless communications have no further to go and is dubious about whether man will really fly through the air. Sir John Wolfe Barry, the engineer of Tower Bridge, believes we will see wave power and hydro-electric power in the twentieth century; though he also predicts 'moving platforms' above and below the streets to ease congestion. Sir William Crookes suspects telephones will become popular, and is interested in 'radium' as a new source of energy – predictions which he rather spoils by suggesting that all London will be covered by a large glass lid to deal with the weather. Sir Henry Roscoe, president of the Chemical Society, believes the 'annihilation of distance' cannot be carried much further in the twentieth century: 'The Atlantic voyage, for instance, which we can now accomplish in five days, is not likely to be reduced to one.'

If the scientists were hit and miss about the future, the political visionaries were mostly miss. There was a general assumption, which extended to self-proclaimed radicals and liberals, that the Empire would continue to be huge while government would be small. Income tax had shot up, because of the Boer War, to the unseemly figure of a shilling in the pound – that is, 5 per cent. The war had increased public spending as a percentage of national income to nearly 15 per cent. It would fall towards 10 per cent until the First World War sent it rocketing to levels closer to those of the 1970s. The reformed and quite efficient civil service stood at around 116,000 (500,000 now, despite computers) though it would double in size in the Edwardian period. The House of Lords was still the cockpit of aristocracy and the prime minister sat there, not in the Commons – though Lord Salisbury would be the last British leader to do that. The richest peers lived on a scale barely comprehensible even after the age of hedge-fund managers and internet moguls. They had hundreds of personal servants. One had a private army, another a large private orchestra which travelled abroad with him. At Chatsworth, 300 torchbearers stood on the main avenue to welcome royal visitors. In London, the great ducal town houses were more like the palaces of lesser continental monarchs. Yet the wealth of the industrialists and financiers had eaten deeply into the landed gentry, diluting the old aristocrats. Their handbook, *Debrett's Peerage*, was vastly swollen by new baronets. In the Commons, the party of the left, the Liberals, was still dominated by aristocrats or by commoners who had done so well they sounded like aristocrats. There were barely any working-class MPs.

The greatest crisis at the start of the century was the South African War, in which a struggling British army was trying to exert imperial domination over small Dutch-speaking republics. At home it uncorked a fizz of patriotism, with city workers queuing to sign up as volunteers, noblemen financing their own detachments, and all kinds of adverts taking on a military theme. Drab khaki (the word comes from an Indian one for dust), which had replaced easy-to-hit scarlet as the British army's field colour, was being worn by fashionable women. When the isolated town of Mafeking was eventually relieved, the scenes of rejoicing were so exuberant that 'mafficking' became a word meaning, roughly speaking, to go wild in public. When Winston Churchill escaped from Boer captivity, the papers had a field day and the music halls satirized the bumptious young man. Yet all this enthusiasm could not hide the fact that Britain fought ineffectively at first, and then only achieved her victory by brutal new strategies, which made other Europeans shiver with detestation.

Early on, the heavily laden and cumbersome British forces found themselves outsmarted and at times cut to ribbons by Boers who knew the land, understood the value of digging trenches, and could attack in fast-moving formations they called commandos. This was as shocking for the Empire as Viet Cong guerrilla successes would be for the United States later. Eventually, under Lord Kitchener, the entire area of fighting was divided up with barbed wire fences and blockhouses, and Boer farms were burned to the ground in order to deny these early guerrillas food and shelter. The Boer women and children were homeless and were transported to badly run camps, soon called concentration camps. There, in conditions of squalor, 26,000 Boers died, most of them children. France, America, Austria and Germany expressed their horror. A brave woman, Emily Hobhouse, the daughter of a Cornish vicar, travelled to South Africa to investigate conditions there and returned to tell the British public about the flies, malnutrition and typhoid, what she described as 'wholesale cruelty' and 'murder to the children'. She enlisted political support and is only one of many radical and feisty women who set the tone of Edwardian Britain. This was a land still bestriding much of the world, but angrily self-questioning at home. And it was a well-informed nation too.

In newspapers and magazines of the day the quantity of foreign news – from the Empire, but also from the United States, continental Europe and Russia – is staggering. Not needing passports, emigrants were flooding out of British ports to Australia, Canada and South Africa. A cascade of talented Britons, fed up with class distinction, grimy towns and lack of opportunity, was flowing into America. In the other direction, refugees from Czarist pogroms or Latin poverty were coming into Britain, mainly to London but also to manufacturing cities and the great ports. There were large German colonies in

Bradford and Manchester, Italian merchants and Polish-Jewish areas. For the lucky rich it was a great age of travel and adventure. The better off set out by motor yacht or train to spend months on the Côte d'Azur, at one of the German spas or in Venice. Sporting aristocrats were busy slaughtering antelope, bison and tigers further afield: a whole dedicated class of civil servants and administrators were running the greatest imperial possession, India. With Britain controlling a quarter of the world and the world's peoples, the planet seemed open and pliant. Literate people, and most were, may well have been better informed than people today, in the age of the internet and twenty-four-hour news. They were probably more interested, because in other ways Abroad was menacing. The German threat was rising, but the danger of invasion by the French had been discussed just as fervently. America was regarded as a hugely wealthy and energetic but politically unimportant power.

Our world is visible, struggling to be born, in one of the most vivid, teeming, fast-changing, exhilarating periods in British history. London was the world's largest city, a global capital which lured anarchists and revolutionaries on the run, millionaires from America and countless poor migrants from Poland, Ireland and Italy. The speed of technological change was at least as disorientating as it is now. It was not simply cars and motorcycles and soon the first aircraft, but also impossibly large and fast ships, ocean liners and new Dreadnought battleships, so expensive they changed how Britons were taxed, as well as the new telegraph systems, electric lights and, bobbing on a distant skyline, Germany's magnificent Zeppelins. Yet the upper classes and their middle-class copy-cats were still insisting on the primary importance of a classical education. More people read ancient Greek and Latin than German or French, though thrusting and ambitious youngsters were opting for science and engineering as the new frontier.

What were these people like? Still photographs of the Edwardians, like photographs of the Victorians, chemically paint just the wrong picture. For they are still. To ensure a likeness, sitters are caught in a rictus or trance, their faces frozen and serious. They seem impossibly stern, or sometimes merely vacant, whereas we know from the written record that this was a jokey, argumentative age. The jerky energy of early film is more useful. What about 'the arts'? Are they a way into the reality of Edwardian life? This was a great age of story-telling. The Edwardians lived in the shadow of the great Victorian novelists – though both Meredith and Thomas Hardy survived into the twentieth century, the latter with his greatest period as a poet still ahead of him. But in the ripping yarn, the Edwardians were and are unsurpassed. This decade and a half saw Conan Doyle's *The Hound of the Baskervilles* and some of Sherlock Holmes's greatest cases. It was when John Buchan published *Prester John* and was working on *The Thirty-Nine Steps*; when Joseph Conrad's great sea adventures and his anarchist thriller *The Secret Agent* appeared, and the hilarious, acid-drenched stories of Saki; when H. G. Wells's finest novels were written, after his invention of modern science fiction; when Kipling was at his most famous if not at his finest. These were the years of *The Wind in the Willows*, *Peter Pan* and *The Railway Children*, which would spawn further wonderful decades of English children's stories, so that a golden glow settled on our memory of Edwardian life that has never quite been tarnished by the facts. Today an academic priesthood divides these story-tellers into a hierarchy of seriousness, but it did not seem so then, when Henry James helped Kipling at his wedding, and Conrad dedicated books to Wells. Many of their stories appeared in the teeming magazines and journals of the age such as the *Strand* and the *Illustrated London News*. The country needed entertainment. There was no broadcasting. As a result, the Edwardians had richer internal lives than most of us today; their writers will appear throughout what follows.

Something similar can be said about the graphic arts and architecture. The Edwardians were a riotously consumerist lot, just like us. Photography was not yet available on a large scale, or in colour. So advertising and illustration depended heavily on drawing and painting. And at illustration, the Edwardians were also unsurpassed. Alfred Munnings, the Victorian miller's son from Suffolk whose horse and gypsy paintings would make him rich, got his first break doing advertising posters, notably for Caley's chocolate factory. William Nicholson and James Pryde, two gloriously talented artists encouraged by Whistler, set up J. & W. Beggarstaff making posters for the theatres, woodcuts and adverts for Rowntree's cocoa. Everywhere there was drawing, from the political caricatures of *Spy* to the *Punch* work of G. D. Armour and Phil May, the latter one of the greatest geniuses of simple line drawing ever. In general Edwardian artists drew far better than artists are able to now. They were properly trained and specialized in bold, striking and often funny designs. The cities were brightly decorated, spangled with colour and wit. In grand painting, for the richest patrons, Britain was under the spell of an American, John Singer Sargent, whose technical skill and bravura still leave the observer breathless today. He had the same sort of status that Van Dyck, another incomer, once enjoyed. Below him there were confident artists such as Philip de Laszlo, who has not lasted well, and William Orpen, who has. As the decade advanced, so did the march of post-impressionist painting, then Fauve and cubist influences, as well as the Scottish Colourists. The history of art inevitably celebrates the new, but British Edwardian art was much richer than follow-the-French.

A similar flash confidence ripples out of many Edwardian public buildings. Town councils, major companies and government officials picked a bewildering number of styles, from ornate Dutch gothic to Venice-in-brick, English-cottage-on-steroids to Loire-by-gaslight. But with steel frameworks they created large, stone- and brick-fronted structures of complexity, grace and sometimes humour, which are much more enjoyable than the peevish, meaner buildings which followed between the wars. Their style was less heavy than that of the encrusted Victorians, but showed an innocent enjoyment of decoration which the theorists and minimalists would later banish. Just as Sargent's portraits show grand financiers or title-loaded aristocrats who smile back with wholly human self-mockery, so the best Edwardian buildings have the scale of an imperial age while somehow managing to avoid pomposity. One way of gauging quality in buildings is to ask how many of a certain age are later torn down and replaced. In general, we have elected to keep Edwardian buildings, including the first really popular generation of semi-detached houses, well made with 'arts and crafts' influences that flow back to the Victorians.

So, Edwardian Britannia touches modern Britain repeatedly. They were struggling with small wars abroad. They were convulsed by new technologies: the motor car, the aircraft, the motion-picture camera and the undersea telegraph cable, rather than biotechnology, digital platforms and the web. They were deeply engaged in the wider world yet sentimental about family and home, highly patriotic yet also sceptical about politicians, obsessed with crime stories and jostling each other in crowded city centres yet remarkably law abiding. They were divided by class and income and united by common prejudices and jokes which baffled outsiders. This was a roaring, unstable, fast-changing time but highly self-critical, too. Edwardian Britain was unfair and strange in many ways. But the Edwardians were evolving fast. The past is not a foreign country.

The Great Paperweight Is Lifted

Queen Victoria had died in bed, holding a crucifix. If there to ward off evil spirits, it was not powerful enough. She was being supported from behind by the Emperor of Germany, Wilhelm II, her dangerous grandson, his arm by her pillow. Immediately after she had gone, Kaiser Bill reflected: 'She has been a very great woman. Just think of it; she remembers George III and now we are in the twentieth century.'[1] Cousin Willy, as the family called him, would do his bit to ensure that it became the bloodiest century in human history. Nor was his history accurate. Though Victoria was alive when George III died, and so provided a kind of human bridge to the age of Nelson and Samuel Johnson, she was just eight months old at the time. Still, the length of her reign had been extraordinary. It made her death, coming so soon after the start of the new century, and though hardly a surprise, one of those moments which sent a shudder of awe through most of the world.

In the year of her birth, 1819, Europe had still been adjusting to the aftermath of Waterloo, British cavalry massacred eleven protestors in Manchester, Keats was writing 'Ode to a Nightingale' and Beethoven was beginning his great *Missa Solemnis*. In the midst of all this, the pregnancy of the wife of old King George's fourth son, the fat, garlicky, sadistic and fifty-year-old Duke of Kent – 'the greatest rascal left unhung' in the summing-up of one contemporary – was of significance for only one reason. Though the British crown would pass to the atrocious Prince Regent, later George IV, there was then a problem: of fifty-six grandchildren, not one was legitimate. To ensure that his child would become Queen one day, the Duke and his heavily pregnant wife, who had been living in Germany, careered across France with borrowed money in a nine-coach convoy of doctors, dogs, songbirds, maids, footmen and cooks, so that the girl was born in London – 'plump as a partridge' – as she would remain. Her uncle, soon to become George IV, hated the very idea of her and when her father died of pneumonia in Sidmouth, Devon, the outlook for the baby and her German-speaking mother had been bleak. But he mellowed. Victoria remembered his grease-painted face and wig. The next king, the cheerful old William, tried quite hard to get her outlandish name changed for the day she ascended the throne.

Had he had his way, the name he wanted, she would have been Queen Elizabeth II. Instead, she became Queen Victoria at the age of eighteen in 1837 and her name became familiar to everyone who speaks English. She was a politically active, opinionated and talented woman, who not only spoke German, French and some Italian, but later learned Hindustani too. She survived periodic outbreaks of republicanism, several assassination attempts and the death of her adored German husband, Albert, though this threw her into a decades-long gloom, earning her the dismissive moniker the Widow of Windsor. Earlier, she had been an earthy creature, who gobbled her food and had a loud laugh, particularly when her first prime minister, Lord Melbourne, was teasingly scandalizing her with his cynical stories. But slowly, as the wilder Britain of the 1840s gave way to the more ponderous, self-important imperium of the later nineteenth century, she too became a solemn, heavy-lidded presence. This is how she is remembered, a kind of fat, white queen bee, gorged on the royal jelly of imperial pride by buzzing flatterers such as Disraeli and surrounded by sleepy-eyed progeny.

Yet the nearly sixty-four years of her reign had seen Britain changed from a country ruled by a few mainly aristocratic families, still dominated by the values of landowners and protected by oak-sided sailing ships, to the centre of a global empire and an industrial urban nation in which workers had become voters. Waves of political reform in 1832, 1867 and 1884 had brought successive groups of men – property-owning, then 'respectable middle class', then working class – into the franchise. No women, yet, of course: the only woman in the land with any real political power was Victoria herself. She was well aware of the hideous conditions of industrial Britain. As a girl, she had travelled through the mining country of the Midlands, noting in 1832, the year of the first great Reform Act, that 'men, women, children, country and houses are all black ... The grass is quite blasted and black. Just now I saw an extraordinary building flaming with fire. The country continues black, engines flaming, coals in abundance, everywhere smoking and burning coal heaps, intermingled with wretched huts and carts and little ragged children.' Blake, Engels or Orwell could hardly have put it better. But 'democracy' was seen as an enemy by the Palace and most of her titled ministers, a menacing, mysterious force that could not be wholly resisted but must somehow be tamed. When she became queen, politics was mainly conducted among a few families, behind closed doors, on handwritten notes and in self-consciously classical speeches in the Commons and Lords. When she died, political rows were being fought out among titled renegades, self-made men from the Midlands and uppity lawyers with a talent for rough talking, at raucous public meetings or through newspaper columns.

By then the vast gap between how Britain saw herself, and how she really was – the chasm in which twentieth-century life would be lived – was already clear to anyone with eyes to see. Vast fleets of ironclad battleships, the clatter of lancers and hussars, the giant public celebrations, jubilees and durbars, could not hide the massive embarrassment of the British army being humiliated by the sharpshooting Dutch farmers of South Africa. In the Foreign Office by the light of gas lamps, aristocratic young men with beautiful Greek were worriedly studying German and Russian plans to drive south through the Muslim Middle East towards India itself. That great scattering of white settlers in Africa, Canada, Australia and New Zealand might have produced satisfactory washes of pink colouring on the map, but it was a thin scatter: in 1900 there were already fewer white people in the British Empire (54 million) than in Germany (56.3 million)[2] and far fewer than in the United States, which had a population of 75 million. The onetime workshop of the world was struggling too with high tariff walls overseas and old-fashioned industries. When Victoria died, Britain was importing huge quantities of German and American steel, and trying to plug the difference by digging and selling more of the coal on which these islands partially sat, hardly the sign of advanced industrial success. The shipyards were still ahead, but not always in technology. Four years before the Queen's death her son Bertie, the Prince of Wales, had retired from his favourite sport of yacht racing at Cowes. His nephew the Kaiser had beaten Bertie's *Britannia* with his new boat, and had taken to parading the latest ships of the German navy off the Isle of Wight at the same time. Bertie complained that 'Willy is a bully' and retired in a huff. In the same year the Blue Riband for Atlantic crossing times had been lost for the first time to the German liner *Kaiser Wilhelm der Grosse*, followed by the *Deutschland* in 1900. Everywhere one looked, from Gottfried Daimler's new high-speed internal combustion engine to the new electric trams, British ingenuity was failing and falling back.

So there was a grey undercurrent of melancholy and uncertainty when the Queen, in her lead-lined coffin, with a photograph and lock of John Brown's hair by her, was finally taken to Portsmouth. The Countess of Denbigh watched the Royal Naval fleet and the visiting German warships give salute after salute as the Royal Yacht *Alberta* passed. By 3 p.m. the blue sky was fading and 'a wonderful golden pink appeared in the sky and the smoke rose slowly from the guns . . . like the purple hangings ordered by the King'. She observed 'the white *Alberta* looking very small and frail next the towering battleships. We could see the motionless figures standing round the white pall which, with the crown and orb and sceptre, lay upon the coffin. Solemnly and slowly it glided over the calm blue water . . . giving one a strange choke, and a catch in one's heart.'[3] Days on, after a massive military commemoration in London which involved more men than set off in 1914 as the British Expeditionary Force to France, the Queen was finally taken to the Royal Chapel at Windsor – but because of faulty equipment (a broken trace), her horse-drawn final journey had to be completed by sailors hauling her home using the communication cord from a train, hurriedly removed for the purpose. This was hailed as a great sentimental British moment. Whatever it was, it certainly wasn't Prussian, or American, efficiency.

L. F. Austin, editor of the *Illustrated London News*, thought that when the old century had ended 'nobody was heart-stricken, for the world does not grieve over an imperceptible point of time. But at

the end of the Victorian era, who is not conscious of a great blank?'
The very words to 'God Save the King' would, he thought, sound
odd, 'a phrase so strange upon our lips that it almost makes a
stranger of him. Within the last few days, I have heard men
murmuring "the king" as if they were groping in their memories for
some ancient and unfamiliar charm.'[4] Yet others were already
impatient and keen for change. Beatrice Webb, co-founder with her
husband Sidney of the Fabian Society, Britain's successful socialist
think-tank, wrote to a friend a few days later with bitter irony: 'We
are at last free of the funeral. It has been a true national "wake", a
real debauch of sentiment and loyalty – and a most impressive
demonstration of the whole people in favour of the monarchical
principle. The streets are still black with the multitudes in mourning,
from the great ladies in their carriages to the flower girls, who are
furnished with rags of crêpe. The King is hugely popular . . . as for
the German Emperor, we all adore him!'

The science-fiction writer H. G. Wells felt frank relief. He
thought the old Queen had been like 'a great paperweight' and, now
that she was removed, he expected all kinds of new ideas to blow
around. So they would – though, as we shall see, they were not
always good ones. Henry James, the expatriate American novelist
and exquisite snob, thought 'Bertie', the new king, 'a vulgarian' and
believed Victoria had died after being sickened and humiliated by the
Boer War: 'I mourn the safe, motherly old middle-class queen who
held the nation warm under the folds of her big, hideous Scotch-
plaid shawl.' He admitted to feeling her death deeply and predicted
that 'the wild waters are upon us now'.[5] Young Winston Churchill
heard the news in snowy Winnipeg, where he was raising cash on a
lecture tour. His father had clashed with Bertie in the past and
Churchill showed no trace of sentiment in a letter to his mother: 'I
am curious to know about the King. Will it entirely revolutionize his
way of life? Will he sell his horses and scatter his Jews [a reference
to Bertie's financial friends] or will Reuben Sassoon be enshrined
among the crown jewels and other regalia? . . . Will the Keppel
[Bertie's mistress] be appointed 1st Lady of the Bedchamber?'[6]
And the vulgarian himself? Judging by the speed with which he
destroyed many treasured statues of Brown, cleared out her photographs and papers, sold her beloved house, Osborne, and tramped

around his new palaces in a trail of cigar smoke, he was not in a sentimental mood. Bertie had been a Victorian, he felt, for quite long enough.

The Chocolate Warrior

Saturday 7 July 1900 was a warm, sticky day in the narrow back streets of York. By first light, there were already plenty of people out and about. One of them was a quiet, soberly dressed man discreetly holding a notebook, standing in the shadows, watching the door of a small, dirty pub, one of fourteen nearby. Shortly after 6 a.m., people were already rattling the door of the pub, though it was slow to open this morning. Everyone who entered, and everyone who left, was noted down in the little book. In all, 550 people went in, including 113 children. After twelve hours of standing, the watcher scribbled down: 'Between 5 and 6 p.m., a woman was ejected. A row immediately ensued, the woman using language unfit for human ears. As usual, a crowd of children were keenly enjoying the scene, which lasted for about three quarters of an hour.' Just over a week later, on Sunday 15 July, the investigator was back. Even on the Sabbath, in an area with its share of Irish Catholics, all the small shops were open, doing a brisk business, particularly the fried-fish shops. Most of the women standing gossiping in the streets were in *'déshabillé'*, which in this context probably means open shirts, without hats. 'Children simply swarm . . . In the evening there were several wordy battles between women neighbours, the language being very bad . . . Between seven and eight, three men endeavoured to hold a gospel meeting, but retired after singing a hymn and giving a short address; the people apparently took no notice, but continued their conversations.' And the notetaker slipped sadly away.

What was happening in York as the old Queen lay ill would play its part in explaining why her son and grandson never faced the kind of revolutionary upheaval that ousted their cousins Czar Nicholas and Kaiser Bill. A large, mustachioed man in his late twenties had become outraged at the conditions of the poor. Benjamin Seebohm Rowntree, of mixed Danish and Yorkshire descent, was no kind of rebel. He came from a powerful, energetic strain of English life, utterly alien to London politics, grown rich on cocoa and sweets. Though clever, he did not go to one of the public schools which had sprouted up all over the country. He did not go to Oxford or Cambridge, either, though his father could easily have afforded it. The Rowntrees were Quakers. So Benjamin went to a local school in York, and then to Owens College in Manchester, set up specifically to educate people who didn't want to make that little curtsey to the Church of England needed in a country whose spiritual life was dominated by frilly bishops, vicars and the Book of Common Prayer. Rowntree's father, Joseph, had also written about the poor, and been witheringly critical of 'British civilization' while he built his cocoa and crystallized-fruit empire. It was a time of investigations into the conditions of the poorer Britons, with government Blue Books, the work of social investigator Charles Booth in London, and socialists such as the Webbs. But Rowntree, working quietly up in York, was the man who would really shock Westminster.

The way he did it was to concentrate not on one of the infamous areas of a great industrial city, which everyone knew about, but on a relatively normal, middle-sized English town known best for its great minster and quaint medieval streets. His work was astonishingly meticulous and careful. He and his investigators went from house to house from the autumn of 1899, finally reaching 11,560 families in 388 streets. The notebook jottings still provide one of the most remarkable and vivid portraits of life as it was being lived at the heyday of the British Empire by a vast swathe of native-born Britons. First, there were brief notes, house by house, going from shoemakers to labourers, widows to factory workers: 'Five children (three by first wife). Husband not quite steady, wife delicate-looking. Respectable: one boy sent to truant school . . . Father has lost an eye. House not very dirty . . . Disreputable old woman. Hawks when able. House very dirty, probably used as a house of ill-fame . . . Four boys, three girls (young). Very poor, little work. House dirty, very little furniture . . . Nine young children. Had parish relief stopped for illegitimate child. Children dirty and unruly. Query: how do they live?'

As the investigators homed in on housing conditions, again street by street, the descriptions become more detailed, and horrifying. In one street, for instance, they report of a pair of houses: 'There is only one water-tap for the whole block. There are no sinks, slops being emptied down the street grating. There are two closets [toilets] in the yard but only one is fit to use, and it is shared by fifteen families.' As the investigators dig deeper through the streets of York, their nausea and anger become more clearly visible through the dry notes. A lady inspector, probably a tough-sounding woman called May Kendall, who refused a salary and seems forgotten by history, makes her way across a brick floor, slimy with filth: 'Dirty flock bedding in living room placed on a box and two chairs. Smell of room from dirt and bad air unbearable.' Nearby, she finds no fewer than sixteen families sharing one tap: 'the grating under this water tap is used for the disposal of human excreta and was partially blocked with it when inspected . . . When inspected the table and floor were covered with crumbs, potato parings, scraps of meat on newspaper, dirty pots, etc.'

There would be a spate of similar surveys of villages and towns across England. What made Rowntree's work different was that he dug into the causes of poverty. The way wealthy Britain had dealt with it so far was to mix voluntary and religious help with a great deal of moralizing. The slums were disgusting, yes, but they were rare (Rowntree showed they were everywhere) and they were the fault of thriftless, drunken or immoral people. As *The Times* put it, responding to the furore caused by Rowntree's book, which was finally published in the year of Victoria's death: 'their wages would suffice to keep them strong and healthy, but they are thriftless; they drink and bet, or they are ignorant and careless in housekeeping'.[7] Rowntree was no stranger to moralizing – he was, after all, a teetotal Quaker – but he set out to clinically destroy the argument that poverty was the fault of the poor. He found two-thirds of people who literally did not have enough to live on 'were women deserted by men, or widowed, or people no longer able to work through illness or old age'. Others were people in work whose families were too big to feed properly. As he pointed out, he was writing at a time when the trade cycle was up, and business was good, yet for workmen at the bottom of the heap, their position 'is one of peculiar hopelessness. Their unfitness means low wages, low wages means insufficient food, insufficient food means unfitness for labour, so that the vicious circle is complete.' Again and again he finds women who tell him they hide the desperate lack of food from their husbands in order to keep them strong enough to carry on working. Hunger happened in private, among the women and children: 'Jim ollers takes 'is dinner to work, and I give it 'im as usual; 'e never knows we go without, and I never tells 'im.'

But what is enough food? Rowntree talked to experts in nutrition, and studied the diet handed out in the York workhouse to destitute people there. He then cut that back to produce the basic needed for 'bare physical efficiency' – and found that in York the wages paid for unskilled labour were not enough to provide food, clothing and shelter to sustain a family of moderate size at merely physical efficiency. Rowntree's book, called simply *Poverty: A Study of Town Life*, is generally written without apparent anger, but at times he simply lets rip:

> And let us clearly understand what 'merely physical efficiency' means. A family living upon the scale allowed for … must never spend a penny on railway fare or omnibus. They must never go into the country unless they walk. [Rowntree himself was a great lover of nature.] They must never purchase a halfpenny newspaper or spend a penny to buy a ticket for a popular concert. They must write no letters to absent children, for they cannot afford to pay the postage … The children must have no pocket money for dolls, marbles or sweets. The father must smoke no tobacco, and must drink no beer. The mother must never buy any pretty clothes … Should a child fall ill, it must be attended by the Parish doctor; should it die, it must be buried by the Parish. Finally, the wage earner must never be absent from his work for a single day.

Break any of these conditions, and the family would not have enough food to keep them going. Rowntree worked out that any labourer with three children or more, 'must pass through a time, probably lasting for about ten years when … he and his family will be underfed'. He also demonstrated, with exhaustive tables and diagrams, that almost a third of the population of York were by his definition sunk in such poverty.

Yet there were moments of jollity. Rowntree and his investigators left a vivid picture of the poor making their own entertainment in the year 1901 which deserves its place as a contrast to the unbearable bleakness of the rest of his report. He found a lot of singing:

> The rooms are, as a rule, brilliantly lit, and often gaudily, if cheaply, decorated. In winter they are always kept temptingly warm. The company is almost entirely composed of young persons, youths and girls, sitting round the room and at small tables. Often there are a considerable number of soldiers present. Everyone is drinking, but not heavily, and most of the men are smoking. At intervals, one of the company is called on for a song, and if there is a chorus, everyone who can will join in it. Many of the songs are characterized by maudlin sentimentality; others again are unreservedly vulgar. Throughout the whole assembly there is an air of jollity and an absence of irksome restraint that must prove very attractive after a day's confinement in factory or shop. In a round of public houses which the writer made one Sunday evening in May 1901, the fact of their social attractiveness struck him very forcibly.

And Rowntree pads back for his cocoa with the brave thought that it all pointed to the need 'for the establishment on temperance lines of something equally attractive'.

Rowntree's book arrived like a bomb in British politics. It showed that at the heart of the Empire, with all its pomp, wealth and self-satisfaction, around a third of people were so poor they often did not have enough to eat, and many were sunk in utter poverty as bad as that of the Czar's empire against which the communists raged. It did this clinically and statistically, in a way that was impossible to refute. Its influence, with repeated reprintings, would last until the First World War and it would later be seen as one of the seminal works of sociology, undoubtedly one of the most important books of the Edwardian age. David Lloyd George, another nonconformist shaker-upper idolized by Rowntree, would wave it at meeting after meeting. Rowntree himself, though a rather more nervous speaker, lectured across Britain, from Glasgow to Bristol, spreading the message. When he reached Birmingham and patiently explained his figures, the local screw manufacturer Arthur Chamberlain, brother of the great politician Joe, got slowly to his feet and announced that, try as he might, he could not find a hole in Rowntree's argument. Therefore, first thing the following morning, he would find out how many people in his engineering companies were getting less than 22 shillings a week, and put it right. He did just that. (There was then a strike by workers paid more than 22s, who wanted their differential maintained; but it was still an extraordinary tribute to the book.)

In the cloisters of Balliol College, Oxford, the master told a young student called William Beveridge that once he had learned all the university could teach him, he must 'go and discover why, with so much wealth in Britain, there continues to be so much poverty'.

Winston Churchill went straight out for a copy and was soon telling an audience in Blackpool about how it 'fairly made my hair stand on end'. In one review he wrote about the York poor: 'Although the British Empire is so large, they cannot find room to live in it; although it is so magnificent, they would have had a better chance of happiness if they had been born cannibal islanders of the Southern Seas ... this festering life at home makes world-wide power a mockery.' Writing to the chairman of the Midland Conservatives, Churchill returned to the theme. American labourers were better fed and more efficient than British ones: 'this is surely a fact which our unbridled Imperialists, who have no thought but to pile up armaments, taxation and territory, should not lose sight of. For my own part, I see little glory in an empire which can rule the waves and is unable to flush its sewers.'[8]

Rowntree had begun to show that the condition of the poor was not simply a matter of their moral failure. Dickens himself, followed by others, had turned Victorian sensibility round from a purely moralizing hardness to a dawning awareness of the real lives of the people of the gutter and the swamp. Yet most turned their eyes away and dreamed of finding some way of dealing with the poor that did not involve either the danger of revolution, or the character-rotting effects of more generous levels of welfare. These are the years when the Labour Party is beginning to appear as Liberal trade unionists come together, and when socialist ideas are filtering through parts of Britain via the activities of small bands of intellectuals and agitators. But most thinking people were not socialist and, before Lloyd George and Churchill broke through the crust of complacency, were against a welfare state. So what could be done? This takes us to a second character, working busily away as the old Queen expired.

Basset Hounds and Breeding

Francis Galton was one of the last survivors of the heroic period of Victorian science. He looked a little like a smaller version of Charles Darwin, which was appropriate, because he was Darwin's half cousin. They shared in Erasmus Darwin as grandfather one of the great luminaries of generous, ambitious eighteenth-century science, and Galton's family tree was festooned with genius and public service. He had been an explorer and statistician, a renowned mathematician whose discoveries ranged from the bizarre to the useful – it was Francis Galton, for example, who showed that fingerprints were unique and did not change during life, a discovery immediately put to good use by Scotland Yard. Though disagreeing with Darwin about some aspects of evolution, he was also fascinated by the subject, particularly as it applied to people. At the Science Galleries of South Kensington – a place which will recur in this book – Galton had been collecting the heights, weights, strength of squeeze and pull of English schoolchildren, trying to establish a human database. But his breakthrough moment came when he stumbled upon a book by the son of the Pre-Raphaelite painter, the sturdy squire Sir John Everett Millais. This was not a work of science or fiction, but rather more down to earth. It was the Basset Hound Club Rules and Studbook of 1874–96. Sir John kept himself amused by detailing the limited number of splodges and colours of each puppy from each pairing of basset hounds. Galton took from this what he believed to be a foolproof theory of heredity – how much of each parent, grandparent and so on, we each possess. The crucial discoveries of Mendel were not yet known in Britain, so this cannot be called in any real sense genetic science. Galton invented a new word, instead: eugenics.

   In October 1901 Galton stood up and delivered the second Huxley Lecture (in honour of 'Darwin's bulldog' and defender, who had recently died) to the Anthropological Institute. He called it 'The

Possible Improvement of the Human Breed under the Existing Conditions of Law and Sentiment'. An intellectual link between the basset hound studbook and the policies of Nazi Germany was about to be forged. Galton had created, he believed, a statistical bell curve of human qualities – the proportion of the population that was very bright, healthy, middling, and so on. This was done in detail and went far beyond easily observable differences such as height. He classified people by their 'civic worth'. Galton then applied his theory to the vast statistical and highly opinionated survey of the London East End poor by Charles Booth. As with the Poor Law Guardians and much ordinary debate at the time, economics and morality were inextricably mingled. Thus 'Class A' consisted of 'criminals, semi-criminals and loafers' while Class B comprised 'very poor persons who subsist on casual earnings, many of whom are inevitably poor from shiftlessness, idleness or drink'. The largest class, E, were 'All those with regular standard earnings of 22 to 30 shillings a week. This class is the recognized field . . . for trades unions . . . essentially the mediocre class, standing as far below the highest in civic worth as it stands above the lowest class of criminals.'[9] At the top, of course, were the rich and clever.

Galton tried to calculate the worth of children in each group, subtracting what it cost to bring them up and look after them 'when helpless through old age' from lifetime earnings. Thus: 'The worth of an average baby born to the wife of an Essex labourer . . . was found to be about five pounds.' By contrast, the worth of a child of the top class 'would be reckoned in thousands of pounds . . . They found great industries, establish vast undertakings, increase the wealth of multitudes and amass large fortunes for themselves. Others, whether they be rich or poor, are the guides and lights of the nation, raising its tone, enlightening its difficulties and imposing its ideals.' (People, in short, like Galton himself.) But where radical Liberals and socialists argued against the unfairness of these great divisions, Galton thought them natural. Society should stop the lower sort from breeding so enthusiastically, and encourage the elite to breed more. It would be 'a great benefit to the country if all habitual criminals were resolutely segregated . . . and peremptorily denied opportunities for producing offspring'. The better sort, meanwhile, should be given grants, diplomas and encouragement to marry each other and produce children, as early as possible. Male fast-breeders would be chosen through exam results and inspection of their family trees. 'The opportunities for selecting women in this way are unfortunately fewer ... In the selection of women, when nothing is known of their athletic proficiency, it would be especially necessary to pass a high and careful medical examination.' Galton wondered whether the aristocracy might help encourage high-value couples without much cash: 'It might well become a point of honour ... for noble families to gather fine specimens of humanity around them, as it is to procure and maintain fine breeds of cattle and so forth, which are costly, but repay in satisfaction.'[10]

It is tempting to dismiss all this as irrelevant ravings, forgotten in the yellowing pages of *Nature* magazine, where they sit between a discussion of agriculture in Tibet and a paper on ocean currents. Nothing could be more wrong. Galton was a scientific superstar of his day. Through the early years of the twentieth century, though elderly (and childless) he was energetically promoting eugenics, often through lectures to the newly formed Sociological Society, then carried and publicized widely through the newspapers. Demanding social pressure to stop unsuitable marriage was vital: eugenics had to be 'introduced into the national conscience, like a new religion' so that 'humanity can be represented by the fittest races'. He chose Valentine's Day 1905 to proclaim his optimism that laws restricting the freedom to marry would eventually come about: *The Times* lavishly recorded his words. Supporters came from left and right. George Bernard Shaw, at the height of his reputation as progressive dramatist and sage, proclaimed that nothing but a eugenic religion could save our civilization. It was important, he went on, 'that we never hesitate to carry out the negative side of eugenics with considerable zest, both on the scaffold and on the battlefield'.[11]

H. G. Wells had been persuaded by his agent J. B. Pinker to collect some essays about the future that he had published in British and American newspapers. In 1901, alongside Rowntree on poverty, Wells's resulting *Anticipations* was one of the talking-point books of the year. It ran to eight reprints in the first twelve months and was one of the bestsellers for the powerful circulating libraries and booksellers Mudie's and Smith's. Beatrice and Sidney Webb both thought it their favourite book of the year and were so impressed that they went to visit Wells at his Kent home to help draw him into their circle. He was introduced to A. J. Balfour, about to become prime minister, and fêted by the director of the Natural History Museum. Churchill bought a copy and liked it. As one of Wells's biographers put it, *Anticipations* 'catapulted Wellsian thought into the drawing rooms, railway cars and clubrooms of the upper and middle classes'.[12] So what was in the book? Parts are surprisingly accurate about the future. He predicts that English will be the world language by 2000 and that servants will disappear through technology. But his other messages underline the gap between Edwardian thought and ours. 'If the Jew has a certain incurable tendency to social parasitism and we make social parasitism impossible, we should abolish the Jew, and if he has not, there is no need to abolish the Jew.' Wells accepted that 'there is something very ugly about many Jewish faces but there are Gentile faces just as coarse and gross ... Many Jews are intensely vulgar in dress and bearing, materialistic in thought and cunning and base in method, but no more than many Gentiles.' And, he pointed out, Jews died earlier anyway. But there was no such shilly-shallying when it came to other races: 'And the rest, those swarms of black and brown, and dirty white, and yellow people, who do not come into the new needs of efficiency? Well, the world is a world, not a charitable institute, and I take it they will have to go. The whole tenor and meaning of the world is, they have to go ... it is their portion to die out and disappear.'

It is only fair to add that Wells revised his views on race a few years later, but the eugenics remained unapologetic when it came to drunkards, gluttons and others with inherited diseases. In his follow-up book, *Mankind in the Making*, published in 1903, he said it was 'absurd to breed our horses and sheep and improve the stock of our pigs and fowls, while we leave humanity to mate in the most heedless manner'. For people with hereditary diseases, or alcoholics, the state should use everything 'short of torture' to punish those who tried to breed. (Wells's own exuberantly unfaithful sexual habits made the finger-wagging about people mating in a heedless manner particularly hypocritical.) The point is that he was then splashing along self-confidently in the mainstream of advanced political thinking. Lord Rosebery, the former Liberal prime minister, expressed his great interest in Galton's eugenics. In 1907 the British Eugenics

Education Society, with at least half its members professional women, was launched and became hugely influential. Middle-class conversations were reported to Galton: a badly behaved child, or delinquent youth? 'Well, it wasn't a eugenic marriage, you see.' A few years later a Mrs Bolce named her daughter Eugenette, thereby boasting about her and her husband's excellent breeding stock.

In July 1912, six months after Galton's death, the First International Congress of Eugenics opened at the grand Hotel Cecil, overlooking the Thames. Its vice presidents included the Lord Chief Justice, the president of the College of Surgeons, the Lord Mayor of London, the vice chancellor of London University, the Bishops of Ripon and Birmingham, the inventor Alexander Graham Bell, the First Lord of the Admiralty ... and Winston Churchill. Major Leonard Darwin, the great scientist's last surviving child, gave a rousing opening speech calling for action against the genetically undesirable. The purpose of the congress was 'to spread far and wide the great new creed with its glittering goal of race and class improvement through selective breeding'.[13] Tragically, in this it was successful. Compulsory sterilization of different groups of people began in some American states and President Calvin Coolidge explained his 1924 Immigration Act: 'Biological laws show ... that Nordics deteriorate when mixed with other races.' Worse still, the message was well heard on the continent of Europe, in France and Scandinavia but above all in Germany, where papers on eugenics were soon being written and where, in 1905, an organization called the Race Hygiene Society was formed.

Joe's Great Rebellion

One hint of greatness is when a person attracts phrase-makers. Two of the most overused phrases used about a politician today are that all political careers end in failure and that so-and-so 'makes the political weather'. Both were first said about that party-smashing comet of late-Victorian and early-twentieth-century British politics, Joe Chamberlain. Enoch Powell, a later iconoclast, just as dangerously tempted to see ideas through to their logical conclusion, said of his fellow Midlands platform-strider: 'All political lives, unless they are cut off in midstream at a happy juncture, end in failure, because that is the nature of politics and of human affairs.' And according to Winston Churchill, Joe's sometime admirer and enemy, he 'was incomparably the most live, sparkling, insurgent, compulsive figure in British affairs . . . "Joe" was the one who made the weather. He was the man the masses knew.' Today his surname is used as shorthand reference to his younger son, the man who tried to appease Hitler at Munich. This would have staggered an Edwardian: Joe could hardly have been more famous in his day. His cartoon image was everywhere, his name was sung in music-hall songs, his speeches attracted tens of thousands and the next day filled page after page of the newspapers. His views were followed in Berlin and Moscow; he was vilified in French cartoons and he was front-page news in New York. But it did all end in failure, smashing electoral defeat in 1906, and worse. On his seventieth birthday he was greeted by a vast celebration in his political citadel, Birmingham, an orgy of processions, speeches, meals and cheering crowds – something like the civic welcome a cup-winning football team might expect today, but more so. Two days later, back home at his London house, the hero failed to appear downstairs for a dinner appointment. He was stuck on the bathroom floor, hit by a stroke which condemned him to a pitiful afterlife, lolling voiceless on the Commons benches where once he had commanded.

In the course of his career, Chamberlain had been a radical tyro, the greatest reforming civic leader in England, the man who split the Liberal Party in protest at Gladstone's decision to grant Irish self-government, and an imperialist statesman whose leadership in the South African war had made him even more famous and divisive. But in this story, it is Chamberlain's last and most dramatic campaign that matters. 'Tariff reform' meant building a wall of taxes around the British Empire and ending free trade. Like Third World campaigners today who call for 'fair trade' to help struggling farmers, the tariff reformers wanted less competition and brutal efficiency. It was an attempt to bind the Empire together in an increasingly dangerous world, to close off a struggling Britain from her European and American rivals. Had the tariff reformers, led by Chamberlain, succeeded, the story of modern Britain, and of the Western world in the early twentieth century, would have been very different.

In his early life Chamberlain had been nothing but useful. He grew up in London as the son of the owner of a shoemaking firm, and made useful shoes, before going to Birmingham and making the useful nuts and bolts that held together Victoria's industrial empire – and in particular the screws. At one time his company was making two-thirds of all the screws manufactured in England. Like many Victorian entrepreneurs, he was able to retire early and devote himself to politics. In Birmingham he became a leading man in nonconformist and radical circles, a classic middle-class modernizer, arguing for votes for all, taking up the causes of compulsory and free secular education and campaigning against rural poverty. As he put it, 'free church, free schools, free land, free labour'. This was also useful. But Chamberlain's greatest early triumphs came after he was elected Liberal mayor of Birmingham in 1873. He dealt with lethally unhygienic water, incompetent and competing gas suppliers, a dangerous lack of proper sewerage, foul slums and more in a prolonged exhibition of energy, optimism and practical municipal politics that is still used today as the best example of what good local government can achieve. Joe's Birmingham was soon sporting museums, libraries, cleared and rebuilt public spaces and noticeably healthier citizens.

Brilliantly equipped to fling himself into the wilder politics being created by the successive Reform Acts of the Victorian age, Chamberlain adored a crowd and marketed himself for a mass audience. His dandyish black velvet coat, soon adorned with an orchid, his scarlet necktie, and above all his monocle, became as well known as Churchill's hat and cigar, Harold Wilson's pipe or Margaret Thatcher's handbag would be. He had a talent for the vivid phrase any advertising man would kill for. Once in the Commons, he set about creating a national organization to make the Liberals more effective, and under Gladstone produced useful legislation on such down-to-earth issues as electric lighting and bankruptcy reform. But Joe turned darker and dangerous, dreaming of a new politics that bound the most aggressive imperial tub-thumping with jobs and social reform at home. Patriotism plus cash in the hand has always been the two-card trick of the demagogue.

Wild men looking for a new politics took note. Among those watching him with awed admiration were Winston's father Randolph, and the young Lloyd George – not to mention Joe's unlikely friend Henry Hyndman, a leading early English Marxist and revolutionary. These were times of far more fluid and fast-changing political sympathies than the sepia pictures of impassive men in top hats suggest. In 1886 Joe broke with Gladstone and most Liberals over home rule for Ireland, setting up his rival Liberal Unionist organization. Going into alliance with the Tory leader Lord Salisbury (whom he had once denounced as a useless excrescence), he became a leading statesman in the days of the rush for African colonies, the confrontations with China and the growing rivalry with Germany. Joe's populism left behind the beliefs of many traditional Liberals while distancing him from the plutocrats and aristocrats of old Tory England. He was routinely called a turncoat, which he was, and seemed to enjoy the blood-sport side of politics just a little too much, revelling in one famous Irish Commons debate when the arguments degenerated into fist fights, leaving torn clothing and broken teeth on the floor. His relish for the Boer War led to it being called 'Joe's War', and his conduct of the 1900 'khaki election', attacking Liberal opponents as traitors and whipping up a frenzy of imperial self-righteousness, led to that being called 'Joe's election'.

A sample of the tone can be tasted in Lloyd George's expedition in December 1901 to speak against the Boer War in Birmingham, Chamberlain's back yard. Having long lost his admiration for the radical imperialist, the Welshman was under ferocious, sometimes physical threat, as a leading 'pro-Boer'. Chamberlain was asked to make sure that when Lloyd George arrived in the city he was at least given a fair hearing. He replied: 'If Ll G wants his life, he had better keep away from Birmingham . . . If he doesn't go, I will see that it is known he is afraid. If he does go, he will deserve all he gets.' Lloyd George, never a coward, went and faced a seething mob. A pro-war crowd estimated at an astonishing 100,000 surrounded the town hall before smashing every window, overwhelming the police and using weapons to break into the building before Lloyd George had a chance to utter a full sentence. Fearing for his life, he donned a police uniform, put on a helmet and was smuggled to safety: forty people were injured and two killed. Chamberlain expressed disappointment that his foe had escaped when his spies sent him a telegram at his London club, telling him that the traitor had at least been prevented from speaking.[14] At times it seemed as if Joe had little sense of where the clear boundaries of parliamentary and political behaviour lay, something shared with other rising stars of the new democracy.

By now he had put together in his mind a set of ideas about Britain's problems and future solutions. Since the great battles over the Corn Laws in the 1840s, free trade had become synonymous with British power and Britain's industrial revolution. The fundamental policy was to let in cheap food from America and Argentina to feed the cities, and leave the farmers to survive as best they could. The corn fields of Sussex had been out-shouted by the terraces of Oldham. But shrewd observers knew that once a tax on imported corn was announced in spring 1902 to help pay for the Boer War, the argument for a much larger wall around the British Empire was bound to return. Chamberlain had spent much of the past decade worriedly observing Germany, whose industry, prosperity and social welfare had been built up behind high tariff walls; the same was true of France and Italy and the Austro-Hungarian Empire; America's tariffs were even higher, and her growth was even faster. So perhaps it was now time to accept that the world was one of rival trade blocks, and build a barrier round the British Empire too? Real wages were stagnating and British industry was growing too slowly. Chamberlain proposed that food should come in cheaply from South Africa, Canada, New Zealand and Australia; anything else should be taxed severely. Meanwhile, British industry could again thrive, supplying the markets of the Empire, which had been effectively closed to outsiders. It was 'Sinn Fein' – Ourselves Alone – on a global scale.

There was one obvious problem. The cost of food was bound to rise. Chamberlain tried to deal with this by arguing that more prosperous British industries and the use of the tariff money for welfare to help the poor would counteract this. There were bigger political questions, too. If Britain went protectionist, and the tariff walls went ever higher, would not the whole world become poorer, and more mutually hostile? Was this not an admission of defeat, stark evidence that British industry, which had been so recently a wonder of the world, could no longer compete on equal terms? On the other hand, the domestic politics of protectionism were intriguing. Those who might benefit were not only the struggling industrialists but the cold-shouldered farmers and landowners – the bulwarks of old Liberalism and of old Toryism brought triumphantly together. Among those who would certainly cheer to support the Empire were the imperial beneficiaries, the military families and colonial administrators. The sharp-tongued Margot Asquith, wife of the Liberal leader, knew what was up. Tariff reform, she said, 'caught on like wild fire, with the semi-clever, moderately educated, the Imperialists, Dukes, Journalists and Fighting Forces'.[15] That was, for the time, quite a coalition.

Winston Churchill realized it too, during his final days on the same side of the Commons as Chamberlain. Speaking in the Budget debate of April 1902, he said people would soon ask why 'should we not kill three birds with one stone – collect our revenue, support British industries, and consolidate the Empire'. He went on to wonder, 'what will happen in this country if the fair trade issue [the euphemism for protection] is boldly raised by some responsible person of eminence and authority. We shall find ourselves once again on an old battlefield. Around will be the broken weapons, the grass-grown trenches and neglected graves . . . and party bitterness, such as this generation has not known. How is it going to split existing political organizations . . . ?' His biographer son called Churchill's speech 'unbelievably prescient', but young Winston was moving in well-informed circles. A week later, Churchill and his young-gun friends, who called themselves the Hooligans (after Hugh Cecil, one of their number), had Chamberlain to dinner. At the end of it he thanked them for a splendid meal and offered in return 'a priceless secret. Tariffs! These are the politics of the future, and of the near future. Study them closely, and make yourselves masters of them, and you will not regret your hospitality to me!'[16]

By then, Joe was well on the way to destroying the Conservative government that had come in under Salisbury, but was now led by that great bison-like grandee's nephew Arthur Balfour. A sprig of one of the oldest and grandest political dynasties, Balfour had seemed an effete creature to fellow MPs. When he was given his first political job by Salisbury, it was widely assumed to be an act of family patronage extreme by the standards even of late-Victorian England and it gave the English language the phrase 'Bob's your uncle'. Known as 'Pretty Fanny', Balfour was a member of the 'Souls' group of bright, self-consciously elitist young aristocrats who met, flirted and exchanged clevernesses. His philosophical writings were admired but the strain was a dying, elegiac one. Among his best-known sayings was 'Nothing matters very much, and few things matter at all', while his best-known book was entitled *Defence of Philosophic Doubt*. In an age of vigorous social and scientific debate, he seemed languidly pessimistic to the point of fatalism. He took the long view: 'The energies of our system will decay, the glory of the sun will be dimmed, and the earth, tideless and inert, will no longer tolerate the race which has for a moment disturbed its solitude.' This, while undeniably true, is not the stuff most prime ministers are made of.

Yet once getting into office, in charge of Ireland, Balfour had proved ruthless enough to get a second nickname, 'Bloody Balfour', and became one of the leading Conservative statesmen of the age, a natural successor to his uncle. As prime minister he was tested by a series of crises but was mostly merely struggling to keep together his coalition of Conservative and Liberal Unionists, as Chamberlain's rampaging threatened to tear it apart. Chamberlain had already lost one important battle, against Balfour's Education Act of 1902, disliked by nonconformists because, although it created a unified school system in England, it also made local ratepayers subsidize Anglican schools. Balfour, who had worried that Chamberlain might snatch the premiership away from him, was simply trying to keep his administration afloat. On tariffs, he had few strong views. He prevaricated, offered delays, including the promise of an imperial conference, and produced vaguely reassuring forms of words – behaving as John Major did while trying to hold his Conservative cabinet together when it was riven by Europe in the mid-1990s. He then trickily cajoled both his cabinet's hard-line free traders and Chamberlain into resigning, and survived himself, undignified but placid, for longer than seemed possible.

Just as the row was hotting up, Churchill wrote to a constituent:

> It would seem to me a fantastic policy to endeavour to shut the British Empire in a ringed fence. It is very large, and there are a good many things which can be produced in it, but the world is larger & produces some better things than can be found in the British Empire. Why should we deny ourselves the good and varied merchandise which the traffic of the world offers . . . Our

planet is not a very big one compared with the other celestial bodies, and I see no particular reason why we should endeavour to make inside our planet a smaller planet called the British Empire, cut off by impassable space from everything else.

Churchill had but recently returned from making money in America, and had an American mother, but it was not self-interest that led him to worry in another letter, this time to a free-trade Tory in Chamberlain's back yard, that a tariff wall would cut off Britain from the United States if it ever came to a European war: 'I do not want a self-contained Empire.'[17] For a man often caricatured as a simple-minded imperial jingo in his earlier career, it was a lucid and noble argument which would soon lead Churchill to desert not just Chamberlain – who was hurt by Winston's defection – but the Conservative Party itself.

Five days before Churchill wrote his 'smaller planet' letter, Chamberlain had fired off the first shot in what would be one of the most gripping political duels of the young century. On 15 May 1903 in a speech at Birmingham Town Hall – its glass repaired from Lloyd George's friendly visit – he swept aside all other issues, telling the Liberal chief whip, with magnificent contempt, 'You can burn your leaflets. We are going to talk about something else.' The country duly divided, with rival leagues, rival newspapers and rival arguments. Chamberlain, backed by most of the press, raised huge sums for posters, leaflets and full-time workers.

It was now a choice, he said, between defending the Empire and sticking with the free-trade beliefs of 'a small remnant of Little Englanders'. His language about Britain's future without protection was apocalyptic, as in this typical speech, made at Greenock on 11 November: 'Agriculture, as the greatest of all the trades and industries of this country, has been practically destroyed. Sugar has gone, silk has gone, iron is threatened, wool is threatened. The turn of cotton will come. How long are you going to stand it?' These industries, he said, 'are like sheep in a field. One by one they allow themselves to be led out to slaughter.' In an initial dozen major events Chamberlain took his arguments from Glasgow to Newcastle and Tynemouth, then west to Liverpool, down to Cardiff and Newport, and back up to Leeds. His language shifted as the influence of the worried manufacturers grew – less of empire, more about saving those industries. A typical Tariff Reform League poster showed a cowed John Bull being pelted from above by American trains and trams, German cars, Austrian furniture and Belgian steel. In Limehouse in London he opened a new line of attack, on recent immigrants. Chamberlain the social revolutionary was gone. His Liberal Unionists were middle class and hostile to grand reforms, and he dropped, for instance, his enthusiasm for old-age pensions. Having joined forces with the right, he now became right.

Against him the Liberals, who had been divided by the Boer War, came together and went on to the attack. Lloyd George, who had been burned in effigy after the relief of Mafeking, and relishing the chance to punish his old enemy, was particularly virulent and witty. You had to go back fifty years to the time when the people's bread was taxed, he told one audience, 'and over three thousand years, to the time when a great Empire was governed by a man called Joseph . . . But there is this difference – the ancient Joseph in his dreams made provision for an abundance of corn for the people. This modern Joseph is dreaming about a scarcity of corn.' (There is nothing like a biblical education to raise the quality of vituperation.) And again: Chamberlain fancied himself a little Bismarck, 'the man of blood and iron'. Instead he was 'the man of screws . . . that is all the iron in Mr Chamberlain's Imperialism'.[18] Yet it was not Lloyd George but the duller Liberal Henry Herbert Asquith who really scuppered Joe. For this stolid-seeming lawyer also criss-crossed the country, to Clydeside, Newcastle, Paisley and Worcester, patiently knocking down Chamberlain's arguments with hard facts, challenging his grasp of history, essentially out-thinking him, as he had always supposed he would. Immediately after Chamberlain's opening Birmingham blast, Asquith had taken the newspaper into his wife's bedroom and exclaimed: 'Wonderful news today; and it is only a question of time when we shall sweep the country.'[19]

For a while it seemed that Chamberlain was winning. His canvassers went from door to door, explaining the arguments and ticking off support. The young P. G. Wodehouse turned out pro-Chamberlain verses for the *Daily Express* featuring a parrot, parroting the cheap-food line of the Liberals. These were so successful they became a music-hall turn and parrot competitions were held.

Another music-hall song went: 'When wealth and mirth refill the earth / Let each man tell his neighbour / All this we owe to Chamberlain'. The whole country seemed to be caught up in what was, after all, an argument about economic theory. Yet this was an argument bigger than governments. Modern Britain became a country with a strong financial and City tradition, always trying to break down trading barriers and shaped by outside connections, not least with the United States. That Britain was the one that tariff reform would have killed at birth.

And in the end Asquith was proved right. Chamberlain was pulverized. It was partly that the business climate improved, so that the spectre of unemployment and mass bankruptcies that had helped him in the early days faded away by 1905. But it was also that he simply lost the argument. When the election was finally called in 1906 it produced a huge Liberal landslide. Even Balfour, the prime minister, lost his seat, though another was soon found for him. The Liberals would stay in office deep into the First World War and, so far as Edwardian Britain was concerned, the Conservatives became merely an embittered opposition. Chamberlain had smashed his second party. After his stroke, what Beatrice Webb called his 'mechanically savage persistence' would keep him going until 1914, when he finally died of a heart attack. A new age in politics was dawning, when the problems of the poor, and the Empire, would be dealt with in very different ways by the men who had beaten him: Asquith, Lloyd George – and Winston Churchill, who had now left the Tories on a long, strange journey of his own.

Death by Three Million Roses

Even *The Times* thought that three million roses might be overdoing it, but conceded that on the evening of 1 July 1912 the blooms, together with the wisteria, the flower-wreathed coloured lights and the gold Renaissance ornaments, produced an effect of 'light and airy elegance'. The Palace theatre in London's Shaftesbury Avenue had originally opened as a grand opera venue in 1891, with Arthur Sullivan's *Ivanhoe*. But the London public's thirst for opera was limited. It soon moved briskly down market, becoming a 'theatre of varieties' famous for its high-stepping showgirls. It was for variety theatre that the endless boxes of roses had been ordered, but that night the crowd was not dressed in the usual jackets and cheap glad-rags, but in formal evening dress. For this was the first ever Royal Command performance at a music hall. King George V and Queen May were among the guests to see the Palace Girls kick, Vesta Tilley do her male impersonation, Harry Lauder sing 'Roamin' in the Gloamin'', the great comedians of the day George Robey and Little Tich perform their famous sketches, the sensational juggler Cinquevalli, and many more. It was, in its way, a historic moment. For seventy years or so, a working-class tradition that had begun in the back rooms of pubs had been slowly forcing its way into the heart of the cities, into ever more lavish venues. Sneered at, campaigned against, brimming with broken marriages, alcoholics and fortunes lost as well as made, by Edwardian times music hall could not be ignored. From its hippodromes, palaces, empires, coliseums and palladiums, the songs poured out that you heard in the street, in the railway carriage and in the parlours. Now, even the other palace had come to pay homage.

Except that there was something wrong on that warm July night. Someone was missing. And though the newspapers wrote up the experiment as a great success, it is clear that it was not quite as sparkling as a really good music-hall night should be. The *Times* man thought some of the performers 'a little overawed' and therefore lacking 'the sparkle of the oddity which endears them' to their usual crowd. Another found it 'a rather dull performance'. Was there a feeling, despite the presence of the King and Queen and the stellar list of performers – 150 took part in the 'garden party' finale – and the three million roses, that somehow the real action was taking place somewhere else? It surely was. Just a few hundred yards to the west, in fact, at the London Pavilion theatre (its shell is now the Trocadero) a very angry, very proud woman was on stage all by herself. The crowd were going wild. She sang and sang, one hit after another, and they would not let her stop. Marie Lloyd had been considered too rude, too 'blue' to appear at the Royal Command, despite being the most famous variety singer of them all. Snubbed, she had hired the rival Pavilion and, according to legend, put out her own posters announcing: 'Every Performance Given by Marie Lloyd is a Command Performance by Order of the British Public'.

Music hall could not be tamed or aimed at the respectable middle classes – not without losing its soul and dying, which it soon would. It was a working-class entertainment, for the people by the people. Its humour was sentimental, patriotic and bawdy, its most celebrated circus acts eye-popping and its songs simple but infuriatingly difficult to dislodge from your ears. 'Daisy, Daisy, Give Me Your Answer, Do', 'The Boy in the Gallery', 'I Belong to Glasgow' are still being hummed across the English-speaking world today. Yet the songs, which survived in print and in some scratchy recordings, are only a small whiff of the spirit of music hall. Most of the great performers never recorded. Most were never filmed. A few were, but long after their heyday. We cannot really hear what the great comics said in their 'patter', partly because it was often thought too rude to write down. We can't quite imagine the noise, smell and sound of the Victorian and Edwardian halls. They stank of sweat and dirty clothes. Most of the men in the stalls and galleries would have been smoking pipes or cigars; many customers would have been drinking heavily and eating during the performances. The gaslights were extremely dangerous and a remarkable number of the halls burned down.

Performers had seconds in which to grab people's attention. Different towns had different traditions about what to do when an act failed. Shipbuilding cities like Glasgow or Newcastle used to specialize in throwing steel rivets. In the East End of London, trotter bones and vegetables were apparently more common. Heavy pewter mugs also made good missiles, which could cause a satisfyingly bloody wound on a struggling singer. Dead cats and dogs were not unknown. Some patrons removed their boots and threw those. In many of the rougher halls, the small orchestra performed below a wire mesh to keep them safe.

The music-hall age had started when Victoria was still a small girl, in rooms of taverns where professional entertainers and amateurs performed, known as 'free and easies'. The money came from the drink sold, as much as the admission prices. They could be found in basements across London from the 1840s. The Star Inn at Bolton, which was in business by 1842, is often spoken of as the first music hall outside London; ten years later the town had ten free and easies. In Scotland, by mid-Victorian times, there were protests about the almost-naked women dancing, the coarse and blasphemous songs and the audience – many of whom were barefoot girls and boys under thirteen. The early purpose-built entertainment halls were wholly different from the respectable theatres of the day. They had tables laid out for eating and drinking, plus a chairman raised at one end by the stage, whose job was to both boost the next act – a juggler, a singer, a comic turn, a ventriloquist – and try to keep some kind of order. By the final years of Victoria's reign the capital had more than 500 halls of different sizes and varieties, with names like Gatti Under-the-Arches, the Cosmotheka, the Old Mo and the Falstaff, and at least fifty grand, specially built music halls, with a further 200-plus round the rest of the country.

The technologies of the time – trains, newspapers and pianos – pushed music hall forward until the First World War. Now that the country was covered with an intricate web of railways, performers travelling in railway carriages bedecked with their own promotional placards could go almost anywhere, and the hit London songs could be heard within days in Exeter, Belfast or Dundee. Some of the most famous acts had come originally from Europe or Australia, while British singers were much in demand in the United States. Towns which had seen almost no outside entertainments coming to them regularly were introduced to people with the exotic accents of Scotland or cockney London, suitably toned down to aid understanding; for by late-Victorian times the rough diversity of regional English was just beginning to be softened. And these remote stars were turned into national celebrities, with their own foibles, catchphrases and tangled private lives, thanks to the explosion of the popular-newspaper market from the 1890s onwards. Finally, the arrival of cheap mass-manufactured pianos, mostly German, meant that a vastly increased number of families had a chance of learning and playing the new songs as they arrived. This in turn fed the music-hall star system. The singer would buy his or her own songs direct from the composers: if the songs went well, they could recoup a small fortune in sheet-music sales. Cheap pianos had the same kind of impact on music-hall Britain as electric guitars and transistor radios would have in the age of pop.

The greatest architect of British music halls was a prolific Devon brewery manager's son, Frank Matcham. He had a hand in no fewer than 150 theatres between 1879 and 1920, but of the forty-odd that have been listed as his major music halls, twenty-seven have been demolished, several have burned down and most of the rest altered beyond recognition.[20] Only a few of the grandest, such as London's Coliseum and Hippodrome, the Shepherd's Bush Empire and the Bristol Hippodrome, remain. We have some no doubt useful spur roads, bingo halls and office blocks instead. In Matcham halls, the classic tiers and stalls arrangements of conventional theatres were copied, and ever more fantastic decorations added. His grandest confection, the Coliseum, boasted the first lift in any theatre in the world, a revolving stage for horse-races and other spectacles, and a small railway to convey the King and his party directly to the royal box. Physicians and others who might receive urgent messages left their seat numbers at a cubicle and would be fished out by messengers. Inside the new halls, thanks to early electric lighting and ventilation, the old scenes of cat-throwing and eating were replaced by something more like a theatrical experience. Even so, during failed or unpopular numbers the noise of hecklers and jeering was often so loud that the performer couldn't be heard. This could gather to 'being given the bird' – hissing so widespread that the act was instantly stopped. A typical evening might include as many as twenty individual acts, each pretty short – jugglers, blacked-up 'nigger singers', romantic ballads, comics mocking the new fad for motor cars, and conjurors. In the provinces there were customarily two performances a night, the first more genteel and the second, for obvious reasons, much rowdier. In London and a few other cities, performers would dash from theatre to theatre, covering quite a few in a single evening. On Friday nights many halls allowed amateurs to try their best, in much the same way as TV talent shows today. In some halls, in place of a verbally sadistic panel of celebrity judges, there really was a manager standing watching in the wings with a long hooked pole to pull failures off-stage by their necks.

The parallels with pop culture are intriguing, going beyond the impact of technology. The subjects of the music-hall songs – love and heartbreak – were not so different, though sentiment ruled, rather than personal rebellion. The structure of the songs, with simple lyrics and pounding chorus, was not so different either. Nor were the temptations. There were plenty of teenage stars tearing their way towards ruin through drink, promiscuity and even drugs. Despair was felt as keenly. Mark Sheridan, the man who had a huge hit with 'I Do Like to Be Beside the Seaside' in 1909 but later saw his career on the slide, was so depressed by being booed at the Glasgow Coliseum that he went to the city's Kelvingrove Park and shot himself. If modern celebrity culture depends on stunts, then again this was nothing new to the music-hall performers. Harry Houdini made a practice of getting himself locked in the local jail wherever he was booked to perform, and then escaping – including from the triple-locked condemned cell in Sheffield, even after the police had added a further seven-lever lock to the cell block. Singers would arrive with pipers or carriages and make grand civic entrances. The rewards could be spectacular, particularly for the singers who were prepared to go on tour to Australia, South Africa, Paris and New York. Though only in her twenties, Marie Lloyd kept a huge establishment of carriages, servants and hangers-on. Recklessly generous, she would shower lesser artists with cash, bought her parents a pub each in Soho and travelled everywhere in high style. Fred Barnes, a gay singer who got his first break at the London Pavilion, was soon earning a fortune, splashing out thousands of pounds a night in Monte Carlo, keeping four cars when they were very expensive toys, and a substantial staff of servants. Florrie Forde, the Australian singer whose hits included 'Down at the Old Bull and Bush' and 'Has Anybody Here Seen Kelly?' – which in 1909 seems to have been as ubiquitous as a Beatles hit sixty years later – became a very wealthy woman. Several music-hall singers married into the aristocracy. Harry Lauder was knighted.

But for most music-hall performers, like most rock singers, life was an endless trail from provincial date to date, always on the road, sleeping in lousy rooms and dreaming of a real hit. The music-hall singer had no records and therefore no way of knowing what might be a hit, other than by the immediate reaction in the hall. The advantage was that, in the pre-recording age, a star only needed a handful of hit songs to continue his or her career for years. In between the live performances, nobody heard you. This also meant that established performers could continue for as long as their strength held out. The easiest way of gauging success was simply to see what the theatre manager would pay. Harry Lauder first realized he was a star when offered an American tour. Not wanting to go, he asked for a fee he thought ludicrous, and got it. Another way was to chart sheet-music sales. 'It's a Long Way to Tipperary', written by a composer and a semi-professional singer who ran a fish stall, was a sheet-music hit when it came out in 1912 and two years later, towards the end of the first year of the war, was selling an astonishing 10,000 copies every day. But most music-hall stars simply listened. If the audience was joining in the chorus after a week or two, the song was a hit. If not, it would be dropped. Katie Lawrence, who sang 'Daisy, Daisy, Give Me Your Answer Do', said that having sung it for several weeks and found it was not catching on, she was about to drop it. Then, back in London after a provincial tour, she heard someone humming it at the station: 'A few minutes later, I heard it again and found that it was all over London. I was completely surprised and, as you may imagine, I did not drop the song.'[21] But the random nature of the business meant there was a voracious demand for ever more songs. Harry Dacre, who wrote 'Daisy', said that in his first two years as a songwriter he had penned 700, and sold 600 of them.

We must beware golden-ageism. Most music-hall songs, inevitably, were unmemorable. The 1960s novelist Colin MacInnes, a lover of music-hall tradition, concluded that they were not as strong as older folk songs, or the blues: 'They're too inhibited emotionally, too limited intellectually, too frankly commercial in their intentions. I think the highest one can claim for them is that they are a sort of bastard folk song of an industrial-commercial-imperial age.'[22] Yet they were also, as he acknowledged, the voice of working-class Britain through more than half a century of fast change. Almost every simple assertion about them can be contradicted. They were jingoistic? Yes – the very word 'jingo' came from a music-hall song about the Russo-Turkish war. But the other point of view was heard as well. 'We don't want to fight, but by jingo if we do . . .' was soon countered by another singer proclaiming: 'I don't want to fight, I'll be slaughtered if I do, I'll change my togs, I'll sell my kit and pop my rifle too. I don't like war. I ain't a Briton true. And I'll let the Russians have Constantinople.' Were the songs sentimental? Many

were, but others were hard-boiled cynical. Were they dirty? Well . . .
that takes us back to the great Marie Lloyd.

Marie Lloyd was a star for thirty-odd years, even though she
died at fifty-two. Born Matilda Wood in the East End of London
to parents whose job was to make artificial flowers, she made her
debut at fifteen under the name Bella Delmere. Her stage surname
was taken from a popular newspaper of the time and her private
life was catastrophic: three husbands, two of them violent bullies. She
was loved for her famously sharp wit and cheek and the sense that
she never left her class. On an ocean voyage, snubbed by the posh
travellers, she refused to sing for the first-class deck, but only for the
second and the people in steerage. In the 1907 theatre strike she was
on the picket line supporting lesser-paid performers. What many
people thought about first, though, when they heard her name, was
that she was somehow improper. Genuinely filthy jokes were
repeated as if from her mouth. Although she had a famously sharp
wit, this seems hard to understand. If you read the lyrics to her best-
known songs, such as 'Oh Mr Porter, what shall I do? I wanted to
go to Birmingham, but they've carried me on to Crewe', they seem
innocent enough, though there is plenty of innuendo of a gentle,
winking nature and many of her songs were meltingly romantic.
Clearly, though, Lloyd's style, her corrupted-girl knowingness, could
send audiences of the day into squirming paroxysms. Summoned by
the London County Council licensing committee during a major
inquiry into indecency in the music halls, she sang her way through
three songs with a butter-wouldn't-melt little-girl innocence which
had them completely perplexed. They expressed their bemusement.
Marie then chose another song, Lord Tennyson's 'Come into the
Garden, Maud', about as proper a poem as any middle-class parent
could wish for. But she sang it in a way that made it seem instantly
filthy, looked them in the eye and then – as with any audience –
laughed at them as they blushed. That story probably tells as much
about the nature of music hall as a dozen treatises.

Here was another secret of Edwardian public behaviour. Innuendo can be more subversive than outright smut, because to
acknowledge that you understand the meaning is to show you
understand the hidden world of pre-Freudian rhyming slang and
body-part images. To blush is to admit. The LCC let Lloyd alone

and their campaign focused instead on the Empire theatre in Leicester Square which, like many music halls, had a considerable number of prostitutes openly working the back of the large horseshoe 'promenade' at the back of the auditorium. The prospect of this being closed caused protests by theatre workers and London cabmen – who passed a motion 'to prevent those persons who were taking such a great interest in the morals of Londoners ruining, not only public places of amusement, but the cab industry'. It provoked a great argument between libertarians and those they called 'prudes', particularly once a decision was made to place a large screen round the back of the theatre, effectively destroying the boozy, smoky, libidinous promenade. Among those who were outraged was the young Winston Churchill, then a Sandhurst cadet, who came to London to protest and produced his first ever letter to a newspaper, telling the *Westminster Gazette* that 'in England we have too long obeyed the voice of the prude'. He was then, by his own account, at the head of a mob of several hundred people who stormed the screen, or barricade, and tore it down, boasting to his brother, 'It was I who led the rioters'. He then made his first public speech, appealing to the crowd from the top of the debris: 'You have seen us tear down these barricades tonight; see that you pull down those responsible for them at the coming election.'[23]

Yet if the LCC was briefly confounded by this unlikely seeming alliance of young Churchill of the hussars and Marie Lloyd of the wiggles and winks, the steady smothering of the spirit of the old music hall continued – death by patronage and respectability as much as death by cinema. Though the 'bioscope', or early films, were offered to music-hall audiences from 1900 onwards, they were little regarded by the performers and certainly no match for the colour and noise of the live acts. As the writer J. B. Priestley, who saw these things first from the perspective of Bradford and the industrial north, put it: 'What began in Coketown finally triumphed close to Piccadilly Circus'; but though the middle classes began to pour in, 'Variety came from the industrial working class and never really moved a long way from it.'[24] Almost everywhere we look in Edwardian Britain, we find a surge of democracy sweeping round the old order. But wherever we look, we also see British society incorporating, and calming, the popular tide. That is true of the early Labour Party, to a lesser extent of trade unionism . . . and it is certainly true of music hall too. West End audiences meant self-censorship, not bawdy, and even short plays. Music hall would continue well into the 1920s, but become a sugary, sanitized mimicry of its earlier self. Those roses had fatal thorns.

Captains and Kings

One of the things that must strike anyone reading Edwardian political memoirs is just how important were the views of the monarch. The papers of Churchill, Asquith and many others are scattered with royal telegrams and accounts of difficult meetings with Edward VII and George V. Both men were natural reactionaries, tempered by more Liberal-leaning advisers and, in Edward's case, by a pro-Liberal mistress. Though this is the beginning of the democratic age, the old web of royal marriages still spread across Europe, making diplomacy familial. Since both 'Edwardian' kings were not merely monarchs at home but enjoyed the fine title King-Emperor, they followed imperial affairs very closely. Edward VII was, as we have seen, highly suspicious of his cousin the Kaiser. He much preferred France to Germany. His wildly successful visit to Paris in 1903, which came when Britain was unpopular there, was followed by the momentous *entente cordiale* of the following year. It was the last ever significant diplomatic act by a British monarch and helped pull Britain into the Great War. Edward knew Paris very well, having sowed enough wild oats there as Prince of Wales to feed most of Europe. He was a great frequenter of Parisian brothels and knew many of the most famous whores, appearing in Belle Epoque naughtiness like a figure in a Toulouse-Lautrec poster, with top hat and bulging belly. This Falstaffian side of Edward also helped make him popular at home, where his many mistresses ranged from cockney girls to one Mrs Keppel.

Of the regiment of strong women that populated Edwardian life, Alice Keppel is worth remembering. Of all Edward's mistresses, none was as important as she, none better known, none more politically significant. She was by Edwardian standards rather on the left, an opponent of Chamberlain and a moderate supporter of Lloyd

George. She was present at the Liberal dinner when Edward was reconciled to the idea of the anti-war Liberal leader Sir Henry Campbell-Bannerman becoming prime minister. When Edward died Queen Alexandra invited Mrs Keppel to his death-bed in 1910. Something of her fame can be surmised by the tale of her getting into a hansom cab and announcing, 'King's Cross'. The cabbie turned round. He was sorry to hear it, he said – but never mind, she'd win him round in due course. (Cabbies featured in many Edward stories. Another had his bawdier cockney mistress Rosa Lewis and the future King enjoying a wild time in a closed hackney coach. The Prince of Wales handed over a miserable payment, leading to the angry cabbie protesting until Rosa gave him two sovereigns. 'I knowed you was a lady as soon as I seen you,' said the cabbie, 'but where did you pick 'im up?')

Campbell-Bannerman would become the Great Caresser's great reassurer. Frequently going for spa treatments at the German resort of Marienbad, where he met Edward both as Prince of Wales and King, the politician worried about 'the extraordinary number of tainted ladies' around the royal person. If Edward VII had been concerned about having to put up with a government of damned Liberals and radicals then owlish, mustachioed 'C-B' was the very man to calm him down. His most famous moment of radicalism had happened during the Boer War, which he vehemently opposed, when he attacked British 'methods of barbarism'. Yet within a few years this was forgotten by all except the military commanders against whom the comment was aimed and Campbell-Bannerman seemed the ultimate safe pair of hands. He memorably said of his health regime, perhaps alluding to his political philosophy too: 'Personally I am an immense believer in bed, in constantly keeping horizontal: the heart and everything else goes slower, and the whole system is refreshed.' Not refreshed enough, however, for in 1908 he became ill, resigned and died three weeks later in Downing Street – the only prime minister to do so.

Asquith's succession meant a steelier, tougher figure at the top, and a much harder time ahead for the monarch. Known to admiring cartoonists as 'the Last of the Romans' and later, to colleagues alarmed by his convivial habits, as 'old Squiffy', his deep learning awed other MPs just as much as his private life intrigued them. He had been happily married to Helen, a quiet, gentle woman who had produced five children; but in the same year he met Margot Tennant at a Commons dinner party, Helen caught typhoid and died on holiday in Scotland. Asquith was by then a rising political star and successful barrister, but Margot was slow to yield. It seemed a very strange match. Asquith had come from an austere middle-class Bible-reading family in Yorkshire and had propelled himself upwards through his academic brilliance and a formidable appetite for hard work. He was of the non-flashy, impassive, middle-class breed of Victorian Liberals, winning great plaudits as home secretary under Gladstone. Stocky, earnest and conventionally dressed, he was the opposite of the aristocrats with whom Margot had mingled. Yet she had always been a fervent Liberal, interested in politics, and had always admired high intelligence – which the Asquiths possessed in spades. Their marriage, which intrigued Westminster, did not prove as happy as either hoped.

Margot Asquith seems to have been a tremendously frightening woman. One of eight surviving children of a rich brewer, she had been brought up in a tempestuous, clever household living in a modern baronial mansion in the Scottish borders. Her great tragedy had been the death of her adored elder sister in childbirth. One of the 'Souls', those arch clever-clever aristos, among the statesmen she knew were Gladstone, Salisbury, Balfour and Rosebery. Her passion was hunting. In 1906 she reflected: 'I ride better than most people . . . I have broken both collar-bones, my nose, my ribs and my knee-cap; dislocated my jaw, fractured my skull, and had five concussions of the brain; but – though my horses are to be sold next week – I have not lost my nerve.'[25] Her tongue was even more dangerous than her horse riding. She had some odd beliefs. Among them was that a full set of teeth was an invariable sign of insanity which would lead to early death – in later years her butler and footmen were encouraged to have all their teeth extracted. As one of the great hostesses, she was a friend of the King and part of the network of high society that kept Liberalism and the Palace in touch.

But by the time of Asquith's arrival as prime minister, relations between Edward and his Liberal ministers were fast deteriorating. As we shall see, it was the great crisis over the Lords and the People's Budget that really brought this to a head, but royal sniping over issues from taxes to the Czar to Ireland required careful attention, both before and after the accession of George V in 1910. Not all ministers reacted well. Churchill was always cheeky and particularly infuriated King George by some of his comments in the gossipy daily reports from Parliament that it was his duty to send to the Palace. In one, in February 1911, Churchill wrote that 'tramps and wastrels' should be sent to labour colonies to work, adding, 'It must not however be forgotten that there are idlers and wastrels at both ends of the social scale.' King George was so angry he instructed his secretary to write to 10 Downing Street: 'The King thinks that Mr Churchill's views, as contained in the enclosed, are very socialistic . . . HM considers it quite superfluous for Churchill in a letter of the description he was writing to him, to bring in about "idlers and wastrels at both ends of the social ladder".' Churchill wrote to the King apparently apologizing, but with perfect insolence suggesting that, if the King did not like his chatty style, he might try reading the parliamentary debates in the newspapers, and effectively resigning. The King's secretary replied that 'he regrets that your feelings should have been hurt' and added: 'The King directs me to add that your letters are always instructive and interesting and he would be sorry if he were to receive no further ones.' Eventually the little dispute was smoothed over. But the Liberal politician's disinclination to be browbeaten by the King is significant. It would not have happened that way in Berlin or St Petersburg; which may be why those monarchies went, and that of fat, wicked Edward and his son, the stamp-collecting, apologetic George, kept chugging forwards.

Daisy in the Time of Nightmares

A good-looking fifteen-year-old boy was in the garden one morning in October 1900, digging in his old jacket and knickerbockers. The big balconied house is gone now, burned down, but the gardens remain, in the south-east London suburb of Eltham. Then, there was a moat and rambling flowers, huge cedars full of owls and old brick walls, dating back to an ancient Tudor house where, by legend, the severed head of Thomas More had been buried by his daughter. It was a place of magic and darkness. At around eleven that morning, a doctor and an anaesthetist arrived at the gate. The boy's mother, still asleep, was woken up. She made him bathe and get into some clean clothes for the simple operation to come – a removal of his adenoids because of the heavy colds he had had. Two hours later, the boy's father emerged white-faced. After the doctors had given the boy chloroform, done their work and left, the boy, whose name was Fabian, had died. There were two grieving women present. One was known as Mouse. The other was Fabian's mother, Edith, who in her despair tried to warm up and revive the child with hot water bottles. Later, talking of the thirteen-year-old girl who was also part of the family, she raged at her husband: 'Why couldn't it have been Rosamund?' Terribly, Rosamund overheard the words. And her world started to fall in as well. For she began to realize she was not the daughter of Edith at all. She was Mouse's daughter. The patriarch of the family, a monocled, mustachioed man named Hubert, was living with his wife and his mistress together. And Edith, his wife, had taken in both the children of his mistress and brought them up as her own.

Edith was already famous, as she still is today, as E. Nesbit, the great children's author who gave the world *The Treasure Seekers*, *The Wouldbegoods*, *Five Children and It*, *The Railway Children* and many other wonderful stories. Some say she invented the modern children's novel. When Fabian died, she was forty-two, a striking woman much addicted to long silk dresses and silver bangles. As the child's name suggests, she was a fervent socialist, one of the founder members of the Fabian Society. Known to her family as Daisy, she had grown up in a rambling, insecure family. Her father had died before she knew him and her mother had taken the children from place to place, through France and Germany as well as England, and from school to school. Daisy emerged as a wilful, sharp, impetuous girl who was soon earning small amounts of cash supplying poems and sentimental stories to the booming magazine market of Fleet Street. She fell for a dashing businessman and sometime writer called Hubert Bland. He had promised to marry someone else, but failed to tell Daisy. When she was seven months pregnant he married her instead, and she decided to make friends with her rival. It would be the start of a pattern. The contradictions of hippie living, mixing politics and sex, high theory and low practice, were known well before the 1960s.

Hubert and Daisy began married life with little money. His brush-making firm, in the hard climate of the 1880s, went bust. She was soon producing children and also helping to keep them afloat through her writing – until slowly he too became a successful journalist. She was unconventional from the start, hacking off her long Victorian hair into a tomboyish crop, refusing to wear the tight corsets and flounces of fashion and smoking cigarettes and cigars in public. It was the first flowering of socialist thought, and Daisy would spend days in the British Museum reading room, working at her stories. Among the friends she made were Annie Besant, who was living with the notorious atheist Charles Bradlaugh. They had gone round the country lecturing on birth control and she had lost custody of her children because of it. Besant would lead the famous strike of the London match girls and was a driving force among Fabian socialists before defecting to the limp mystical creed of Theosophy. Another of Daisy's new friends was Eleanor Marx, daughter of Karl. She had nursed him, helped finish *Das Kapital* and then thrown herself into socialist politics. She lived with Edward Aveling, another socialist, in what the Victorians would call 'sin'. Aveling married an actress without telling Eleanor and then proposed a joint suicide pact, leaving her with the prussic acid. Eleanor killed herself while he quietly left, very much alive. Which was a sin.

This is a suburb of English life full of idealistic but badly behaved men and strong but tormented women. Hubert was an insatiable sexual predator and Daisy responded to his multiple infidelities by taking many lovers of her own, including George Bernard Shaw and a string of devoted younger men. When Shaw was approached by Edith Nesbit's first biographer, his secretary replied for him: 'Mr Bernard Shaw desires me to say that as Edith was an audaciously unconventional lady and Hubert an exceedingly unfaithful husband, he does not see how a presentable biography is possible as yet; and he has nothing to contribute to a mere whitewashing operation.' Hubert may have been behaving in a traditional male fashion, like so many other Victorian and Edwardian males from Edward VII to Lloyd George, but Edith, or Daisy, was struggling to find what life as a freer, more independent woman might mean. How should women conduct themselves in this in-between world of traditionalist and voracious men and a glimmering new idea of freer relations outside the confines of unhappy marriage? It was a real dilemma. At the top end of the social scale, adulteries were so frequent they were taken for granted by the hostesses organizing country-house weekends. Among working-class families, as Rowntree, Booth and others had shown, huge numbers of children were born out of wedlock, often to mothers unsure of the father's identity. The middle classes, pressed by both sides, hung on all the more doggedly to notions of respectability, casting adulterers and unmarried mothers into social darkness.

One way of approaching the dilemma was to ask whether divorce should be allowed without disgrace, thus at least freeing some men and women from relationships they had come to loathe. In 1890 the second Earl Russell had married a woman called Mabel Scott but the marriage had not worked and she returned to live with her mother. Ten years on he went to Nevada, the only place he could get a divorce, and then remarried. This was illegal in Britain, and in 1901 he was tried and imprisoned for bigamy. Out of this and his moving defence of his position came the Divorce Law Reform Association of 1903 and a Royal Commission in 1909. The commission even included some women, despite the protests of the King, who complained that this was 'not a subject upon which women's opinions can be conveniently expressed'. Arnold Bennett's novel *Whom God Hath Joined* in 1915 dealt directly with the misery of unhappy marriage and the dangers of the divorce court: 'It was the most ordinary thing on earth! Two people had cared for each other and had ceased to care for each other, and a third person had come between them. Why not, since they had ceased to care?' The novel reaches its climax in the gloomy Divorce Court on the Strand: 'And gradually the secret imperious attraction of the Divorce Court [to bystanders] grew clearer to the disgusted and frightened Laurence . . . Here it was frankly admitted that a man was always "after" some woman and that the woman is also running away while looking behind her, until she stumbles and is caught . . . All the hidden shames were exposed to view, a feast for avid eyes. The animal in every individual could lick its chops and thrill with pleasure.'

Two others stuck in failing marriages were Tolstoy's dashing, bearded translator Aylmer Maude and the married woman in whose house he was lodging, a striking thirty-three-year-old biologist. She had been the youngest Doctor of Science in Britain and suffered an intense, failed love affair with a Japanese scientist while she was studying in Germany. Now she was married to a rage-prone Canadian geneticist who was entirely impotent. She was desperate to escape into Aylmer Maude's arms but, like Lord Russell, found it impossible to get a divorce. Like so many women, including her own mother, she had married with very little knowledge of sex. She was genuinely puzzled about what was wrong. And so one morning, in the best scientific spirit, she marched into the British Museum reading room and asked for every explicit book on sex they had.

For six months Dr Marie Stopes sat there working her way through sexual treatises and manuals in English, French and German, including at least one kept locked in the cupboard of pornography. Most useful of all were Havelock Ellis's sexual studies, which had been published between 1894 and 1910 but were only available to most men (never mind women) with the help of a doctor or lawyer's certificate. Ellis believed it was time to stop thinking of women as somewhere between angel and idiot, and for men to work to understand their partners' sexual needs. The vagina was like a lock which required the right moment, the best conditions and some skill to enter: 'The grossest brutality may be, and not infrequently is, exercised in all innocence by an ignorant husband who simply believes that he is performing his "marital duties".' Slowly Stopes accumulated the knowledge she needed to divorce her husband on the grounds of 'nullity'. But as she returned from her library sessions and teaching job at London's University College, he would be waiting to abuse and taunt her. She said she felt as if she was drowning in sewer filth, had a permanent headache and was thinking of suicide.[26]

Eventually Marie Stopes would get her divorce, though only after further horrible rows and a physical retreat from London – the outbreak of war found her living in a tent on a beach in Northumberland, where she was suspected by local militia of being a spy. But the real fruit of her personal search would be a book, *Married Love*, which was not published until 1918. By then she had met the

American birth-control pioneer Margaret Sanger. A virgin, Stopes knew very little about the practicalities of this and the two women, after meeting at the Fabian Hall, sat down over a supper of roast lamb to discuss condoms. Stopes would become the great liberator for innumerable women, though she fell out with Sanger. Her later views would become odder and odder, but *Married Love* fired the imagination of people who felt trapped in sexless or joyless situations. It was hailed by suffragette leaders who wanted to push women's liberation beyond the vote. In private letters and public campaigns, novels and scandalized newspaper articles, there was a rising debate about sexuality and gender. It was still a debate at the edges of society, and under its surface. Even most Fabians maintained highly respectable and conventional marriages. The darkest secrets of Edwardian family life, the beating of women by drunken or simply violent husbands, rape, and the unconsummated marriages of homosexual men, were never publicly discussed and only emerge as knowing hints in letters and memoirs. But the arrival of more women in the workforce, and a greater understanding of human biology, were facts which could not be brushed away.

The socialism of those days was one which relied wholly on future visions and dreams, not on any established model. Fiction was essential to it. H. G. Wells set his science fiction tales in places like Woking. He wrote fantasies but it was fantasy about the future, with its boots on the dust and pavements of Edwardian England. Bubbling under was sexual fantasy. Wells was a keen Fabian socialist and soon frequently visiting the Nesbit–Bland household in Eltham. Just as sexually predatory as Hubert Bland had been, Wells began an affair with Rosamund, Bland's daughter by Mouse who had learned of her true origins on that dreadful day eight years earlier. She and Wells ran off together, Rosamund reportedly dressed as a boy, but were caught at Paddington station by Bland, who pulled Wells off the train and thumped him.

The row that followed, when Wells was already fighting with the other Fabians about politics, was sensational. Wells suggested that he was saving Rosamund from the unfatherly attentions of her father: 'I conceived a great disapproval of incest, and an urgent desire to put Rosamund beyond its reach in the most effective manner possible, by absorbing her myself.' Nesbit and Bland, he told Bernard

Shaw, oversaw an 'infernal household of lies'. And when Shaw tried vainly to make peace between the warring parties, he received a double barrel-load of H. G. Wells's invective at its most entertaining. The more he thought about Shaw,

> the more it comes home to me what an unmitigated middle Victorian ass you are. You play about with ideas like a daring garrulous maiden aunt but when it comes to an affair like the Bland affair you show the conscious gentility and judgement of a hen . . . The fact is you're a flimsy intellectual, acquisitive of mind, adrift and chattering brightly in a world you don't understand. You don't know, as I do, in blood and substance, lust, failure, shame, hate, love and creative passion . . . Now go on being amusing.[27]

Abominably though Wells had behaved, it is hard to deny that he had a point. Yet the clotted story of male predation among the idealists, vegetarians and socialists was only just beginning.

The great contemporary novel of the suffragette age was Wells's *Ann Veronica*, the story of a frustrated, clever young woman scientist who runs away from her father and suburban home to try to live freely by herself in London. She pitches herself into the world of predatory men – one of them suspiciously like Hubert Bland – and militant women which Wells, the author, knew all too well. The near impossibility of women surviving independently in Edwardian London, finding work and supporting themselves without being menaced and insulted, is eloquently explained. And Wells's satirical take on the Fabian-and-friends crowd is unsparing. The Goopes, for example, are not just vegetarian but fruitarian. Mrs Goopes, childless and servantless (itself evidence of eccentricity in 1909), writes for a journal called *New Ideas* on 'vegetarian cookery, vivisection, degeneration, the lacteal secretion, appendicitis and the Higher Thought generally . . . Their very furniture had mysteriously a high-browed quality.' But *Ann Veronica* was an easily identifiable fictional portrait of a real-life woman, Amber Reeves – Wells's latest conquest – a dark-haired and brilliant beauty in her late teens known as 'the Medusa', a socialist economist and philosopher. Her affair with Wells included a vigorous session in the open air when they apparently lay under a tree on a copy of *The Times* newspaper featuring an attack on modern immorality by the popular novelist Mrs Humphry Ward. Others say the naked buttocks pressed against Mrs Ward's prose were in fact those of Elizabeth von Arnim, another Wells lover. Just to complicate things hideously, Mrs Ward's attack in the newspaper had been aimed at Rebecca West . . . who would herself later become another lover of Wells.[28] Amber became pregnant with Wells's child. Another of her admirers agreed to marry her to save her from disgrace. Something strikingly similar would happen later with Rebecca West. (Amber, Elizabeth and Rebecca all became novelists too.) The similarities with Nesbit and Bland's ménage earlier are too close for comfort.

Edith Nesbit had chosen love affairs and heroic tolerance as her way out. Others made unhappy marriages to keep their respectability. These are the real stories behind some of the cascade of great children's story-telling. Most were bland school romps but the best reflected much more. In *The Railway Children* of 1906, not only is the father absent, wrongly imprisoned, and the mother struggling to pay the bills by hack journalism, just like Nesbit, but a runaway Russian socialist appears, rather like the extraordinary Prince Kropotkin, who was a family friend. In *Five Children and It*, which Nesbit published in 1902, there are references, albeit joking, to the Fabians' agenda. The It of the title, a prehistoric sand fairy who can grant wishes, begs the children not to reveal its existence to adults because 'they'd ask for a graduated income-tax, and old-age pensions and manhood suffrage, and free secondary education, and dull things like that; and get them, and keep them, and the whole world would be turned topsy-turvy'. In *The Amulet* of 1906 the Queen of Babylon is transported to Edward VII's London and complains about the wretched and neglected condition of the slaves in east London's Mile End Road: 'You'll have a revolt of your slaves if you're not careful.' In the writings of Nesbit and others, the possibilities of fantasy, magic and childlike wonder arrest the attention because adult life around them is dangerous and unpredictable, unfair and often broken. Children become clear-eyed observers of the failures of the adult world.

We cannot begin to understand the Edwardian age unless we see it partly through the eyes of children, and then through the eyes of some of the extraordinary, tough, self-confident women challenging the male hierarchies. It was hardly surprising, perhaps, that some of them became men haters. In *Ann Veronica*, the militant suffragette activist Miss Miniver is a vinegary, anti-sex creature who believes men are beasts and that maternity has been women's undoing: 'While we were minding the children they stole our rights and liberties. The children made us slaves, and the men took advantage of it . . . Originally in the first animals there were no males, none at all. It has been proved. Then they appear among the lower things . . . among crustaceans and things just as little creatures, ever so inferior to the females. Mere hangers-on.' Though the libidinous Wells supported votes for women, you can hear the grinding axe of the sex war. In fact, he was barely exaggerating. The suffragette Frances Swiney believed that male sperm was toxic and male sexual desire was 'a pathological excrescence – not a natural impulse'. The League of Isis argued that women should have intercourse only for reproductive purposes, once every four or five years. Christabel Pankhurst herself came to believe that up to 80 per cent of the male population was riddled with gonorrhoea and had to be restrained – her 1913 book on the subject was titled *The Great Scourge*. There was a lot of anger in domestic Edwardian life.

Rebel Girls

Boggart Hole Clough in Manchester, on a beautiful Sunday morning in July 1906: a young, determined-looking girl has been addressing a huge crowd in this ancient park, shaped like a bowl, or primitive amphitheatre. She and her fellow speakers are at the bottom, talking upwards to a large crowd, not entirely friendly. Then a large group of young men, local footballers many of them, charge downhill with sticks. As the crowd begins to panic, the men link arms and surround the women. The young female speakers in particular are singled out, grabbed by their arms and dragged around the park, passed from man to man as if they were rugby balls. Their clothes are half ripped off, they are beaten across the face until bleeding. Older men shout obscene suggestions and the crowd begin yelling 'like savages'. Eventually the girls are rescued by a counter-attack of other men and women and dragged to a house nearby for refuge. The young woman speaker was Adela Pankhurst, youngest of Emmeline Pankhurst's daughters. She always felt her mother had not given her enough love and support but now, for once, she had earned respect. Adela had been imprisoned for disrupting meetings and was addressing a suffragette crowd about her experiences. Her redoubtable mother had come from London to hear her in a park where Emmeline herself had confronted the authorities a decade earlier in a row about free speech.

The Edwardian suffragette campaign was extraordinarily violent. It involved arson and death as well as marches and window-smashing. Members of Emmeline Pankhurst's WSPU – the Women's Social and Political Union – disrupted meetings of Liberal politicians, heckled, petitioned and sold their newspaper on the streets. But they also rushed Parliament, challenged the police with mass marches which turned violent, smashed huge numbers of shop windows, set fire to letter-boxes, slashed famous paintings in art galleries, disrupted courtrooms and deliberately got themselves arrested, refusing to pay fines and therefore facing imprisonment, during which many went on hunger strike and had to be force fed. They attacked politicians. The prime minister, Asquith, was punched, had an axe flung at him and had slates thrown at his car. Winston Churchill was attacked at Bristol railway station by a riding-crop-wielding woman who hit him on the face. 'Take that, you brute, you brute,' shouted Theresa Garnett. 'I will show you what an English woman can do!' Lloyd George's half-built house at Walton Heath in Surrey was partly destroyed by a bomb. The suffragettes did not try to take human life – they were not terrorists in any serious modern sense – but their actions were considerably more vigorous than the later Gandhi style of passive and peaceful protest. Most of the violence was the violence they deliberately allowed to be inflicted on themselves; and it was this more than anything which discomfited and shook traditionalist Edwardian Britain.

The most famous incident occurred at the 1913 Epsom Derby when Emily Wilding Davison killed herself under the hooves of the King's horse. Emily had been, by all accounts, a determined and idealistic girl, one of nine children of a middle-class Hertfordshire family. Her early life shines with promise, like a Wellsian heroine's: a gold medal-winning swimmer, keen cyclist, deeply religious Christian, a theatre lover and admirer of Shaw's plays, who managed to get herself to college and eventually achieved a first-class degree from the new St Hilda's College, Oxford. But, like the Pankhurst girls and many other prominent suffragettes, she lost her father early – creating not just a personal but an economic problem, which meant she worked unhappily as a teacher and more happily as a governess. Emily may or may not have been a lesbian. The suffragette story is full of passionate relationships between women who live together but the reticence of the age generally leaves their private lives just that. People were less explicit, asked less, knew less and perhaps speculated less. At any rate, she was drawn into the cause by friends and quickly became a militant, moving from speaking in public to heckling Liberal politicians and then rushing the Commons, where she also hid overnight three times, sustained by bananas and chocolate.

All this meant prison, force feeding and rough treatment. Not forgetting her religious faith, she would write 'Rebellion against Tyrants is Obedience to God' on the cell wall. She became involved in arson, including possibly the attack on Lloyd George's house, and in November 1912 in a bizarre incident attacked with a dogwhip a harmless Baptist minister in Aberdeen, apparently mistaking him for the Liberal chancellor. When she went to Epsom racecourse she may have not intended to kill herself – she had bought a return ticket – but was fired up by thoughts of martyrdom. She watched the first two races and even marked her race-card before running out into the course and trying to grab the reins of King George's horse, Anmer, as it raced past. Unsurprisingly, the horse trampled her. The jockey suffered concussion and Emily died four days later in Epsom Cottage Hospital from concussion of the brain. Entirely predictably, while there was national interest in her fate – shared by the royal family – the mail that poured into the hospital was savagely hostile: how dare she risk the life of the poor horse? (Anmer, it should be recorded, suffered nothing worse than slightly bruised shins.)

This is the incident almost everyone has heard about, partly because it was caught on film and partly because Emmeline Pankhurst decided to make Emily a great public martyr to the cause, and her funeral a major WSPU event. But she was by no means the first suffragette to have given her life.[29] At least two other women had by then died prematurely, almost certainly of injuries inflicted by the police. The force feeding of women in prison who had gone on hunger strike was itself a brutal business. Trying to force mouths open to accommodate metal contraptions resulted in broken teeth and ripped gums; alternatively the passages of the nose would be bruised by rubber tubes shoved down and into the stomach. In Holloway Prison in London, a twenty-one-year-old working-class girl from Leicester who had trained as a dancer, Lilian Lenton, was subjected to force feeding and had the tube accidentally pushed into her windpipe. Her left lung was filled with sloppy food and she nearly died from septic pneumonia. Hurriedly released, her case led to the 'Cat and Mouse' Act which provided for very ill suffragettes to be released from prison, watched until they recovered, and then arrested and jailed again. But Lilian herself, a slight, striking girl, was also a completely committed arsonist. After her birthday she had embarked on a programme of window-smashing before visiting the suffragette headquarters to announce a change of tactics: 'my object was to burn two buildings a week . . . whenever we saw an empty building we would burn it'. They included Kew Gardens pavilion. Pursued by police, Lily proved adept at disguising herself as a boy and making dramatic escapes when cornered.[30]

These and many similar stories have made the militant suffragettes one of the best-known political successes of twentieth-century British politics. Yet several aspects of their story need to be added to get a complete picture. First, most women supporters of the suffrage campaign were never 'suffragettes' (a term originally meant as derisive, coined by the *Daily Mail*) at all. By the height of the agitation, just before the First World War, the Pankhursts' WSPU had around 2,000 members but Millicent Garrett Fawcett's National Union of Women's Suffrage Societies (NUWSS), which had been formed as early as 1887, had around 100,000 members and branches almost everywhere. The larger organization was more democratic internally, and did not split, as did the WSPU, which, had war not intervened, might well have fallen apart entirely. The less militant suffragists were often friendly towards their more aggressive rivals, and brave too. For many middle-class women, taking part in outdoor protests such as the 'mud march' on Parliament was traumatic in itself, and in many households they were confronting obdurate and

bewildered male relatives. There were many parallels between Millicent Fawcett and Emmeline Pankhurst. Fawcett, like Pankhurst, had
married a Liberal politician, though her husband rose to be a cabinet
minister under Gladstone, while Pankhurst's never achieved worldly
success, either as a radical Liberal candidate or later as a socialist.
Both women were inspired by the new thinking of late-Victorian
England – Fawcett was a friend of the early women's rights politician
and philosopher John Stuart Mill. Both lost their husbands relatively
early. Both were good organizers and both utterly determined. But
Fawcett and her movement worked inside the system, quietly
converting MPs until by the early 1900s she had a Commons majority
in favour of giving women the vote.

Her problem was that MPs smiled and nodded but never quite
got round to the subject, which kept being delayed; this led to
suffrage campaigners first splitting away from the formal Liberal and
Independent Labour organizations, and later actively targeting them.
In addition, Edwardian MPs were not prepared to contemplate any
vote for working-class women. The newly formed Independent
Labour Party and radical Liberal MPs were deeply worried that the
vote would eventually be given to middle-class women only, the
wives and daughters of their class enemies, and so would result in
Britain becoming more conservative, not less. Keir Hardie, despite
this, staunchly supported votes for women. That other titan of early
Labour history, George Lansbury, even went to prison and endured
force feeding for the suffrage cause, later attacking Asquith in the
Commons at the height of the agitation: 'You will go down in
history as the man who tortured innocent women. You ought to be
driven from public life.' Yet when Lansbury resigned his seat in east
London's Bow and Poplar in 1912 to stand on the specific cause of
votes for women, he was easily defeated. The tension between male
Labour leaders and suffragettes was always there and, as we shall
see, when war came the suffragettes gave the socialists good reason
to be bitterly disappointed.

The strongest rebuke to radical Liberal and Labour worries about
the cause being essentially middle class came from the growing
number of working-class militants, the so-called 'rebel girls' of the
suffragette story. Few of them left much in the way of books or
diaries but a rare exception was the Manchester radical Hannah

Mitchell, whose memoir *The Hard Way Up* was discovered among her papers when she died in 1956 and published only in 1968.[31] It is from there that the description of the Boggart Hole riot comes, and Hannah is worth dwelling on, because she reveals much about the suffragette and socialist story which is missing from the lives of the movement's better-off leaders. She came from a remote farm in Derbyshire and suffered under a mother driven to furious temper tantrums by housework and drudgery. Refreshingly straightforward in her memoir about how she dislikes the heavy routine of house-keeping, Hannah loathes cooking too and is not much enthused by motherhood. Missing formal education, she runs away and becomes a seamstress in various northern cities, eventually marrying a young fellow lodger, beginning to read and going to socialist meetings. As to marriage, she reflects that it was probably for her a mistake. She wanted comradeship and soon believed birth control was vital – 'by far the surest way for women to obtain some measure of freedom. I had seen many pretty, merry girls who had married on a small wage, and whose babies had come fast, turned into slatterns and prema-turely aged women.' She herself gives birth to a son, which without anaesthetic and with forceps was 'sheer barbarism and ought to be regarded as "wilful cruelty" and dealt with accordingly'. But after that her husband 'had the courage of his socialist convictions' and no more children follow. In mining villages and then in Ashton-under-Lyne, Hannah becomes a speaker at socialist meetings, attends the 'Labour church' and by 1904 is a Poor Law Guardian – one of the few positions women could take in public life. The following year, almost inevitably, she becomes involved with the Pankhursts and the suffrage issue, speaking outdoors 'on the steps of shows or roundabouts, on the market grounds, or at a street corner, on a chair, on a soap box from the nearest shop, often lent only in the hope of seeing some fun'.

Hannah Mitchell was the anonymous woman described as heck-ling Winston Churchill at the Manchester Free Trade Hall during the 1906 election, when he had her pulled up to the platform and briefly debated with her. She then passed through most of the rituals of the suffragette. She was imprisoned – the clothes were horrible, she reported, and 'the absence of garters and knickers made one feel almost naked' – but possessed such energy that she survived without the ordeal of force feeding. She took part in a famous raid on the Commons, fly-posted propaganda and, above all, spoke, endlessly, touring the country until she suffered a complete breakdown. The biggest impression left by her book was that the suffragette cause provided her with an escape route from the dreary, repetitive manual work required by the Edwardian home. A rebel against the role of mother and wife which, for the vast majority too poor for servants of their own, meant grinding toil – the scrubbing, washing, mangling, ironing, cleaning, baking and feeding that underpinned Edwardian respectability – she eventually joined the breakaway and more democratic Women's Freedom League. Hannah stands for a spectral army of unrecorded domestic dissidents.

Until the recent release of census information, the full story of the suffragettes of the Yorkshire and Lancashire mill towns and northern industrial cities has been underplayed.[32] Many came from homes in which the father was drunk or absent, and the mother the leading figure. In Hannah's case her mother was a termagant and her father nice, but very weak. Other families were more dramatic. Nellie Gawthorpe of Leeds effectively kicked her alcoholic and sexually aggressive father out, and set up home with her sister and mother. Annie Kenney, who with her heroine Christabel Pankhurst heckled Churchill in Oldham in 1905, was the daughter of a textile worker in the West Riding of Yorkshire whose early life was dominated by a strong mother. Annie herself tore off a finger as a ten-year-old mill girl and, when her mother died, was left bereft: for her the suffrage cause was a new all-female family. Edith Key was the daughter of a mill worker and a mill owner straight out of pulp fiction, who had seduced his employee and then stalked off. This was a time when women who had been let down by the male social system – through death, drink or desertion – could begin to glimpse wider horizons. The Pankhurst daughters themselves, though comparatively well off, had had a hard time because of their father and mother's endless radical politicking. Their lives were changed for ever by his early death from a perforated ulcer. Rebecca West, as a young teenage girl in Edinburgh, was writing pro-suffrage letters to the *Scotsman* and parading to school wearing Votes for Women badges. Her father, a rackety adventurer, right-wing journalist and gambler, had long before abandoned his family and lived alone in a

Liverpool tenement. In his final illness he sent a pathetic letter to Edinburgh: 'Good bye Lettie, Winnie, Cissie. I am dying. I loved you. Papa.'[33] His wife, who had not seen him for five years, went to bury him alone.

Clearly, many suffragettes and more moderate suffragists had happy upbringings, stable marriages and were supported by men who enthused about the cause too. Yet Edwardian life was economically risky, with yawning holes in the pavement for the unlucky and grimly constrained lives for, in particular, women who failed to make a good marriage. And the suffrage campaign was understood at the time to be about more than just the vote. Cartoons, postcards and anti-suffragette propaganda show them as men-haters who want to dominate weak husbands, wear the trousers and generally upend the social order – as unnatural and mannish freaks. There were lesbian and man-hating suffragettes, which is hardly surprising, and stoutly independent characters such as the composer Dame Ethel Smyth, in her tweeds and pork-pie hat, who did not care a fig what any man thought. But in a traditionalist society the psychological pressure on women attacked for their sexuality and lack of femininity was intense and may help explain why, later, so many suffragettes would make a point of their conservative and traditionalist views about other issues, from child care and venereal disease to the beastliness of Germans. The courage it took to stand up publicly to hardened male politicians, egged on by crowds of jeering men, never mind the physical protests and arrests which followed, should never be underestimated. Suffragettes smashed the complacent face of Edwardian Britain, and gave the lie to the world's view of Britain as a hidebound, conventional and stable society.

The Welshman and the Dukes

The Edinburgh Castle in the depths of London's Limehouse was the scene of Lloyd George's greatest speech, one of the most dramatic in the politics of radical Britain. Generally called a pub by historians, it was a strange, whitewashed building with battlements and turrets, flagpoles and slit windows. Once reeking of gin and tobacco, it had been converted into a centre for evangelical meetings in the East

End and so was appropriate for Lloyd George's provocative sermon against the aristocracy. On the evening of 30 July 1909 a large body of police was on duty outside, struggling to repel suffragettes who had mustered in force. Inside around 4,000 men were waiting. The windows were open and the chants of the angry women outside could be easily heard. Inside, male suffragette sympathizers had infiltrated themselves, and one managed to climb one of the columns on the stage, dressed in suffragist green and purple, tying himself to it. He was soon followed by half a dozen stewards. One climbed up to him and, pulling out a knife, cut the ropes and straps and hauled him down. As he and other protestors were hustled out, punches were thrown by the Liberal crowd. Then, to loud applause, up got the small, wiry, long-haired and instantly recognizable figure of the Chancellor of the Exchequer. Today and for many decades chancellors have been accustomed to defending their Budgets in the Commons and broadcast interviews. This was a rare thing, a chancellor obliged to take his Budget, already being called the People's Budget, to the people themselves. But Lloyd George was no ordinary Treasury minister. He was by now the most controversial and, to many, the most dangerous, politician in the country.

There were plenty who saw him in his prime who thought he was the greatest orator democratic British politics ever produced – greater than Churchill himself. Among those who seem to have taken that view was Churchill, at that time Lloyd George's follower and acolyte. To the most fervent of his admirers he was the Welsh wizard, the Merlin of radical politics or simply, in the words of one who introduced him at Rhyl, 'the greatest man since Christ'.[34] Yet to many others he came across as corrupt and hypocritical, constantly on the look-out for personal advancement, just as ready as Joe Chamberlain to split parties and very much the deluded egotist who would end up, as he did, crawling to Hitler. The historian Robert Blake asked with genuine bewilderment: 'Was he a man of principle pursuing by devious means a consistent end, or was he an opportunist who relied upon his intuition to gratify at every turn, his love of power and office?'

A young lawyer from a strongly nonconformist, Welsh-speaking coastal village in north Wales – where the Principality pokes a finger out at Ireland – Lloyd George had first made his mark as a Welsh nationalist. Attacking the Tories in the 1880s he spoke of 'the English ogre, this fiendish she-wolf whose lair is in Westminster'. A good early indication of the Lloyd George style came from the obscure-sounding Llanfrothen Burial Case. The law had been changed to allow Welsh nonconformists to be buried in Anglican churchyards, but one rector had held out. Lloyd George searched for, and found, a dying Methodist whose family allowed his cooling corpse to be used to challenge the rector. They literally broke down the church-yard gate and buried him, against the Llanfrothen vicar's will, alongside his daughter. Lloyd George then took the family's side in the case, and won. It made him a Welsh national hero. This mixture of ingenious controversy-stoking, bad taste, courage and self-promotion will recur. As a Liberal MP he had quickly established himself on the radical wing of the party, supporting the Boers as if they were simple Welsh farmers and the Irish Catholics as if they were nonconformists, and generally taking a very high moral tone while engaging in ever more enthusiastic adulteries while his wife Margaret was left behind in Wales. He was a Liberal, however, not a socialist, warning as early as 1904 that if his party did not push social reform successfully, the newly formed Labour Representation Committee would one day sweep them aside: 'the Liberal Party will be practically wiped out'. He was, of course, right about that. When, after the tariff row, Churchill stalked out of the Conservative Party, it was to the seat next to Lloyd George in the Commons that he stalked. And when the Conservatives under Balfour finally expired, Lloyd George became a member of the cabinet, President of the Board of Trade and, as his biographer put it, one 'of the board of directors of the greatest Power on earth'.[35] Yet his radical instincts appeared as sharp as ever. In 1906 he said in Birmingham that if the next Liberal government had done nothing after a Parliament 'to cope seriously with the social condition of the people, to remove the national degradation of slums and widespread poverty and destitution in a land glittering with wealth ... then a real cry will arise in this land for a new party and many of us here in this room will join it'.

Pulling the teeth of dangerous radicals is an old British establish-ment sport. Lloyd George was cautiously welcomed at the Palace, flattered by the mainstream press and turned into a genial 'card', a buzzing, amusing Welsh 'character', by the caricaturists. In turn, as a cabinet minister in Sir Henry Campbell-Bannerman's Liberal government, he was generally a reassuring figure. A radical reformer, yes, and one with a sharp wit, but a practical, sensible man who worked hard to reform the conditions of seamen and the safety of ships, to improve industrial statistics, to modernize patent law and to resolve dangerous industrial disputes, notably on the railways. It was, if not humdrum, the kind of thing any modernizing government in an age of international trade and growing industry had to do. The Welsh firebrand quietly plugged away. Fine fellow! Then Campbell-Bannerman died. Asquith made Lloyd George Chancellor of the Exchequer, a job he would hold continuously for longer than anyone else until Gordon Brown arrived in 1997. The fun began: Lloyd George turned to his wild side.

There were plenty who believed the real radical in the new Liberal government was Asquith, not Lloyd George. As the outgoing chancellor, Asquith had prepared the ground for the early version of old-age pensions, and had begun to find the money to pay for them. Lloyd George too had been a long-time campaigner for some system of relief for the old. As we have seen, he was hugely impressed by Seebohm Rowntree's book. During the Boer War he had complained at the waste of resources: every large shell exploding in Africa was money taken away from old-age pensions. The first reform was a minor, rather botched one. Determined to go further, Lloyd George used his summer parliamentary break in August 1908 to travel to Germany and Austria to find out at first hand what a really good system of welfare looked like. Germany hangs over Edwardian Britain in so many ways. The rising military and naval threat, she was in the forefront of industrial inventions. But she was also where radicals went to see the future of a fairer, better-organized way of treating people. Her coal miners had enjoyed some protection in hours worked and conditions since 1776; child and juvenile labour had been restricted since 1839. If there was no German Dickens, perhaps that was one reason. And from 1881 to 1889 Bismarck's Germany extended insurance against sickness, old age and unemployment far more widely and rigorously than any other European power had so far even contemplated.

Lloyd George visited German factories, old-age insurance offices, seamen's organizations, harbours and social democratic politicians.

Back at Southampton he told a waiting reporter for the *Daily News*: 'I never realized before on what a gigantic scale the German pension scheme is conducted . . . no amount of study at home can convey to the mind a clear idea of all that state insurance means to Germany.' Churchill, now promoted to Lloyd George's old job at the Board of Trade, was if anything more evangelical still, badgering Asquith for labour exchanges, unemployment insurance, health insurance, public works to mop up unemployment, compulsory education until seventeen and state control of the railways – in fact, much of the agenda of his later enemy Clement Attlee in 1945. Back in 1908 he told the prime minister: 'Germany with a harder climate and far less accumulated wealth has managed to establish tolerable conditions for her people. She is organized not only for war but for peace. We are organized for nothing except party politics . . . I say – thrust a big slice of Bismarckism over the whole underside of our industrial system & await the consequences whatever they may be with a good conscience.'[36] Or as he put it later in one of his happiest phrases, 'we must bring the magic of averages to the rescue of the millions'.

The growing vision of Lloyd George and Churchill, had it been given concrete expression in the Edwardian age, might have transformed the story of modern Britain, and spared the country much of the hardship and despair to follow. Yet there was a strong tradition of hostility to the German way, too bossy and organized for the traditions of small-state freedom-loving Britain. W. J. Braithwaite, a key official sent to study the big slice of Bismarckism in more detail, reported back that it was too bureaucratic. Much better to base insurance on the tradition of the voluntary friendly societies and the private insurance companies, whose members would prevent malingering. Lloyd George wasn't enough of a details man, and perhaps wasn't enough of a socialist, to resist such arguments. So a prologue to the eventual National Insurance Bill of 1911 explained that 'the only really effective check . . . is to be found in engaging the self-interest of the workmen themselves . . . a purely State Scheme . . . would inevitably lead to unlimited shamming and deception'. While there is some truth in this, learned the hard way in more recent times, it discarded the basic principle of the German state-welfare scheme in favour of 'the most trivial level of borrowing of individual devices'.[37] But where would the money come from? Recession and unemployment stalked industrial Britain. Out in the streets, patriotic crowds were chanting for the latest hugely expensive war machines, the British Dreadnought battleships: 'We want eight and we won't wait.' Guns or butter? Welfare or warfare? This was what really set the radical Liberal leaders on their collision course with the old establishment.

Lloyd George needed to find, he calculated, £8 million for the Dreadnoughts, and another £8 million 'to save 700,000 people from the horror of the workhouse and £2 million for 200,000 aged paupers'. Most of the money would come from higher income tax and from estate duties, but also from alcohol and tobacco duties, a rising amount (still small in total) from the new motor cars and from petrol. There would be a super-tax and a land tax, both highly provocative for the small number of the super-rich. Few of the million or so people then paying income tax were earning enough to be hit by the new proposals. Only 12,000 people would face super-tax and only 80,000 estate duty. Yet these, of course, were the people with the influence in Edwardian Britain. The Liberal cabinet was, in the main, horrified. The land value taxation turned out to cost more to collect than it raised and would be withdrawn again, with Lloyd George still in office as prime minister, in 1920. But back then, had it not been for Churchill's unstinting support, Lloyd George would not have survived the weeks of angry ministerial discussion. By this stage, the close political friendship between the Welsh firebrand and the Duke's nephew seemed truly bizarre. Churchill's only political guest at his wedding had been Lloyd George. He had invited this rising class warrior to stay with him at Blenheim, where Lloyd George had walked off to try to find a nonconformist place of worship 'under the shadow of this great palace – found them at last in a United Prayer Meeting in a field. They soon spotted me and were delighted, poor lads.'[38] As the controversy grew about the 'socialistic' measures, Churchill came to be regarded as a class traitor by others in his family and social circle. He may well have been psychologically prepared for this. Forty years earlier his father Sir Randolph had also been ostracized from polite London society, though for threatening the Prince of Wales with exposure in a complicated divorce action, and by some accounts for actually threatening him with a duel. This had been done for reasons of family loyalty: Randolph was protecting his elder brother Blandford, later the Duke of Marlborough, a man who according to newspapers of the day was known for 'brutal and profligate behaviour . . . a foulmouthed fellow, a ruffianly wife-beater, a man who if many in both Houses of Parliament had their way, would have been subjected to the ignominious punishment of the lash'.[39] Nevertheless, the vicious ostracism, including the need for the Churchills to decamp to Ireland since few titled families would receive them, was long remembered by Winston, who never treated King Edward very seriously and whose readiness to step outside the magic garden of the aristocracy began early. By 1909 the Duke of Beaufort thought Churchill, despite his grand connections, as much of a threat as Lloyd George and said he would like to see them both torn apart 'in the midst of twenty couples of dog hounds'.

Lloyd George's Budget speech in 1909 was very long and by all accounts dull listening, yet it would ignite the great confrontation of pre-1914 British public life. He argued that four Dreadnoughts were the minimum needed. Granted, it would have been an act 'of criminal insanity' to throw money required for other purposes 'on building gigantic flotillas to encounter mythical armadas' but for Britain, 'naval supremacy is essential for national existence'. He moved on to praise Germany's national welfare system, call for better use of Britain's land and natural resources and explain in meticulous detail why he was raising particular taxes. He concluded, however, by describing it as 'a war Budget . . . raising money to wage implacable warfare against poverty and squalidness' and looking forward to the time when 'wretchedness and human degradation . . . will be as remote to the people of this country as the wolves which once infested its forests'.

Early reaction was calm, but as the full import of the taxation of the rich hit home, it swiftly became intemperate. The government faced an increasingly self-confident and aggressive Tory opposition, most importantly in the Lords, which had thrown out Liberal measures, notably on the licensing of pubs. Churchill had warned that the Lords would be sent 'such a Budget in June as shall terrify them; they have started a class war, they had better be careful'. Lord Rosebery, the languid grandee and former Liberal prime minister, replied when it arrived that this was 'not a Budget but a revolution' and went on to imply the Commons did not have the authority to impose it. This was 'pure socialism . . . the end of all, the negation of faith, of family, of property, of Monarchy, of Empire'. A campaign began in the press, in the City, among landowners, in the House of Lords, as the establishment began to hit back. Financiers held meetings, aristocratic and wealthy Liberals went to protest in person to Asquith, an Anti-Budget League was formed and the newspaper letters pages were brimming with well-bred bile.

And so Lloyd George was found, that hot July evening, down at Limehouse, with the suffragette protestors finally expelled and the huge crowd quiet and expectant. In the eyes of many, including Tory peers, the Conservatives were successfully beating the elected government by working through the Lords. Their leader, Arthur Balfour, was enjoying the discomfiture of radicals who had beaten him at the polls but were now themselves being thrashed in the gilt and mahogany surroundings of Pugin's aristocratic palace. Lloyd George had always had a strong line in anti-landlord rhetoric. He seems genuinely to have despised the peerage, just as he was an enthusiast for 'new money' and the coarse, pushing-ahead men later called entrepreneurs. He was building on a long radical tradition of opposition to the Lords, which wanted to see the upper house abolished, or at least so neutered that it would never be able to challenge the elected chamber. This was a real confrontation, an historic one, between urban democracy and landed power. It was about more than simply raising money. On that night Lloyd George blew on the fire with all his magic-dragon might and brought the trouble to boiling point.

He had needed the money for Dreadnoughts, he told his audience, and the workmen had 'dropped in their coppers'. But when he went round Belgravia, 'there has been such a howl'. Was it not a shame that a rich country like Britain should allow those who have toiled all their days to die in penury and starvation? In one of the most moving passages, he recounted being down a coal mine, half a mile deep:

We then walked underneath the mountain, and we had about three quarters of a mile of rock and shale above us. The earth seemed to be striving – around us and above us – to crush us in. You could see the pit props bent and twisted and sundered, their fibres split in resisting the pressure. Sometimes they give way, and then there is mutilation and death. Often a spark ignites. The whole pit is deluged in fire and the breath of life is scorched out of hundreds of breasts by the consuming flame.

Yet when he and Asquith went to the landlords and asked for something to keep out of the workhouse 'these poor fellows who have been digging up royalties at the risk of their lives, some of them are old ... they are broken, they can earn no more', the aristocrats scowled, turned away and called them thieves. Well, said Lloyd George, 'I say the day of their reckoning is at hand'.

By this stage some landlords had begun petty protests, such as refusing to pay their customary subscription to the local football club or threatening to sack labourers if the Budget was passed. Lloyd George was merciless and continued the attacks: 'Are they going to threaten to devastate rural England by feeding and dressing themselves? Are they going to reduce their gamekeepers?' What, he asked his working-class audience, would they find to do in the season? 'No weekend shooting with the Duke of Norfolk or anyone.' With the support of the people behind him, he later added, 'we can brush the Lords like chaff before us'. A fully equipped duke, he told his audience, costs as much to keep up as two Dreadnoughts, 'and dukes are just as great a terror – and they last longer'. The typical nobleman 'has one man to fix his collar and adjust his tie in the morning, a couple of men to carry a boiled egg to him at breakfast, a fourth man to open the door for him, a fifth man to show him in and out of his carriage, and a sixth and seventh to drive him'. The chancellor knew his country-house economics: this was incendiary wit.

On his yacht at Cowes, Edward VII, who spent a fair proportion of his time shooting grouse with dukes, purpled with anger at Lloyd George's words. Asquith wrote to Lloyd George warning him that the monarch, whom they would need as an ally in threatening to destroy the Lords by swamping it with peers, was 'in a state of great agitation and annoyance ... I have never known him more irritated or more difficult to appease, though I did my best.' Lloyd George wrote to the King pointing out how much he had been provoked. Edward replied from his royal yacht that, though he personally took no position on the Budget, 'the language used by the Chancellor of the Exchequer . . . the King thinks was calculated to set class against class and to inflame the passions of the working and lower orders against people who happen to be owners of property'. *The Times* was equally condemnatory, saying in a leader two days after Limehouse that he had been 'openly preaching the doctrine that rich men have no right to their property, and that it is the proper function of Government to take it from them' and attacking his 'studious misrepresentations . . . violent invective . . . his sophistry . . . his coarse personalities . . . his pitiful claptrap'.

Neither the royal rebuke nor the one from *The Times* had much impact on Lloyd George. A few months later in Newcastle he demanded to know who was governing the country, people or peers? The Budget had not been formed to provoke a constitutional fight with the Lords but now that had happened, how was it possible that 500 'ordinary men, chosen accidentally from among the ranks of the unemployed' could push aside the will of the millions who made the country's wealth? If there was a revolution, it would be sparked by the Lords but then directed by the people. Edward Carson, the savagely brilliant and uncompromising lawyer who would lead the Ulster campaign, announced that Lloyd George 'has taken off the mask and he has preached openly a war of classes, insult to individuals, the satiation of greed and the excitement of all the passions which render possible the momentary triumph of the demagogue'. Churchill was seen as not much less socialistic. He had already warned that if social reform was halted there would be 'savage strife between class and class' and was just as ready as Lloyd George to mock ducal lifestyles, despite his own Blenheim connections. Dukes, he told a Leicester audience, were unfortunate creatures who ought to be left to lead quiet, delicate sheltered lives: 'Do not let us be too hard on them. It is poor sport – almost like teasing goldfish . . . These ornamental creatures blunder on every hook they seek and there is no sport whatever in trying to catch them. It would be barbarous to leave them gasping on the bank of public ridicule upon which they have landed themselves. Let us put them back gently, tenderly, into their fountains.'[40] Yet again, the court intervened: the King's private secretary wrote a letter of protest to *The Times*, which Churchill thought showed that both he and the King had gone mad.

The Lords kicked out the People's Budget in November 1909,

by 350 votes to 75, breaking a constitutional convention which had lasted since the Glorious Revolution of 1688. It was an act of suicidal stupidity. The landed aristocracy was already in headlong economic retreat, with the sales of great estates in Ireland, Wales, Scotland and England continuing at a relentless pace ever since the great agricultural decline began in the 1880s. Grand houses were being let, scores of fabulous artworks – paintings by Van Dyck, Titian, Rembrandt, superb furniture, historic Renaissance statues – were coming up, year after year, in the London salerooms. The social status of 'land' was beginning to shake, just a little. The number of knighthoods being given out had been rising sharply, so that Lord Salisbury remarked you could not throw a stone at a dog in London without hitting a knight. Army reforms attacked the traditional aristocratic route towards a red coat and braid – buying commissions. Edward VII's circle contained many Jewish financiers and he seemed to enjoy luxury and good living more than the rarefied class distinctions of the old landed set. Behind gnarled hands, in which old blue blood still gurgled, they called him traitor, and thought the same of his ministers. It was easy for paranoia to grab the throats of the old order, particularly when 'squiffy' Asquith, with his young female admirers and love of the bottle, and Lloyd George's already-rumoured love affairs and financial corruption were the talk of the town.

With no Budget the government could not long survive. On the Liberal side, the need for a general election to provide moral authority for a full-frontal attack on the Lords became clear. Under the British constitutional system, the Lords could not simply be abolished. The Tory majority there would have to be diluted out of existence. Then long-discussed plans to bring them forever to heel could be put into place. This meant the formal removal of their power to stop any monetary bill, and powers for the Commons to override them on all other legislation too, after three attempts by the Peers to amend it or throw it out. They would have the power of delay, not of veto. The King thought there would need to be two general elections, the first on the Budget and the second on the future of the Lords, before the latter could have its power taken away, an idea he detested. And this is indeed what happened. For a short time the payment of income tax was voluntary, since the

Budget could not pass. In the first 1910 election the Liberals' huge 1906 majority in the Commons vanished, though with the Irish nationalists brought in as allies they could still beat the Tories. The Budget then passed, and Asquith turned his attention to the neutering of the Lords. In early May, the King had died. He was succeeded by his forty-five-year-old son George, desperate for a compromise. The Tory and Liberal leaders met, trying to find one, but could not. Lloyd George fantasized about the break-up of the party system and a new coalition government of the best of both parties in the Commons, perhaps with him as prime minister. There was talk of putting it all to the people in a referendum.

George V agonized over what to do. Perhaps he should refuse to swamp the peerage but instead call on the Tory leader Balfour to try to form a government? Then in an election, perhaps the people would vote for Balfour, King and Peerage, not for the damned radicals. Then again, if they voted for Asquith and Lloyd George, that might well mean the end of the monarchy, as well as the House of Lords. It now seems that King George was conned by his own adviser, who hid from him the fact that Balfour, if asked, would have tried to form a government. So, eventually, believing there was no alternative, he gave Asquith the promise he was looking for. There would be 500 or so new peers if necessary, but this was to remain a dark secret until after the second general election. In his diary the King, who was not given to overstatement, wrote, 'I agreed most reluctantly . . . I disliked having to do this very much.' The second, winter, election of 1910 produced little change in the Commons and through the first half of 1911 the Parliament Bill, assaulting the old power of the Lords, ground its way through the Commons. In July, Asquith formally announced the deal he had done with the King eight months earlier. He had more than 200 names already drawn up for instant peerages – retired military men, Oxford professors, plenty of knights and businessmen, the list seems dully respectable now. But up in the Lords, they were not quite ready to give up. Not yet.

Compton Verney, a grand Adam house of the 1760s, stands near Stratford-upon-Avon in Warwickshire, the traditional seat of the Willoughby de Brokes. There, for centuries, there had been hierarchy and deference, fox hunting and forelock-tugging by honest farmers and ploughmen. In 1906 Richard Greville Verney, the nineteenth Lord Willoughby de Broke, was innocently clip-clopping along, contemplating fox hunting, his lifelong obsession, when he met an old farmer who told him that the Liberal landslide meant that 'everything I had would be taken away from me and divided among the people who had voted for the Radical candidate. But, of course, I did not believe a single word of it, and went on hunting as if nothing were going to happen.'[41] These were acres which had seen off impertinent requests to allow railways through, where the rude remarks of Joe Chamberlain and the radicals of nearby Birmingham had been treated with disdain. Like so many of his friends, Willoughby de Broke's life was wholly bound up with his county and his land. The modern world was a nasty rumour. Like so many, he was woken up by the People's Budget.

Along with many other 'backwoodsmen' among the Tory peers, Willoughby de Broke attended Lord Landsdowne's grand London house for a brisk meeting to agree to vote down the licensing bill and then adjourned for a decent lunch at the Carlton Club. Even Willoughby de Broke could see this might seem offensive to the elected government of the day: 'a great nobleman, living in a palace in the heart of Mayfair' had written a few letters to his brother noblemen in the country 'summoning them to take private counsel with him under his own roof, where, after a desultory conversation lasting less than an hour, it is agreed to turn down a proposal that has occupied the Liberal Party for something like a quarter of a century'. Yet he confessed to finding the meeting itself 'great fun'. Some of the Tory peers, he reported, were believed to have thought that Landsdowne House was the House of Lords, and that they had been voting formally. Before the Liberals had won their Commons majority, the upper house had been sparsely attended and votes were so rare that, when they happened, the peers would 'cackle as if they had laid an egg'. But with radicals at large in the Commons, all this was about to change.

The fox-hunting peer was soon taking regular early morning trains south from Warwickshire to destroy Lloyd George's Budget and defend the Lords against Asquith's democratic threats. Though Willoughby de Broke and his world have long gone, it is worth trying to understand his motives. In his memoirs, much of them devoted to country pursuits, he argued that the late-Victorian period had been a golden age for the ruling classes:

> Their order still continued to dominate in both Houses of Parliament. The freak, the faddist, the schemer and the doctrinaire were either not returned to the House of Commons . . . or . . . made to feel out of place in an assembly composed of those whom an orator of blue blood once called 'people like ourselves'. In their own counties the squirearchy were supreme, and hunted and shot to their heart's content with no one to say them nay . . . They had a dominating influence in politics, a comfortable balance at the bank, and modern comforts on a scale of which their fathers could never have dreamed.

Yet this long-faced, quizzical aristocrat maintained that in the 18,000 acres of his ancestral home, everyone was happier for knowing their place, from the master of foxhounds to the curate. 'I am prepared to defend the hereditary principle,' he once said, 'whether that principle is applied to peers . . . or to foxhounds.'[42] It was well said of him that he believed England's masses should be 'treated as he treated his gamekeepers, grooms and indoor staff – that is, kindly and firmly. He had quite a gift for writing, thought clearly, and was not more than two hundred years behind his time.'[43]

The Tory leaders of the day, including Lords Lansdowne and Curzon, were first in line in the great reactionary battle but the backwoodsmen were always suspicious that the grandees might eventually sell them out. Curzon was regarded as insufferably pompous even in aristocratic Edwardian England. The story was told that, after it was suggested he try public transport for once in his life, he boarded a bus and gave the driver his home address. He had been Viceroy of India and hoped to become prime minister. He gave the hardliners their nickname by saying, at a dinner in May 1911: 'Let them make their peers; we will die in the last ditch before we give in.' So they became 'ditchers'. The Tories who decided to compromise, indeed to cave in, were known as 'hedgers' – and soon included Curzon himself.

After riotous and vicious scenes in the Commons and an abortive attempt to find a compromise between the party leaders, the final act would be played out in the Lords. The second general election had confirmed the Liberals in power, albeit still only with Irish support. Would the peers accept the democratic will of the country and vote for their own emasculation? The Tory Party itself was now at daggers drawn. The party leaders were calling for surrender. The ditchers were determined to go down fighting and set up their own organization to campaign across the country for the survival of aristocratic government. The beginnings of a breakaway party emerged, with its own typists, campaigners, public speakers and lobbyists. Ferocious rows broke out, families divided and old friendships were broken. On 24 July 1911, with the King's promise to swamp the Lords in his pocket, Asquith arrived in the Commons having been cheered by crowds in the short motor-car ride from Downing Street. But inside the chamber the prime minister was shouted down for nearly half an hour by irate, almost berserk, Tory MPs, screaming 'Traitor', 'Who killed the King?' and (rather more obscurely) 'American dollars' until eventually he had to give up and leave. It was, reported Churchill afterwards to King George, 'a squalid, frigid, organized attempt to insult the Prime Minister'. But like many scenes in the Commons, its effect was the opposite of its intent. It broke the nerve of the Conservative leadership. Asquith was not going to crack. Worried, among other things, about the effect another 500 low-born peers would have on their own social status, 234 Tory peers agreed to throw in the towel. Curzon wrote that anyone who kept fighting deserved to be sent to a lunatic asylum.

Willoughby de Broke and many others preferred Bedlam to Curzon. Most of his troops were horsemen, bred to charge first and think afterwards. A huge final 'no surrender' dinner was held in the Hotel Cecil. Up and down London Willoughby de Broke was taking numbers, making lists. It would be very tight. On 8 August the two factions faced one another in the Lords, many of the ditchers wearing white heather in their buttonholes and the hedgers wearing red roses. After a bitter debate, when the vote was about to be called, some of the ditcher aristocrats were having second thoughts. Willoughby hid the top hat and coat of one noble duke to keep him in the Lords for the vote. But he bolted anyway, running off into the night. In an age when it was unthinkable for a gentleman, never mind a duke, to appear hatless, this is as good an image as any for the final defeat of the aristocratic order. The ditchers lost. Asquith and Lloyd George had won.

This was a parliamentary revolution. It was accomplished without bloodshed but was the definitive defeat for the landowning class, which had believed for centuries that even in the age of 'demagogues' the country could not be run against their vital interests. Its effects are still with us, but it was a very British revolution. Willoughby de Broke was a sentimental, hunting-obsessed believer in the good old days; he was a fanatic with a sense of humour, who knew when he was defeated. In 1921 he was forced to put up his beloved Compton Verney for sale. It was bought – the ultimate humiliation – by a soap manufacturer and Willoughby de Broke died the following year. At the time of writing, his descendant is one of the remaining hereditary peers in the House of Lords, and a member of the UK Independence Party.

Huns in Sussex

The light is failing on a cold sandy island off the Baltic coast. In a corrugated-iron hut a group of men are talking in some kind of code. Outside, crouched down, his heart thumping, is a young Foreign Office employee who has been moving around these treacherous waters in a battered yacht. He makes out a single word which catches his attention – 'Chatham'. Piece by piece, the mutterings about water depths, tugs and weather fall into place. The observer, with the delightfully old-fashioned English surname of Carruthers, follows the muttering strangers and smuggles himself onto a small tug, pulling a barge half filled with coal into the murky seascape. He now understands. He is watching 'an experimental rehearsal of a great scene, to be enacted, perhaps, in the near future – a scene when multitudes of sea-going lighters, carrying full loads of soldiers, not half loads of coal, should issue simultaneously in seven ordered fleets from shallow outlets, and, under escort of the Imperial Navy, traverse the North Sea and throw themselves bodily upon English shores'. Though a fictional scene, it comes in a book which in 1903 felt all too real. The description of the German coast around East Friesland was uncannily accurate, there were detailed charts inside

the book and the clever nature of the German invasion plan
convinced many that it was accurate. The man responsible for the
story was a clerk in the House of Commons and the Liberal leader –
soon to be prime minister – Campbell-Bannerman called him into
his office to ask whether it was true. A former prime minister, Lord
Rosebery, was equally intrigued. Soon MPs with constituencies on
the English east coast, apparently to be targeted for German landings,
were bombarding the government and navy with worried questions,
and the First Lord of the Admiralty was in urgent communications
with the director of Naval Intelligence.

The book was *The Riddle of the Sands*, written by an experienced
amateur sailor and sometime soldier called Erskine Childers. It
remains the best of the 'invasion scare' fictions of Edwardian Britain.
It was the fruit of Childers's own knowledge of sailing round and
exploring the sandy, foggy, treacherous Baltic coast of Germany, and
his determination to alert politicians and public to the vulnerability
of Britain to a forthcoming invasion by the Kaiser's forces. Like many
other serious sailors, he had seen the Kaiser's racing yachts and
battleships up close. In the first months of the new century, illustrated magazines had made much of a new volunteer force being
recruited in the City of London to go off and fight in the increasingly
desperate Boer War. There are drawings of clerks and lawyers
standing in line – the City of London Imperial Volunteers. One of
them was Childers, who found his Tory views being softened and
liberalized by his experiences as an ordinary soldier in South Africa.
In the epilogue to Childers's novel, a memorandum explains: 'We
have a small army, dispersed over the whole globe ... We have no
North Sea naval base, no North Sea fleet, and no North Sea policy.
Lastly, we stand in a highly dangerous economical position.' There
were plenty who pooh-poohed such a grim view of Britain's real
military strength. The prime minister, Lord Salisbury, was a boatman
of a different temper. He was disinclined to panic and suggested that
as soon as every Englishman knew how to use his horse, bicycle,
motor car and rifle for home defence, the invasion threat would
recede.

But the great national jitter about invasion overwhelmed aristocratic scepticism. *The Riddle of the Sands* was reprinted again and
again in the years before 1914. Three years after Childers's book,

men in spiked German helmets and blue-grey uniforms startled passers-by in London's Oxford Street. This was a publicity stunt by the *Daily Mail*, advertising 'The Invasion of 1910', a serial by the sensationalist novelist (much admired at court) William le Queux, which contained a bloodthirsty account of the German army landing after preparations at just the spot Childers predicted. There are firing squads, German soldiers murdering women, Uhlans galloping into undefended British towns and the rest. Le Queux had worked closely with the British field marshal, former Boer War commander and all-round imperial hero Lord Roberts, who in turn boosted the book at Westminster. In fact, their plausible scenario for invasion was judged too boring for circulation purposes by Lord Northcliffe, the paper's proprietor, who ensured the Germans invaded one town at a time, with the *Mail* providing a map for each day's events. In 1909 Northcliffe sent the socialist Robert Blatchford on a tour of Germany to warn Britons of the Huns' 'gigantic preparations . . . to force German dictatorship on the whole of Europe'.[44]

Many other influential journalists pursued the same theme. Leo Maxse, an admiral's son and talented right-wing controversialist, helped foment the spy mania of 1908, going so far as to warn a friend to get rid of his German nanny because, as a keen cyclist, she was almost certainly a military agent. Le Queux entirely agreed, warning his readers that the German high command had a secret civilian army hidden in England, posing as waiters, clerks, bakers, hairdressers and servants: 'Each man, when obeying the Imperial command to join the German arms had placed in the lapel of his coat a button of a peculiar shape, with which he had long ago been provided, and by which he was instantly recognized as a loyal subject of the Kaiser.'[45] It was reported elsewhere that every grocer's shop, dairy, garage, pub and telephone office had been marked down to prepare for the invasion, that German military bands had secretly prepared siege guns in the London suburbs and that – according to one MP – there were 66,000 German reserve soldiers living secretly in the Home Counties with an arms dump at Charing Cross, just along the road from the Commons.

Invasion shudders kept coming. Another began with 'news' that German battleships had bombarded and then destroyed the forts at Harwich, followed by the arrival of 5,000 troops there, Zeppelin attacks on the dockyards at Chatham and the advance of the German army through Colchester and Chelmsford. As they approach the capital, there is panic in London. Terrified citizens try to stop British soldiers being sent to France to try to hold the line there: '*April 7, Afternoon.* – Serious rioting in London . . . Enormous crowds, converging on Westminster, were repeatedly charged by the mounted police, and finally fired on by the two battalions of Guards which had been assigned to the duty of protecting His Majesty's person . . . [the population] endeavoured everywhere to prevent the departure of troop trains by invading the lines, tearing up the rails, or laying themselves in front of the engines.' The government is overwhelmingly defeated in the Commons and is replaced by a new one, with the single purpose of saving London. The Germans arrive in Romford and Woolwich and there is continuous street fighting until they reach Tottenham. Meanwhile the British and French armies in France are totally defeated. On the story goes, in great detail, until finally the tide begins to turn. It is compelling, much more so than Le Queux. So it should be, perhaps. For the author was none other than Winston Churchill, then First Lord of the Admiralty; and its audience was admiring naval chieftains.

Yet five years earlier, Churchill had devoted a major speech to ridiculing war with Germany. The two countries needed each other's trade and the big British colonies were under absolutely no threat from Germans. 'What remains as a prize to be fought over by two great countries? Nothing but tropical plantations and small coaling places scattered here and there . . . although there may be snapping and snarling in the newspapers and in the London clubs, these two great peoples have nothing to fight about . . . Are we all such sheep . . . Are we all become such puppets and marionettes to be wire-pulled against our interests into such hideous convulsions?' Churchill's intimation of slaughter ahead gives the lie to the popular belief that Edwardians had no notion of what a future European war might mean and sauntered towards the trenches. In Wells's book *Anticipations*, he foresees 'the grey old general . . . who learnt his art of war away in the vanished nineteenth century' with his epaulettes, sword and obsolete horse riding at the head of his doomed column: 'Nothing can happen but the needless and most wasteful and pitiful killing of these poor lads who make up the infantry battalions . . .

The scattered invisible marksmen with their supporting guns will shatter their masses . . . It will be more like herding sheep than actual fighting.' Thinking Edwardians knew perfectly well what might happen, the catastrophe of a war of cavalry and young soldiers in the age of machines. As with Churchill in 1908, many were determined to avoid it at all costs.

What changed? For Churchill, it was not simply the move from Trade to the Home Office, with its defence stores responsibilities, and then to the Admiralty itself. Initially he was with Lloyd George in trying to limit the number of super-expensive new Dreadnoughts to four, while the crowds were chanting 'We want eight and we won't wait' – something he later frankly admitted had been a big personal mistake. But the increasingly menacing behaviour of the Germans shifted him, and many more. He knew Germany as well as any senior minister, through friendships with businessmen and having been invited over twice by the Kaiser to watch the German army on manoeuvres. He knew that the Imperial German Navy was expanding very fast and the Kaiser was making it clear that the warships were not for show. The sending of a gunboat to Morocco in 1911, a deliberate provocation to France in a colonial dispute, sent such a shiver through London that serious war preparations had begun. It was only after a menacing speech from Lloyd George, making clear that Britain would come to the aid of the French in any war, that Germany backed down. The famous German Naval Law of 1912 sharply increased the rate of building of warships and the widening of the Kiel Canal to allow free access to the North Sea from the Baltic, both directly challenged the Royal Navy's command of the home seas. The race between German and British shipyards was frantic, despite calls for a halt, or 'holiday', by Churchill, right up to the outbreak of war. In a speech in 1912 which caused grave offence to Berlin, Churchill had pointed out that there was a difference in danger to the two countries. The British navy was a necessity, the German one 'more in the nature of a luxury . . . It is existence to us; it is expansion to them. We cannot menace the peace of a single Continental hamlet, no matter how great and supreme our Navy may become.' But Britain could be defeated and 'swept away utterly' by naval defeat: 'It is the British Navy which makes Great Britain a great power. But Germany was a great power, respected and honoured all over the world, before she had a single ship.'

We are back to the world of Erskine Childers and a planned German strike on Britain. The fact that this never happened, and was ridiculed by Berlin, does not invalidate Churchill's point. As he sailed happily around the ports and squadrons of the navy in his rather grand Admiralty yacht, organizing new strategies and shifting the whole fleet from coal to oil, Churchill was well aware that a single naval defeat could finish everything. By the time the Battle of Jutland took place, a bloody draw, only the Royal Navy could have lost the war in an afternoon. That this did not happen, despite ferocious shipbuilding and the latest submarine technology from the Germans, is partly down to Churchill, and the panicky, Germanophobic mood of the country which supported him. The spy manias and terrors were often silly. Organizations such as the Navy League were on the far right of Edwardian politics and helped foment suspicion of foreigners and radicals in government. Yet the threat was real all along. Long before Edwardian politicians were sure of it, they had to find some way of paying for the ruinously expensive ships, while keeping their promises on welfare alive. By then Churchill had already sketched out the likely strategy of a European war and the numbers of forces on each side, as well as what the German high command would do, with uncanny accuracy. From now on, he seemed to assume that war was likely.

Enter the Workers

A little earlier, a short, angry-looking man in a soft felt hat had sent a letter to Mr Churchill, then home secretary. Ben Tillett said the dock workers 'shall bring about a state of war ... Hunger and poverty have driven the Dock and Ship workers to this present resort, and neither your police, your soldiers, your murder nor Cossacks will avert the disaster coming to this country.' This was written in the hot summer of 1911, as the meat by the wharves began to stink, long rows of butter in barrels turned rancid, huge piles of vegetables rotted, and tempers rose. Edwardian Britain, like Britain today, lived on imported food. Unlike today, it was brought in entirely by boat and unloaded by hand, tens of thousands of ill-paid men – stevedores, lightermen, carmen – trundling barrows and barrels, working cranes, loading drays and unpacking crates for a few pence an hour. For decades they had been pitted against one another, scrabbling for work in mutually hostile groups. Now, under Tillett and his comrades, they were suddenly speaking as one. The government and the capital were helpless before them, unless, like the Czar, Mr Churchill really was prepared to order in the cavalry. The cabinet swiftly buckled and the strike won the eightpence-an-hour victory the dockers had sought.

Tillett was one of a remarkable group of working-class leaders who had emerged in late-Victorian Britain. Bigamous, violent in his language and wildly inconsistent, he was a man who knew what life at the bottom was really like. He was born into a large and poor family in Bristol, and his mother died when he was one. His father worked in a cart factory when he wasn't drinking, which wasn't often. By the age of seven, to pay the bills, Tillett was working in a brick factory cutting slabs of clay from daylight to dusk. Up in Scotland his great rival Keir Hardie, just a little older, had endured early years that were just as harsh and just as typical of Victorian working life. According to family lore he was born to his unmarried farm-labourer mother in a turnip field. After she met and wed a carpenter and moved to Glasgow, the young Hardie, aged ten, worked twelve hours a day delivering bread. Trying to help his mother, he was late for work one morning, and was sacked by his master, whom he remembered sitting at a mahogany table with his family round him, the coffee bubbling and their plates loaded with dainties, as he lectured the boy. The anger he felt then stayed with Hardie all his life, keeping him warm on cold evenings in backstreet meetings for decades to come.

In Bristol, Tillett ran away to join Old Joe Barker's Circus and became an acrobat, until a sister snatched him back and had him taught shoemaking. But Tillett was wild and angry and his father caught him in a theatre and turned him over to the Royal Navy at thirteen. At that age, Hardie was sitting for long hours in a dark room in a Lanarkshire coal mine, operating a trap door to let air into the mine shaft. These were not children who would have needed Seebohm Rowntree's researchers to tell them about unfairness.

Tillett and Hardie would cobble together their education in fits and snatches, Tillett in the navy, until he fell off some rigging and had to be invalided out, and Hardie through his mother and step-father, and with underground exercises in the darkness. They grew up forcing themselves to read and re-read the same books until they understood them – Carlyle and Ruskin, Dickens and Shakespeare. They both attended a Congregational church and began to climb upwards by organizing trade unions for workers in desperate straits. For Hardie, it was the Lanarkshire and Ayrshire miners in the 1880s. Tillett, at just the same time, had left the merchant navy and was living in the vile slums of Bethnal Green working as a docker, one of around 100,000 casual labourers who would queue for work each morning at the gates of the wharves hoping to get hired, when, according to evidence given to the House of Lords at the time, 'men struggle like wild beasts; we stand upon one another's shoulders'.

A sickly-looking man with stubble and a stutter, Tillett taught himself public speaking, co-founding his first union in a Hackney pub. Like Hardie he was roughed up by company thugs and after the epic London dock strike of 1889 he founded the Dock, Wharf, Riverside and General Labourers' Union, which in due course and by merger eventually became the mighty Transport and General Workers' Union. Hardie, meanwhile, had been working for the Scottish miners and founding Britain's first Labour party, the Scottish Labour Party. Neither man began as a socialist; both were radical Liberals. They were attracted to Marxism and each knew Engels, but turned from that to become founding members of the Independent Labour Party, formed in Bradford in 1893. They both ended up in Parliament. They seem, therefore, a matched pair. Yet Hardie and Tillett would veer off in wildly different directions, which together explain a lot about the failures and successes of the socialists before the First World War.

Hardie, a temperance campaigner, preacher and organizer, took the high road of building a parliamentary party. Tillett believed that socialism could come about only through trade union insurgency outside Parliament. For a while the two became rival heroes to millions of workers. In the Commons, Keir Hardie was the first socialist, working-class MP who looked and sounded what he was. In an age when MPs all wore dark frock-coats, stiff collars and top

An eye for headlines and exuberant headwear from the first:
Young Winston, war hero, 1899.

Lizzie Van Zyl: the effect, if not the intention, of Britain's
South African invention – the 'concentration camp'.

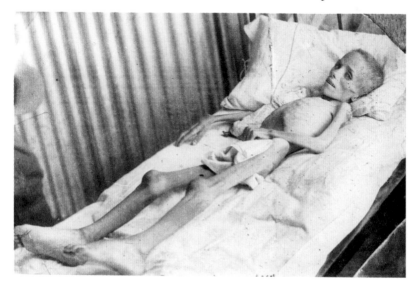

The old world dies:
Queen Victoria's funeral cortège,
1901.

'Pont' of *Punch*, perhaps
the greatest cartoonist
of the thirties, sums up the
entire message of this book
in a few squiggled lines.

*"Now children, I wonder if you realise that you
have inherited the largest and the richest Empire
the world has ever known."*

Radical Joe became the
Great Imperialist. Once among
the most famous, and infamous,
men on the planet.

Below 'Edward the Caresser':
Bertie felt he had been a Victorian
for quite long enough.

Below right A strangely sinister man:
Queen Victoria's grandson, Kaiser Bill,
doing his bit for world wildlife.

Awesome – and awesomely expensive: Britain's 'Dreadnought' leads
a naval flotilla in 1906.

Anti-free-trade propaganda. An economic argument that split Britain
down the middle.

Working-class engineer and salesman toff: Royce and Rolls in the year of their great Silver Ghost, 1906. It went like a silent silver bullet and still remains the world's most valuable car.

Edith Nesbit: a wild, experimental private life.

Peter Pan: Edwardian children's stories provide a key to the inner life of the era.

H. G. Wells: often silly, often wrong, but the most ambitious popular sage of the time.

Britain's got talent: music hall was the Edwardian equivalent of popular television.

Very naughty and a national treasure: the great Marie Lloyd.

One of the forgotten greats: Little Tich in his prime.

hats, he famously arrived in a simple woollen suit with a red scarf, or tie, and a floppy hat, usually described as a cloth cap but more like a deerstalker. More important, he refused to play the usual Commons game, protesting against the time spent on grovelling addresses to the royal family, insisting that MPs had the right, and duty, to discuss the grimy details of working-class life and supporting strikers everywhere. Today those who remember Hardie tend to see him as an almost Christ-like figure, gentle, bearded and modest. In his heyday he seemed to the middle classes a menacing and ferocious character. His very name was used by nursemaids to scare their whimpering charges.

Tillett seemed as threatening. In 1912, during the second great London dock workers' strike, he was openly preparing for violent confrontation. His hat tipped back on his head, he would be found standing in the open air at Tower Hill in front of a silent river and a sea of faces, demanding how many there had some military training and would join the Transport Workers' Civilian Police. As a forest of hands rose his language became wilder: 'Sedition or no sedition, I want to say that if our men are murdered I am going to take a gun and I will shoot Lord Devonport' – he being the leader of the employers with whom he was negotiating. Three weeks later, at Hyde Park, Tillett was again promising violence, and indeed revolvers were used, and men wounded, soon after in fighting between strikers and strike-breakers. Tillett then appealed to God to ´strike Lord Devonport dead and the crowd chanted back: 'He shall die, he shall die.' That strike failed, but there were waves of strikes in 1911–12 in the railways, textile mills, mines and shipyards which shook the Edwardian elite, Liberal and Tory. Revolutionary trade unionism, then fashionable on the left in France and America, was thought a more serious threat than socialist parties.

In November 1910 striking miners at Tonypandy in south Wales began a three-day riot which the police could not control. Churchill, as home secretary, was asked for hussars and infantry. Contrary to his later reputation for impetuous violence against strikers, Churchill refused to allow them to proceed but halted them at Swindon while he telegraphed an appeal to the miners to stop. Instead, he ordered police reinforcements from London. In a telegram to the King he explained that constables were better. Troops would not have arrived in time to stop the looting of shops and 'infantry soldiers can if attacked or stoned only reply by fire from long-range rifles which often kills foolish sightseers . . . or innocent people'. The cavalry and infantry were eventually sent but by then the rioting had stopped. Churchill was angrily attacked for his weakness in *The Times* and defended in the *Manchester Guardian*, which reckoned he had saved many lives by holding back the troops, who would simply have bayoneted rioters. It is curious that about the only fact 'everyone knows' about Churchill's early political career was that he sent in troops to kill strikers at Tonypandy. Liverpool's dock strike was in fact a much more serious affair, with a week of serious violence and appeals from its mayor who told ministers it was not a strike but that a revolution was in progress. Again Churchill urged the use of police, not the army. But the strikes spread throughout Liverpool and, once a national railway strike began, the mood became uglier. The Riot Act was read, the entire Aldershot garrison was sent north and a warship appeared off the coast at Birkenhead. Huge meetings in the city and further rioting left two men dead.

King George V sent a telegram to Churchill warning against 'half hearted deployment of troops'. They should only be used as a last resort but, his telegram ended, 'if called on they should be given a free hand & the mob should be made to fear them. GEORGE R.I.' Meanwhile the panicking mayor of Birkenhead told the Home Office: 'I do not think that I have sufficient resources at my disposal. If you cannot send me more military or naval support, I cannot answer for the safety of life or property.' In the circumstances, though Lloyd George's talks which stopped the national rail strike were the real breakthrough, Churchill's moderation is quite impressive. Elsewhere, there was panic. Upper-class gents rushed to buy revolvers to protect themselves in their London clubs and army encampments appeared in Hyde Park, Regent's Park and Battersea Park. It was reckoned that every soldier in the country was on standby and there was much talk of the coming revolution. The vast coal-miners' strike of 1912 saw 850,000 miners stop working, with another 1.3 million workers affected. This was only halted after most of what they wanted was conceded in Parliament.

It seemed that perhaps the syndicalists were right. Keir Hardie began to argue for a single massive union to batter down the walls:

'The old idea of separate unions has passed away. The colliers, the iron workers, the steel workers, the artisans, the railway men, the shop assistants, the school teachers, the gas workers and the street cleaners have all got to stand together . . . as members of one class.'[46] Tillett's second dock strike was a failure, the men effectively starved back to work, but the strikes and insurrectionary language went on. Over in Dublin another huge and violent transport workers' strike the following year, led by James Larkin and James Connolly, ended with five dead and thousands injured, plus hundreds of strikers arrested and jailed. At the 1913 meeting of the TUC in Manchester, Tillett responded to the slaughter in Dublin by arguing to cheers that strikers had the right to have firearms and use them: 'War has been declared upon the workers . . . This exhibition of Czardom is something we will fight against, even if it is sedition and civil war to do so.'[47] Women factory workers in fizzy-drinks factories, jam factories, cigar factories and chain-making factories all struck during the sweltering 1911 summer. So did schoolchildren, protesting against the use of the cane, and too much homework.[48]

Socialism had begun to emerge as a living idea among working-class people in the 1880s. It was about as unformed, vague and prone to splits as any early religion, and its dreams of a better future were fuzzy. For the followers of William Morris and English socialists like Blatchford it promised paradise on earth, a return to simpler lives with no slimy-walled slums or ear-splitting factories. It is easy to mock, but on the edge of the great cities and beyond, plenty of working-class families did keep livestock, grew vegetables and had their own hens to supplement their income. In the mining villages, the countryside was never far away. Among the innumerable small unions there were plenty of self-educated craftsmen. Morris, with his intricate wallpaper designs and olde-worlde typefaces and parables, seems desperately old fashioned now. To many late Victorians, though, he seemed modern, a herald of the future; perhaps the best comparison is with radical environmentalists of our age. For others, socialism was inextricably linked with Christianity. There were Labour churches and socialist churches operating very like nonconformist chapels all across industrial Britain, often knitted together by travelling speakers, including the cyclists and horse-drawn vans of Robert Blatchford's Clarion movement. In the early days, almost all radicals and socialists were still inside the Liberal family. But it was starting to get harder to see how a party with landowners and mill owners so dominant among its MPs could really be an agent of dramatic social change.

From the formation of the Labour Representation Committee of 1900 there was a formal yoking together of socialists and trade unionists. But it was hard going until a tiny dispute in Wales spiralled out of control. The case had begun with the victimization of a signalman in a village who, having agitated for higher wages, was told he was being moved to another job, uprooting his ill wife and ten children. His treatment at the hands of a violently anti-unionist manager of the small Taff Vale Railway Company provoked an angry response. The railwaymen decided to use sabotage. They smeared grease on the rails of a modest slope, so the trucks' wheels began to spin and the carriages slowed down; at which point the men emerged from bushes along the track and uncoupled the trains. This was dangerous, aggressive and highly effective. It brought the railway company round to talks. But the Taff Vale management were not finished. They sued the men's union and won, getting the then substantial sum of £32,000 in damages. If this stood, any serious strike or action against a company would bust the union involved. This at last persuaded the old-style union leaders that there was no alternative but politics. They would have to be able to change laws, with their own MPs.

After Taff Vale, 'Labour' candidates began to appear in by-elections. In the 1906 general election twenty-nine of them won seats, soon renamed themselves the Labour Party and helped the winning Liberals reverse the Taff Vale judgment. To start with, Labour MPs made little impact. In a chamber dominated by Oxbridge repartee, they were easy to patronize. Where they were heard, it was on the specific issues they knew about at first hand: workmen's compensation and the medical inspection of state schools. Will Crooks, a Labour MP for Poplar, got 'character tests' to limit old-age pensions struck out of the legislation after asking, 'What degree of drunkenness was to disqualify for a pension? Half stewed, half drunk, steadily drunk, talkatively drunk, quarrelsome drunk, maudlin drunk, dead drunk?'[49] In 1907 at a famous by-election at Colne Valley a young and charismatic former divinity student called Victor Grayson won a spectacular victory as an independent socialist over both the main parties, and there was much talk of a revolutionary break-through. But Grayson was an alcoholic and lost his seat three years later. By 1912 the acerbic Beatrice Webb was writing: 'The majority of Labour MPs are a lot of ordinary workmen who neither know nor care about anything but the interests of their respective trade unions and a comfortable life for themselves.'

The industrial scene was more exciting than that. Perhaps Britain was instead heading towards a workers' uprising that was choked off only by the extraordinary circumstances of the First World War? For all the incendiary talk and the movements of ships and troops, and occasional outbreaks of violence, it seems unlikely. The demands of most trade union members were straightforward and modest – another penny or two on the hourly rate, fair differentials, an eight-hour working day, free school meals for their children and a meagre but guaranteed old-age pension. From the first days of Labour MPs, trade union sponsorship had tended to rein in socialist dreamers, rather than spurring them on. Even the miners and railway workers, more militant than most, who favoured a minimum wage and public ownership of industry, were actually hostile to state welfare because it would undermine their own friendly societies and mutual aid organizations.

There were, however, serious revolutionaries abroad in Edwardian Britain: the SDF supporters who would eventually form the core of the Communist Party, plus European and Russian anarchists and Marxists. Britain prided herself on having a liberal attitude to political dissidents and refugees, much to the anger of foreign governments. In 1907 Lenin, Stalin, Trotsky, Gorky and a host of Bolsheviks and others gathered in Islington for a congress to debate differences. Lenin and his mistress Nadezhda Krupskaya stayed in the Hotel Imperial in Russell Square while Stalin and many of the lesser-known comrades bedded down in doss houses and rented rooms in the East End. The future Labour leader Ramsay MacDonald, in white tie and tails, then met Lenin and Stalin at a Chelsea drinks party. The *Daily Mirror* reported that young Bolshevik girls were training themselves with revolvers, but the nearest anyone came to real violence was Stalin, already a hardened gangster and terrorist, who was nearly beaten up in a pub by dock workers. Lenin took the revolutionaries to his favourite pub and ensured supplies of beer and sandwiches for their meetings but few of them seem to have enjoyed London very much.

There is no doubt that the anarchist and communist cause was greatly helped by having a safe refuge in London, just as Islamist terrorism was eighty and ninety years later. In the Sidney Street siege of December 1910, a gang of Latvians murdered three policemen after a bungled East End jewellery raid, and then holed up and held out with rifles. Churchill summoned Scots Guards from the Tower of London to help, and called up artillery too. Then, unable to contain his curiosity and sense of theatre, the home secretary arrived as well, in top hat and astrakhan-collared coat, where he was photographed glaring at the house and later ordered it to be left to burn when it caught fire. He excitedly told Asquith later that it had been a striking scene – 'firing from every window, bullets chipping the brickwork, police and Scots Guards armed with loaded weapons . . . I thought it better to let the house burn down rather than spend good British lives in rescuing those ferocious rascals.' But Churchill was widely mocked for his grandstanding. He proposed a tightening up of the law against illegal immigrants and 'aliens', for which he was much attacked by other Liberals. One MP warned him that 'human life does not matter a rap in comparison with the death of ideas and the betrayal of English traditions'.

The end of the old landed order, the apparently corrupt and cosmopolitan plutocracy of Westminster, the socialistic demagogues, looming revolution and the failure to build a stronger army – all this flashed and flamed on a paranoid canvas that at times seems very reminiscent of post-war Weimar Germany. But there is an instinct for moderation, compromise and pulling back wherever one looks. Leo Maxse, who had run the Balfour Must Go campaign and encouraged talk of treachery, had his way by the autumn of 1911. When Balfour stepped down he ruefully commented that he and Maxse 'are probably the two happiest men in London'. Lloyd George, up to visit the royal family at Balmoral at the same time, found King George 'a very, very small man . . . all his sympathy is with the rich' and complained the court was civil to him 'as they would be to a dangerous wild animal'.[50] Yet Balfour could joke about inviting 'Leo' to dinner and Lloyd George did hobnob with the King and Queen.

In its revolt, the Tory leadership had pulled back at the last moment; the King had unhappily accepted that democracy could not be thwarted; nobody had died in the last ditch; and the Lords carried on contesting Commons bills for a long time to come. Fudging and hesitation were also old British traditions.

Those Magnificent Men

Lenin, including during his visits to London, used to ask the question, 'Who, whom?' He was asking about the universal power relationship: who could do what to whom? But you can narrow the question, making it physical and asking rather, 'Who goes to whom?' In a school, office, business negotiation or affair, who summons and who answers? That tells you where power lies. And the point about the first meeting of Rolls and Royce, which took place at the magnificent new Midland Hotel in Manchester in May 1904, was that Rolls went to see Royce. It is not what you would have predicted. The Rt Hon. Charles Rolls was not only the son of a titled landowner on the Welsh borders, who had been to Eton and Cambridge, he was also already a well-known figure to newspaper readers for his feats in new motor cars, and to high society as a successful purveyor of Panhard cars, London driving instructor and all-round petrol-age adventurer. He had a West End showroom and a garage in an old skating rink at Fulham with space for 200 vehicles. Quite naturally, he did not feel it was up to him to leave London and pay court to Henry Royce. For Royce was, by Rolls's standards, barely educated at all and very bottom drawer. A failed miller's son, he had left school at nine and struggled to make ends meet delivering telegrams, working in factories and briefly enjoying an apprentice's training at a rail yard in Peterborough. He had walked the lanes of northern England looking for work, lived on bread and milk, known bitter cold and poverty and had very slowly worked his way up until he owned a tiny electrical engineering works in Manchester, making lamp-holders, dynamos and small electric cranes.

If Rolls symbolized the derring-do of the moneyed Edwardian male, a posh petrolhead thrilled by the adventure of speed technology, Royce was a prime example of the grimly obsessive working-class man who had clawed his way up. He was an industrial engineer of genius. As his business had grown, he had bought his first car. Unlike Rolls, who had been an early convert to the Panhard cars created by the French pioneer, Royce was instantly dissatisfied with the quality of the second-hand car he had bought, also French, a Decauville. So he took it to pieces and bit by bit, from the cylinders to the carburettor, the ignition system, distributor, cooling system, gear box, suspension, brakes and lubrication, completely redesigned it from the inside. By the time he had finished . . . except that the lanky, bearded, workaholic Royce never finished, and was soon building an entirely new car. It did not look like much but when the new vehicle, registration number M 612, began to trundle round the roads of Cheshire, it was very unusual: it was remarkably quiet, it was comfortable, and it did not break down. Back in London, Charles Rolls was having increasing trouble selling his Panhards. Though they laid down the basic design followed by most car makers for the next fifty years, the French machines were by 1904 looking rather old, box-like and slow. So when Rolls heard about the new car from a friend, Henry Edmunds, he was instantly intrigued. Perhaps Royce might like to come down and see him? On 26 March 1904 Edmunds wrote a note to Royce: 'I saw Mr Rolls yesterday, after telephoning to you, and he said it would be very much more convenient if you could see him in London, as he is so very much occupied.' But no go. Royce would not budge.

So Rolls took the train north to Manchester. Who, whom? On the way, in the dining car with Edmunds, he confessed that what he really wanted was a car connected with his name, 'so that in future it might be a household word, just as much as "Broadwood" or "Steinway" in connection with pianos; or "Chubbs" in connection with sofas'. This tells you much about Rolls, just as Royce was later revealed in his true colours when it was put to him that success in the car industry would come from making reliable vehicles at a low price for a mass market, and he replied that no, he was only interested in making the best car in the world, regardless of price.[51] Henry Ford and young William Morris, who had started his tiny Oxford Automobile Company the previous year, would take the other road. Meanwhile, Rolls and Royce found their common enthusiasm removed any social stiffness. Their lunch was a roaring success, as was the trip in the car that followed. From this meeting came, of course, one of the great British engineering success stories of modern times. Rolls-Royce would get its first breakthrough in the frequent car races of the time, and its second with the extraordinary Silver Ghost of 1906, which with 40 horsepower could do a top speed of around 80 m.p.h., yet was remarkably quiet. Though such cars became symbols of wealth and status, when they were first produced it was their performance that flabbergasted even hardened automobilists. One wrote later: 'There arrived before my house the most astonishing motor car I had yet seen. The length of it, the silence, the stately form of it were beyond anything the motor world had yet known. It was, I was told, the work of a great engineer, one F. H. Royce ... We glided through the traffic with an ecstasy of motion which left the passenger astounded. We floated up hills at top speed.'[52]

A year after Rolls and Royce had started working together, the plugged-in marketing aristocrat and the obsessed engineer, the number of cars on British roads had risen to 16,000, and through the Edwardian age they would start to become common, if not quite ubiquitous. By the time the First World War began there were 132,000 registered motor cars in Britain, and observers described roads 'swarming' or 'alive' with traffic. A century earlier Britain had been a pioneer in the 'horseless carriage' but had long since fallen behind. As early as 1803 a Cornishman was running the London Steam Carriage Company and in the 1830s large steam-driven coaches owned by 'Squire and Macerone' ran between Paddington and Edgware to the north-west of London, reaching speeds of 20 m.p.h. – probably about today's average. Glasgow and Paisley had a steam-carriage route, carrying up to sixty people at a time, and by the early 1830s parliamentarians were predicting the replacement of horses by steam cars.[53] Boiler explosions and the arrival of the railway age proved them wrong, though steam-powered cars, early ancestors of new vehicles being developed for the global-warming age, remained popular well into the twentieth century. The early garages in Edwardian Britain sold a wide range of electric cars. Even the King had one.

But apart from the pneumatic tyre, invented by the Scotsman John Boyd Dunlop, all the key developments in the car were made in the 1880s by Germans – famously Gottfried Daimler and Karl Benz – or Frenchmen. This was partly because of the state of British roads. The railway age had left the country with badly tended, slippery tendrils of ancient roadway, quaint and looping but hardly efficient. It was also because of the equally out-of-date state of transport law. In the 1860s self-propelled vehicles had been given speed limits of 2 m.p.h. in towns and twice that in the country, in both cases to be preceded by a walking man carrying a red flag or (at night) a red lantern. The flags were later made voluntary but the enthusiasm of the British police for apprehending and fining early motorists was vigorous long before the arrival of the speed camera. In 1895 John Knight successfully built his own petrol-driven car and triumphantly rode it through the streets of Farnham at eight miles an hour. He was promptly arrested and fined for speeding.

Like many other new things, from passenger air travel to home cinemas and mobile phones, cars began as a toy of the rich. Their promoters included men like Sir David Salomons, the first Jewish Lord Mayor of London. He founded the attractively named Self-Propelled Traffic Association in 1896, which merged into the Automobile Club a year later, stuffed with peers and grand politicians such as Rosebery and Balfour. When a bill was introduced into the House of Lords in 1903 to raise the speed limit to 20 m.p.h., it was attacked as being legislation 'of the rich, for the rich and by the rich'. Yet the car drivers felt they were persecuted by outdated laws and officious policemen. In 1905 the Automobile Club was splitting, with the breakaway Automobile Association representing the more militant motorists.

Some sense of how it felt to be an early motorist comes from a remarkable book by Lord Northcliffe, founder of the *Daily Mail*, and others. Produced in 1902, though it ran to regular later editions, *Motor Cars and Driving* was full of advice about which car to buy – an Argyll, perhaps, or a Napier? – and what to do when things went wrong. The usefulness of the motor car was demonstrated by its ability to get you to fox-hunting meets, to remote parts of the countryside for pheasant or snipe shooting, and to Scottish trout lochs. Sir Henry Thompson, Bart, FCRS, contributed an essay on the health benefits of motoring: 'Personally, I have found my drives to improve general health. The easy jolting which occurs when a motor car is driven at a fair speed over the highway conduces to a healthy agitation; it "acts on the liver", to use a popular phrase, which means only that it aids the peristaltic movements of the bowels and promotes the performance of their functions.' It was as effective for constipation, in other words, as was vigorous horse riding. (When next you see film of Edwardians riding, or driving their fine horseless carriages, you can reflect on what they were hoping for.) But, acknowledged Sir Henry, horse-riding also helped develop the leg muscles. This disadvantage in motoring 'may be to some extent overcome by alighting at the end of a drive of twenty miles and running smartly for about two hundred, or three hundred, yards'. Good advice, no doubt, if perhaps slightly undermined by the fact that by the 1904 edition of the book, game old Sir Henry had become the late Sir Henry.

Motoring was an outdoor sport. Few cars had proper coverings and much debate took place about what to wear. Baron de Zuylen de Nyevelt, president of the Automobile Club of France, pointed out that motorists' clothing was the subject of 'much irreverent ribaldry and . . . in many cases, the chaff has been merited'. Ordinary tweed and cloth were useless, he explained, because 'the air will be felt whistling round the ribs, and coats become distended behind like balloons'. On the other hand, 'a leather jacket and trousers are objectionable because the moisture from the body cannot escape, with the result that underclothing becomes dangerously moist and disagreeable'. The baron recommended tightly belted cloth suits, lined with punctured chamois leather, and also rugs split down the middle to wrap around the legs, snow boots, and India-rubber kilts, the latter particularly useful in cold weather because when you alighted to make adjustments, 'the hot envelope of air is still retained under it'. Best of all, however, was a fur coat worn with the fur outside, and a very high collar, despite the fact that 'these coats have been a source of very considerable amusement to onlookers and small boys in England'.[54]

By the beginning of the First World War, however, cars were almost ordinary machines for getting about in. Car factories sprang up. Laws were changed. Races and processions of cars round the country allowed people everywhere to watch, touch and sometimes ride in the new machines, whose characteristic 'toof, toof' noise was no longer causing beasts and people to jump in fright. Famous men such as Field Marshal Lord Roberts, Rudyard Kipling and Winston Churchill were keen motorists, much photographed. In the cities, horse-drawn omnibuses began to disappear in favour of petrol-driven buses. Hansom cabs were replaced by motorized taxis. Lorries replaced carts. Petroleum spirit, which had been available mainly from chemists, was being sold at the new garages. Country taverns began to tout for motorists' custom, turning their horse-yards into car parks. The victory of the car was faster than the victory of the Labour-voting working classes or the victory of the suffragettes. Rolls-Royce Ltd moved to a sprawling new factory at Derby, lured by the promise of cheap electricity and land. It would soon build military cars and its engines would be used for aircraft too.

Royce was never much impressed by flying but Charles Rolls was smitten. By June 1910 he was the best-known aviator in the country, famous for his long-distance flights. He negotiated a strictly private deal with Royce and the other directors which saw him retire from day-to-day work as the car firm's technical managing director. A few days later the thirty-two-year-old Rolls set off for Bournemouth by train because he had been booked for speeding in Hyde Park. He was on his way to that town's centenary celebrations, which featured musical concerts conducted by Sir Edward Elgar, masked balls, processions of Boy Scouts – and an air show. A new aerodrome had been created in the town's Southbourne suburb. Hedges had been torn up and more than forty vegetable allotments removed. A system of multicoloured flags had been prepared for tests of aerial derring-do. Large cash prizes were on offer. Later an over-excited journalist claimed that Rolls arrived in the resort with 'a look of doom, some strange prognostication of a sudden and fearful end that turned his cheeks grey'. It was very gusty, bad weather for the flimsy biplane, a Wright, that he had brought. A French rival, Edmond Audemars, who had already been up and had crashed without injury, went over to warn him to delay. But Rolls refused and took off, planning a circular flight to be followed by a landing on the appointed mark, close to the judges' tent. Those watching thought he was coming in too high and reported 'a sickening snap' as part of the aircraft came away. He plunged down and crashed. He was thrown to one side of the wreckage and at first sight looked untouched, perhaps only knocked out. But he had been killed instantly. Friends and admirers formed a circle around the body. A news photographer who tried to snap him was set upon; his camera was grabbed and smashed.[55]

So a pioneer of British motoring died a pioneer of flying, one of a small band whose efforts would produce the world's first air battles four years later. He was clearly bored with Rolls-Royce by then, though Royce's infamous lack of interest in air travel did not stop the company itself playing a dominant role in the aircraft age. Its engines would power the first plane to make a transatlantic crossing, and the Spitfire, and one day Concorde. Rolls had played a key part in creating the company, however. He might have had a short attention span, and never quite understood the fanatical attention to detail and management displayed by Royce, always giving the older man full credit as the engineering genius. But Rolls understood that breakthrough consumer products needed allure, a sprinkling of the magic dust of media attention. His circles and connections ensured that Rolls-Royce cars were winning prizes, were admired and written about by the new mass media, and had a patriotic flavour in a market until then dominated by German, French and American competitors. Had landed wealth and élan worked with northern engineering grit a little more frequently, the industrial history of modern Britain might have been rather more sparkling.

Rider and Rud: How Shall We Live?

Many times in the years before the First World War, had you been able to peer through the mullioned windows of a Jacobean house in the Sussex weald, or through the windows of one of London's men's clubs, the Savile, you would have found two men talking passionately about the future of the English race and the Empire. One was fat, in his fifties, and thickly bearded, a squire-like figure. The other had a jutting jaw, a thick moustache and equally thick spectacles. Sir Rider Haggard and Rudyard Kipling were among the most famous men in the English-speaking world and firm friends. Haggard's yarns such as *King Solomon's Mines* and *She* had made him a celebrity, courted by US presidents and cajoled onto royal commissions. Kipling was the poet of the Empire, a short-story writer and author of children's tales which were (and are) loved everywhere. Though Haggard had been brought up in East Anglia, he had grown up, fast, in South Africa in the days of the Zulu wars. Kipling had been born in India, and had spent his years of early adulthood as a journalist and poet in Lahore and Simla. Both, now unsettled but settled back in rural England, were in unsatisfactory and dutiful marriages. Both had lost a loved child to illness. By now their most vigorous work was behind them, but as public figures their views on the future of the British in the world were urgently sought.

In Edwardian Britain the Empire was emphatically not the sole property of the public-schoolboy adventurers, proconsuls or 'flannelled fools' (Kipling's term). Only a few people expressed openly anti-imperial thoughts – some Christian radicals, some Marxists, some Irish nationalists and free spirits such as Wilfred Scawen Blunt, the adventurer and diarist. Progressives and Conservatives both still believed that the Empire was in principle a great civilizing achievement. They might differ about when different parts of the Empire could advance towards self-government; about whether Canada was fated to be incorporated into the United States and about the way to treat 'native' peoples with their own legal and religious cultures. But the sense that Britain had a civilizing mission was general. By the Edwardian age the most violent expansionists were history. Cecil Rhodes had been buried in 1902 with a Matabele salute. Only very rarely, as with Francis Younghusband's assault on Tibet a year later, did the Empire push outwards. A lust for more land and dominion was more likely to be found in Teddy Roosevelt's Washington, or the Kaiser's Potsdam. The British heroes were explorers, Captain Robert Falcon Scott and Ernest Shackleton with their reinforced ships in the Antarctic, or Howard Carter and Lord Carnarvon searching through the dust and stony piles of Egypt. Once the British had climbed or slogged with a flag, to take territory and make fortunes; in the years before the First World War they were more often climbing and slogging for the sake of it.

Haggard and Kipling were more interested in turning imperialism inwards, to change the British, who they both felt had become soft and corrupted by politicians. Haggard admired the Zulus, with their ancient laws and clear morality: 'Where they differ from us mainly is that they do not get drunk until the white man teaches them to do so ... their towns at night are not disgraced by the sights that distinguish ours, they cherish and are never cruel to their children, although they may occasionally put a deformed infant or a twin out of the way, and when they do go to war, which is often, they carry out the business with a terrible thoroughness.'[56] As to the rights of white men to arrive in their land, he said that God could not have given to one race the right or mission of exterminating or robbing the other: 'It seems to me that on only one condition, if at all, have we the right to take the black man's land; and that is that we provide them with an equal and just Government and allow no maltreatment of them ... Otherwise the practice is surely indefensible.' If the Empire was to work, then more able-bodied, bright, tough people had to emigrate. Yet meanwhile Britain herself was in a horrible state – declining agriculture and filthy, rotting cities.

Kipling took just the same view. In his early years in India he had lauded the selfless administrators, struggling with cholera, female infanticide and the caste system, writing to a cousin: 'For what else do the best men of the Commission die from overwork, and disease, if not to keep the people alive in the first place, and healthy in the second?'[57] For him the Empire was a moral cause, little understood by the enfeebled, swarming masses of the industrial cities at home. Central London he found 'four packed miles of seething vice', a pullulating place of literary and moral corruption, choking yellow fogs and bitchery. Like Haggard he was a believer in the imperial tariffs crusade of Joe Chamberlain, even if he thought most politicians corrupt and democracy a sham. The thrashing the Boers had administered to Britain provoked a bitter poem, 'The Islanders', in which Kipling denounced British feebleness, mocking the ill-prepared soldiers and their political leaders: 'Sons of the sheltered city – unmade, unhandled, unmeet – Ye pushed them raw into battle as ye picked them raw from the street'. He was equally derisive about the cricketers and footballers footling at home – the 'muddied oafs' – and the pheasant-shooting squires. Once he had returned from India, Kipling became increasingly convinced that the soul of the nation was in the soil and timeless agricultural wisdom.

Like Kipling, Haggard was worried about the condition of England and saw land-plus-empire as the only way out. Young men were crowding to the towns 'to seek a living there, sometimes to succeed, sometimes to sink to misery, or the earning of bread by hanging round the dockyard gates in the hope of a casual job'. The answer was to recreate the England of yeomen. To give people a stake in the land, without setting class against class, as the radicals would, he 'earnestly advocated the division of land amongst about ten times as many as hold it at present, thereby spoiling a great many estates and often interfering with the interests and pleasures of those who shoot and hunt'. He was soon being talked about in rural Suffolk as a dangerous socialist. At a time when General Booth's Salvation Army was running training camps to redeem broken urban alcoholics and prostitutes, Haggard proposed something similar on a much larger scale in the colonies. The government sent him to Canada to investigate further. Because the Empire disappeared, it is easy to forget how influential the imperialists once seemed. For much of thinking Britannia, Haggard and Kipling represented a clear vision of the future – not the socialists, Liberals and other confused types. Kipling, however, was entering his 'decade of hating'. His 'range of loathing' encompassed Indian nationalists, Irish nationalists, the Germans and all Liberal or soft-Tory politicians. But by 1912 'in England it encompassed trade unions, democracy, liberalism, Free Trade, socialism and bungalows'.[58] Did the Empire still count? It would be a challenge to the Empire, one close to home, that would rouse Kipling to his most extreme passion.

The Provisionals at War

War preparations were well advanced. Some 100,000 men had enlisted, and been drilled and trained by hardened, experienced officers, veterans of many a dusty campaign fighting for the Empire. They were veterans of many marches. They had half a dozen of the latest Vickers Maxim machine guns and 50,000 rifles, many of them brand new. They had paraded beneath the largest Union Jack ever made. They had no artillery yet, nor any air force – this was 1914 – but alongside their regiments and mounted forces they had a motorized corps, more advanced than the enemy could boast, despatch riders, signallers, field telephones and sabotage squads. In their khaki uniforms and caps, the men had already gone through the camaraderie-forming experience of hard training, better-off professionals in civilian life cheerfully learning to take orders from their social inferiors, and all of them bound together by patriotic fervour. Women had been recruited into a large nursing auxiliary for the conflict. Other families, women and children, were already being evacuated. Stocks of food and ammunition had been prepared, plans had been laid for martial law and there were even plans for a wartime currency. Nobody underestimated what lay ahead. The latest warships were ploughing up and down off the coast and large formations of enemy troops were uncomfortably close.

If this seems a familiar picture of the British preparing to resist German aggression in the summer of 1914, one further fact needs to be added: the enemy here was the British army. This was the Ulster Volunteer Force on the edge of full-scale rebellion. Its political leaders were eminent MPs who had had to scurry fast from Westminster to avoid arrest. Warrants were thought to be being prepared to seize and imprison more than 200 people regarded as traitors by half of Britain, and heroes by the other half. Their cause was supported by the leader of the Conservatives, Andrew Bonar Law, by the great national composer Sir Edward Elgar, by Kipling, by Lord Milner, the former grandee ruler of South Africa, by many of the most important newspapers, much of the House of Lords, an admiral of the fleet and by Lord Roberts, motorist and military hero. The Ulster cause was fervently backed by many less eminent Britons too: its 'British Covenant' attracted nearly 2 million signatures. Embarrassingly for the government, many serving British officers and men also supported the rebels. More than the trade unions, the suffragettes or the rebel peerage, this was the crack that threatened to break Britain in two.

By the summer of 1914 it seemed to well-informed opinion in Berlin, Moscow, Washington and Paris that the United Kingdom was on the very edge of civil war, and that fighting could not long be delayed. A despairing King George V agreed. So did the army's director of operations, Sir Henry Wilson. Even Churchill thought so. Having misplayed almost every part of this drama, he angrily told the Commons that if it came to rebellion and civil war, the government would fight to win it. Edward Carson, the stone-faced Dublin lawyer who personified the implacable determination of the

Ulster cause, now saw 'no hopes of peace'. Carson, holed up at Craigavon, the ugly house overlooking Belfast Lough which had become the Unionist rebels' headquarters, guarded by UVF sentries, told his followers they would have to 'assert the manhood of our race'. In a 1913 Unionist Council meeting, an anonymous but authoritative-sounding assessment had been given: 'The British Army will hate it, but as a whole I believe they'll fight against you . . . To impress the English you must not only put up a fight, you must put up a good fight, and I cannot see how you can put up a good fight unless you seize the first move.' In another paper, the UVF's 'No. 1 Scheme' of early 1914, subtitled 'The Coup', plans were duly laid for the cutting of railway, telegraph and phone lines, the capturing of arms and ammunition depots, attacks and capturing of field artillery guns, the closing of roads and blowing up of bridges.[59] These were laid by ex-British army commanders with access to plenty of money and tens of thousands of weapons, the best smuggled in by ship from Germany and Austria in a daring operation out of the Kiel Canal and through the sandy Baltic murk of Erskine Childers's novel. All over Britain, young men had quietly slipped away to join the rebel army.

It seems outlandish. People in Sussex or Glasgow taking up arms because of Belfast – surely not? Yet it did not seem so strange at the time. At Blenheim Place, birthplace of Churchill, Bonar Law, the Tory leader, had told the Duke of Marlborough and the assembled worthies that Winston and his Liberal government were nothing less than 'a revolutionary committee which has seized upon despotic power by fraud' and promised there was 'no length of resistance' which he would not support. If force was used, the Conservative Party would support it. At another demonstration in London, peers and highly respectable old gents from their clubs, in top hats and astrakhan coats, joined to cheer the rebels. *The Times* was in support. In Liverpool shipyards and Hammersmith pubs, working men had stored huge quantities of smuggled arms for Ulster. On Tunbridge Wells Common a pro-Ulster demonstration began, according to the *Times* reporter, with 'a mounted escort of sturdy Kentish yeomen' leading a long procession round town, with bugles and hymn-singing. Then Kipling spoke in the most extraordinarily incendiary terms. After attacking the corruption of the government, he said the Home Rule Bill had broken the faith of generations: 'it officially recognized sedition, privy conspiracy and rebellion; it subsidized the secret forces of boycott, intimidation, outrage and murder'. It meant, said the poet, 'life or death – and better death than the life it would impose on [Ulster's] sons'. There were cheers. Kipling went on that it was also a matter of life or death 'to every freeman in these islands. Ireland is sold today. Tomorrow it may be the turn of the Southern counties to be weighted off as a makeweight in some secret bargain. Why not?'

This life or death crisis, causing troop movements and something close to paranoia throughout Conservative Britain, had been provoked by a bill proposing a form of home rule for Ireland (a Dublin-based parliament) that was very far short of independence and would have kept Ireland well inside the UK and empire. It was little more than devolution, since defence, trade, foreign policy and imperial issues would all be kept by London. Yet Ireland had been England's first colony. Dublin rule would mean Roman Catholic domination, and the end of the Protestant ascendancy. At the very least, Protestant Ulster must be allowed to go its own way. Kipling and his friends – including perhaps half of middle-class Britain – thought it meant the beginning of the end for the Empire. Ireland was not a foreign country – not, at least, to the great Tory landowners and aristocrats who bulked so large in Edwardian London. In the *Punch* stories and cartoons, in the Irish hunting season, in the grand houses of the Protestant ascendancy and in the Irish baronetcies so freely scattered through polite society, the world of southern Ireland felt close to home. Even the Irish nationalists in the Commons, fierce men in their day, had become part of the familiar furniture of political life, grand witty fellows, most of them. Now it was all to be spoiled because the damned Liberals relied on Irish nationalist votes in the Commons and Asquith had done a devil's deal.

In the 1910 general elections, Asquith had barely mentioned Ireland. Now he was suddenly threatening the very future of the UK, as the price of power. The fact that Lloyd George had just escaped by the skin of his teeth being caught corruptly dealing in shares, and that the Lords had finally been neutered, added to this obscure but real sense of political grievance, of being cheated, so eloquently exploited by Kipling. Carson's great Ulster covenant, signed by nearly half a million people, and the flag-draped ceremonies in town halls

and in Belfast, made a big impression on British minds. For years the
nationalists had indulged in violent attacks, jeered at the British flag,
complained about their lot and now seemed to have Asquith in some
kind of parliamentary armlock. The Ulster Unionists flew the flag
and practised, in their quiet Scottish way, the virtues of hard work
and thrift while appealing quietly to their King. So how had it come
about that, as a result of a parliamentary deal, Britain was backing
her critics against her friends?

Churchill had not helped. Earlier in the crisis, he had insisted on
trying to address pro-home rule Ulster Catholics in the same Belfast
Hall where his father had promised to fight Gladstone on Ulster's
behalf. Despite Churchill's increasingly pompous self-justification, it
did seem a strange act of filial blasphemy. He was warned that Ulster
workers were stockpiling bolts and rivets and taking revolvers out of
pawn in preparation for his arrival and was eventually persuaded to
speak instead in a tent at a football ground in a Catholic part of the
city. Even so, he was jostled by furious crowds who managed to lift
the back wheels of his car well off the ground before the police beat
them away. Four battalions of infantry were needed to protect him
and, after addressing a rather wet gathering, he had in effect to run
away. Though Churchill was characteristically triumphalist about his
adventure – 'It was splendid, the wicked dug a pit and they tumbled
into it themselves' – he had in fact handed the Unionists a major
propaganda victory. From then on he tended to use inflammatory
language in public while in private looking for ways of excluding
Ulster, at least for a while, from the Home Rule Bill.

That was a dangerous game. The Irish nationalists, not unnatur-
ally, listened to Churchill's speeches and were greatly heartened.
They thought they were getting all Ireland. In Bradford Churchill
had mocked the Tories for suggesting the Irish nationalist majority
might be coerced to stay. 'There you get a true insight into the Tory
mind – coercion for four-fifths of Ireland is a healthful, exhilarating
and salutary exercise – but lay a finger on the Tory one-fifth –
sacrilege, tyranny, murder!' Referring back to the Lords dispute, he
said that 'the veto of violence has replaced the veto of privilege' with
the Tories vying with 'the wildest anarchists' in their attack on the
constitution. If it came to civil war, the government would not hold
back. The Irish leader John Redmond expressed delight. Behind the

scenes, however, Churchill was quietly talking with his old Tory friends about the exclusion of Ulster, and indeed the creation of a Belfast parliament. Churchill's double game can be seen as wise statesmanship, yet it looks more obviously like an unhappy mix of public provocation and private pass-selling. From the Admiralty he was despatching ships to confront Carson's preparations for a provisional government, while on various yachts and in private houses he was suggesting deal after deal.

The most significant acts of the Ulster drama happened not in the Admiralty, Downing Street or the streets of Belfast, where the columns of armed men were marching. They occurred in a cavalry barracks near Dublin, the Curragh, and then in the gloomy grandeur of the War Office in Whitehall. Lieutenant-General Sir Arthur Paget, the commander of British forces in Ireland, was not a splendid soldier. When the Liberal government decided to start putting pressure on the UVF, believing plans were afoot to seize and raid army depots, the army was told to be ready to move first, seizing strategic sites across Ulster. The suspicion grew that this was the start of a military strike against Carson's provisional regime. Paget was summoned by the secretary of state for war, a bumptious former soldier called Sir John Seely, and warned that troops would need to be sent north. This was undoubtedly ticklish. The army included many Irish officers from Unionist families who would feel they were being sent to intimidate, and possibly kill, their own. When a British column was marching and came across UVF men by the side of the road, they saluted and turned 'eyes right' as they passed by.

In London, Seely told Paget and his colleagues that army officers whose families lived in Ulster could be excused – they could simply disappear while the operation was going on and return to their posts afterwards. But everyone else would be expected to carry out orders. Paget returned to Dublin. He summoned his seven most senior officers and told them not only their likely orders but about his own fears and doubts. He insisted that nobody would be asked to shoot unless they had been shot at first and sustained casualties and indeed, according to a later memorandum by Churchill, 'that he intended himself to walk out in front and be shot down by Orangemen before any firing in reply would be ordered of the troops'. However attractive this prospect might have been, it had no effect on the senior officers around him. After a series of meetings, most officers, led by the commander of the 3rd Cavalry Brigade, General Hubert Gough, said that if the choice was to march on Ulster or resign – well then, they resigned. Paget telegraphed to the War Office. His first telegram read: 'Officer commanding 5th Lancers states that all officers except two, and one doubtful, are resigning their commissions today. I very much fear the same conditions in the 16th Lancers. Fear men will refuse to move.' No reply came. A second telegram went off: 'Brigadier and 57 officers Third Cavalry Brigade prefer to accept dismissal if ordered north.'

A debate began then, and continues in the army today, about whether this was outright mutiny. The case against is that the hapless Paget had offered his officers a choice and they had merely made it. The case for is that the British government had told the army to take an action it regarded as politically essential and senior soldiers had refused. As one MP told the Commons shortly afterwards, the implication was that if ordinary soldiers did not want to fire against strikers during disturbances, they would be allowed not to. The second phase of the army revolt happened more quietly but was in some ways more telling. Summoned to London, the rebel officers were confronted by their commander-in-chief Sir John French, and then by War Secretary Seely, and faced them down. Gough insisted he wanted a signed guarantee that his men would not be asked to enforce home rule on Ulster – a wholly unconstitutional request for a serving officer. Seely began almost to beg, saying there had been a misunderstanding and the move north was only to safeguard supplies. French said that maybe having this in writing would help Gough with his officers and Seely pretended that this made the request acceptable. A note was written, agreed by the cabinet. But it did not go quite far enough, so Seely added more in his own handwriting, promising that the government had no intention of using the army 'to crush political opposition to the policy or principles of the Home Rule Bill'. Gough looked it over. Still not good enough, he thought. He added his own sentence, asking 'In the event of the present Home Rule Bill becoming law, can we be called upon to enforce it on Ulster under the expression of maintaining law and order?' and told French that unless the answer was no, he and the colonels would leave the army. French picked up his pen and wrote, 'That is how I read it, J. F.' Gough then pocketed this documentary evidence of the government caving in to military blackmail, and returned to his post. This was more than the government had actually agreed to and in the ensuing storm both French and Seely had to resign. Even so, the government had been humiliated, the War Office had backed down and the army rebellion had achieved its aim. They were watching in Berlin.

The King was watching too. In the south of Ireland, the Irish National Volunteers had observed the increasing militancy of the UVF and begun gun-running and training on their own account. As events moved towards a climax, Churchill had ordered a battle fleet off the Ulster coast, loaded with field guns. He was accused of preparing a 'pogrom' for the Ulstermen. One Unionist leader, Lord Charles Beresford, called him an unbalanced egomaniac and Carson added that he would be remembered as 'the Belfast butcher'. Meanwhile Churchill and his colleagues were deep in debate about possible border solutions, village by village, if Ulster was excluded. A wearisome conference was going on in Buckingham Palace to try to find a compromise, which nobody by then believed possible. The cabinet, wrote Churchill later, had been toiling round the muddy byways of Fermanagh and Tyrone when he heard the quiet voice of the foreign secretary Sir Edward Grey reading a document which had just arrived. It was the Austrian ultimatum to Serbia. Initially, Churchill struggled to disengage his mind from Ulster: 'We were all very tired, but gradually as the phrases and sentences followed one another impressions of a very different kind began to form in my mind. This note was clearly an ultimatum ... it seemed impossible that any state in the world could accept it ... The parishes of Fermanagh and Tyrone faded back into the mists and squalls of Ireland, and a strange light began immediately, but by perceptible gradations, to fall and grow upon the map of Europe.'

Ireland would be soaked in blood but the cause of Ulster triumphed. It did so for the most terrible of reasons. The slaughter of the UVF men, reorganized into the 36th (Ulster) Division at the Battle of the Somme in July 1916, was so overwhelming, heroic and mesmerizing that the idea of 'betraying' their memory and accepting a single united Ireland disappeared from the British mind. After the suicidal attacks on German positions at Thiepval, the 700 men of the West Belfast Battalion from Shankill had been reduced to just seventy survivors. The long days of drilling in quiet, dripping fields or village halls paid off in keeping the Ulstermen together as they walked slowly into the machine-gun bullets. The blood price was paid. A century after the events which began the Ulster revolt, Northern Ireland remains part of the UK and Carson stands on his plinth outside the Stormont parliament. Yet the ironies ripple out in all directions. The gun-running heroics of the UVF were soon copied by the Irish nationalists: they were landing rifles outside Dublin a few days after the assassination of the Archduke at Sarajevo. Carson had all the trappings of a provisional government and was preparing for a besieged Ulster state. The Kaiser had shown a close interest. In the event, it was to be the provisional government of Dublin's Easter Rising, with minor German help, that followed. And it may be that the Ulster revolt helped convince Germany that, when war came, Britain would not fight, or not effectively. German generals expected civil war in Ireland and the headquarters staff of the Austrians also discussed this as one factor which probably gave them a free hand in dealing with the Serbs. Lloyd George, speaking at a dinner party, thought the Germans 'have been stimulated by extravagant and erroneous reports regarding the state of affairs in Ireland'. Ulster's voice had been heard. But in all the wrong places too.

The Coming of War

Churchill's colleagues always suspected he wanted war. It was not that he was particularly bloodthirsty, though the Marlborough blood was red enough, but rather that, since becoming First Lord of the Admiralty in 1911, his creation of an ever stronger navy had led him to want to see it in a proper fight. Always fascinated by detail, he had become embroiled in airships and seaplanes, gunnery and boilers. Always long-winded, he was the despair of the cabinet as he harangued them on the need for more Dreadnoughts. Some sense of his argument has been given earlier. Yet he became, if not monomaniac (Churchill was never that), at least obsessed. His colleagues dreaded being caught by him in corridors. From being

Lloyd George's closest political ally he became his enemy, fighting the chancellor for the money he needed. This may have been Asquith's ruse to ensure that the dangerous radical alliance in his cabinet was weakened; but it meant that in practice Churchill had to rely on only a couple of others to keep growing the navy in its race with Germany. One was Asquith himself. The other was Sir Edward Grey, the foreign secretary who had been working hard but fruitlessly to find diplomatic solutions to the Balkan and central European tinderbox. Despite the doubts of most of the cabinet, Churchill got his way through the key years of 1912–13. Over in Germany, great warships poured from the yards – eight battleships alone. But in Britain, in the same period, thirteen were launched. Germany hailed the *König Albert*, *Grosser Kurfürst* and *Markgraf*. Britain hit back with the *King George V*, *Conqueror*, *Ajax* and *Iron Duke*. And on it went.

Was this a gross waste and a provocation, run by an overgrown schoolboy too in love with his toys, as Lloyd George and others were inclined to think? As ever with Churchill, vision was adulterated by glee. He knew himself. A few days before the declaration of war he wrote to his wife: 'My darling one & beautiful, Everything tends towards catastrophe and collapse. I am interested, geared up & happy. Is it not horrible to be built like that? The preparations have a hideous fascination for me. I pray to God to forgive me for such fearful moods of levity.' His attitude to the new craze for flying showed this character he understood so well. Germany had a world lead in the great rigid Zeppelin airships, which would later bombard London. Churchill, meanwhile, was desperately building up a Royal Naval Air Service, designing uniforms, haranguing officials about the design of engine controls and learning to fly himself, to the utter despair of his political friends and his wife. By the time he stopped because of the large number of deaths from accidents, he had been up almost 140 times. The naval pilots treated the whole thing partly as a joke – the planes were used to pick up fresh oysters and, on one occasion, to shoot wild duck from the air for the First Lord's supper. Churchill surprised them by telling them of the coming air war, which would eventually mean the arming of aircraft, something that had not then been considered. The notion that Churchill got to grips with rearmament and the importance of fighters only in the years before the Battle of Britain is wholly wrong. He was behaving in much the same way at the close of the Edwardian age. The naval build-up has been forgotten, by comparison with the heroics of the RAF in 1940. But Churchill was tactically right in 1911–14 too. Had the German Imperial Navy been strong enough to defeat Britain's home fleet, as it very nearly was, then the Channel would have been closed and the war would have been over.

The bigger question is whether he was right about the need for war at all. On 1 August 1914, one of the darkest days in European history, Lloyd George and Churchill spent part of the cabinet meeting throwing hastily scribbled notes to and fro. Lloyd George tore most of them up but they were gathered up and saved by his mistress (and later wife) Frances Stevenson. They show Churchill exerting all his cajoling charm and eloquence on the older man, still unsure about war. If Lloyd George was for resigning rather than fighting, 'All the rest of our lives we shall be opposed. I am deeply attached to you & have followed your instinct & guidance for nearly 10 years' and 'Please God – It is our whole future – comrades – or opponents. The march of events will be dominating.' The replies from Lloyd George are fewer than the blizzard of Churchill notes, and almost coquettish in their brevity. But he was coming round. Less than a fortnight earlier, after the assassination of Archduke Franz Ferdinand, he had been telling a City audience that, although 'you never get a perfectly blue sky in foreign affairs', and though there were clouds 'even now', things were better than in 1913. Lloyd George had never been a pacifist. He was strongly pro-French and felt that, in the end, Britain and France, the two democracies, had to stand together.

Because we know how the cabinet debates ended, and we have the images of cheering, bellicose crowds lining the London streets – as they were in Paris, Berlin, Vienna and Moscow too – it is easy to pass over the argument about whether or not Britain would fight. Yet Asquith himself thought three-quarters of his own party in the Commons were against intervention. Had it been a straight cabinet vote at the beginning of August, there was almost certainly a majority against declaring war, even if Germany violated Belgian neutrality. So the arguments of Churchill, Grey and Asquith were of great importance. Once Lloyd George had come over, that was effectively that: whatever the numbers game, if the prime minister, chancellor, foreign secretary and leading war minister had agreed, it was hard to see a cabinet cabal of lesser creatures overcoming them. Those who thought war was inevitable were, Churchill apart, deeply depressed. Grey is remembered today for what he apparently said while standing in his Commons office looking at the lamplighters at work in the streets below: 'The lamps are going out all over Europe and I doubt we shall see them lit again in our lifetime.' More eloquent still were the thoughts he jotted down in July 1914 when he predicted that 'a great European war under modern conditions would be a catastrophe for which previous wars afforded no precedent. In old days nations could collect only portions of their men and resources at a time and dribble them out by degrees. Under modern conditions whole nations could be mobilized at once and their whole life-blood and resources poured out in a torrent. Instead of a few hundreds of thousands of men meeting each other in war, millions would now meet, and modern weapons would multiply manifold the power of destruction.'[60]

Right to the end Britain was making attempts at peace. At 1.30 on the morning of 1 August, three days before war was declared, Asquith had driven to Buckingham Palace, where 'the poor King was hauled out of his bed' to appeal to the Czar to stop Russian mobilization, and therefore perhaps halt the German plan too. The prime minister described King George 'in a brown dressing gown over his nightshirt & with copious signs of having been aroused from his first "beauty sleep" – while I read the message'. After the King had topped and tailed the appeal with 'My Dear Nicky' and 'Georgie', the message was sent and the prime minister returned to Downing Street. Grey was doing his best with the German ambassador, who in turn was still trying to persuade the British government that Germany was the victim, terrified of being crushed between Russia and France. So why did the argument for war become so apparently irresistible? Grey's explanation to the American ambassador on the day war was declared was as plain as any. If Germany won, he said, she would dominate France. The independence of Belgium, Holland, Denmark and perhaps Norway and Sweden would be 'a mere shadow'. Their separate existence as nations would be a fiction, Germany would have their harbours and would dominate the whole of western Europe. 'We could not exist as a first-class state under such circumstances.' Lord Kitchener, the famously handlebarmoustached imperial soldier, appointed war minister by Asquith, and who had actually fought with the French in the last war against the Germans in 1871, said the Germans would 'walk through the French army like partridges' and if Britain failed to support France, she would never exercise real power in the world again.

So although the Kaiser's Germany was in no way an earlier version of the evil force of Hitler's, the calculation about a continent under German control, and Britain's future if that happened, was the same in 1914 as it would be in 1939. Could Grey have found a compromise? He tried very hard. He has been criticized for not making it clear enough early enough to Berlin that invading Belgium would lead to a British declaration of war. But the extraordinary gamble of the German military plan utterly depended on cutting through Belgium, and assumed as well that victory over the French would have been secured before Britain could intervene properly. Whatever Grey said, the Germans had to spring their plan to have a good chance of victory; and it nearly worked.

So the preparations clicked into place in Britain as elsewhere. Armed guards suddenly appeared at railway junctions and ports. Artillery batteries arrived at key sites on the south coast and the mouth of the Thames. The fleet, its lights doused, slipped down the Channel to take up its battle stations in the North Sea. Britain's ambassador in Berlin quietly hurried home. The cabinet was unsure until the last moment about sending troops to France, hoping that this could be Winston Churchill's naval war. In the City there was something close to panic. The Germans had called in their overseas loans and stocked up their gold reserves: Asquith complained that Britain's financiers were 'the greatest ninnies . . . all in a state of funk, like old women chattering over teacups in a cathedral town'. Both the Tories and the Irish nationalists in the Commons assured Asquith they would support war to defend Belgium and France. All this happened so fast, in just a few days, that individuals felt overwhelmed. Grey said later that not even someone like himself, foreign secretary, could make pledges about war or peace on behalf of a great democracy. One of his strongest feelings was that 'he himself had no power to decide policy and was only the mouthpiece of England'.[61]

And on the streets, the crowds were indeed for war. An anti-war counter demonstration in Trafalgar Square on Sunday 2 August was a damp squib. Asquith was disgusted as he heard the King being cheered late at night the next day, a 'distant roaring' half a mile away from where he sat in Downing Street. He wrote to his lover Venetia Stanley: 'War or anything that seems likely to lead to war is always popular with the London mob. You remember Sir R. Walpole's remark: "Now they are ringing their bells; in a few weeks they'll be wringing their hands."' Britain had not fought a war on the continent of Europe since the Battle of Waterloo was won in 1815. She had, by continental standards, a tiny army. Politicians with a sense of history, and those who had studied the growth and power of armies and weapons, had some sense of what war, not against Boer farmers or Afghan tribesmen, but against well-prepared modern forces, might mean. On the street, where the cause of France was popular and the German menace had been luridly discussed in the press for years, it seemed much simpler. Britain was the world's greatest power and it was time to teach the Hun a lesson. And Churchill? He was with the crowds in spirit, as he often was. Margot Asquith recorded with distaste that on the day when war finally broke out, 4 August, as she was passing the foot of the staircase in 10 Downing Street, 'I saw Winston Churchill with a happy face striding towards the double doors of the cabinet room.' Once he was inside, her husband reported the same: 'Winston, who has got on all his war paint, is longing for a sea fight.' What fun was going to be had.

Part Two

THE MEANING OF HELL

1914–1918

The House is crammed: tier beyond tier they grin
And cackle at the Show, while prancing ranks
Of harlots shrill the chorus, drunk with din;
'We're sure the Kaiser loves our dear old Tanks!'
I'd like to see a Tank come down the stalls,
Lurching to rag-time tunes, or 'Home, sweet Home',
And there'd be no more jokes in Music-halls
To mock the riddled corpses round Bapaume.

Siegfried Sassoon, ' "Blighters" ', 1916

There are aerial photographs of the great First World War battle-fields, taken by the earliest military planes. So we can see what the village of Fleury outside Verdun looked like in 1914 as the fighting started. Neat farm buildings are clearly visible, and roads and strips of fields, drains and hedges running in all directions, land-loving patterns that go back to medieval times. Exactly the same place in 1916 is like a photographic negative, or a dead coral, with empty tooth-stumps instead of houses, and the surrounding landscape scarred. Many of the features have gone. By 1918 there is nothing recognizable of Fleury at all. The artillery, the mortars, the wire and the trenches have left by now a blank, with only a rough, pitted texture. You could be looking at a close-up of an elephant's skin. If it wasn't labelled you would have no idea this had been a landscape. This rubbing-out of meaning is also a metaphor. On the day it ended, arguments began about what the war meant, including whether it was a victory or a catastrophe, and whether it needed to be fought at all. They have carried on ever since – far more so than for the war against Hitler. The arguments drew in pacifists and prime ministers, historians of the left and right. They were fought out in plays and novels, television comedy programmes and documentaries, and they continue still.

The arguments about the war's meaning cannot end. The Kaiser's Germany was indeed a militaristic, expansionist and out-of-control polity, determined on war at a scale that would have forced Britain to resist, or to accept fast decline. The Germany of 1914 was not the Nazi Germany of 1939. It had a functioning parliament, with opposition parties, and its anti-Semitism was mainly confined to words. But it was a leader-directed state, determined to expand, prepared for an aggressive war and militarized in a way that no other country in Europe could quite comprehend. A world in which the Kaiser's

Germany had won, dominating the Netherlands, France, Scandinavia and central Europe, with the continent's ports barred to Britain, would have made a very different twentieth century. The British Empire would have swiftly died, rather than living on into the middle of the century. Adolf Hitler would, perhaps, have remained a mediocre water-colourist and bar-room bore. It is impossible to guess what would have happened to Russia. Perhaps Czarism would have been reformed into bourgeois democracy and Lenin left to brood in Swiss exile. The domination of America would have been, perhaps, less dramatic.

Still, it is not hard to see why Britain's leaders mostly thought they had to fight. Once that is conceded, the military historians argue persuasively that although awful blood sacrifices were made, and awful mistakes, the generals cannot be blamed as easily as they once were. This was a new kind of fighting, which nobody was properly prepared for, including the Germans. The trench system could not have been broken by some other, unexplained, but somehow cleverer strategy. But even conceding all this does not subdue the persistent anger and incredulity about the slaughter. It is the front-line tales, the squalor and suicidal bravery, the culling of the youngest and best that has stuck in people's minds, while the smoothly persuasive explanations of the historians slip past us. Study the many accounts of the first day of the Somme from a military perspective. Realize just what Haig's dilemma was, how scanty his intelligence, how pressing his need to relieve the French, being hammered to pieces at Verdun. Dispose of some of the myths about men being made to advance slowly out of mere military stupidity. After all that, one is still left with the trembling lieutenants putting their whistles to their lips and leading their men straight to almost certain death.

It is true that of all the British troops involved in the Somme offensive, three-quarters emerged unharmed – that includes, of course, many well behind the front line. But how powerful is that, compared with knowing about Captain D. L. Martin of the 9th Devons, a former maths teacher, who carefully worked out from drawings and models that he and his men would certainly be killed by enfilading machine-gun fire on 1 July and explained this to senior officers, but who nevertheless led the attack as ordered? He was right – he and 160 men of the Devons were almost instantly killed, and buried in a mass grave over which was written: 'The Devonshires held this trench. The Devonshires hold it still.' There are thousands of 'Captain Martin' stories. This book does not include a detailed account of the battles of the war, month by month and yard by yard. There are thousands of others that do. It will include an account of the main turning-points. But the real problem is reaching back through the arguments about its meaning to try to find the people who fought and endured it. In many ways they have been lost in the mud too. Our attitudes today, to class, to ethnic and religious differences, to suffering and death, to patriotism, make the gap virtually unbridgeable. The patriotic-Edwardian landscape has gone, just as medieval Fleury from the air has gone.

Though the war did not change everything about Britain's story, it changed a lot. During it, we discovered big government, high taxes, working women, and the common use of the word 'fuck'. After the war, women could no longer be denied the vote and the old Liberal Party was broken. After the war, what used to be called 'high politics' – the doings of cabinet ministers and the parliamentary debates – simply mattered less. Grey third-raters trudged through the footnotes of politics while around them a new world would open up, of protest and experiment, hedonism and cynicism. Before the war began, the Ulster revolt had threatened civil war; after it, the Irish Republic broke free. Post-1918, people might still be patriotic but they could not be gaily patriotic in the old way.

A struggle to comprehend the war's meaning began immediately, and has never gone away. During the 1920s many people clearly saw it as a victory from God. The dead were present, on freshly carved memorials, and in the minds of their widows, children and friends. To call theirs a meaningless sacrifice would have been disrespectful, cruel, blasphemous. The man to blame was the Kaiser; it was a shame he was skulking in Holland and couldn't be hanged. For years there were raucous alcoholic celebrations on Armistice Day, even Armistice Balls at the fashionable hotels. Then, slowly, a more mournful tone emerged, and the influence of scarred writers became stronger. Wilfred Owen began his long posthumous march from obscurity – nobody had heard of him in the years immediately after the war – to becoming one of twentieth-century Britain's best known poets. In the radicalized thirties, hostility to the 'Colonel Blimp' military chiefs who had led the war, and disillusion about a land unfit for heroes, caused many Britons to rethink the Great War. When it became clear that the war to end wars hadn't been that, and Britain was fighting her second German war, the first one was remembered mainly as a prequel. Though there was no Somme, at least for the British, during 1939–45, the parallels between the two wars are stronger than is sometimes understood.

But it was after 1945 that the Great War's meaning was most strongly argued over. The creation of the welfare state, and then the great consumer economy, perhaps gave people a sense of superiority over the earlier part of the century. That first war had been far bloodier, fought against a less clearly demonic enemy, and had certainly not produced a fairer, happier Britain. Second time around, the enemy was utterly evil, the war unavoidably one of national survival and the victory belonged to everyone. Post-war leaders such as Attlee, Macmillan and Eden, who had fought in the Great War, had a strong sense of class guilt about the sacrifice of so many troops, and were animated by a 'never again' mentality. On the left, the threat of nuclear war and later the anti-Vietnam War movement made the theme of military incompetence and upper-class callousness popular. The Allied leadership of the more recent war was still beyond reproach, but the conduct of the earlier one became an irresistible target. Thus from the early 1960s, with Joan Littlewood's *Oh! What a Lovely War* and the fast-growing popularity of anti-war poets such as Owen, Siegfried Sassoon and Isaac Rosenberg, the notion of the Great War as the Senseless Slaughter grew. This chimed well with the anti-establishment mood of public schoolboys who had grown sick of pious lectures in the war memorial-decorated chapel. The voices of the class-regimented Edwardians fell silent; the statues could not speak.

It wasn't only the left. Critical conservative historians such as Basil Liddell Hart were now followed by cage-rattling Tory polemicists. Alan Clark's 1961 book *The Donkeys* was hugely successful with the public, however much disdained by academics. The historians' attack on the generals had plenty of raw material to work with since between the wars leading politicians, notably Lloyd George and Churchill, had vigorously pursued their old quarrels with Earl Haig and French in print; but the impact of so much death on so many working-class families helped give the argument a new bite. Television jumped in too, as television does. How could the poets' passionate disgust fail to trump the stale regimental memoirs? Was it not the case that all you needed to remember was that shaking white face of the eighteen-year-old as a subaltern's whistle blows? Were not the Germans just like us, ready to play football and sing carols on Christmas Day, as much the innocent victims of politics as any Tommy? In the empathy culture of today this can seem the end of the argument.

Eventually, counter-attacking in waves, came the Great War revisionists, historians like Gary Sheffield, Gordon Corrigan and Dan Todman, who asked afresh what choices Britain really had in 1914, and whether the generals had really been as stupid and heartless as was being claimed. Instead of standing firmly in today's world and pointing the finger at yesterday, they tried to see the choices and beliefs, illusory or not, as they were understood at the time. 'They should have used tanks.' 'Making soldiers walk with packs towards machine guns was simple murder.' In 1915–17 it was never so easy or clear. In pointing out to a new generation the huge difficulties facing the British commanders, and reminding us that the story of the war includes the British army's 'forgotten' breakthrough victories of 1918 as well as the bloody slogging of earlier years, the revisionists have done a great service to truth. They have also sometimes gone too far in trying to minimize the horror, and been unfair on the politicians, or 'frocks' as the soldiers dismissively called them. Lloyd George may have been a scheming, untrustworthy and self-justifying goat, but in rallying, sustaining and holding together a young semi-democracy through terrible times, he was touched by greatness too.

The Nearness of Hell

This was the first war to touch almost everyone in Britain since the brutal civil wars of the seventeenth century; it had vastly more impact on the homes of the British than the wars against Napoleon or the imperial wars. You could hear it. If you were walking in the Home Counties, or opened a window even in a London suburb when the wind was in the right direction, the air was stirred by the rumble of barrages from guns in France. When the British mines that began the Battle of the Somme exploded, they could be clearly heard in central London. A journalist, Michael MacDonagh, recalled sitting in the sunshine on Wimbledon golf course in March 1918 (when the last German offensive was starting) and feeling 'a curious atmospheric sensation – a kind of pulsation in regular beats. There was not the faintest breeze . . . Yet there were persistent tremors or throbs.'[1] The front line was very close, a short train ride from the Normandy coast. Soldiers sent home dirty linen and letters weekly, and households in Glasgow or Hull sent back home-baked cakes, photographs and newly knitted socks along with freshly ironed smalls. At home, across most of Britain, bivouacs for soldiers occupied parks and squares. School playgrounds and football fields were taken over for drill and bayonet practice. Khaki was everywhere on the streets – though in the early days, when there was a lack of dye, you would have seen plenty of soldiers in blue, because the postmen's cloth had been taken. You would see the recruiting posters and the grim-faced women waiting with white feathers to pounce on men in civilian clothes – enough of a problem for the government to issue armbands and badges to men whose work was essential at home. As the war went on you would see women doing work, in banks, factories or even in the fields, that had once been done by men. Other absences would strike you. So many of the horses had disappeared. As the war went on, a pervasive dinginess spread. Lights went out. By 1916 even Bonfire Night had been banned.

You would feel the war too, most obviously in your stomach. Right at the start there were shortages and rocketing prices, as panicky people stocked up on sugar, flour and tins. But this passed, and for a while few people saw much of a change. Yet Britain imported a third of her food. Atlantic shipping was now urgently needed for war materials and once the German U-boat attacks began in earnest, there was real hunger. In the Second World War, universal rationing was introduced early and basic principles of fairness were set, leading to many poorer families actually enjoying a better diet. In the Great War, rationing arrived late, in 1918, and there was great unfairness beforehand. The journals and letters of people living in the country show a ravenous obsession with collecting mushrooms, trapping rabbits and killing wild birds. Game birds – partridge and grouse – were noisily abundant because the sport of shooting them had stopped. But still there are some accounts of rural children dying of hunger. Everywhere allotments were dug, from public-school playing fields to city parks, and there was also a government-sponsored scheme of 'voluntary rationing' during which the minister of food, Lord Devonport, exhorted the country in May 1917: 'We must all eat less food and, especially, we must all eat less bread ... The enemy is trying to take away our daily bread. He is sinking our wheat ships. If he succeeds in starving us, our soldiers will have died in vain. In the interests of the country I call upon you all to deny yourselves, and so loyally to bridge over the anxious days between now and the harvest.' At one point there was two months' supply of wheat and only four days' supply of sugar left. The familiar white bread disappeared; food riots broke out in parts of London and Liverpool, with much suspicion of shopkeepers for hoarding and appallingly long queues. The crisis passed and a more serious form of rationing followed, using local councils and private companies to police it. Meanwhile in schools, shivering children had to make do with vile slops for their meals and, at home, odder and odder forms of bread were picked apart with trepidation.

It was not just food. There were shortages of most things, and for the first time stern limits on the opening times for pubs and the strength of beer. This is the moment when the restrictions on pub opening hours that were such a feature of twentieth-century Britain first began. The new regulations allowed watering of beer, and a vigorous campaign against drunkenness began because of worries about the amount munitions workers were drinking. The measures appear to have worked very effectively: convictions for drunkenness fell dramatically, even if the country's leaders proved hypocritical on the subject. Lloyd George bullied the King into announcing that he would give up alcohol for the duration of the war, strongly suggesting to him that his lead would be followed by cabinet ministers, clergy, businessmen and judges. In fact, almost nobody followed poor King George, least of all Lloyd George. The then prime minister, Asquith, a notorious drinker, was much alarmed until Lloyd

George assured him that alcohol would be available for those who could get a doctor's note 'to the effect that it was necessary for you to have it', at which Asquith brightened up.

If you were very unlucky, you might see the war at first hand. Scarborough, Whitby, Bridlington and Hartlepool were bombarded by German warships sitting close enough offshore to be clearly visible to those they were trying to kill. This was a huge embarrassment for the Royal Navy and partly hushed up at the time, though many people were killed and a lot of damage done. The German navy's intention had been to keep embarrassing the British Home Fleet so that it could be enticed out and attacked with U-boats and mines, but the shelling was otherwise an act of terror, rather than of any military value. Houses, parts of old Whitby Abbey and warehouses were hit, and panicking people fled for the hills. Later, parts of the south of England were raided by Zeppelins, causing awe and shock if not the devastation their commanders had hoped for. For people still getting used to manned flight, death from the air and the 'baby killer' Zeppelins were a terrible shock. Air-raid warnings involved policemen on bicycles blowing whistles and displaying placards; people died praying beside their beds. Later still, London was attacked, rather more lethally, by Gotha bombers. This was not 1940: only around 850 people were killed inside Britain by all the German raids of the Great War, as compared to 60,000 in the second conflict. But the psychological effect of fearing that the bombers might swarm over at any moment was deep and lasting and would contribute to appeasement in the thirties.

The way most people witnessed the war, however, was in the bodies of the wounded men returning and the faces of those who had received a letter or telegram informing them of a bereavement. Above all, these were the years of visible death. A little over 6 million men were mobilized to fight in the war, and more than 722,000 died (41,000 of them after the Armistice from their wounds), though an accurate figure will never be found. But the danger was unevenly distributed. One in eight fighting soldiers was killed, and nearly a third wounded. Including those taken prisoner almost half, 47 per cent, of the army were casualties. The worst place was Flanders: for every nine men sent there from Britain, five would be killed, wounded or reported missing. In the navy people were half as likely to be killed (though few were wounded: ships sank, and that was that). In the air force the death rate was just 2 per cent. Nor was the danger equally distributed by class and geography. Scots took a disproportionate share of the deaths, as did the Ulstermen: both were used as shock troops in some of the worst battles. Officers were disproportionately more likely to be killed, and junior officers especially so (though seventy-eight British generals also died). From the main Oxbridge colleges the ratio of deaths was twice the national average. A survey of peers aged under fifty and their sons concluded that a higher percentage of ducal families had suffered violent death over the fifty years from 1880 than during 1330–1479 – the period of the Hundred Years War and the Wars of the Roses. And being a front-line subaltern, the lowest-ranking officer, was particularly dangerous. Those who think of painters and writers as effete might be interested to know that no regiment, battalion or division of the British army suffered higher casualties than the Artists' Rifles, the 28th Battalion of the London Regiment, which specialized in training subalterns – so much so that they were known as the Suicide Club.[2]

Of the whole adult male population of Britain, one in seven aged under twenty-five died. Half a million British men under thirty died.[3] Astonishingly, given the myths about a lost generation, the British population actually continued to rise, partly because people stopped emigrating during the war. One historian has pointed out that 'of all those counted in 1911 and who were of military age between 1914 and 1918, eighty-six per cent of them were still there when they were counted again in 1921'.[4] The other side of this coin is that the huge numbers of deaths and maimings were focused on particular parts of the country, from the 'Pals' battalions of Bradford and Liverpool to the Scottish regiments. Despite the higher death rate of officers, the vast bulk of the dead and maimed were working class. As the army was expanded, and then expanded again, recruitment was partially sub-contracted to local councils and business leaders, who naturally made much of the value of men joining up alongside their friends and neighbours. As discussed below, it probably helped morale. But because of the swift slaughters during specific attacks, the dreadful envelopes would also arrive simultaneously at house after house in just a few adjacent streets. The intensity of what happened in some places is not lessened by the fact that it did not happen everywhere.

Here again we have to have steady fingers and humility in trying to reach back to touch the past. Death was better known ninety years ago. The average life expectancy for a man, before the war, was in the late forties and for a woman the early fifties. Disease, as we have seen, killed far more people. Many of the soldiers digging trenches or working underground in Flanders were coal miners or engineering workers at home, where fatal industrial accidents were routine. Before easy access to anaesthetics, people were more used to pain. Before plastic surgery and abortion on demand, there were far more disfigured and disabled people in civilian life. These were tougher times. And when one compares Britain's losses to those of the other main Western Front belligerents, they recede statistically a bit: the French lost nearly twice as many dead (and 3.7 per cent of the population, against Britain's 1.5 per cent) and the Germans three times as many (3.2 per cent). Yet nothing really cancels the brute facts, such as the 20,000 British soldiers killed on the first day of the Somme or the terrifying nature of the experience of industrial war. Clearly, no comparison, or any reflection on life's inherent hardships, had much impact on people at the time. With their imperial wars, the British were simply unused to anything like this.

The British Expedition

Tales of the British Expeditionary Force, or BEF, tell us quite a lot about the country that sent it. The BEF is a battered mirror to life as it had been, as well as providing gritty glints of the world that is to come. Though we talk of the 'British army', in this fight there were successive armies. The first, the original British Expeditionary Force, was small, professional, well trained and badly equipped. It helped save France from the German onslaught but was more or less wiped out in doing so. The next army was of Territorials and auxiliaries, quickly swollen by the third army, the vast volunteer forces created by Kitchener. Finally, there was the conscript army of those who had not volunteered before. For a long time, through these different armies, traditional class distinctions remained, the rivalries between counties, trades and professions survived and some of the failures of pre-war Britain, particularly in organization and technology, were mimicked. This would be a war not just of soldiers against soldiers but of system against system. It would pit the organized, disciplined Prussian traditions against the more chaotic and unfairer Edwardian British way, greatly to the latter's disadvantage, until Britain learned the hard way and began to change.

Recruitment showed how powerful class loyalties were. As Wilfred Owen discovered, in the early years of the war commissions were available for people from 'good' public schools, not for your average grammar-school boy. There was even a special University and Public Schools Brigade for those who could not face serving alongside working-class soldiers, as well as an Old Boys Corps and 'sportsmen's' battalions, advertised 'for the upper and middle classes only'. In many other places, at open-air gatherings in city centres, public-school men, barristers and clerks found themselves lining up with labourers and factory workers, sharing a queue and a chat with people across the class divide for the first time in their lives. In percentage terms, those most likely to enlist as volunteers came from the professions, banks, offices and the entertainment world. Agricultural workers and factory workers were needed more at home, of course, though coal miners were also particularly likely to enlist. As with the Boer War, medical inspections of volunteers showed a nation still badly fed and poorly doctored. To start with, because the medical examiners were given a shilling for every man they passed, large numbers of unfit men were sent into uniform. Later, worryingly high percentages of men with curved spines, poor eyesight, rotten teeth or bad lungs were noted. Perhaps the most revealing statistic of all is that *on average* serving soldiers were five inches shorter than officers. 'Bantam' battalions were formed in which every man was less than 5 foot 3 inches tall.

Once in France, at least in the early years, these divisions remained. Among the upper fighting classes, school songs were sung, founders' days celebrated and jokes exchanged in Latin or Greek. Public-school officers sent vividly descriptive letters home while ordinary soldiers had to leave theirs unsealed for censorship. Officers had servants – 'batmen' – and handmade clothes. They ate well. One artillery officer serving at Vimy Ridge in 1916 recorded dinners of 'soup, fish (if possible), meat (or fowl when poss.) asparagus, vegetables (always fresh); savoury (always), pudding (always), Whisky, Perrier, Port (every night), Vermouth, Sherry, biscuits, cigarettes and cigars, coffee, tea or cocoa, fruit'.[5] During his short period as an officer in France, Winston Churchill wrote to his wife to send two bottles of old brandy and one of peach brandy every ten days, plus 'Stilton cheeses: cream: hams: sardines – dried fruits: you might almost try a big beef steak pie: but not tinned grouse'. Yet the 'noblesse oblige' tendency among the upper- and middle-class officers was also impressive. Unlike their French counterparts, front-line officers lived with their men as well as leading them into battle, and organized football matches and other games to keep them occupied, very much in the tradition of the muscular Christian. Famously, one officer, Captain Nevill of the 8th East Surreys, prepared his attack on the first day of the Somme by painting a football with 'The Great European Cup-Tie Finals. East Surreys versus Bavarians. Kick off at zero.' Another football was painted with the words 'No referee' and both were kicked over the parapet when the attack started, Nevill having offered a prize for whoever dribbled a ball to the German lines. He was killed straight away.[6] His widely reported behaviour was regarded as marvellous back home and lunatic in Germany.

British soldiers were often eating well for the first time in their lives, albeit on dull fare. Their rations were more generous than the French or German ones, and included fresh meat and vegetables where possible, with biscuits, cheese, bacon, bread, cigarettes and a daily tot of rum. This would have been much more than many working-class men would have had at home, and was a source of envy and astonishment to German troops when they broke through British lines later in the war – though by then Germany had had to cope with a long British blockade and the so-called 'turnip winter'. British troops had shorter spells at the front line too and were comparatively well looked after medically. But, because the army reflected the country, they were much less well educated than the German troops they were facing and, to begin with, in worse physical shape. Mostly industrial workers, they were dogged, tough and obedient, while also being cynical and scabrous. Some had joined the army early because there were few practical alternatives; in the first weeks of the war, it is estimated that half a million men were made redundant. For many they had the solidarity of living and fighting alongside others from their street, village or factory.

Though the war was relatively mechanized, it reflected a horse-drawn Britain too. At its peak, the army in France was using around 450,000 horses and mules to get around, to carry and occasionally to attack with. Many had been brought across the Atlantic from Canada, the United States or South America but almost a fifth of the horses and mules at home had been taken from the farms, stables and streets. What awaited them was not pleasant – the army mules had their vocal cords cut to stop them braying and giving away their position to the enemy, while grey or dappled horses were dyed dark. Both would then be at high risk of being blown up as they took men, messages and equipment back and forward from the front lines. All the armies fighting had large cavalry contingents, though apart from a few attacks at the 1917 Battle of Cambrai (involving Sikhs and Canadian cavalry, along with English hussars) the British cavalry was little used. Still, with the horses, the aristocratic officers and the lack of socialist or suffragette rhetoric, it is easy to see why so many conservative-minded Britons found much that was reassuring amidst the dirt, the boredom and the fear.

For officers and men the 1,000-strong battalion, defending its own little piece of the front, became a community, a wartime village or firm, with its own class divisions, but where everyone knew everyone else. The badges, the accents and the characters produced an intense sense of belonging which veterans would remember all their lives. But this was an unreal Britain without unions, strikes and political divisions (for all the politicians were pretty much despised, along with the red-tabbed staff officers, allegedly living it up in châteaux far back from danger). It was coarse and the songs sung were famously very rude, as well as very funny. It is somehow reassuring to know that the famous 'Hymn of Hate' written by Ernst Lissauer, and sung by the German troops to express their loathing of the British, was promptly translated and sung by the BEF too, with a chorus, 'Oo do we 'ite?' and a full battalion replying: 'England!' One vivid source for the tone of the trenches was created by a captain from the 12th Battalion of the Sherwood Foresters, who found himself in the worst place of all, the Ypres salient (which means it jutted into German lines and was under attack from different directions) in February 1916. Captain F. J. Roberts, who would go on to win a Military Cross on the Somme and who survived the war, came across a half-smashed old printing works in the ruins of Ypres, with the type scattered outside in the mud. Though no journalist, he promptly decided to rescue and repair it, and produce a newspaper for the troops around him. This he did, first from the old building and then, when it had been finally blown to pieces, from a rat-infested cellar sheltered below the seventeeth-century ramparts of Ypres, built by the military architect Vauban.

Roberts's paper was first called the *Wipers Times* – 'wipers' is supposed to be how Sir John French, the BEF's first commander who spoke no French, pronounced Ypres. The name would later shift as the Sherwood Foresters were moved around. It is a thin production, facetious, angry and gossipy by turn. But to get some sense of the extraordinary circumstances in which it was written, printed and distributed, it is worth turning to Philip Gibbs, a journalist who described the salient at the time as a sea of red liquid mud composed of brick dust and 'bodies, bits of bodies, and clots of blood, and green, metallic-looking slime, made by explosive gases . . . Human flesh, rotting and stinking, mere pulp, was pasted into the mud-banks. If they dug to get deeper cover, their shovels went into the softness of dead bodies who had been their comrades. Scraps of flesh, booted legs, blackened hands, eyeless heads, came falling over them when the enemy trench-mortared their position.'[7] These are Stalingrad conditions, possibly the worst that any British soldiers have ever experienced for a prolonged time. So how did they see themselves, in the pages of their own little paper?

The first thing to say is that it is all terribly British. The horrors around them are referred to only in cod advertisements with wild typography about flame-throwers, gas and mortars. There is anger present, but it is mostly directed at officers behind the front line and blow-hards at home who keep writing about how well the war is going. Censorship at home is mocked: the newspaper promises to refer to the war 'which we hear is taking place in Europe, in a cautious manner'. More satirical adverts target the officer class: 'Are You Miserable? Are You Unhappy? Do You Hate Your Company Commander? Yes! Then buy him one of our New Patent Tip Duck

Boards . . . *If he steps on to the end/'Twill take a month his face to mend.'* But most of the miseries are made light of. A Nature Notes column explains: 'Birds . . . are of two kinds only – The Carrier Pigeon (a delicacy for front line trenches), and the nameless, untamed variety usually collected by junior officers.' There is plenty of gossip, which must have meant something at the time, about an unnamed major and his Belgian friends and his wallpaper. It is striking to find complaints about 'an insidious disease . . . affecting the Division, and the result is a hurricane of poetry. Subalterns have been seen with a notebook in one hand, and bombs in the other absently walking near the wire in deep communion with the muse.' Above all, there is a great deal of dreadful verse and awful puns, Limericks about girls from the Somme sitting on number five bombs, and the rest of it. The *Wipers Times* is a fascinating record because it reminds us that in the middle of the horror, many people were not reflecting on religion, or politics, or the meaning of war, but were just trying to get by with the same facetious humour and gossip they always liked. Edwardian Britain was a place of bad jokes, bad verse and horsing about, as well as a country in crisis; and the BEF was like that too. One extract of anonymous doggerel perhaps tells us more about how the poor bloody infantry was really thinking, than the protest poetry of Owen or Sassoon:

> Three Tommies sat in the trench one day,
> Discussing the war in the normal way,
> They talked of the mud, and they talked of the Hun
> Of what was to do, and what had been done,
> They talked about rum . . .
> But the point which they argued from post back to pillar
> Was whether Notts County could beat Aston Villa.

The Old Ways of Love

The nineteenth of April 1915 was a busy day during a perplexing time in the war. The tragic and bloody landings at Gallipoli were in the final stages of preparation and, despite passionate arguments at the heart of the government, would start six days later. In France,

Britain had just lost 13,000 men in the Battle of Neuve Chapelle; in three days' time the Germans would counter-attack at Ypres using for the first time a new weapon: gas. Failure in Flanders had led Kitchener to make one of his most chilling remarks of the war, complaining that the British commander Sir John French had wasted shells, rather than men. The men could be easily replaced, he said; the shells could not. A crisis in the supply of shells and other armaments was hanging over the whole government. This, the last Liberal government Britain has had, would soon be destroyed by it, and by a row boiling at the Admiralty between Churchill, hot for the Gallipoli adventure, and his old friend, the brilliant and unstable First Sea Lord 'Jackie' Fisher. Lloyd George was, of course, intriguing, and was meanwhile in vigorous debate with other ministers about whether it would be right to ban alcoholic drinks entirely. This was, to put it mildly, an important time for the British cabinet.

Yet that morning, as the cabinet talk went on, covering munitions, strategy in the Mediterranean and the possibility of prohibition, the prime minister was distracted, as he often was. He was writing to the twenty-eight-year-old woman with whom he had been deeply in love for three years. He wrote to her most days, and sometimes several times a day, letters crammed with gossip and, though from a sixty-three-year-old man, as wildly passionate as any from a brimming youth. Meanwhile, as Asquith was scribbling with only one ear on the cabinet debate, a few feet away another minister was also writing. Edwin Montagu had long been one of Asquith's most trusted supporters and now, still in his mid-thirties, had recently been brought into the cabinet. A coming man, he was being talked of as someone to take over the munitions problem. Montagu, or 'the Assyrian' as Asquith jokingly referred to him in private letters, had a strong jaw and a large square face, with a vigorous black moustache. He too was only half paying attention to the cabinet debate. In fact, he too was writing a love letter: 'My very dear one, I have never received, I need not tell you, a letter so thrilling and delicious as yours this morning. God bless you for it!' And his letter was to the same woman as the prime minister's letter.

Venetia Stanley came from a rich, clever, argumentative family and was regularly described as boyish and dark-eyed. She does not look extraordinarily beautiful in pictures but something of her vigour and liveliness is clear. Among those who had been much struck with her was Winston Churchill, whose wife was her cousin. Her letters to Asquith have disappeared, probably destroyed by him, but his to her are some of the most moving and detailed accounts of the politics of the time, and show Asquith as a profoundly romantic, witty and complicated man. Ecstatic confessions of adoration are followed by wicked gossip and details of military matters, such as Britain's breaking of German codes, which even other members of the cabinet knew nothing of. As Asquith begins to contemplate the idea that Venetia will marry someone else he writes in pencil, late at night, that fate will cut him off from 'the richest plenitude of love and happiness that has fallen to the lot of any man of my time'. But he wants to think of 'the Promised Land' 'with its milk & honey & grapes & the rest, wh. I am not allowed to taste, as possessed and enjoyed by someone, more love-inspiring & heart-filling & therefore worthier than I could ever hope to be'.

The biblical reference shows perhaps that Asquith subconsciously knew, though he was not then sure, that his rival was Montagu. For Montagu was Jewish and it was essential to him that Venetia convert before they married, which she agreed to do. To make things more complicated, Montagu and Asquith were in one another's company continually, across the table at meetings, walking together through London, sitting side by side on train journeys, and Montagu adored the older man. In that same cabinet meeting he continued his letter to Venetia: 'I do not know what to do. I simply can't face, and that's an end of it, hurting the PM . . . I owe it all to the PM. I love him. I can't be guilty for my own happiness of hurting him.' Self-hating, he berates himself as 'a coward and a Jew' unfitted for politics but concludes: 'I do not see how we can invent a new triangle. I cannot share you, nor can he,' before ending on a note of bathos, which confirms much about cabinet meetings of the period: 'Yours very disjointedly and disturbedly (Winston is gassing all the time) . . .' Yet eventually Edwin and Venetia agreed they must marry, dropping the bombshell on Asquith – though perhaps in the circumstances of 1915 that is not the best metaphor. After hundreds of pages of garrulous, self-analytical, literary and loving letters, his final one to her is bleak and tiny. It reads, in full: 'Most Loved – As you know well, *this* breaks my heart. I couldn't bear to come and see you. I can only pray God to bless you – and help me.'

What, one might ask, of Margot, Asquith's tough and brilliant wife? She had always taken a tolerant attitude towards Asquith's weakness for younger women, what she once called his harem. But a few days before that cabinet she had confronted him about Venetia. She wrote, explaining how she felt, to Montagu: 'I have as you know often wondered if Venetia hadn't ousted me faintly – not very much – but enough to wound, bewilder & humiliate me.' She always invited Venetia to dinners and meetings and her jealousy was not small or wounded vanity but out of love for Asquith and the knowledge, 'alas! That I am no longer young'. But she went on to describe her 'absolutely unique' relationship with Asquith: 'Every night however late I go & sit on his knee in my nightgown & we tell each other everything – he shows me *all* his letters & all Venetia's & tells me every secret.' This does not seem likely; or if true makes Margot a most unusual person. But to demonstrate her point she sent Montagu a letter from her husband after their row in which he insists that he is not transferring his confidence to the younger woman: 'My fondness for Venetia has never interfered & never could with our relationship.'[8]

It is as hard, looking backwards, to fully understand Edwardian attitudes to love and sex, as it is to understand much else about that age. For one thing, men regularly speak of their love for one another without there being any evidence of erotic or homosexual instinct. For another, as we shall see, there seems to have been much cuddling and even nights spent in bed without intercourse because of the dangers. The lava-flow of Asquith's heated prose would say to us instantly today that his relationship with Venetia must have been sexual. The young diplomat Duff Cooper, who knew the family, thought so, recording in his diary that his lover, Lady Diana Manners, had had a letter from Asquith in July 1915 when the Venetia–Edwin marriage was taking place: 'Diana is quite certain that Venetia was his mistress which rather surprises me. This letter, which was rather obscurely expressed, seemed practically to be an offer to Diana to fill the vacated position.' Diana, like Venetia, wanted to stay close to the prime minister but without 'physical duties that she couldn't or wouldn't fulfil. I advised her to concoct an answer which should be as obscure as his proposal and leave him puzzled – the old lecher.'[9] Yet it is wholly possible that Cooper and Diana, both of them wild enough, were wrong about Asquith and that this is another example of that now-outlawed perversion, the passionate friendship.

Apart from casting a unique shaft of light on the world of high politics through its trail of undestroyed letters, does the love triangle at the heart of the 1915 cabinet matter at all? While it was peripheral to the political crisis that was beginning to engulf Asquith, it badly winded him at a critical time. It would not lead to a newly moral 10 Downing Street when Asquith finally went since Lloyd George also had a mistress, Frances Stevenson, who lived with him most of the time, later becoming his wife. If Asquith was an elderly romantic and possibly a lecher, Lloyd George was a famous goat. Kitchener once said that he objected to discussing sensitive military issues in cabinet because they all went home and told their wives – except for Lloyd George who went home and told somebody else's wife. The Asquith revealed in the Venetia Stanley letters was without doubt a man from another era. Though he might confess to moments of anger and even self-hatred, he was the frock-coated intellectual, romantic and political cynic he had always been, too easily distracted from the grim and grinding business of trying to win a world war. For nine years he had been the most important Briton. But by 1915 he was starting to look as dated as the Edwardian age itself. Coarser times had come and coarser men were needed.

The First Crisis

The war can be divided into several phases, each changing the politics of Britain. In the first, there was still popular optimism about a short, easy victory. Asquith's Liberal government was not much remodelled. His was still a free-trade ministry which was highly sceptical about government taking too many powers and had absolutely no concept of the state revolution that would be needed to fight war on the coming scale. The land war, it was hoped, would be mainly fought between the French and Russians on one side and the Austrians and Germans on the other: Britain would control the seas and finance her allies, contributing only a modest land army. Yet Britain's chief enemy was a thoroughly militarized, centrally directed and war-directed power, with a vast land army and a sophisticated general staff almost outside civilian control. This, of course, was part of the point – a 'Prussianized' imperial power against a sort-of democracy. Anyone who had taken a close interest in Germany's rise, which meant anyone vaguely interested in public affairs, must have realized that laissez-faire was hardly going to be enough to beat the Prussians, but the old lot carried on in the old way. There was no talk of bringing in the Tory-Unionists or Labour to a government of national unity, as happened in the next war.

Some hard decisions were made. The Defence of the Realm Act, known as DORA, which would allow almost dictatorial powers over the press and many aspects of civilian life, was passed almost immediately. The most vigorous and warlike speeches by far came from Lloyd George, who had been so slow and cautious about supporting the conflict in the first place. From the beginning, by instinct rather than as political manoeuvring, he was speaking like the war leader Asquith plainly was not. He urged generosity to the German people while having no illusions about the scale of the struggle ahead. He told a recruiting meeting in London, in a speech described at the time as the finest in the history of England: 'They think we cannot beat them. It will not be easy. It will be a long job; it will be a terrible war; but in the end we shall march through terror to triumph.' The purpose of the war was to free Europe from a military caste determined to plunge the world 'into a welter of bloodshed and death'. And already he was looking forward in exalted terms to higher war aims:

> There is something infinitely greater and more enduring which is emerging already out of this great conflict – a new patriotism, richer, nobler . . . I see among all classes, high and low, shedding themselves of selfishness, a new recognition that the honour of the country does not depend merely on the maintenance of its glory in the stricken field, but also in protecting its homes from distress. It is bringing a new outlook for all classes. The great flood of luxury and sloth which had submerged the land is receding and a new Britain is appearing.

This was 1945 optimism thirty years early and it was Lloyd George's Treasury, in sharply raising taxes and authorizing the first paper one-pound notes in case of gold hoarding, which was most active on the home front.

Asquith's most dramatic political response to declaration of war was to accede to a public and press campaign for the imperial war hero Lord Kitchener, bringing him into the cabinet as war minister. Kitchener had been home on a visit from Egypt, which he was ruling, and was summoned from the deck of a cross-Channel ferry back to Whitehall. Like Lloyd George, Kitchener thought it would be a long and bloody war and was immediately clear that the small professional British army would be nothing like big enough to win it. The field marshal knew the French army well and was rather more interesting than his waxy, glazed-eyed image, but he would prove a disastrous cabinet member, who tried to act almost alone and regarded the views of elected leaders as impertinent piffle. In the insolent words of one of Asquith's children, however, he made 'a great poster' and proved the inspirational creator of the mass volunteer armies of the first part of the war. 'Your Country needs YOU' and his accusing finger had a dramatic effect. He had reckoned on 100,000 volunteers responding. In the first week alone, 175,000 did and by the end of that month, September 1914, three-quarters of a million men had signed up. By the time conscription arrived in spring 1916, 2.5 million people had enlisted. Yet Kitchener himself would end up fighting with generals in the field and with politicians in London, and would become a prime scapegoat for failures in supplying ammunition, and the military disaster of Gallipoli. This was partly because he had fallen out with the other great force in wartime Britain, the popular press; but when he was drowned on his way to Russia in June 1916, he was mourned as a great national hero.

In this early period, the full cabinet continued to meet in the old relaxed way, as in peacetime, and even when a 'war council' was formed in November 1914, chaired by the prime minister, it met irregularly and was within a few months too big to be effective as a quick-acting executive body. This first period was brought to an end by a succession of military failures and a growing realization that the war would be long and hard. At sea, German warships managed to evade the Royal Navy and shell towns on the east coast. There were other naval failures too, with ships lost to U-boats and mines, and a German naval victory off Chile. None of this was disastrous, but after Churchill's hyperactive work preparing for a showdown at sea it was very disappointing. He responded by bringing back a man who would nearly destroy him, Lord, or Jack, Fisher, to be First Sea Lord.

More important was the fate of the BEF. This was not the army of keen public-schoolboy lieutenants and scrawny workers of later years, but a highly trained, mobile and wholly professional force. Its shooting was outstanding – when the Germans first met them they thought they were facing machine guns, so fast and accurate was the rifle firing – and it had been thoroughly reorganized after the defeats of the Boer War. It had a large quantity of cavalry but less in proportion than the Germans or French, and British cavalry were trained to dismount and fight as infantry; they were less archaic than the Prussian Uhlans or the French Cuirassiers, with their horsehair-plumed helmets, gleaming breastplates and sabres. On the other hand, they lacked any trench mortars and enough machine guns, usable grenades and high-explosive shells for their scanty artillery.

Above all, the BEF was tiny. It comprised five infantry divisions, against a hundred raised by Germany and sixty-two French divisions. It had one division of cavalry. The German army had twenty-two of them and the French ten. The BEF was slightly smaller than the Belgian army, which had made a brave stand earlier but had collapsed and was now clinging on to a tiny remaining strip of land. As one military historian has pointed out, 'In August 1914 the BEF held twenty-five miles of the Western Front, the French 300 miles.'[10] Criticism of British strategy has to take account of the fact that for most of the war, really until its final stages, the British army was very much the junior partner and had to respond to what the French suffered, hoped for and at times demanded. So although the first encounter, and indeed the second at Le Cateau, shocked and halted General von Kluck's First Army and demonstrated British skill, when the French fell back, so did the BEF. This became one of the British army's great retreating successes. Unlike the fallback to Dunkirk, the French and British line held and soon it was the Germans retreating. Much has been made of the failure of the British army to realize that there was a gap in the German line, available for an old-style war-of-manoeuvre push – the last time this happened until after the main slaughter. But communications were terrible and commanders sensibly cautious. With both sides trying desperately to outflank each other, the front quickly extended to the coast. Churchill, absurdly if bravely, had personally seized control of the defence of Antwerp with some sailors but that port fell and the two sides ended up facing one another from just outside Ostend to the Swiss border. The digging began, though the first trenches were paltry scratches in the mud compared with what came later. The machine-gun posts and wire went up. The rain came down, for months. So did the German shells, proving that the enemy was far better equipped with artillery. The world of war had suddenly changed. The consequences would change Britain, as well as continental Europe, for ever.

It is not true that Britain's war leaders were slow to realize what had happened, and the likely consequences in loss of life. The first attempts at headlong attack had been bloody enough and just before New Year 1915 Churchill wrote to Asquith saying, 'I think it quite possible that neither side will have the strength to penetrate the other's lines ... my impression is that the position of both armies is not likely to undergo any decisive change – although no doubt several hundred thousand men will be spent to satisfy the military mind on that point ... Are there not other alternatives to sending our armies to chew barbed wire in Flanders?'[11] Churchill had been converted by his admirer Lord Fisher to the idea of attacking the German sea coast, seizing the Kiel Canal and/or then taking the Russian armies through the Baltic to within a hundred miles of Berlin. Fisher had long dreamed of such a coup, ever since a German general had told him how vulnerable the coast was. He had even talked to the Kaiser about it before the war, who dismissively joked that he would send the Prussian police to arrest the British navy. Undeterred, Fisher had devised, and had built, special shallow-bottomed warships to attack Germany. They were called *Courageous*, *Furious* and *Glorious*, and were so odd that the navy rechristened them *Outrageous*, *Spurious* and *Uproarious*. But Fisher was in deadly earnest and had prepared bombardment plans and had landing craft for the Czar's soldiers built as well. Churchill, sharing his daring, was profoundly excited by the Baltic plan.

Lloyd George was thinking along parallel lines. He too wrote to Asquith saying that more trench warfare would destroy the morale of the troops and that any attempt to force the well-defended German lines would end 'in failure and in appalling loss of life'. His preferred alternatives were to attack Austria through the Balkans, rousing the Serbs, Greeks and others; or to attack Turkey via Syria, thereby helping the Czar's army, which was in dire trouble in the Caucasus and begging for help. These political searches to avoid mass slaughter in France led to increasingly bitter rows with the military, above all Lords Kitchener and Fisher. The army high command believed that, bloody as it was, the only way to defeat Germany was full-frontal in Flanders and many historians today agree. Lloyd George and Churchill have been attacked as romantic, know-nothing busybodies, distracting the men properly in charge of the war and diverting vital soldiers and guns to hopeless causes.

Indeed, Lloyd George's hopes for some kind of Balkan uprising showed little understanding of the politics of the region, or of Greece. Whether an attack could have succeeded across the North Sea and whether the disastrous attempt on the Dardanelles, meant to shake Turkey out of the war, could have worked with better luck and leadership can never now be known. Both Lloyd George and Churchill were men who tended to believe they knew more than the experts and the latter was schoolboyish enough to rouse the cabinet to mocking laughter at some of his antics. He had a very odd attitude to the war, telling Margot Asquith at a dinner party in January 1915, 'I would not be out of this glorious delicious war for anything the world could give me . . . I say, don't repeat that I said the word delicious but you know what I mean.' Yet he and his old Welsh leader were democratic politicians, acutely aware of the difficulties of sustaining public support for a long blood-sacrifice without hope of breakthrough. Both, but particularly Lloyd George, were slogging up and down the country making speeches to keep up morale and offer hope – something military historians tend to easily dismiss as mere politicking. They had a duty to try to use their ingenuity to look for alternative strategies. Inevitably, however, this pitted them against those who were sure that the war would be won or lost in France, and that any diversion would simply prolong the killing.

These arguments were being thrashed out in the War Council

and between ministers. And it seems that the views of Maurice Hankey, a brilliant official who was secretary to the War Council and later the man who effectively created the modern Cabinet Office system, proved decisive. He argued strongly against Churchill's northern attack and in favour of the Dardanelles assault. The cabinet agreed, initially authorizing a naval attack through to Constantinople, which could be threatened with bombardment, possibly then bringing down the Ottoman Empire. Though the battleships' bombardment was ferocious and quite effective, they sailed straight into a minefield. One French battleship and two British were sunk and the entire fleet withdrew, giving the Turks time to reinforce and prepare land that would have been relatively easy to seize. Now it was decided to make this a full landing of troops. Kitchener, who knew the Middle East well and easily understood the luscious prospects for the Allies if Turkey surrendered, became a supporter of this Churchillian adventure at least. The eventual landing by British and Australian troops at Gallipoli, badly organized and poorly supported, ran into ferocious and deadly Turkish defence led by Kemal Ataturk, who would later become the founder of modern Turkey. Just getting ashore was murderous, near-impossible: troops drowned, were killed by their own side or easily fell prey to well-sited machine guns. In the early stages they had to use bayonets against the guns, with predictable results. Pinned down on the beaches, with little cover and at the mercy of Turkish artillery, the slaughter was terrible; some 50,000 British, Australian and New Zealand troops died of wounds or disease. As the disaster continued, conditions became ever more horrible, a corpse-scented, fly-covered landscape as bad in its way as anything in Flanders, and even more hopeless militarily. One eyewitness was the father of the modern media tycoon Rupert Murdoch, who, despite having his notes seized and destroyed, sent a savage report about British incompetence to Australia and London. Though Churchill blamed the admirals and generals at the scene, it was he who was most blamed by the public, and the disaster nearly destroyed his political career. At the time the *Daily Mail* called him 'guilty in the first degree'.

One of those who died in the adventure was the poet Rupert Brooke, who had become a gleaming symbol of British manhood, despite his generally second-rate verse. He dreamed of a second

Trojan war, and of another British crusade. But he was bitten on the lip by a gnat before he reached the Dardanelles and died of blood poisoning. He was buried on Skyros, the Greek island which reputedly had produced Theseus, 'some corner of a foreign land' – which would have pleased him. His epitaph in Greek read: 'Here lies the servant of God, a sub-lieutenant in the British navy, who died for the deliverance of Constantinople from the Turks', thus extending Britain's war aims even beyond Churchill's wilder dreams. At home, Asquith, whose daughter Violet had loved Brooke, told Venetia his death 'has given me more pain than any loss in the war' and spoke of a 'dazed, dim, premonitory feeling' that the next loss would be even closer to home. His son Raymond would be killed on the Somme the following year. Churchill took it upon himself to write Brooke's obituary for *The Times*, piling up clauses to help build one of the iconic reputations of the time. Brooke's lush late-romantic style, his unabashed but self-conscious patriotism and his blond good looks made him a perfect pin-up for the 'lost generation', even though he was always a tricky character, half way between Lawrence of Arabia and Sassoon. Had he lived, he might of course have developed into a tougher, angrier war poet. Dead, he was safely frozen rigid as England's young Galahad – the only time a gnat has turned a man to marble.

Meanwhile, in the great old Admiralty, almost a state within a state, Fisher and Churchill were at each other's throats. Theirs was one of the strangest relationships of the British wartime story. Fisher had always been charismatic and had known almost every interesting ruler of late-Victorian and Edwardian times: czars, kaisers, grand dukes and presidents. He had a strangely oriental face, which led many to doubt whether he was really fully British, and a charm so intense that both men and women fell for him. The admiral had first met Churchill at Biarritz, the favoured pleasure promenade of Edward VII, and noted: 'Fell desperately in love with Winston Churchill,' who in turn apparently told Fisher, 'You are the only man in the world I truly love.' As we have noted before, it is dangerous to read Edwardians with twenty-first-century spectacles, but Fisher's adoration of Churchill was intense enough to make him the enemy of Clementine, Churchill's wife. During the Gallipoli crisis, when Churchill was briefly in France without taking the First Sea Lord and she had invited Fisher to lunch, he lurked round afterwards before leaping out to suddenly inform her: 'You are a foolish woman. All the time you think Winston's with Sir John French he is in Paris with his mistress.' She was very upset and bundled him out. Much later, when Fisher had long gone from the Admiralty and so had Churchill, but the two of them seemed to be in cahoots again, Clemmie shouted at the little old man: 'Keep your hands off my husband. You have all but ruined him once. Leave him alone now.'[12]

So this was no humdrum office alliance. Fisher's return to the Admiralty was greeted with something like the applause for Kitchener at the War Office, and in his first weeks he encouraged a speedy revenge attack by British cruisers which resulted in the Battle of the Falklands, a notable and crushing victory over five German ships which effectively put the Kaiser's surface fleet out of contention across most of the world's oceans. But Fisher was by now an old man. His furious rate of work and his eccentric, often brilliant thinking came up against a younger man, Churchill, who was just as brilliant and just as hard-working but who now was not his adoring protégé but his absolute boss. Churchill did little to calm or cultivate Fisher. The latter did not like the idea of the Dardanelles campaign, partly because it was not his thrust at Germany and partly because he wanted to keep the whole fleet ready for a coming Trafalgar-like confrontation in the North Sea. He was won round for a while but became increasingly irascible and unpredictable. At the key War Council meeting he had to be physically stopped from walking out by Kitchener and led back to the table. His memorandums became violent and, in the view of Hankey, completely mad, and he announced his resignation no fewer than eight times. The worse things went at the Dardanelles the more he ranted about how he had been against the affair all along.

On the morning of 15 May 1915, as the bloody disaster of Gallipoli was becoming apparent, he simply disappeared. He went to see Lloyd George to tell him he was going off to Scotland and then vanished . . . later it turned out that he had taken refuge in a hotel room at Charing Cross, within a few hundred yards of the Admiralty, whose officials were desperately combing central London and railway stations to find him. When at last a note from Asquith reached him, commanding him in the King's name to return to his post, along with an emollient letter from Churchill, he was unmoved. He returned to Downing Street, telling Asquith and Lloyd George he could stand 'it' (Churchill) no longer. Meanwhile he had tipped off Andrew Bonar Law, the Unionist leader, to what he was doing. This was further treachery. And in the middle of it all reports began coming in suggesting that the German High Seas Fleet might be finally coming out to do battle. By now all London was ablaze with rumour. The Queen wrote to Fisher asking him to remain at his post like Nelson. Churchill said he regarded the Sea Lord's behaviour as desertion and the King agreed, saying later that Fisher should have been 'hanged at the yardarm for desertion of his post in the face of the enemy' or at least punished by 'dismissal from the service and degradation'.[13]

Fisher, unaware of all this, was riding on a wave of euphoria. He sent an ultimatum to Asquith saying he would stay only if Churchill was kicked out of the cabinet, and he was given absolute control of the war at sea, all naval appointments, fleet dispositions and 'absolutely untrammelled sole command of all the sea forces whatsoever'. He would not serve under Balfour, either. Furthermore he wanted this published to the fleet so that everyone would know of his victory. Meanwhile he sent a letter to Bonar Law telling him that Churchill 'is a bigger danger than the Germans by a long way'. It was the kind of fantasy of a constitutional coup by the military over the politicians that many generals and admirals may have entertained but nobody before or since has proposed to a British prime minister. Even Fisher's highly partial biographer called it a deranged letter and it finished him. Asquith told the King that Fisher was 'somewhat unhinged'. Some of the papers agreed, though others championed his cause. Fisher's resignation was, however, devastating for Churchill. He, after all, had appointed him in the first place and then been unable to work with him. If a coalition with the Tories was to be the result, then he knew he was likely to lose the Admiralty, for the Tories still loathed him. He desperately petitioned Asquith to keep him on, bombarding him with letters and personal pleas, but Asquith was thinking of other things, including his own survival as prime minister. And this was only one part of the crisis breaking over him. Fisher was a lethal torpedo, but the heaviest bombardment had come from another force which was itself reshaping British public life.

The May Coup

On the morning of Friday 21 May 1915 there was unaccustomed uproar on the floor of the London Stock Exchange. More than a thousand men of all ages were shouting, jeering and carrying bundles of newspapers to the middle of the floor, where they were piled up and set alight. This bonfire blazed to choruses of cheers and groans. The cheers were for Lord Kitchener. The groans were for Lord Northcliffe, owner of the *Daily Mail* and *The Times*, and one of the most powerful men in Britain. The burning papers were copies of that day's *Mail*. Some painted a message and carried it round the corner into Throgmorton Street to the City offices of the newspaper and hung it outside: 'The Allies of the Hun', it read. A little further west, in London's clubland, pinstriped, frock-coated servants gathered up copies of the papers published by Northcliffe, which included the *Evening News* and the *Weekly Dispatch*, and threw them in waste bins. The reaction was not confined to a few walrus-suited clubmen or City clerks. Similar protests followed in Bristol and Liverpool and across Britain, the circulation of the *Daily Mail*, the best known and most successful newspaper in the country, fell by more than a million overnight, from 1,386,000 to just 238,000. No article in the history of British journalism has ever had such a dramatic negative effect on circulation. The man responsible, Alfred Harmsworth, Lord North-cliffe, liked to say he had the hide of an elephant. When the news was brought to him he was sitting surrounded by his senior journal-ists – they always stood while he sat, to show respect. He took off his glasses, told them he didn't care what they thought but that he was right. Then he turned to the news editor and asked about the next day's news: 'Fish, what's on the schedule?'

The article that had caused the uproar was written by Northcliffe himself, in pencil at his country home, and was a culmination of his campaign to shake the government into taking seriously the shortage of high-explosive shells for the Western Front. This was no academic or merely personal vendetta. It went to the heart of how a government needs to work in wartime. Sir John French in Flanders had already lost unimaginable numbers of casualties trying desperately to break the German line. He could be blamed himself, but he blamed the lack of the right number and quantity of shells. Shrapnel shells, sending out a hail of small metal fragments, were devastating against troops in the open but of little use in demolishing trenches or deep bunkers. Kitchener, who had made his name in South Africa, had overseen the supply of the wrong kind of shells and, once he had accepted the idea of the Gallipoli attack, had diverted a fifth of French's shells to the Dardanelles. Furthermore, until recently, the British navy had done nothing to obstruct the supply of cotton to Scandinavia and other neutrals, from where it had gone directly to Germany to manufacture 'gun cotton', the essential raw material of the day for high-explosive shells. The German artillery was much more effective. Sir John and the British high command were right. Kitchener, fussing about wasting ammunition, was hopelessly wrong. Lloyd George knew it, but Asquith and the majority of the government – what one *Mail* journalist called 'a Cabinet of tired lawyers' – were still backing the war minister. The *Mail* had been campaigning aggressively about the shell problem, with headlines such as 'Killing our Men by Cotton'. At Neuve Chapelle, the shells had run out. Asquith made a speech pooh-poohing the idea that there was a shortage and at that point Sir John French's patience snapped.

He did something widely regarded as reprehensible but which led directly to the *Daily Mail* crisis. He showed the *Times* war correspondent Charles Repington the secret War Office correspondence which backed up his belief on the shells shortage and led to Repington reporting that the British failure had been directly caused by a 'fatal' lack of high explosives. It infuriated Kitchener, questioned Asquith's veracity or grasp of facts and led Northcliffe to assault the 'tired lawyers' head-on. His *Mail* leader asserted bluntly that

> Lord Kitchener has starved the army in France of high explosive shells. The admitted fact is that Lord Kitchener ordered the wrong kind of shell . . . He was warned repeatedly that the kind of shell required was a violently explosive bomb which would dynamite its way through the German trenches and entanglements and enable our brave men to advance in safety. The kind of shell our poor soldiers have had has caused the death of thousands of them . . . We are growing callous about the size of the daily lists of killed, wounded and missing . . . Thousands

of homes are mourning today for men who have been need-
lessly sacrificed.

Apart from the fact that 'thousands' was a wild underestimate, this
was a deliberately brutal assault on the reputation of the man who
until then had been seen by most Britons as the greatest soldier and
leader the nation possessed. People knew Kitchener from the posters,
and they knew he had recruited the huge new citizen armies, and
they were outraged. Yet Northcliffe was absolutely right. His attack,
combined with the efforts of another press owner, Sir Max Aitken –
soon to be Lord Beaverbrook – convinced the Tory leadership and
some leading Liberals, notably Lloyd George, that things could not
carry on this way. It was time to sweep aside what Northcliffe
referred to as the Edwardian country-house style of government.

He did not get his way immediately. Denounced up and down
the country as a reptile, a traitor and worse, Northcliffe watched
while Asquith brought in Bonar Law and a coalition government.
The resignation of Fisher had been the final blow, but the shells
crisis had weakened Asquith fatally – and, as Churchill reflected later,
there had been no victories to compensate, or carry the government
through. The coalition was still dominated by Liberals. Unionists
accepted surprisingly low positions, though Balfour got Churchill's
old job at the Admiralty and Churchill had to take a junior role
before he quit politics, briefly, for the trenches. Kitchener would
hang on, denouncing Northcliffe and the press, comforted by his
national status, working busily on his rose garden, until he drowned
while on a mission to Russia. Above all, as we shall see, Lloyd
George was put in charge of munitions and began to entirely reshape
the relationship between the state and the people before finally
ousting Asquith and becoming prime minister himself. Northcliffe
and his later rival Beaverbrook, now pulling the strings of the *Daily
Express*, were both involved in the destruction of the last Liberal
government. There has been a nonsensical argument ever since
about which had done more to bring this about – the full-frontal
attacks of Northcliffe on the shells crisis or behind-the-scenes plotting
by Beaverbrook, the friend and protégé of Bonar Law, who was
finally persuaded by the resignation of Fisher that the government
must change. Was it the shells or was it Fisher? The *Daily Mail* or

the *Daily Express*? The true answer was that it was both. After a year of disappointing and tragic war-making, the press ended the Liberal age. Asquith, like Kitchener, despised journalism. But journalism, while not more powerful than the politicians, had grown so strong it could now, given the right circumstances, destroy a government. How had this happened?

There is a widely believed myth that popular British journalism was essentially imported from America. It was not. American journalism was sharper, faster and more aggressive but the British variant developed separately. It was largely created by a single genius, Alfred Harmsworth. A golden-haired, strikingly handsome boy from a poor family, by 1915 he had grown into a swollen ogre, demonized in Germany as the man who had taken Britain to war, the real power behind the façade of Parliament and court, manipulating the whole empire. Harmsworth, born in Dublin to a tough mother and a feckless, hard-drinking father, had been brought up in north London, the eldest of a large family. Mid-Victorian England was a hard place for families on the edge of economic survival: the Harmsworths' neighbours went bankrupt and the whole family committed suicide. Alfred was bright, ebullient and obsessed by technology. Whatever was new – bicycling, motor cars, aircraft – thrilled him. And he had an uncanny understanding of what the huge newly literate lower-middle classes would be prepared to read. He learned his trade first with cycling and sporting magazines, but his empire started with what could be called snippet-journalism, an amalgam of quotes, pieces of information, curious facts, news and jokes. The first paper, *Answers to Correspondents*, was a direct copy of an earlier and highly original publication, *Tit-Bits*, for which Harmsworth had worked. But Alfred's energy, promotional stunts and talent for controversy soon outstripped it and his success was assured when he ran a simple competition: guess the amount of gold in the Bank of England and win a pound a week for life – enough in those days to allow you to marry and set up home. He received more than 700,000 responses and was soon expanding, first with boys' and women's magazines, and then by buying the ailing London *Evening News*. Harold, his younger brother, had been persuaded to leave a safe civil-service job, which was lucky because he had the organizational ability and financial nous that Alfred lacked. Thus a late-Victorian publishing empire was built up, with nerve, chutzpah and a certain amount of vulgarity, out of almost nothing at all. This was the prologue. The main act was the *Daily Mail*.

It is impossible to quite explain the novelty and shock value of the now-familiar *Mail* when it first appeared in May 1896. So much of what it pioneered is what we now think of simply as journalism. It junked the word-for-word reporting of dull political speeches. It introduced first-person-singular 'I was there' reporting. Its stories were short and dramatic. It delighted in controversy, arguments to get people angry and get them talking. When most papers were grey and crammed, hard to read, it was printed on bright white paper with enough space to make it easy on the eye. It was aimed at what one harrumphing politician (Lord Salisbury) dismissed as 'office boys' but what Harmsworth called 'the busy man' – though he insisted on features to appeal to women, too. It was right-wing, patriotic and optimistic about progress. He told his journalists to 'explain – simplify – clarify' and coined the now well-known phrase, 'When dog bites man, it isn't news; when man bites dog, it is.' He told another reporter: 'The three things which are always news are health things, sex things and money things' – which remains, broadly speaking, true. He told Thomas Marlowe, an early *Mail* editor, that it was not made 'by licking Ministers' boots . . . I have a natural horror of that sort of journalism' and that it was 'no good printing long articles. People won't read them. They can't fix their attention for more than a short time.' The whirling radicalism of the Harmsworth style was a revolution in popular culture that can reasonably be compared to the arrival of the radio or the internet. Before broadcasting, this was the voice of the new democracy.

Alfred had sales stunts of all kinds, from jigsaws to sky-writing, from free books to prizes for pilots. When the Boer War started, his paper brought back thrilling despatches from South Africa and tangled with the authorities. It used pictures early, used them big and used them often. And it was cheap, half the price of its rivals. It was an almost instant success, causing Alfred to exclaim on the second day of publication that he had struck a gold mine.

Within a few years it was such an established part of British life that there were music-hall songs and jokes about the *Mail*, or the *Daily Liar*. Harmsworth was called the enemy of the human race and the man who was ruining the Empire. In turn, he shunned the establishment, though he accepted a peerage in 1905, at the time the youngest person to get one. The Edwardian political elite did not know quite how to respond to Northcliffe and the 'new journalism' which he represented. It was possible to demonize the man, but it was not possible to brush aside his readership, because it was identical to the newly enfranchised rising classes. He represented a fresh force in Britain, unpredictable and crude but rising, while the aristocracy and 'country-house government' was falling. Politicians would woo him in private and denounce him in public – Churchill was particularly guilty of this – but they understood that the popular press was now far more important than the old political journalism. And in 1908 the two collided, when Harmsworth bought *The Times*. This made him one of the most powerful people in Britain, above all because he not only had the means, he also had an agenda to push. A passionate imperialist, he was an early and relentless Cassandra about German invasion. He can best be described as a maverick, anti-party right-winger who believed in technical progress and getting things done and who had little time for Parliament or the political classes. Harmsworth and his newspapers were at least as complacent and flat-footed in July 1914 as the politicians were, but as soon as the war came, he was brimming with ideas about how to win it and had a network of informants across Europe that made him much better informed than any minister. The clash with Asquith and Kitchener was all but inevitable.

The confrontation was worse than it might have been because Kitchener despised journalists and was determined to fight the war without any news coverage at all. In the early days, most of the papers sent correspondents to the front and some brought back stories that were extraordinarily vivid. They were there when Kluck's First Army crashed head-on into the BEF and they described the retreat from Mons, and the first stages of trench warfare, sparing the reader very little. The *Mail*'s Hamilton Fyfe wrote bleakly about shattered British soldiers with no trench protection under constant shelling. Another reporter, G. Ward Price, watched the bombardment of Rheims Cathedral, reported the phlegmatic courage of the advancing Germans, mown down but still coming on, and described what it was like to be shot at. At home, a Press Bureau under the

Tory politician F. E. Smith had been set up to censor what was published and was soon being called the Suppress Bureau by journalists. Philip Gibbs, one of the greatest reporters of the time, then working for the *Daily Telegraph* and the *Chronicle*, managed to get out to the front disguised variously as an orderly, a stretcher-bearer or a French correspondent, and many more did similarly. Gibbs was arrested five times trying to get his stories back. Yet stories kept getting out, via American papers, or thanks to ingenious reporters who tucked their reports into their caps and smuggled themselves back to London. Kitchener then announced that no reporters would be allowed at the front, and threatened to shoot any who were found there. Fyfe was exiled to Russia. The *Daily Mail*, a favourite among the British troops, responded by printing letters they had sent home, and which were passed on for publication by their families.

It was a classic confrontation between military thinking and democratic thinking and, in the conditions of the Great War, a hard one to disentangle. The more people at home knew about the atrocious conditions and losses being sustained at the front, the greater the danger of morale crumbling. Unrestricted reporting would, of course, give Germany, through her agents in Britain, vital information. Yet this was a war which could not be won without the support of the civilian population, and the less people knew, the wilder the rumours. The often-told tale of Russian troops being seen landing in Scotland with the snow still on their boots and marching through to France was one example. And over time, as the slaughter mounted, the yawning gap between official reports of victories and the tales told in letters, or by the returning wounded, would cause more anger and despair than truthful reports would have done. Kitchener, who had been a kind of military dictator in Egypt before the war, had no conception of the needs of a parliamentary democracy at war. Interestingly, although Germany was in most ways far more authoritarian and regimented than wartime Britain, her armies were far more open to journalism, including that of neutral countries, so that at times it seemed easier to find out what had happened from the enemy.

Eventually, Kitchener relented enough to allow a small number of accredited journalists at British headquarters behind the lines, and some of their reports were brilliant. Here, for instance, is Philip

Gibbs describing life in the trenches during a quiet phase in the first Ypres campaign, as the rains came.

> In 'Plug Street' and other lines of trenches they stood in water with walls of oozy mud about them, until their legs rotted and became black with frostbite, until many of them were carried away with bronchitis and pneumonia, and until all of them . . . were shivering, sodden scarecrows, plastered with slime. They crawled with lice, these decent Englishmen from good clean homes, these dandy men who once upon a time had strolled down the sweet shady side of Pall Mall, immaculate, and fragrant as their lavender kid gloves. They were eaten alive by these vermin and suffered the intolerable agony of itch.[14]

The war poets were not the only people describing to the public the reality of what was happening. Gibbs sometimes sounds absurdly cheery to modern ears, but his day-by-day reports of the Battle of the Somme make absolutely clear that, victory or not, many of the British attackers had to march steadily into scythe-like machine-gun fire, that the ground was soon strewn with corpses and that the Germans, far from being demoralized by the huge bombardment, were fighting with huge courage. He also reports captured Germans saying there will be another war with Britain in ten years' time. This is not the simple propaganda of legend. The Great War was not the finest hour of British journalism. No war involving the state so deeply is likely to produce notably daring or critical reporting. But working under very difficult burdens, including threats to close down their papers and arrest individual journalists, many papers responded well. Politicians might fume. But if they were to survive, they needed the press. Two men understood this intuitively. One was Churchill, though he was still learning. The other was his master, Lloyd George. But before they would rise again, Britain faced a return to the issue which had nearly destroyed them before the war – Ireland.

Cruel, Promising Easter

The story of the sad, brave and incompetent Easter Rising of 1916 could begin almost anywhere – among the money-raising Fenians in

America, the foundation of the Irish Republican Brotherhood, or even in Germany. But since it was a rebellion against the very idea of empire, one could also begin it far from Europe. In the year 1890 in a corrugated-iron shed in the humid, greedy heart of the Belgian Congo, in a dirty little town called Matadi, two white men met, both lean, both bearded, both seething. Surrounded by adventurers, drunks, sadists, prostitutes and desperadoes hoping to make a fortune from the slaughter of elephants for their ivory, the great Joseph Conrad met a British consular official whose story would rival anything in his fictions, Sir Roger Casement. The novelist, whose *Heart of Darkness* would become the most powerful fictional denunciation in English of the evil of colonialism, found his companion intelligent and sympathetic. They sat for ten days and talked. Later, when they met again in London, Conrad wrote about his new friend. This official of the Empire, said Conrad, 'could tell you things! Things I have tried to forget. Things I never did know.' In the early years of Edwardian Britain Conrad and Casement were on the same side, ardent for justice.

Casement had travelled with a Belgian officer who collected human heads. He had seen the beatings, murders and amputations visited on local people ordered to gather rubber. He had travelled on foot, with his bulldog, deep into the jungle to gather first-hand accounts of atrocities. He had rented an iron steamboat and sailed deep inland to see for himself the heart of darkness. He had learned native languages. He had bombarded the Foreign Office with furious and interminable letters about the cruelties visited by rapacious whites on defenceless blacks. At home his style is well described by another writer, Ford Madox Ford, who said: 'I have myself seen in the hands of Sir Roger Casement who had smuggled them out of the country, the hands and feet of Congolese children which had been struck off by Free State officials, the parents having failed to bring in their quota of rubber or ivory.' (Even Conrad doubted such a thing could be true: Conrad was wrong.) Casement wrote to the Belgian officials too, predicting that their rule could only lead to the semi-extinction of the people and the effective destruction of the whole region – a prediction that by the twenty-first century, when the Congo has become lawless, semi-deserted and isolated, seems bleakly vindicated. This was no ordinary imperial official. Still, he had official backing, however nervous: his 1904 'Casement Report' on the Belgian Congo atrocities was commissioned by the government and shocked public opinion around the world.

Casement's campaigning led him to fund and covertly support one of the most vigorous radical organizations of Edwardian England, the Congo Reform Association. Its organizer was a young half-French radical and former shipping worker, E. D. Morel, and between them they roused much of British opinion against King Leopold's personal fiefdom in Africa, with its forced labour and confiscation.[15] They recruited aristocrats, famous writers such as Conan Doyle and Galsworthy, the Archbishop of Canterbury, many MPs, philanthropic businessmen and retired colonial governors. They made enough noise for the Belgian king to become a hate-figure in *Punch* and spread their influence to America. Most importantly, the Casement Report was eventually accepted by the Belgian Parliament, which began moves to take the Congo under formal Belgian rule, and away from the King. The CRA would eventually be wound up in 1913, by which time a constitutional change for the Congo and a series of reforms could allow it plausibly to declare at least a temporary victory. Casement had moved on. In 1906 he was sent to Brazil, and then to Peru, where he campaigned on behalf of natives kept in a similar state of murderous subjection by rubber-planters, founding the Anti-Slavery Society in Britain and eventually achieving, as in the Congo, some real successes. By the time he retired from the Consular Service in 1912 he was a well-known, decorated and esteemed figure, connected to a wide range of politicians and writers – a radical, but an establishment radical. Yet there were a couple of things about Casement which would change the way he is remembered – and change it utterly.

For Casement was no more English than Conrad. He was Irish. His father had been a typical soldier of the Empire, a dragoon who had served in the first Afghan campaign, but his mother was a Dubliner, a Catholic, and he was born just outside the city. When his parents died early, he was brought up by relatives in Ulster, and never ceased to think of himself as fundamentally Irish. We have already seen how the events of 1912–14 split Ireland and forced tens of thousands of people to rethink their loyalties. Casement joined the Irish Volunteers, the pro-home rule movement set up to confront the Ulster Volunteers under Carson. His experiences in Africa and South America had made him a determined critic of imperialism. That was unusual. What was more unusual still was that he consciously began to connect the injustice of British rule over Ireland to the rule of the British in Africa, Egypt and India. The Irish, he believed, were 'the white slave race of Europe'. Casement went to America in 1914 to try to raise money for Irish revolt from the Fenians there, but once war was declared he decided that, if Ireland was to free herself, she could do it only with German help. His enemy's enemy was his friend. He sailed back to Europe and made his way to Berlin. There, in November 1914, he persuaded the Kaiser's men to declare that 'under no circumstances would Germany invade Ireland with a view to its conquest or the overthrow of any native institutions in that country. Should the fortune of this great war, that was not of Germany's seeking, ever bring in its course German troops to the shores of Ireland, they would land there not as an army of invaders to pillage and destroy but as the forces of a Government that is inspired by goodwill.'

This was important for Casement as he believed the Germans would inevitably win, and would therefore be able to dictate Ireland's future. In Dublin, the leaders of the Irish Republican Brotherhood had decided within days of the war starting that their best chance would be a rising at some point helped by Germany. They had infiltrated the Irish Volunteers and other bodies and were planning for a bloody revolt. At the very least this would force the British to draw troops away from France and hasten their defeat. They too were soon in touch with Berlin, via Switzerland. Meanwhile, in Germany, Casement tried to recruit captured men from Irish regiments – all of whom had volunteered to fight for Britain – into an 'Irish Brigade', modelled on the 300-strong force that fought with the Boers against Britain a dozen years earlier. His overtures were largely met with scorn, however. In Limberg prison camp, he was struck, pushed and asked how much the Germans were paying him. Out of many thousands, only a few hundred ever signed up to wear the iron-grey tunic with a harp and shamrock badge. Nor were the Germans much impressed with his strong anti-colonialist views as he pressed on, insisting on meeting the German chancellor, Bethmann-Hollweg, and on getting promises for around 100,000 rifles, German officers and men, plus ammunition, for the planned uprising. The question was, when? In Berlin, Casement had little knowledge of the tiny conspiracy being hatched by the IRB, who had agreed to proclaim their republic at Easter 1916.

The IRB, lately allied to the socialist leader James Connolly, had begun to bring round large sections of the more moderate Irish Volunteers to join the uprising – a plan Casement learned about quite late. Though Germany had eagerly watched the pre-war Irish crisis, its military leadership did not believe the chances of success were high. In a series of increasingly desperate letters from the Hotel Saxonia in Berlin, Casement wrote to his handler, Count Georg von Wedel, insisting that without troops and serious amounts of fire-power, any uprising was doomed. He soon realized he was trapped. Germany would offer 20,000 rifles and enough ammunition for only a day or two of heavy fighting. If Casement agreed, he would be returning to Ireland to take part in a disaster. If he pulled back, he would seem a coward. He wrote to the count, 'I do not think anyone was ever put in a more atrocious position. Whatever I do must of necessity be wrong ... My instinct as an Irish nationalist is to be with my countrymen in any project of theirs, however foolhardy, to stand or fall with them.' So he was put into a U-boat with a couple of companions, while 20,000 rifles and a few machine guns were sent separately on a German freighter, disguised as a Norwegian ship. Thanks to the Admiralty's code-breakers, this was intercepted and scuttled. Later, through messages from Germany sent via the Vatican, and the testament of a priest who sheltered him, it became pretty clear that Casement had gone to try to stop the rising, not to lead it. Having landed by rubber dinghy in Tralee Bay, delighting in the 'primroses and wild violets and the singing of the skylarks in the air', he was promptly captured. He still had the ticket stub from his German train journey to the U-boat base in his pocket, and was charged with treason and sabotage before being taken to London.

The priest who had briefly sheltered him, Father Ryan of Tralee, duly warned the leaders of the planned rising that the Germans were not sending troops. They were determined to go ahead. Some, at least, saw things differently from Casement. These were brave men, but also visionaries and fanatics. It is a curious thing that so many of them had English or Scottish connections. James Connolly, the great mustachioed socialist, was born to Irish parents in Edinburgh, where he began work for the city's evening newspaper before joining the British army. He had returned to Scotland before settling in Dublin in his late twenties. Tom Clarke, one of the guiding figures in the IRB, was the son of a British army sergeant. He had been imprisoned for trying to blow up London Bridge, and later earned his living as a Dublin tobacconist. Eamon de Valera, the later president, was born in the United States to an Irish mother and a Cuban father. He was brought to Ireland and educated there from the age of two, becoming a teacher and a passionate supporter of the Celtic revival. Joseph Plunkett, who travelled to Germany seeking arms and who devised the military plan for the rising, was Irish born and educated, but he got his first military training at Stonyhurst College in Lancashire, in the OTC. Padraig Pearse, who read out the declaration, had an English father, a Birmingham stonemason in his case, and had also come to nationalism through the Irish language and culture, founding a bilingual school. His nationalism was unhealthily martyr-fixated: after the war began, he hailed the patriotic bloodletting: 'It is good for the world that such things should be done. The old heart of the earth needed to be warmed with the red wine of the battlefields. Such august homage was never before offered to God as this.'

This was the language of blood-sacrifice, not so different from some of the more gruesome poetry being written by young English patriots destined for France. The IRB men knew even as they gathered their bullet-fodder that they had little chance of success. A real uprising would have required artillery, plenty of machine guns and German soldiers – 25,000 of them, in Casement's reckoning. Worse, since the rebels would need plenty of men of their own, the official leaders of the Irish Volunteers, unaware of the IRB's infiltration of their organization, disapproved of the revolt. In a confusion of contradictory orders, only some 1,600 men actually took part and most of the fighting would be confined to central Dublin. The mixture of IRB intellectuals, well-drilled but under-equipped Volunteers and the couple of hundred working-class Dubliners of Connolly's Citizens' Army, formed in 1913 to defend trade unionists after the great lock-out, had little prospect of holding their target buildings, the General Post Office, the law courts, a biscuit factory and others, once the British army arrived in force. A serious uprising, meant to strike at the heart of the Empire, was hurriedly redefined as a glorious gesture. Perhaps, by proclaiming the Republic and by giving their lives, the rebels would so transform the politics of Ireland that after the war, independence from Britain would become inevitable.

This, in turn, was implausible if the British behaved logically. Forewarned by the broken German codes of what was intended to happen over Easter, one might have thought that the authorities would have been waiting to strangle the rebellion before it started. Not a bit of it. Astonishingly, despite the evidence of the Volunteers training, and the intercepted codes, and the arrest of Casement, the rebels were able to seize their targets, which were undefended. There were only about 1,200 British soldiers in the area, none of them in central Dublin. Again, one might have thought the British army, with its bitter experience from France, would be able to counter-attack effectively. Again, they did not. Soldiers ran at well-protected sandbag emplacements and, as if it were Flanders, were promptly mown down: in one engagement, just twelve Irish Volunteers killed or wounded scores of soldiers. The British artillery was so inaccurate that British forces returned fire on their own guns, assuming they must be rebel ones. Connolly, wounded but commanding from his bed, which was carried from place to place, provided inspirational leadership once Pearse had proclaimed the Republic. But as soon as major reinforcements arrived, and the British artillery had the range of the rebels' headquarters at the GPO, the end could not be long delayed. On 29 April 1916, five days after the rising had begun, Pearse gave the order to surrender. On the British side, 132 soldiers and policemen had been killed. On the Irish Republican side, 64 fighters had died, as well as nearly 250 civilians.

Even at this stage it had been a small-scale rebellion, relatively quickly contained. It did not look like the lit fuse for Irish independence its leaders had hoped it would be. By comparison with the 1,600 rebels, around 150,000 Irishmen had volunteered to fight for the Empire in Flanders by 1916, and Irish opinion, certainly as reflected in the newspapers and in the booing of crowds, was hostile to the Republicans. Having looked at some of the leading Republicans, it is worth remembering others who took the opposite course. Take the case of William Orpen, one of the most talented painters in Britain. With a long lower lip and a tendency to strike poses he looks in his self-portraits rather like the later comic actor Kenneth Williams. By 1914 he was already a hugely fashionable portraitist, who would go on to paint Churchill, Field Marshal Haig, the French commander Foch and a swathe of rich aristocratic society. But he was also an Irishman, who had started at Dublin Art School aged twelve. He painted and supported the Irish home-rule leaders, and had seen nationalists running guns into Howth in 1913. He supported the strike of Dublin transport workers under Larkin too, and among those who had sat for him was a beautiful Irish painter he had met at the Slade called Grace Gifford, whom he painted as 'young Ireland'. She would later marry one of the leaders of the rising on the night before he was executed, and serve time in prison herself. So Orpen, like many more, faced a personal conflict when war came. Sean Keating, another Irish painter who later became well known in the Republic, begged Orpen to leave London and return to Ireland. Keating told him: ' "Leave all this. You don't believe in it." But he said: "Please. Everything I have I owe to England . . . It was the English who gave me appreciation and money. This is their war and I have enlisted. I won't fight but I'll do what I can." ' And so it all followed, said Keating sadly, 'the horrors of trench war, block headed generals, political crooks and rich Americans and finally [for Orpen] two bottles of whisky a day, amnesia and death at 52'.[16]

What this leaves out is that Orpen became the finest war artist on the Allied side, whose superbly painted images of trench warfare, done rather traditionally, are much more unsettling than the more famous paintings by the modernists and cubists of shells going off. In Orpen's pictures you see the yellowed corpses of dead German soldiers, a raped woman going mad, a soldier standing stark naked having had his uniform blown off by a shell-blast. You see injuries and horror in the sunlight. By the time the war ended, Orpen was bitter about the politicians, whom he derisively called 'the frocks'. Yet he was commissioned to paint the huge official recording of the victorious leaders signing the Versailles treaty afterwards. It is a monumental picture, but the war leaders look strangely small in the great Hall of Mirrors, and this is no mistake of perspective by the artist. As he said, there was no dignity there: 'People talked and cracked jokes to each other . . . the "frocks" had won the war. The "frocks" had signed the peace! The army was forgotten. Some dead

and forgotten, others maimed and forgotten, others alive and well –
but already forgotten.'[17] Orpen was only one of the great artists
who told the truth about the war. (His friend William Nicholson
made an almost equally savage official portrait of the Canadian
general staff posing in front of a huge blown-up photograph of a
shattered townscape. Sargent himself painted *Gassed*, showing a
column of blind men tottering through the devastation. Stanley
Spencer's images of army hospitals are among his finest work.) But
had Orpen not decided his duty lay with Britain and the war, then
our understanding of it would have been less. We owe him much.
And in making his choice, he was far from alone. The 'Irish airman'
whose death was memorialized in a famous poem by Yeats, was
another Slade art student, like Orpen. Where the fighting was
actually happening, old Irish enmities simply seem to have collapsed.
Ulster Volunteers and Catholic nationalists, not to mention the
Curragh 'mutineers', would end up fighting and dying alongside each
other.

All this would be squandered by British stupidity. Having ignored
their own original intelligence, then failed to stop the rising quickly,
the authorities now went on to make their worst mistake of all. Sinn
Fein had not been involved in the rising. Yet all 'dangerous Sinn
Feiners' were rounded up by the army and police – more than 3,500
men and women were arrested – and many of those who had taken
part in the rising were court-martialled for treason. Ninety were
sentenced to death, of whom fifteen were actually shot, all but one
in Dublin's brooding old Kilmainham gaol. Connolly was so badly
injured that he had to be tied to a chair to be executed. Plunkett was
married in jail to Orpen's muse. These and the others were shot
privately in the gaol's stonebreakers' yard, adding to the air of fear
and horror which was felt by English bishops and MPs as well as by
Fenians in America and the Vatican. The blood, in the words of one
bishop, seemed to be seeping out from below the prison door.
Another 1,500 men were interned in camps that became hot-houses
for Irish revolution. The killings turned Irish opinion round and
made martyrs of men who had been in danger of being regarded
as marginal and failures. Sinn Fein, having not been involved in the
rising, would transform itself into the core party for full-on independence and win a huge harvest of votes by the end of the war.

And Casement? His trial did not go as smoothly as the authorities had hoped. As a British subject he had certainly been a traitor, and admitted it. His faith in the Germans had gone, indeed he regarded them now as 'cads' who were bound to be defeated. The Treason Act would not normally apply to crimes committed in Germany but it was closely reinterpreted to catch Casement – people said later he had been 'hanged by a comma'. There was a major campaign for clemency, led by famous writers such as Sir Arthur Conan Doyle, Arnold Bennett, G. K. Chesterton and John Galsworthy. Bernard Shaw wrote privately. Yeats wrote to Asquith. The Archbishop of Canterbury, remembering the Congo campaign, saw the home secretary. What of Conrad? He was patriotically disgusted by Casement. The last time he'd seen the man, he told an American lawyer, was on the Strand, where 'he was more gaunt than ever and his eyes still more sunk in his head . . . He was a good companion; but already in Africa I judged that he was a man, properly speaking, of no mind at all. I don't mean stupid. I mean that he was all emotion.' Given the letters he had written to Casement this was unkind, and perhaps cowardly too. Meanwhile any hope of Casement escaping the noose was being snuffed out by photographed pages of handwriting and shocked whispers circulating through London clubs, Parliament and newspaper offices. In his Ebury Street rooms, rented before the war, the police had found Casement's diaries.

Casement had always been homosexual and haunted by the fate of others who had been discovered and disgraced, or who had killed themselves. He seems to have kept, alongside his public diaries, the 'black diaries' which listed and described his sexual exploits. These fell into the hands of the British secret service. The Home Office set to work. Asquith was sent them. The Archbishop was told about them. So was the American ambassador. Newspaper editors were briefed. Casement's supporters were quietly tipped the wink. There has been a long argument about whether these diaries were, in fact, forgeries, but recent research tends to suggest they were genuine. Casement probably never knew quite what was happening outside his prison cell, but it is grimly ironic that this man whose life was a torrent of explanation and advocacy was being finished off by his own handwriting. His appeal to the Lords would have had to have been approved by the attorney general – the same F. E. Smith who had done so much to support the illegal Orange revolt of earlier times. But it would not have saved him and he would duly go to the gallows, with the hangman commenting that he was 'the bravest man it fell to my unhappy lot to execute'.

Before he died, however, Casement had given a passionate speech from the dock, denying the right of an English court to try him and hoping for reconciliation between Ulstermen and the rest of Ireland. He then made a declaration about every people's right to self-rule, one that would echo:

> If we are to be indicted as criminals, to be shot as murderers, to be imprisoned as convicts because our offence is that we love Ireland more than we value our lives, then I know not what virtue resides in any offer of self-government held out to brave men on such terms. Self-government is our right, a thing born in us at birth; a thing no more to be doled out to us or withheld from us by another people than the right to life itself – than the right to feel the sun or smell the flowers or to love our kind . . . If there be no right of rebellion against a state of things that no savage tribe would endure without resistance, then I am sure that it is better for man to fight and die without right than to live in such a state of right as this.

Overwrought it may be, but the speech echoed and resonated for years afterwards, affecting other opponents of British imperialism. Wilfred Scawen Blunt found it 'finer than anything in Plutarch'. A young, sensitive trainee lawyer in London thought it 'extraordinarily eloquent and moving': he was Jawaharlal Nehru and he would, one day, lead an even larger part of the British Empire to independence.[18] Casement's body was buried in quicklime at Pentonville Prison and finally returned to Ireland in 1965, for a huge state funeral attended by the elderly de Valera. His cause, however, thanks to the British executions, was smoking and fizzing all the way to civil war.

The Wizard Circles towards Power

The rise of Lloyd George to become prime minister is one of the most unlikely tales in modern political history. He had been a radical, natural democrat, scourge of the rich, the foe of military imperialists during the Boer War and the man Ulster Unionists and their English Tory allies liked to hate the most. He would become a war leader whose speeches brimmed with fire and patriotic defiance, holding near-dictatorial powers and supported by the very people who had been among his sharpest enemies – Bonar Law, Unionist leader Carson, and Milner. By doing this, he would destroy the Liberal Party, which divided into Lloyd George-ites and Asquith-ites, and ensure that there was no effective left-of-centre party throughout the inter-war years – since Labour was still a feeble infant. Having been the individual most responsible for progressive politics in Britain before the war, he would become the man most responsible for the conservative politics of Britain after it. He is mercury and smoke, glitter and varnish. There are clues to the mystery. He was always an outsider, not part of the networks of power in Liberal England and as uninterested in the philosophical underpinnings of Liberal thought as Tony Blair was later bored by socialist ideology. He believed in himself, and in doing. He was increasingly drawn to self-made and 'go-ahead' business people, rather than party loyalists or other MPs. His power came from his actorly self-projection, his ability to connect with millions of voters in a mimicry of intimacy and above all in his formidable, astonishing zest for action. In Asquith the country had a philosophical parliamentarian as its leader, who famously believed in 'wait and see' – in peacetime a perfectly sensible tactic of allowing situations to disentangle themselves where possible. By 1916 what Britain needed was a leader far more on the front foot – someone with the energy of a dozen devils and the tongue of as many angry angels. Such men have faults. Lloyd George was, for instance, corrupt, libidinous and unscrupulous. But these men don't grow on trees.

For Lloyd George, the immediate effect of Asquith's coalition government was that he was handed the hardest job of anyone then in politics: he was put in charge of munitions. It sounds almost humdrum. But during Britain's first industrial war it meant revolutionary action throughout much of the realm of labour and capital. He would have to deal with the industrial disputes that were erupting across the country, as trade unionists fought the idea of bringing in less qualified or experienced workers to fill the gaps left by recruitment – 'dilution', as it was called. That would mean more training of new workers, new pay agreements and more labour-saving machines. He would have to speed up the particularly sensitive employment of women in factories. He would have to bring together the haphazard network of small industrial concerns into a single efficient production system for guns, shells, vehicles, aircraft, ships and engines. He would have to shake up the transport system. He would have to find ways to make munitions employees work harder and better. He would have to deal with their food and housing. And he would have to do all of this when things were at their bleakest, cheering, and inspiring, and leading in a way the nominal leader, Asquith, could not manage.

None of this was easy, and it did not go smoothly. When Lloyd George went to the Clyde, where socialists, including some genuine revolutionaries, were influential among shipyard workers, and where rent strikes against greedy private landlords had inflamed feelings, he had a very rough time. He ended up arresting and imprisoning leaders of the Clyde Workers Committee. But he learned and, under the influence of Seebohm Rowntree once more, began to extend the welfare help for munitions workers and their families further and further, until his new department became a far more ambitious social-reform machine than anything dreamed of in pre-war politics. It built more than 11,500 houses and flats and provided double the number of hostel places. It set up 900 canteens for factories, in which a million people could eat. The government's official history lists some of the things considered by his department's welfare section. They include providing cows to produce milk for explosives workers, deciding 'the relative merits of cocoa and milk as beverage for such workers; the energy value contained in suet puddings; the cost of hockey sticks and boxing gloves; the erection of swings; the purchase of flower seeds; the establishment of play centres for children . . . the requirements of a boys' holiday camp . . . the area of washing trough required per worker . . . the overcrowding of tramcars and the supply of ferry boats; the equipment, down to the last saucepan and floormat, of hostels' and much, much more. Lloyd George himself ruminated on the odd fact that the making of weapons of mass destruction had led to a humanizing of industry, and if one searches for the real origins of the modern welfare state they can be found most clearly in what he was up to in 1916.

He was in the job for only a little more than a year. But by the time he left, the manufacture of heavy guns, for instance, was up by 1,200 per cent and deliveries of them to the army were at ninety-four times the previous rate.[19] The number of medium shells which had taken a year to produce when he took charge was being turned out every eleven days by July 1916, and the rate for heavy shells was even faster. When told that Kitchener thought four machine guns for each British battalion would be enough, Lloyd George replied: 'Take Kitchener's maximum . . . square it, multiply the result by two; and when you are in sight of that double it again for good luck.' That was an exaggeration of what was actually achieved, but the army got all the machine guns it needed. New ways were found of filling shells; new trench mortars, which had been rejected by the War Office, were ordered (and proved highly effective). Though strikes continued throughout the war, new deals were struck with union and labour leaders. By the end of the war the ministry had 3 million workers under its direct control. This was a kind of Liberal Stalinism, except that profits continued to be made and it was rather more effective than its successor. By no means all the credit was Lloyd George's. He had hired and encouraged some excellent business people, and some of the improvement would have happened anyway. But this was Britain's first experience of a war economy. It was the polar opposite of the laissez-faire economic thinking the Liberals had once championed. It showed what could be done by energetic leaders prepared to break the old rules. And it made Lloyd George the hero not of Welsh nonconformists, or of the left, but of the fire-eating war party he increasingly seemed to be leading.

Asquith could have survived Lloyd George's frantic energy had the war been going better, but these were among the worst months for Britain. The Czar's armies were in terrible trouble. The Battle of Loos had been another scene of butchery for little gain, which led to Sir John French being replaced by Sir Douglas Haig in December 1915. Conscription finally arrived, though in a bungled form which led to much anger, since married men were called up before many single men. In February 1916 the German assault on the French fortress of Verdun began. It would continue for most of the year, a deliberate attempt to suck the French army into a battle which would 'bleed them white': it nearly succeeded. Carson resigned from the government in protest at its lackadaisical approach. Then came the Easter Rising in Dublin, an utter shock to London. The news continued to be terrible, not just from the Dardanelles but from the Balkans, where a British army landed at Salonika in Greece became trapped and useless because of the defeat of her allies Serbia and Romania. Then came the meat-grinder days of the Somme, a direct consequence of Verdun but very hard to sell as victory. As Asquith's power dwindled – other ministers remarked on his shaking hands, pendulous cheeks, watery eyes and twitching face – Lloyd George's stock was rising.

Was he plotting? Of course he was plotting. He could no sooner stop than a hare can restrain itself from leaping. He had become something of a favourite of Harmsworth, which helped, but more generally the papers were boosting him – and in ways which got under Asquith's apparently impermeable skin. In a letter to Venetia he wrote about a gloomy walk back to Downing Street: 'I sometimes think that Northcliffe and his obscene crew may perhaps be right – that, whatever the rest of the world may say, I am, if not an imposter, at any rate a failure, & *au fond* a fool. What is the real test?' Meanwhile Lloyd George was convinced things could not go on this way. He would need the full support of the opposition Unionists if a more efficient coalition regime was to take over, and he was forming a steadily stronger relationship – though they had been golf partners for some time – with Bonar Law. After Kitchener's drowning, something Northcliffe described as the greatest luck the British Empire had had in its history, the Unionist leader and Lloyd George debated which of them should become War Minister. Bonar Law, characteristically, gave way, so when Asquith was confronted by their done deal he duly offered it to Lloyd George. He in turn had been on the edge of resigning but took the new promotion, though it gave him little real power.

The final confrontation which finished off Asquith in the winter of 1916 was on the central issue of how modern politicians should fight a modern war. His War Council was too big and unwieldy. He himself persisted in his old ways: the long country-house weekends, the lengthy letters to women friends, the unabashed enjoyment of cards and gossip. He was still a formidably clever man and in many ways a far more attractive one than Lloyd George – certainly deeper and richer in his understanding of life. Yet he was out of time. Lloyd George wanted the whole conduct of the fighting put in the hands of a tiny team, to give the kind of focus and direction British politics had never before thrust at a war, or indeed anything else. Bonar Law agreed. Asquith did not. He was badly hit by the death of his eldest son Raymond in yet another murderous attack in September 1916. (It is sometimes suggested that those running the war were removed from the reality it brought to tens of thousands of homes by letter or telegram, but Asquith was ordinary in the loss of a son. Bonar Law lost both his eldest and second sons, Jim and Charlie. His friend Kipling famously lost his boy Jack. Lloyd George had been nervous about his children fighting but was so horrified by visiting the brain-damaged son of a friend in France, shot through the head and dying in agony, that he came close to a nervous breakdown. The Northcliffe family lost several boys. Aristocrats, tycoons and politicians who tried to keep their sons out of the fighting were shunned.)

It was the press baron who first plunged in the knife. He told his *Daily Mail* editor: 'Get a smiling picture of Lloyd George and underneath it put the caption "Do it now" and get the worst possible picture of Asquith and label it "Wait and see".' He then ordered that from now on, the word government must only be used with inverted commas round it and penned an editorial chastising 'government' by 'some 23 men who can never make up their minds'. To crown it all he wrote a headline, reading simply 'Asquith – A Limpet'. Politicians today who complain about being roughed up by the press should try a little history. The Tory leader Bonar Law realized, after a rather obscure parliamentary revolt, that his own MPs were growing restive about his leadership, and would not put up with the Asquith style much longer. Bonar Law, with the future press baron Sir Max Aitken acting as go-between, was now ready to join hands with Lloyd George. It would be clear that not only a bruised and bitter Asquith, but also most of the old clique of Edwardian Liberals who had served with him, would have to go. In their place would come a government of a few Lloyd George-supporting Liberals, the odd Labour man and, in the majority, the Unionists and Tories who had been out of real power since 1906. With no election, this was a wartime parliamentary coup. Beatrice Webb wrote in her diary that Britain was getting 'a brilliant improvisation – reactionary in composition and undemocratic in form', the first dictatorship since Oliver Cromwell, created by 'a powerful combination of newspaper proprietors'. Lloyd George himself seemed unbothered by the dictatorship assertion – which of course did not then have its darkest meaning – asking what a government was for, if not to dictate? From both radical right and radical Liberal, it was a coalition of the raw and edgy, all the impatient men together. Against them were the embittered Liberal majority and the Irish nationalists, plus a few pacifists. This was a national government, though nothing like as broad as Churchill's would be in 1940.

Speaking of whom – what had happened to Churchill, the one impatient man still outside in the cold? He had been to the front, serving briefly with the Foot Guards, during which time he escaped death only by chance, being called back to see a general at the very time his dugout was destroyed by a shell. He then commanded a battalion of the Royal Scots Fusiliers, serving in the trenches for only five weeks in early 1917 before returning to politicking in London when his battalion was amalgamated. During his time in France he became friendly with Max Aitken, Bonar Law's friend, the Canadian tycoon and go-between. It would be a highly significant and lifelong relationship. Churchill did not take part in any battles and, of another man, one might wonder whether his return to the capital was cowardly. Churchill, however, was always physically brave. In this case he was bored and deeply frustrated. He was sure he should be helping command not some soldiers but the British Empire. By the time his friend Lloyd George was in the final stages of manoeuvring to replace Asquith, Churchill had good reason to hope that his time had come again. But it had not, not yet. Churchill heard the bad news after spending time steaming with his Tory friend F. E. Smith in the Turkish baths at the RAC Club in Pall Mall, during which he was invited to dinner with Smith, Aitken and Lloyd George. After Lloyd George had left, Aitken, who knew Churchill would not be asked back into the cabinet because of the hostility of the Tories, hinted as much, telling him: 'The new Government will be very well disposed towards you. All your friends will be there.' Churchill instantly realized what was happening and flew into a terrible temper. 'Smith,' he told his friend, 'this man knows that I am not to be included in the new Government.' Then he stormed out into the street carrying his hat and coat and shrugging off Smith's attempts to calm him down.

Lloyd George would have liked to include Churchill, and would bring him back later. But in early 1917, with Britain facing defeat in the war, the Germans still in the stronger position in France, Russia collapsing and the Balkan allies fallen, he had more important things on his mind. It has been plausibly argued that Britain was closer to national defeat when Lloyd George took over than she was in 1940. To cope, he resolved to radically reshape British government. His biographer John Grigg described his solution as being nearer to the Committee of Public Safety in the French Revolution than to a conventional British cabinet. In charge of the fighting would be a War Cabinet of just five men – Lloyd George, the Tory leader Bonar Law, the Labour leader Arthur Henderson, and two right-wing Tory imperialist peers: the grand Lord Curzon and South Africa's former ruler, the part-German Lord Milner. Bonar Law would be leader of the Commons, but for the rest of the war Lloyd George did his best to ignore ordinary parliamentary business entirely. He made rousing speeches – before broadcasting, speeches which were then reported by newspapers were really the only way a war leader could reach the population. He occupied himself increasingly with high-level diplomacy, what a later age would call summits. Not all were happy or successful, as when he conspired to downgrade Haig, whom he distrusted, by making the unsuccessful Frenchman General Nivelle supreme commander. But the whirlwind which had been promised duly appeared.

So we have had this new regime compared to Cromwell's and to Robespierre. What was the truth? It was a wartime expedient, scooping up the most vigorous people, pushing Parliament mostly aside and using an improvised national leadership which brought in experts and military leaders when necessary. The War Cabinet was not only small and free to concentrate on what mattered, it was also hyperactive, meeting at least once a day. More mistakes would be made. Decisions would be made – about Palestine and Iraq as well as the shape of Europe – which would resound into the twenty-first century. And when the war was over, with the czarist regime toppled by revolution and the Kaiser in exile as Germany seethed, it would not seem such a wild innovation. In due course, in the conditions of peacetime, MPs would rouse themselves and shrug off both Lloyd George and his Whitehall revolution. But for now, at last, Britain had her first modern leadership for her first modern war. The Edwardian Age finally ended, not with the death of King Edward VII or even with the declaration of war in 1914, but with the formation of the Lloyd George dictatorship.

The War at Sea: Titans and Logic

The First World War at sea has made too small a splash. It is mostly reduced to a couple of items. After the great story of the Dread-nought race before the war comes the Battle of Jutland, described boringly as a draw, and then the final Wagnerian act by the Imperial German Navy, which scuttles itself at Scapa Flow. Our tales of great sea-fights between the Royal Navy and the Germans all come from the Second World War – the desperate struggle against the U-boats, the Arctic convoys and the chasing, then sinking of the *Bismarck*. Had it perhaps been pointless, that massive Edwardian effort to build ever greater oil-fuelled steel-plated armadas? The answer is no. Had the Royal Navy not bottled up the German fleet, or had it been defeated in a confrontation at sea, then Britain would not have been able to feed and fuel herself through the war, and would soon have been unable to sustain her armies in France. Lloyd George and Churchill had looked for swifter, less bloody ways of beating Germany by attacking from the Balkans or knocking over Turkey. Similarly, the German high command hoped that by seizing control of the seas they could starve Britain out very quickly. That was part of the point of the Kaiser's pre-war naval expansion. It nearly worked. The greatest danger to Britain from U-boats came in 1917, not in the next war, while Jutland was a far greater, more tragic and important event than the pursuit of a single battleship, however glamorous.

In the early stages of the war, the Royal Navy had not been the great success the average Briton had expected. Ships were lost in small engagements, German cruisers slipped through its fingers, and great British ships were lost to mines and torpedoes. Yet a British blockade of Germany became steadily more effective and the German response, using U-boats to sink merchant shipping, was a big factor in bringing the United States into the war. The senior British admiral, John Jellicoe, was well described as being the only man who could lose the war in an afternoon. If the Germans lost their fleet, it would be a national disaster but they would be able to continue fighting on land almost as before. If Jellicoe lost his, Britain would have to sue for peace. Knowing this, he and his great ships spent much of the war at Scapa Flow, in the Orkney Islands, with other concentrations in the Firth of Forth and the Cromarty Firth, waiting. It was frustrating, despite the many opportunities for golf and fishing, particularly as the grim news from the trenches came in. The German admirals did little more, being in a weaker position, until the arrival in February 1916 of the brilliant, aggressive Admiral Scheer, a cool, cheerful and popular leader who was determined to draw the British into battle on his terms. That meant ruthless U-boat warfare and sending German ships on raiding missions designed to lure out the fleets of Jellicoe and his junior rival, Admiral David Beatty. At the end of May 1916, Scheer's strategy finally worked.

Though it is called the Battle of Jutland, it happened right in the middle of the North Sea, about 100 miles south of Norway, and a little more than that from the Danish (Jutland) coast. Scheer had sent his second-in-command, Admiral Hipper, with forty ships to lure out the British; he followed behind with the main German High Seas Fleet to close the trap. Jellicoe and Beatty had some advance warning. Thanks to a German ship running aground and being taken by Russians, and another being boarded off Australia, the British had access to their enemy's most secret naval codes, which were collected and interpreted by a secret team of boffins in the Admiralty's Room 40. Luckily for Scheer and Hipper, the Royal Navy was too contemptuous of the civilian code-breakers and too suspicious of the messages to use their advantage well, but it did allow the British fleets to head out to meet the Germans, knowing that this was indeed the long-awaited breakout. The fleets on both sides were enormous, with the Dreadnought battleships at their core and huge flanks of smaller vessels. This would be a Somme on the high seas. As one naval historian has written: 'Now, on both sides, the orders were given. Fifty-eight moving castles of grey steel – thirty-seven under one flag, twenty-one under another, the dreadnoughts of the two greatest navies in the world – were about to collide.'[20]

The full story of the battle is too complicated to be told here. In essence, the smaller British fleet, led by Beatty with his battle-cruisers, met Hipper coming north, and in a furious engagement came off worse, with two of Britain's finest ships blown to pieces. The German gunnery was better and the German ships were better protected, and could absorb more punishment: as Beatty put it in the middle of the fight, 'There seems to be something wrong with our bloody ships today.' At this stage, the Germans did not know that Jellicoe, with his far larger force, was heading towards them, and as he sailed back north, much bloodied, Beatty was able to lead not only Hipper but also Scheer, with his main force, straight towards Jellicoe. The full force of the Royal Navy's Dreadnoughts inflicted such damage on the German navy that they could stand it for only a few minutes. Then Scheer performed a brilliant parade-ground manoeuvre and turned his ships away at such speed the British admirals did not know what was happening. Oddly, Scheer then turned and attacked again, taking further appalling punishment. As he finally decided to flee, he loosed his destroyers with their torpedoes at the British battleships. Jellicoe responded by turning his battleships round so they presented their sterns to the torpedoes, and managed not to lose a single ship. The price was that he had let the badly mauled Germans get away, and he never found them again, since they sliced through a weaker British force by night and made it back to harbour. Jellicoe was endlessly attacked for this un-Nelson-like behaviour – the navy's tradition was to attack, attack, attack – but he had always argued that since Britain had command of the seas, he could not risk his main force. By the time the British Grand Fleet returned to Scotland, the centre of the North Sea was covered with oil, corpses, wreckage and acres of dead fish, killed by the explosions.

Both navies had performed astonishing acts of heroism. Some of the most damaged German cruisers had engaged in a semi-suicidal death charge against the British battleships to help the rest of their fleet escape. Later, tiny British destroyers behaved equally recklessly in attacking German Dreadnoughts, even ramming them – something akin to a soldier trying to knock over a tank. There were bad tactical mistakes on both sides, not helped by great confusion about what was actually happening. The British had seaplanes as spotters, and the Germans their Zeppelins, but the weather allowed neither to operate. Just as on land, the commanders had only a vague notion for much of the time about what was happening in the thick of fighting. By the standards of a day in Flanders, the numbers killed or wounded were small – 6,768 on the British side, and a little over 3,000 on the German. The Royal Navy lost six cruisers of different types, and eight destroyers, fourteen ships sunk to the loss of eleven German ships. Like the Somme or Ypres, there was no breakthrough, rather the appearance of deadlock – but here too, the battle affected the course of the wider war.

In Germany, when Scheer's fleet returned home, it was treated as a great national victory, with flags, a national holiday and German newspapers trumpeting the 'annihilation' of the British. In Britain, partly because of confusion and censorship, the German verdict was initially accepted and there was deep gloom. Flags were lowered to half mast. Theatres had their lights turned out. The two British admirals, Jellicoe and Beatty, began a long war by proxy about which was more to blame. At Jutland, both Jellicoe and Beatty had made major mistakes, though Jellicoe was treated worse and felt it more – Beatty was a far more astute and apparently dashing manipulator of the media. Yet the Germans had made as many mistakes and, in the end, theirs was the fleet unable to sail again, while the Royal Navy was prepared and waiting for the next confrontation within four days of returning. Jutland was not pointless. Had Britain won, she would have been able to dominate the Baltic as well as the North Sea, supporting Russia, and perhaps the outcome of the 1917 revolution would have been different. Had Germany won the battle, she would probably have won the war.

Her next move at sea very nearly did win her the war. From the start, naval strategists on both sides knew that mines, torpedoes and submarines were changing war at sea – making it far harder, for instance, for surface ships to sail up and down blockading ports. Fisher had been an early advocate of submarines, though there was much naval hostility to such an 'under-handed' way of fighting and one admiral proposed that any submarine crews caught should be hanged as pirates. Germany, meanwhile, had been slow to develop submarines and in the early stages of the war was sceptical about these unhealthy little craft. But when in September 1914 a single small submarine, *U-9*, sank three British cruisers, killing 1,400 men, there was national jubilation and the reputation of the U-boat was made. The strategy of starving Britain, not only of food but of fuel and raw materials, was a reasonable one for the Germans – and the British blockade was simultaneously trying to do the same to them. But to be effective they must sink not only British ships but any ships sailing into British ports, including famously the liner *Lusitania.*

This was one of the great Cunarders, fast enough to have won a Blue Riband for her pre-war darts across the Atlantic, and in May 1915 she was carrying 1,262 passengers from the United States, mostly British but also many Americans. What was not advertised was that in her hold she was also carrying shells, rifle cartridges and high explosives for the war. Caught by *U-20* ten miles off the south coast of Ireland, she was torpedoed and sank so fast the lifeboats were mostly useless. Just over 1,200 people died, including ninety-four children, a third of them babies. Also among the dead were 128 American citizens. Photographs of the drowned children helped cause a wave of anger and revulsion, though in Germany the sinking was hailed as a triumph. A fierce propaganda fight about the rights and wrongs of the sinking began. American opinion was outraged and President Woodrow Wilson expressed deep anger, enough to per-suade the Kaiser to change the rules for U-boats, in turn angering the German admirals. A medal struck by an obscure German in Munich commemorating the sinking was copied by an American in London, Gordon Selfridge – the owner of the famous Oxford Street shop. He produced 300,000 of them as a memento of German barbarism. To keep the United States out of the war, the Germans moderated their attacks through the rest of 1915. The following year, determined to try to strangle the British supply route for most of their food, the U-boat campaign was stepped up again. Almost inevitably more Americans were drowned. Wilson became more threatening still and again the Kaiser ordered the U-boats to attack cargo ships only in special circumstances. Scheer, newly appointed to command the High Seas Fleet, was so angry he ordered all U-boats back to base.

Through 1916 relations between the Germans and the Americans improved. Wilson won re-election to the White House on his success in keeping the United States out of the war. There were continued arguments about the high seas, but the U-boats were restricted in their work. It was over the winter of 1916–17 that things changed. Germany was by now hard pressed, shorter in manpower than her enemies and with hunger biting hard into the civilian population. The country was short of coal, oil and meat. The potato harvest had failed, meaning that even that staple had to be rationed. Starvation beckoned; the Austrians were warning that hunger and revolution were marching together. It was obvious that not only was the British blockade working, but also that Germany's enemies were winning because their war-making supplies of food, oil, cotton, iron, wood, horses and ammunition were coming across the Atlantic from America. 'Unleash the U-boats' became the cry. The problem, of course, was that doing so with sufficient ferocity to drive Britain out of the war would almost certainly mean dragging America into the war. The gamble depended upon either the United States somehow being deflected or persuaded not to declare war or, more likely, on the submarine campaign being so successful that by the time US armies had been assembled the British would be beaten and the Atlantic controlled by Germany. Rolling such dice may seem wild, but by then Germany was running out of options. The two warlords, the old Junker-general Hindenburg and his second-in-command Ludendorff, who would later help Hitler towards power, were rising in influence. The Kaiser's oldest adviser, his chancellor Bethmann-Hollweg, who was more cautious, was losing ground.

In December 1916 the head of the navy, Admiral Henning von Holtzendorff, told Hindenburg and the other warlords that it was only because of 'the energy and force of England' that France and Italy were still fighting: 'If we can break England's back, the war will be immediately decided in our favour.'[21] The backbone was her shipping: 10.75 million tons of shipping, much of it neutral, was needed to keep Britain in business. Holtzendorff reckoned the U-boats could sink 600,000 tons of ships a month and put off another million tons. A properly unrestricted campaign could put Britain out of the war in five months – that is, by the summer of 1917. To do that would mean sinking without warning any ship trying to get to or from Britain, American ones included. The decision to go ahead was taken in a remote Silesian castle, despite Bethmann-Hollweg's entreaties, and on 31 January 1917 Germany announced that unrestricted attacks by her U-boats would begin the following day. These were now formidable craft, some 140 of them, with sixteen torpedoes apiece, able to stay at sea for up to six weeks and to travel under water for eighty miles at a time. Soon liners and cargo ships were exploding and sinking in large numbers, killing Americans, as well as British, Scandinavians, Dutch and others. Even then, America might have stayed out, confining herself to outraged protests. The Germans, however, did something spectacularly stupid. They intrigued to draw Mexico into a war with the US, promising her Texas, New Mexico and Arizona. The 'Zimmermann telegram' – named after the foreign minister who sent it – was sent via Washington, decoded in the Admiralty's Room 40 and passed to President Wilson, who promptly declared war. Now it was a race to the finish: could the U-boats defeat Britain before American intervention changed everything?

It was a very close-run thing. Within weeks the Germans' target for sinkings was being approached and by April it had been easily beaten – not 600,000 tons of shipping sent to the bottom but 860,000 tons. It was a true slaughter of merchant shipping and, before long, Britain was running out of fuel oil, sugar and many foods. A series of desperate remedies was tried. At sea there had been some success with 'Q-ships', which had been disguised to look like unarmed merchantmen but which carried guns to ambush the U-boats when they came to the surface. This involved a lethal pantomime in which Royal Navy sailors and officers pretended to be panicking Dutch or Norwegian sailors, with some abandoning ship while others stayed hidden behind, often having to endure shelling from a U-boat to maintain the illusion, until the trap was sprung. But although a dozen U-boats were destroyed in this way, the ruse depended on their captains deciding to save torpedoes and blow up the merchantmen after surfacing, and by the summer of 1917 the U-boat captains had learned their lesson and were sticking to surprise and torpedoes.

Another answer was simply to hunt round the world for extra ships – all sorts of ancient rust-buckets and unlikely vessels were bought and sent across the Atlantic to brave the U-boats. Another was to build more ships in Britain, and that happened. A new Shipping Ministry took control of all British merchant ships, another blow to laissez-faire. New weapons, including better underwater listening devices and depth charges, were developed. Destroyers were taken from the main fleets and used to patrol the most dangerous approaches. Yet none of this was enough to stem the rate of losses. By the early summer of 1917, as the short nights gave the U-boats even more opportunity for carnage, it looked as if Britain would have to sue for peace.

What saved Britain was a simple case of lateral thinking. Admiralty strategy had long been clear: convoys did not work. The merchant ships were too slow and ill captained to hold together in convoy and could not make the necessary joint manoeuvres. Most obvious of all, the convoy, being big, made too easy a target for a U-boat. As the Admiralty itself said in January 1917: 'It is evident that the larger the number of ships forming the convoy, the greater is the chance of the submarine being enabled to attack successfully.'[22] Finally, there were too few destroyers to protect every convoy every mile of the way. Yet there was something odd about this thinking. The navy itself used convoys very successfully. It used them to transport men across the Channel, losing very few ships to U-boats, and it used them when its own fleets of Dreadnoughts set out, surrounded by a protective ring of destroyers. Inside government, the argument for trying convoys began to grow, with Lloyd George and Hankey pitted against the traditionalists. And almost as soon as the convoy system was used, the U-boats' toll started to fall. For the final piece of the intellectual jigsaw was now clear. Convoys might be larger than individual ships, but in the context of the vast space of the ocean, this was really irrelevant. A U-boat looking for prey was almost as likely to miss a convoy as to miss a ship. But with huge numbers of scattered ships, it was likely to come across one of them. If it missed the convoy, it missed scores. And even if it came upon the convoy, there would be little time to fire more than one or two torpedoes, which in any case became more dangerous because of the destroyers. The answer was simple and effective. The U-boat threat never went away, but never again was it so lethal. American destroyers now joined British ones and Germany's last best chance of victory disappeared. There would be titanic battles in France to come, including a final German break-out towards Paris; but once the Atlantic lifeline was secure, and once the Americans were in the war, there could be only one outcome. Yet at home, this was little understood.

The Women's War

The attempted strangling of Britain had made one thing plain: women could not be excluded from a modern economy or state. When the war started, the suffragettes were still in full revolt. More than a thousand had been imprisoned and the leaders of the WSPU were mostly either in jail or on the run. Both Emmeline and Christabel Pankhurst were taking refuge in France when war was declared. There is a common belief that votes for women were finally won only because of the Land Army girls and the female munitions workers; but this is wrong. Behind the impression of 'mayhem as usual', the suffrage case had been winning ground in 1913–14. Labour was likely to insist on all its candidates supporting women's suffrage at the next election. The Unionists had been talking to the less aggressive suffragists about some kind of electoral promise too; and now even Asquith was beginning to drop hints that he was coming round. As for Lloyd George, he was talking privately to Sylvia Pankhurst, the sister who had left the WSPU and was now leading the socialist wing of the movement. The vote would have been won without the war. Indeed, probably, the war delayed the breakthrough. It also split the Pankhurst family irretrievably and broke the WSPU. But it meant that when women finally won the vote in 1918 there was almost no opposition left standing; by then even Northcliffe and the *Daily Mail* had become enthusiastic if unlikely suffragists.

That is partly due to Emmeline and Christabel, who turned themselves round in remarkably short order from being feminist rebels to patriotic cheerleaders of spectacular stridency. As soon as the government announced a general amnesty for suffragette prisoners and those on the run, they were petitioning hard to do their bit for the war. Emmeline addressed a meeting in London on the German Peril. When the retired Admiral Charles Penrose Fitzgerald organized in Folkestone 'the Order of the White Feather', calling on women to present these traditional symbols of unmanliness or cowardice to men in civilian clothes thought to be 'idling' or 'slacking', WSPU members took this up too. Their newspaper the *Suffragette* ceased publication briefly, returning with articles fiercely attacking some ministers for being allegedly pro-German, and foaming with aggression. When it was replaced in 1915 with the *Britannia*, the new paper carried the masthead slogan 'For King, For Country, For Freedom' and made a point of viciously attacking left-wing pacifists like Ramsay MacDonald who had staunchly supported the suffrage cause. With government money they organized a march of 30,000 women, insisting on their right to do war work, and later they toured the country haranguing meetings of workers, attacking strikers as pro-German or Bolshevik and helping the Kitchener recruitment campaign.

Sylvia would have nothing to do with any of this, supporting a negotiated settlement and doing practical work with working-class families in east London – which did not stop her being booed and showered with rotten vegetables when she spoke in public. Later, in 1917, Emmeline travelled on a government mission to Russia to try to rally support for the war there (Ramsay MacDonald was supposed to go as a balancing voice but the ship's captain refused to take him). She arrived just as the Bolsheviks were about to oust the Provisional Government and did little good, or harm. Sylvia, by then, was ardently supporting the Bolsheviks. The movement, like the family, was splintered beyond repair. The strident nature of their propagandizing, combined with Christabel's simultaneous ranting about venereal disease, made many soldiers view them as anti-male. In the war poets you can find strands of misogyny which are in part a reaction to all those self-certain women handing out white feathers (including, often, to wounded or serving men back on leave) and lecturing them about syphilis. Meanwhile many members of the WSPU became convinced that Emmeline and Christabel were snaffling the moribund organization's funds for their trips to America and France. At meetings they were heckled and many walked out.

Though the Women's Land Army got the most coverage, relatively few women went to work full time in agriculture. Farmers preferred to pay less to child workers. But they swarmed into munitions factories, into transport jobs, into offices and into general industrial jobs vacated by men. The total number of extra women in employment in industry during 1914–18 rose by around 800,000 to just under 3 million; some 400,000 more women found jobs in offices; another 200,000 women's jobs were created in government and banks employed a further 50,000 or so.[23] From Glasgow trams to Liverpool shell factories, the London Underground to women police officers patrolling urban parks, Britain suddenly started to look a little different. Skirts became a little shorter. Some women in factories or on farms took to wearing trousers. Cigarettes became popular with women as well as men. Moral attitudes shifted: when it became clear that the exodus of men to the front had left thousands of unmarried mothers pregnant, their children were declared patriotic 'war babies' and money raised to support them. Other forms of support made breakthroughs too: the bra began to oust the old-fashioned camisole. One diplomatist said later that when he had left England in 1911 'contraceptives were hard to buy outside London or other large cities. By 1919 every village chemist was selling them.'[24] One way and another, the Edwardian woman had gone.

The suffrage victory came about, however, by Westminster accident, the kind of random clink of billiard balls that often happens there. The men's franchise included an occupational qualification. But with the upheaval caused by the war, not only for the fighting men but for those who had moved job to help maintain industry, the register was useless. It would need to be rethought. To hold an election while disenfranchising the nation's heroes was patently absurd. The old rules would have to be torn up. This gave Asquith cover to announce a semi-conversion to votes for women. In early 1917 a committee of peers and MPs suggested a universal franchise for men and for all women over a certain age who were able to vote in local government elections or were married to a voter. When the age was fixed at thirty, this would give around 8.4 million women the vote, many more than the suffragettes had hoped for before the war. The Commons voted overwhelmingly for this in June 1917 and, under the influence of the new patriotism, that arch reactionary Lord

The strange allure of speed: British pioneer skiers virtually invented the sport of downhill ski racing.

We're off to the movies – well, some of us are. The Fred Karno vaudeville troupe, including Charlie Chaplin and Stan Laurel, en route to America, 1910.

Above One of the most successful agitators: Ben Tillett addressing strikers in 1911.

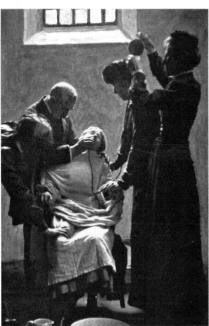

Left The brutal reality: a suffragette prisoner being force-fed. Holloway Prison, 1909.

Opposite, top Sylvia Pankhurst in full flood in the East End, 1912.

Opposite, bottom The Pankhursts fighting to present a petition to the King, 1914.

A better poster than a warlord? Kitchener in 1915, shortly before he was lost at sea.

War hero, poet and protestor: Siegfried Sassoon.

The 'Baby Killer' looms over London. Zeppelins brought London's first Blitz, now little remembered.

Unimaginable horror and courage:
an early British trench attack,
Flanders.

A Disunited Kingdom and
a shocking political blunder:
British troops subdue Dublin's
Easter Rising of 1916.

Belgium, 1918: British dead line the trench after the German breakthrough.

'Gurgle, gurgle, fizz . . .': the German Navy's final two-fingered salute to Britain. Scapa Flow, the Orkneys, 1919.

The woman who dared to ask: Marie Stopes, who brought sexual knowledge to millions.

The original anti-sleaze campaigner who vanished into thin air. Was Victor Grayson murdered?

The smile of a jackal? Maundy Gregory was a slander-monger, influence-peddler and Lloyd George's sinister middle-man for the sale of peerages.

Curzon only recommended abstention and the Lords too passed the measure, which became law in February 1918. Were the women workers pleased? Probably, but they had other worries too. In the munitions factories, so many were turning yellow through poisoning that they were popularly known as 'canaries'.

A Plague on Haig?

The man who from Christmas 1915 until the end of the fighting was in charge of Britain's main struggle on land has seen his reputation plummet from national saviour to bloodsoaked fool. Sir Douglas Haig, later Earl Haig, was a cavalry officer who had started his service in India, fought with Kitchener in the Sudan and then taken part in the Boer War. As aide-de-camp to Edward VII he was well connected at court, abstemious, brief of speech and strongly religious. Though he cordially despised politicians, particularly Lloyd George, he was a highly political man and a born intriguer who had effectively knifed his predecessor, Sir John French, before getting command of the British forces in France for himself. The ultimate 'donkey', the very image of the unimaginative and stubborn general sending his men to the slaughter, at the time he had a huge reputation. Partly because of his post-war work for veterans and the wounded, Haig's funeral in 1928 was one of the biggest modern Britain has ever seen – more people turned out to pay their respects to him than would for Churchill, or indeed Princess Diana.

The case for Haig is that he was always more flexible in his thinking, keener on new weapons of war such as tanks and aircraft and a better administrator than the critics understand. He fought against any diversion of the war into other theatres, such as the Middle East or Italy, and always understood that Germany had to be defeated in France, where her main power was concentrated. He might have suffered from excessive self-belief, even a complex about being God's instrument, but commander-in-chief is no job for the introspective or indecisive. And the job was particularly hard. Nobody had fought a war like this one before. When he took over as commander the British Expeditionary Force had about 600,000 men and held thirty miles of front line; by 1918 he was commanding three times as many men holding 123 miles. As one pro-Haig military historian has put it: 'It was Haig who had to manage that expansion; and train, equip, deploy and fight the largest army Britain has ever had ... in a coalition war with difficult allies.'[25] By the final stage of the war it was Haig's army which alone was able to mount a sustained attack and which eventually defeated the German army decisively. As to his strategy in the bloodiest battles, including that notorious first day of the Somme and then the bloody slog of Passchendaele, it is argued that Haig's massive use of artillery and belief that the Germans would be broken by waves of infantry attack after the bombardments may have been wrong but was entirely logical.

The case against him is that he lacked the flexibility to learn from his mistakes, and had insufficient imagination to understand the human cost of what he was attempting. Too often in Haig's diaries, the loss of 10,000 or more men is described as 'very small'. The Passchendaele attack, which drew horrified protests from some more junior commanders, was intended to retake a coastal strip of Belgium and deprive the Germans of U-boat bases in a bold move Haig described with such theatrical bravado that the cabinet was briefly entranced. By the time the British and Canadian forces attacked, the terrible weather had made their job all but impossible. The Germans were terribly mauled – 'Flanders 1917' is to Germany what day one of the Somme is to Britain, or Verdun to France – but their line did not break. The British gained some higher ground but at the cost of 250,000 casualties, of whom more than 50,000 were killed. One of Haig's closest aides is said to have wept when he saw the conditions, and asked: 'Did we send men to fight in this?' Haig persisted in the attack long after it was obvious to those fighting that no break-through would be achieved, and if he takes credit in part for the eventual victory in Flanders then he must be blamed for the fact that there, at Tyne Cot, stands the largest Commonwealth cemetery in the world.

The question that is ultimately unanswerable, of course, is whether the war could have been won without such slaughter. Other generals thought so. Lloyd George had always believed the war could have been won without such a dark blood-sacrifice and this was the source of his hostility to Haig throughout the second half of the war when he briefly put a French general, Nivelle, over Haig's head until Nivelle was discredited by his failed offensive. Eventually Lloyd George had had to give way to Haig. The alternatives to slogging in Flanders had collapsed. The Italians were badly beaten at Caporetto, the Dardanelles and Salonika expeditions had been failures and, although the war in the Middle East had gone well, it was hardly the high road to Berlin. And Lloyd George could not keep sacking commanders-in-chief, or falling out with a military top brass which still had the support of the country. Trying to think through alternatives was the job of a humane democratic leader, but Lloyd George's skills as a military strategist were negligible and both he and Haig knew it.

Haig's moment of glory, and partial vindication, came in 1918, when the Allies had little hope of the war ending soon. On the Russian front, after the seizure of power by the Bolsheviks, Germany had imposed a punitive peace. The March 1918 Treaty of Brest-Litovsk took from Russia a third of her population, half her industry and almost all her coal. A savage warning to France and Britain about what to expect if Germany won in the West, it allowed the German commander Ludendorff to hugely reinforce his armies in Flanders, giving him a sudden superiority in numbers over the British and French. He would only have this for a while, however, since the Americans were on their way. Realizing that by now his main enemy was Haig's BEF, he gambled everything on smashing through the British lines in a final push. This was always going to be hard. On the rare occasions when some kind of breakthrough had been achieved – such as the Battle of Cambrai at the end of 1917, when British tanks had briefly seized the initiative – following through, dragging artillery and supplies across ravaged trench lines, had proved almost impossible. But Ludendorff had a simple idea. He refused to use the word strategy: 'We chop a hole. The rest follows.'[26]

Ludendorff nearly did chop his hole. Using specially selected shock troops, the first time 'storm troopers' appeared, carrying the new sub-machine guns as well as their traditional grenades, flame throwers and trench mortars, and preceded by the usual artillery barrage, the Germans fell upon the British. Haig's army was at the time relatively weak: Lloyd George, mistrusting him, had held back all the reinforcements he had wanted. Later, this would cause a significant political crisis for the prime minister when a major general, Sir Frederick Maurice, wrote an open letter to the press accusing Lloyd George (and Bonar Law) of lying to Parliament about the relative strengths of the British army at the beginning of 1917 and 1918. It was a tangled affair, but Lloyd George saw off his enemies in the Commons in a speech combining guile, chutzpah and bluff. For the two British armies concerned, the effects were rather more dramatic. Ludendorff's men heavily outnumbered the British Fifth Army under Sir Hubert Gough, who had twelve divisions facing forty-two German ones, and had clustered his men too far forward. The Germans, using gas and high explosives, broke his defences and would quickly gain forty miles, taking more than 1,000 square miles of territory. On 21 March 1918, the Germans took around 21,000 British prisoners, one of the largest British surrenders ever. Six days later Gough, protesting bitterly about his treatment, was sacked by Lloyd George.

The British Third Army, north of Gough, better prepared for in-depth defence, gave far less ground. But it still seemed likely that the Germans would succeed in breaking through between the British and French. As the BEF retreat continued, Haig issued his famous 11 April Order of the Day, insisting that victory would be won by whoever held on the longest: 'There is no course open to us but to fight it out. Every position must be held to the last man: there must be no retirement. With our backs to the wall and believing in the justice of our cause, each one of us might fight on to the end.' By this stage in the war it was a matter of who was left standing. And though German advances continued, Ludendorff began to turn his attention to the south, and to the French, forgetting his original determination to break Haig. Paris seemed in imminent danger, at the end as it had been at the beginning. But ferocious British defensive fighting took such a toll on this final 'Kaiser Battle' attack that the German army's spirit began to break. In its way it was a great victory, albeit one made while walking backwards. By July the Germans had been stopped and by early August the Canadians and Australians were counter-attacking with such success that Ludendorff's own spirit was broken. By September a ferocious British-French counter-attack was destroying the German lines and by the following month the German army was collapsing as the BEF, with the Americans now in the war too, drove deeper and deeper behind the original scenes of carnage and stalemate.

For all this, at the time Haig was much praised, along with Lloyd George who never lost his nerve. Haig was in his way just as brave a man, and as dedicated a leader as the prime minister. Later his name was indelibly linked to the murderous frontal assaults of the war as a whole. Haig was dogged without flair, brave but unimaginative. He was not a fool. But he was not a great military genius at a time when Britain sorely needed one. In a way, Britain's victory was a victory for Haig values – resilience, refusal to give up. But as the surrenders of March 1918 hint, it was a close-run thing.

The Ribbon in the Mersey: Protest

The endless beach at Formby, where the Mersey meets the Irish Sea, was a quiet place even in wartime. On it, alone, in July 1917, a tall and striking-looking officer was walking. Stopping by the water, he first shook his fist at the sky. Then he began to tug at the small ribbon sewn onto his tunic, showing he had won the Military Cross. It fell weakly on the water and floated away. The man turned back. He was Siegfried Sassoon, a hero from the trenches, who was in the middle of the worst crisis of his young life. Back in Britain after being wounded, he had decided that the war was being fought for the wrong reasons, and that he would refuse to serve any longer. He was well aware that this would probably mean a court martial and possibly even the death penalty, though disgrace and imprisonment were likelier. He had written to his commanding officer 'with the greatest possible regret' to tell him 'it is my intention to refuse to perform any future military duties'. Nobody could call him a coward. Indeed, he himself likened the protest to his earlier recklessness in the front line. Now, summoned at once to his regiment's base at Litherland on the outskirts of Liverpool, he had been sent to await his fate in a nearby hotel, where he was mainly occupying himself learning poetry off by heart to keep him going in prison.

Sassoon was no ordinary objector. His family was one of the better-connected of the great Jewish dynasties of Edwardian England who mingled with the set of the Prince of Wales. Sassoon had been brought up in a classic old-fashioned English gentry way, part of the Sussex landed set, reading the imperial adventure stories of G. A. Henty and Rider Haggard and riding obsessively to hounds. These were days when hunting was central to upper-crust country life and considered so important for developing manliness and horsemanship that the army did not count time off for fox hunting as leave. Educated at Marlborough, where he was said to have carried knuckle-dusters to repel anti-Semites, and at Cambridge, Sassoon wanted to be a writer. But when war came it seems all but inevitable that he instantly enlisted in the Sussex Yeomanry, quickly switching to the Royal Welch Fusiliers to get to France more quickly.

All this would matter when his great rebellion started because, unlike many, his friends would be well connected and powerful. In the fighting, Sassoon had shown himself not only a charismatic front-line leader but spectacularly brave. He shared the usual front-line distaste for staff officers and politicians, but it was not until he arrived back home that his distaste turned to a wider disgust. It is best sampled, not from his excellent lightly fictionalized autobiography *Memoirs of an Infantry Officer*, in which he appears as George Sherston, but from his diaries, articulating a feeling that must have been widely shared but which was mostly buttoned up and suppressed by those serving. On 19 June 1917 he wrote: 'The soldiers who return home seem to be stunned by the things they have endured. They are willingly entrapped by the silent conspiracy against them. They have come back to life from the door of death . . . They vaguely know that it is "bad form" to tell the truth about the war.' Then his anger turns on the politicians:

> The rulers of England have always relied on the ignorance and patient credulity of the crowd. If the crowd could see into those cynical hearts it would lynch its dictators . . . Of the elderly male population I can hardly trust myself to speak . . . They glory in the mechanical phrases of the Northcliffe Press. They regard the progress of the war like a game of chess, cackling about 'attrition' and 'wastage of manpower' and 'civilization at stake'. In every class of society there are old men like ghouls, insatiable in their desire for slaughter, impenetrable in their ignorance.[27]

This is the same disgust that can be found in poems of the time, such as the memorable suggestion that a jingoistic crowd in a music hall would be well served by the arrival of a spouting tank lumbering down the aisles.

Sassoon decided to make his protest public, by writing a 'soldier's declaration' against the war. He announced that he was now 'in wilful defiance of military authority, because I believe that the war is being deliberately prolonged by those who have the power to end it'. What had begun as a war 'of defence and liberation' had become one 'of aggression and conquest' and, had the war aims been published, then it would be clear that a peace settlement could be negotiated. He was writing on behalf of the soldiers against 'the callous complacency with which the majority of those at home regard the continuance of agonies which they do not share, and which they have not sufficient imagination to realize'. It was a powerful denunciation, and made strong points – not least in tacitly drawing attention to the war in the Middle East and Africa, little debated, but where Britain was indeed extending her influence and empire. Yet his argument about war aims seems odd. By this stage in the conflict, the question was whether Germany could be beaten and would withdraw from captured territory if she was not; there was no evidence that she would, and indeed the most dangerous German attack was still to come. Nor was it fair to tar all civilians and politicians with the same brush. Millions knew pretty clearly what was happening. They could talk, and hear, even if they could not yet read it all. Sassoon's own poems, published during the fighting, contained vivid descriptions of the filth and degradation of Flanders. Even among the Colonel Blimp types in their clubs, there were many heartbroken men.

Sassoon was speaking for a small minority, but by 1917 it was a growing one. We have already met Edmund Morel, the half-French campaigner who fought for the natives of the Belgian Congo with such success. Many radical Liberals had been aghast at the declaration of war and had formed what they called the Union of Democratic Control, calling for Parliament, not the Crown, to be supreme in all matters of war-making and treaties; for an 'international council' to be formed – a first draft of the idea that would become the League of Nations – for general disarmament, and for there to be no changes of boundaries without referendums. By November 1914 they had broken with the Liberals, begun to form branches around the country and had the support of eighteen Liberal and Labour MPs, including Ramsay MacDonald. Backed by the *Manchester Guardian*'s editor C. P. Scott and rich Quaker families, they began to hold meetings, issue pamphlets and publish their own journal. Radical suffragettes, the Independent Labour Party and pacifists would join them.[28] It is very hard to gauge how many people supported the UDC and the No-Conscription Fellowship which followed it. This took courage. Bertrand Russell was stripped of his Trinity College, Cambridge, lectureship and later imprisoned. The Liberal MP Charles Trevelyan's local council passed a motion calling for him to be 'taken out and shot'. MacDonald was barred from his golf club, which complained that 'we are tainted as with leprosy'; he was later beaten up and narrowly escaped being thrown in a canal. Ferociously attacked by newspapers, their meetings were broken up by hostile audiences and at one, in Farringdon, London, in November 1915 soldiers stormed the platform and drove the speakers off.

As the full bloody cost of the war began to become apparent to everyone, the UDC found itself more popular, and the government started to consider it more dangerous. During the wave of strikes it attracted 3,000 people to a meeting in Merthyr, south Wales, in September 1916; more big gatherings took place the following month in Glasgow and Bradford. By the spring of 1917 the Russian Revolution had enthused the left of the Labour Party and the UDC campaigners felt they were making headway in what until then had been a pro-war party. The government cracked down. At the end of the war, the MPs who had supported the UDC would be swept from the Commons in the 'khaki election' of 1918, but the movement, by welding radical Liberals and Labour people together, helped snap the old Liberal Party and led to the post-war rise of Labour.

This was the tense political situation into which Sassoon had walked. He knew little of politics, but he was determined to be a martyr. The army was equally determined that he would not be. His well-connected friends divided between those who cheered his stand and those who were appalled by it. There then began a fascinating struggle for his conscience. Fellow officers wrote from France begging him to say he had been sick, had a nervous breakdown, and would withdraw his attack on the war. Fellow poet Robert Graves travelled up to see him to persuade him to attend a medical board. Though alike in some ways, they had differing ideas about bravery. Graves told Sassoon he was losing the respect of his brother officers, still fighting in France. Sassoon told Graves that by not speaking out he was the coward. In the end, Sassoon capitulated and allowed himself to be sent to a hospital for mentally damaged officers, Craiglockhart, on the southern outskirts of Edinburgh. There he came under the care of a podgy, balding, stammering but brilliant man, Dr William Rivers of the Royal Army Medical Corps. An early specialist in psychology and neurology who had travelled the world and studied in pre-war Germany, Rivers was influenced by Freud, though he did not agree with his theories on sex. He became closely involved in the Sassoon case, seeing him sometimes three times a day as he steadily tried to persuade him to return to the war.

Famously, Sassoon was interrupted while cleaning his golf clubs by a nervous younger man from the Manchester Regiment who had suffered a nervous breakdown after being shelled on the Somme. This man, Wilfred Owen, had bundles of handwritten poems and would be much influenced by Sassoon before returning abroad and being killed in the final days of the war. Sassoon eventually decided he had to return too. He had not recanted his views in the place he called 'Dottyville', nor ever did. He simply felt his place was with the fighting men, not with the uncomprehending civilians, particularly when he heard in November 1917 that his battalion was having a terrible time. His return to France was circuitous, via service in Ireland and the Middle East. On 10 July 1918 he finally got his wish and was reunited with his comrades on the front line. The following day, attacking a German machine-gun post, he incautiously stood up to get a better view and was promptly shot by his own side. Luckily for poetry and for posterity, he survived this second wound.

During the war, unlike the French, the British army would not mutiny. Unlike Russia, there would be no revolution. In Britain there were just 7,000 people who registered as conscientious objectors but who agreed to do other work, such as in ambulance units. Another 3,000 were sent to labour camps and 1,500 'absolutists' who refused any compulsion were treated particularly harshly. These are tiny numbers. But Sassoon's indecision was shared by many. He was torn between intellectual contempt for the war and for its leaders on the one hand, and his feelings of exhilaration and comradeship on the other. He had no great loathing for Germans, except when a friend was killed. He was engagingly open about how proud he was of his medal, the MC he threw into the Mersey. However vile and dangerous the fighting was, it gave him at times a stronger sense of being alive than anything at home. In all this he stands for countless others who were neither enthusiasts for the war nor found they could evade it. He could express this tragic tension as few others could. Nor was he alone in hoping for a negotiated peace. At just the same time as Sassoon was rejoining his regiment, at the end of November 1917, a Unionist statesman published a letter in the *Daily Telegraph* calling for just that. Lord Lansdowne had been a last-ditcher against Lloyd George in pre-war politics, was a close ally of Balfour's and had not been asked to join Lloyd George's government. His letter, proposing a compromise peace, spawned much outrage in the national papers and a torrent of abusive mail, never mind anger in the cabinet. But it was supported privately by many individuals, including the Archbishop of Canterbury. The war drew a kind of snarling bulldog mask across the face that the British people presented to the outside world. Behind that mask, however, many thousands were having second thoughts.

Shadows from the Hall of Mirrors

For Germany, the end had come suddenly. Faced with a final death-or-glory mission against Britain, the High Seas Fleet had started to mutiny. Red flags were raised, officers shot and trains commandeered. A revolutionary situation spread through the coastal cities. Workers' and sailors' councils were formed, much as in Russia, and for a short time there was a communist Republic of Oldenburg with a stoker as president. Communist crowds were marching through Berlin. German officers in uniform were chased by angry civilians. Ludendorff resigned. The Kaiser, pressed by President Wilson, eventually agreed to abdicate and a German republic was declared. Wilhelm fled to the neutral Netherlands where he was consoled with 'good hot English tea', shortbread and scones. Despite demands for him to be handed over to be tried, the Dutch gave him sanctuary and he settled down in a small castle at Doorn, chopping wood, playing the country gentleman and later observing the rise of Hitler with mixed feelings. Wilhelm's army had hoped for a ceasefire on the field, followed by cautious negotiations about the future. However, when the German delegation had made its way tortuously by car through the front line, waving white towels, and finally reached the Allied commander-in-chief Marshal Foch in his train carriage in the forest of Compiègne, they were confronted with instant demands for disarmament and withdrawal. Faced with revolution and after fruitless protests, they signed. This was only the first part of Germany's march of humiliation.

Unlike in 1945, in 1918 Germany was not occupied or disarmed. Indeed, she still had troops in France and had decisively won her war in the East. She thought she was getting a negotiation when in fact she was getting an ultimatum. This was perhaps just deserts for a country which had imposed such a brutal settlement on Russia a year earlier. Yet the leaders who gathered in Paris, led by President Woodrow Wilson, who had arrived by ship from the United States, Lloyd George, Clemenceau and Italy's Vittorio Orlando, were not nearly as powerful as they seemed. The war had shaken the world, and their reach was short. The Russian Bolshevik revolution was something they did not understand and with which they could not negotiate. In other places, including Budapest and Munich, there were further communist uprisings, and the delegates in their frock coats and top hats were all too aware that hunger and anger could yet upend all Europe.

The Treaty of Versailles has not been fondly remembered. Above all, it is blamed for the huge reparations heaped on defeated Germany, and thus for the rise of Hitler and the next German war. It managed to humiliate Germany while not sufficiently tying her down to avoid the next confrontation. Its guiding principle of self-determination for all peoples, proclaimed by the American president, raised hopes that would be quickly dashed. For self-determination, if it means anything, means an end to imperialism, and this was a war won by empires, the British one most obviously. Americans might have disliked and resented the British imperial system, and the old gang of European leaders, but they could do very little about it.

Among those who left Paris in 1919 with a deep sense of grievance were the would-be empires of the future, notably Japan and Italy. The United States Senate, understanding at least some of this, refused to ratify the treaty. So America never joined the League of Nations, Wilson's great project. In France, public opinion thought that the treaty was too kind: Clemenceau, their great war leader, was voted out of office the following year. Barely had the ink dried before there was fighting again, in Poland, Ireland and Turkey. Meant to put a full stop to the old ways of war, Versailles proved only a comma.

For Britain, after the jubilation of the Armistice, not much of this was clear. Whatever trouble would be faced at home by Wilson and Clemenceau, Lloyd George was riding high. In December 1918 he had won a crushing general election victory. Liberals who had supported his coalition and Unionists agreed not to stand against each other, thus prolonging the wartime alliance. With many women now voting, and a fresh register, twice as many people took part as at the last election, in 1910, and the result was a massive personal triumph for Lloyd George, 'the man who won the war'. Unionist and pro-Lloyd George candidates won 473 seats and the Asquith Liberals were reduced to a pitiful twenty-nine – Asquith himself being among those who lost his seat. Labour lost its pacifists, but won an extra twenty seats, now becoming the second largest party. Although women were now eligible to stand, not a single female MP was returned to Westminster – the only woman elected had been the aristocratic Sinn Feiner Countess Markiewicz, who, like the other Sinn Feiners who had swept southern Ireland, took her place in Dublin's self-proclaimed Dáil. Lloyd George would live to regret both his dependence on the Unionists, who again dominated the new government, and his wilder promises during the campaign, when he pledged a land fit for heroes. But this fickle, brilliant, corrupt and charismatic man was for the time being at the very peak of his popularity and power.

The war had changed him from a radical to a pillar of the establishment. He was more moderate than many in wanting a fair settlement with Germany and retained his old interest in welfare. But now on the world stage, he was an imperial leader. Britain had been more admiring of her allies, France and America, than she had ever been before. But people felt this had been a victory for the

British Empire; there were no US troops stationed in Britain and the Americans had, after all, arrived late. When there was precious little good news from Flanders or Gallipoli, there had been cheer from sideshows such as T. E. Lawrence's involvement with the Arab revolt against the Turks and the defeat of German forces in East Africa. In the war's darkest days, Lloyd George had created an Imperial War Cabinet. The sacrifice and success was that of Canada, Australia, New Zealand, India and South Africa. The Commonwealth was closer and meant far more, after the heroics of the Canadians and Australians, and the Indians too. People such as Jan Smuts, the South African who had led commandos against the British in the Boer War but who went on to be a member of the War Cabinet, a British field marshal and a founder of both the League of Nations and the UN, were public heroes. The same went for the former trade unionist (and, like Smuts, deeply racially prejudiced) Australian prime minister Billy Hughes – cheered and lauded on the streets of London as no Australian leader would be now. And indeed the Australians lost more soldiers than the Americans. Now the war was over, the position of the Empire seemed if anything stronger. Ireland was clearly a problem that could not be long delayed. There were ominous rumbles in India. But this seemed a time to expand, not contract.

The worst British decisions affected the Middle East. The story of the Empire in the early twentieth century itself is too large and tangled to be dealt with properly here. But the tale of Britain's bumbling incompetence and double dealing with the Muslim world has left too much of a legacy to be ignored. It is a narrative of greed for land, greed for oil and ignorance about Islam, combined with some heroic and ludicrous military moments; it has done its bit to create the wound of modern Iraq and some of the extremist and authoritarian regimes of the region. To start with, Britain's involvement had been mainly with Egypt, effectively run as a subsidiary of the British Empire because of the importance of the Suez Canal to Egypt and the oil-rich Persian Gulf. Since Churchill had switched the British navy from coal to oil before the war, the oilfields there, and the refinery at Abadan, built in 1913, had been a vital national interest – and a source of huge wealth to the shareholders of the Anglo-Persian Oil Company. But the decision of the Ottoman Empire to side with Germany in 1914 opened up other possibilities. Early in the war, to protect the Persian oil, a British-Indian force invaded that part of the Ottoman Empire we now call southern Iraq, seizing the sleepy mud-built town of Basra which until then had been forgotten by the modern world. A major expedition north through Mesopotamia was first successful and then disastrous when an over-stretched and cut-off British force was obliged to surrender to the Turks after a siege at Kut el-Amara, south of Baghdad. In 1917 a larger British army did capture Baghdad.

More dramatically, another British army, after early reverses, spent 1917 pushing back the Turks and their German advisers through Palestine and Syria. General Allenby, a ferociously bad-tempered, heavy-set and brilliant commander, descended from Oliver Cromwell, had assembled a force in Egypt which included soldiers from almost every part of the British Empire, plus three battalions of Jewish volunteers, many from America. Using 12,000 British, Australian and Indian horsemen, backed up with planes, armoured cars, torpedo boats and much cunning, he outmanoeuvred and outfought the Turks, entering first Gaza and then, after a skirmish involving the Welsh Guards at the Mount of Olives, Jerusalem itself. Allenby took the city as the leader of the first Christian army to get there for 700 years: he arrived on foot and unarmed. He then pushed north into Syria, where he overwhelmingly defeated the Turkish army in one of the last and most decisive battles of the war: it happened at Megiddo, or Armageddon as it is better known. With Allenby was another Englishman touched by myth. T. E. Lawrence, or 'Lawrence of Arabia', the scholar, writer, archaeologist and self-promoting genius, had helped lead the Arab revolt from what is now Saudi Arabia, something he himself called 'a sideshow within a sideshow'. Lawrence persuaded Allenby – probably in spite of his penchant for swaggering around in Arab robes – that a campaign of Bedouin guerrillas on camels led by the ancient Hashemite family and directed by himself could hugely help the conventional war. The price, however, was the promise to Emir Feisal that a great new Arab kingdom would be created across much of what is now Syria, Israel, Palestine, Jordan and Iraq. When Lawrence and Feisal rode into Damascus, along with Allenby's cavalry, this is what they thought would happen.

They could not have been more wrong. For one thing, in his famous Declaration of 1917, the British foreign secretary Arthur Balfour had just promised to support a Jewish homeland. Sent to Lord Rothschild after a cabinet meeting, the very short letter declares British 'sympathy with Jewish Zionist aspirations'. It goes on to proclaim that Britain viewed 'with favour the establishment in Palestine of a national home for the Jewish people' and would try to help that happen, 'it being clearly understood that nothing shall be done which may prejudice the civil and religious rights of existing non-Jewish communities in Palestine'. Quite what this meant has been debated ever since. It seemed to promise the Zionists their own state; yet it also suggested that this could come about without harming the rights of Arab Muslims living there. But however mealy-mouthed, it would certainly mean no independent Arab state could include Palestine; Allenby was worried enough by the Declaration that he tried to hide news of it. Worse was to come, however, for Feisal and the Arab revolt. As soon as the Ottoman Empire had collapsed, Britain and France began to fight over the scraps. Britain had always eyed Mesopotamia. Once it was out of fear that the Russian bear, or the Kaiser, who had proclaimed himself the protector of all Muslims, would move south against British India. Now those threats had gone, but the British had realized that the black, tarry stuff oozing from the grit and sand of Basra, Mosul and Baghdad was almost certainly oil. They wanted it and, after a complex deal to share some of the benefits with the French, the Middle East was duly carved up. Palestine and what is now Iraq went to Britain's sphere of influence, joining her domination of Egypt and Persia. France got Syria and the Lebanon. So much for the self-determination of peoples.

So, at the Paris peace conference, Prince Feisal, with Lawrence in attendance, was humiliated – almost as much as another hopeless petitioner, Ho Chi Minh, then working as a kitchen assistant in the French capital but already dreaming of independence for Vietnam. The Arab humiliation would be partly reversed two years later in Egypt at a conference chaired by Churchill, when Feisal would be declared the first King of Iraq and his brother Abdullah would become Emir of Transjordan – two fake monarchies to serve British interests. This in turn would weaken the Hashemite dynasty: Arab power would start to move across to another rebellious family, that of Ibn Saud,

whose Wahhabi form of Islam has had such an influence on the
modern world. By then the last Caliphate in the Muslim world, that
of the Ottomans which had sided with Germany and declared jihad
against her enemies, had disappeared. Britain had encouraged Arabs
to believe that the Caliphate should be based not in Turkey but where
the rulers of Medina and Mecca could be found. After the war, the
destruction of the Ottoman Empire and its dismemberment would
also mean the end of the Caliphate of Constantinople; this caused a
major movement of protest and outrage in India (including of course
today's Pakistan) with its then 70 million Muslims. These are complicated matters but it is worth totting up the tally so far. We have
made-up countries with imported puppet rulers; Arab nationalism first
encouraged and then mocked; extremist forms of Islam left to flourish;
and the old Caliphate abolished, leading to a debate about what should
replace it throughout the Muslim world. The consequences of the
First World War amount to more than paper poppies once a year;
they are all around us still.

A Final Gurgle

At least Lloyd George, settled in grand style in Paris, with a big
election victory under his belt, could reflect that the British government was still a master of events. He had established himself as
radical firebrand, then reforming cabinet minister, and now wartime
leader and world statesman. His writ ran. The empire had never
been stronger. Above all, the Royal Navy ruled the seas. Its domin-
ance was symbolized by the floating corpse of its enemy, seventy-
four battleships, battle cruisers and other warships of the German
High Seas Fleet, all now safely at anchor at Scapa Flow. They had
been sailed across the North Sea, greeted by the Royal Navy in full
force, with every flag flying, and finally surrendered in the Firth of
Forth before being taken to the Orkneys. There was a debate about
what to do with them. The French wanted some extra battleships,
so did the Italians. The dreaded U-boats had long ago been towed to
Harwich and were being destroyed. But the might of the Kaiser's
navy was still afloat, awaiting the final terms of the peace treaty in
Paris. For seven months skeleton crews of German sailors would

stay on board, bored out of their minds, smoking, playing cards, talking revolution, dancing and combating a growing population of rats while their officers discussed what to do. Rear Admiral Ludwig von Reuter, aboard Scheer's Jutland flagship, had made his mind up already. If the terms of the treaty were harsh, and the fleet was to be handed over, then better to scuttle the lot. The Paris terms would turn out to be worse than the Germans' worst nightmares and as the last days of haggling continued, von Reuter prepared for a final two-fingered salute at Britain.

On the day it happened, the British warships guarding the German fleet were themselves out at sea, practising against destroyer attacks with torpedoes, for some future conflict then barely imaginable. The only British afloat in Scapa Flow were a party of 400 Orkney schoolchildren, on a tug boat for a day trip, and a marine artist on a trawler, making sketches of the German battleships. By all accounts 21 June 1919 was an almost perfect day, the kind of translucent, soft summer weather that can make the Highlands and Islands of Scotland feel like paradise. At 10 a.m. Reuter sent all ships his coded message, by flag, light and semaphore, reading simply, 'paragraph eleven'. The crews went below, opened the sea-cocks and let the chill waters in. Then they wound out the lifeboats and began to abandon ship. Starting with the flagship, *Friedrich der Grosse*, the ships began to list and go down. Some slowly and placidly subsided. Others upended and went down with great gurgles and hissings. Panicking, the little British guard ships fired on the German sailors and tried to order them back. Vain attempts were made to tow some of the stricken vessels. One German captain waving a white flag was shot in the head. All together, nine Germans were killed. None of it made the slightest difference. Soon Scapa Flow was covered with oil stains and bubbles, refuse and little boats. Hissings and roarings came from all around. The British fleet rushed back, far too late: by early afternoon almost every German ship was on the bottom. Petulant and furious, the British commander shouted abuse at Reuter and his officers: they remained calm and stony-faced. For Reuter, it was the last act of the Great War and something which reduced, if it did not remove, the shame of defeat and surrender. The message, for those who chose to think about it, was that Germany was down but not out – defeated but not reconciled.

Part Three

KEEPING OUR BALANCE

1919–1939

Footfalls echo in the memory
Down the passage which we did not take
Towards the door we never opened . . .

T. S. Eliot, 'Burnt Norton', 1935

Great periods of history have names – the Elizabethan age, the Victorian, the Edwardian – but the time between the two slaughters of the twentieth century comes with no monarch attached. We resort to combination: 'the twenties and the thirties', as though they were identical and inseparable. Or we say 'between the wars' or 'inter-war Britain', glossing over these twenty lively years as nothing more than a pause, an intermission between the acts in the twentieth century's great drama. Some have called it 'the Age of Baldwin', after the dominant politician of the time, but few people have much idea who Baldwin was. Those who do remember him have a fuzzy picture of a self-satisfied man smoking a pipe and scratching a pig's back while Hitler rants offstage. Other political figures are either forgotten entirely or remembered as comic incompetents – Ramsay MacDonald entranced by duchesses, Oswald Mosley posturing in boots. Churchill's moment was yet to come. So everything about this time seems unsatisfactorily vague. What's the story? What does it mean for us now?

Only a great banking crisis, mass unemployment and the Depression; only the political class loathed and ridiculed; only the world's power balance changing as new nations rise in the East; only a people at home enjoying new consumer goods and dreaming dreams of a better way of living. These are the years when imperial Britannia is slipping into history and modern Britain, still an ado-lescent, is becoming visible. Our memory of these decades seems oddly concerned with headwear – podgy politicians in pork-pie hats, incompetent financiers in top hats, hard-faced manufacturers in bowler hats, flappers in cloche hats, fascists in peaked caps and endless streams of the unemployed, on street corners or hunger marches, their flat caps pulled down tight. Yet despite the neat classification by headgear, it is also a time when nothing leads anywhere. The General Strike is not a revolution. The abdication crisis has become almost incomprehensible. There are all those Oxbridge types promising not to fight for King and Country, but we know they did anyway. The great events of these decades, which include the rise of Nazism, the hideously cruel Soviet experiment, the triumph of Hollywood and Roosevelt's New Deal, take place far away from our cloudy islands. For Britain, it is the Great Age of Half-Cock. Only with the crisis of 1940 does the country begin to rouse itself and History, properly understood, begin again. One might decide that not only does this period have no name, it does not deserve one.

But what about all those echoes of today? The British of the inter-war years were introduced to Kellogg's cornflakes and Mars Bars, observed the spread of Sainsbury's, Marks & Spencer and Dewhurst the butchers. They were (mostly) united for the first time by a national electricity grid, so that the country became bright at night. This was when the British became a people obsessed with home ownership and mortgages. Despite wonderful writers, a culture based on moving pictures in cinemas began to push books aside. At home, pre-television, it was the great radio age. The British began to travel in large numbers for holidays at the coast in the first Butlin's camps, and some went abroad too. They crammed their narrow roads with cars, became addicted to crime thrillers, began to live in sprawling suburbs and sucked up the new American culture. If you buy organic food, if you have ever been to a nightclub, if you go to a gym, if you take drugs or drink cocktails, read paperback books or listen to the BBC, or ski, or champion the freedom of the motorist, then you have been shaped by what happened in Britain in the twenties and thirties. Many of us live in one of the semi-detached houses or apartment blocks that sprang up; our country is marked by the stalking pylons, roadside pubs, garages and offices built or opened then. Light industry was putting money into the pockets of people we would now call teenagers. Their financial crises and arguments about unemployment feel fresh again today. From the English Midlands to the south coast, at the very least, the thirties felt surprisingly like an early draft of the fifties, or even the early sixties.

For some of the time people were angrier about politics, and with good reason. Foreign policy was what was most likely to kill you. Without a proper welfare state, losing your job or status was much scarier than it is today. The middle classes had servants, not appliances. There wasn't much litter because there wasn't much wrapping, and much less to wrap. No motorways and no supermarkets meant local shopping, with baskets over the arm. There was the scent of cigarette smoke everywhere. Four out of five men smoked, and almost half the women. Boys started early and the brands were high-tar, often untipped ones, such as the famous Capstan Full Strength, Woodbines and Craven A. The thicker smoke pollution of the cities hanging in the air was, by our standards, almost unbearable. Medical science was still primitive. The worst health disaster was the so-called Spanish Flu epidemic immediately after the First World War, not so very different biologically from more recent 'bird flu' viruses, except that it killed around 220,000 people in Britain. Year in, year out, huge numbers of others died from infections or operations which today would be easily treated or routine. Despite the pioneering work of Sir Alexander Fleming, there would be no antibiotics readily available until half way through the next war. Only the children of the middle and upper classes were really well educated. Most left school at fourteen; a tiny handful of adolescents progressed to university. For the poor, hospital treatment was grim and many relied on the kindness of local doctors who dispensed with their fee, sometimes charging richer patients more to make up the difference.

Even when we are following the spoor of something we can all recognize now, such as interest in organic, local food or the need for regular exercise, their origins in the twenties and thirties can seem downright weird. This is a time of cults and crazes – and, it has to be said, of crazies too. Women in flowing gowns doing solemn-faced dances in fields, or men in odd home-made uniforms intoning spiritual gobbledegook at the edge of forests, were trying in their way to find routes to a better future. There was a craze for spiritualism, partly driven by a yearning to contact the 'lost generation' left in Flanders. But in general, before television, people were odder. That is, they could follow their own paths without being nationally observed, commented upon or so easily ridiculed. Less education, and a smaller media, meant there was more eccentricity. That produced its own kind of freedom. Britain was bigger then.

That is, there were around 16 million fewer people in the same space, which seemed bigger too because it was harder to get around. For those with cars and living near cities travel was often faster, but for the majority it was slow and rare. So regional accents were stronger and local habits more diverse. Only the upper classes, and bohemians, knew much about abroad. Yet people who really couldn't take Britain any more could get out. The political elite spent half the year by the Mediterranean. The most reactionary aristocrats decamped to hunt, farm, drink and lord it over the natives in East Africa. Ambitious lower-middle-class or working-class people could go to Canada or Australia. During the twenties, more than half a million people left, though the thirties, which are meant to be so dreary, saw a big change. In net terms, 650,000 immigrants came here.[1] They were, of course, mostly white.

Those living through this period often talked of being a 'post-war' generation. Apart from a few hyper-alert and prescient people, they did not know a worse war was coming. But it was the most important self-description for the period. The Great War seemed to have sliced away most of what went before it. Old habits of deference, old authorities, had gone. The question was now: 'How shall we live?' Not everyone bothered to ask it. But the most interesting people did, whether their reply was to drink and take drugs, or to live in a rural community, or fall for a new political creed. And a word of caution should be said here about the political extremism. An extraordinary number of people appear in this book who are attracted to fascist thinking – Churchill included. A few were real extremists, hostile to democracy, ready for violence. Most were vaguely anti-Jewish in a snobbish but entirely peaceful way. Many more still had been entranced by Mussolini than by Hitler, and thought some kind of strong national regime would help defeat unemployment. It is vital to try to think ourselves back into a world before the Holocaust, before the Waffen SS and before Nazi Germany's violent expansion. They did not know what we know. Something similar can be said about those – never many – who became communists. Sharp-eyed observers brought back accurate stories of the hideous nature of Stalin's regime but thousands of idealists simply refused to believe them. They were blinded in part by their fear of the fascists; just as the fascists justified thuggery by their genuine fear of 'Bolsheviks'.

Let us not be too smug about these great-grandparents and great-great-grandparents. For above all, most of them voted in their millions for moderate and even timid parties. Dull though most of Britain's politicians were, we can thank our lucky stars, or our lucky birthplace, that they presided over a country so complacent, hide-bound, unthinkingly loyal to its increasingly suburban monarchy and so stupefied by the fading glory of its past, that it never fell for thrilling politics as most of the rest of Europe had. Politicians used to compliment one another on having common-sense ballast, or 'bottom'. In the 1931 general election, fifty-five per cent of voters went for the Conservatives. In 1935, the National Government did almost as well. Most other voters opted for middle-of-the-road Labour. Just 0.1 per cent voted Communist. The twenties and thirties were a time of idealism and sparkling visions of new futures, but they were also when the British were saved by a low centre of gravity – by Britannia's vast and heavy buttocks, her unimaginative, tea-swilling, bovine inability to be easily excited. These were the years when, despite every temptation, we kept our balance.

Grief and Gaiety

On 9 November 1920, a few platoons of British soldiers set out once more for the front. Led by one officer apiece, they went to the still-churned, still-slimy ground where great slaughters, at Ypres, Cambrai, Arras and the Somme, had taken place. They marched to a place of rough wooden crosses without markings, where dead Britons too torn about to be identified had been buried. Just one body was dug up from each site, placed in a plain deal coffin and then brought back to a small chapel. Next, an officer was blindfolded and led into it. He reached out and touched one of the four coffins. The other three were returned to be reburied. The fourth was then taken by train to the Channel, where it was met by a warship and placed inside a larger casket of oak, specially made from a tree cut down in Hampton Court forest. With an escort of destroyers and given the admiral's nineteen-gun salute as it passed, the dead man – a Scot or a Welshman, a Nottinghamshire miner or a Devon public schoolboy, a man who had died bravely or in terror – no one knew who he was – was then taken to London. Two days after being dug up in France, he was paraded through the streets, his pallbearers being field marshals and admirals, until he was buried deep in the sand below Westminster Abbey. On his coffin rested an antique sword from the King's collection. In the next days and weeks, more than a million people came to say goodbye. Outside, in Whitehall, 100,000 wreaths had almost hidden the base of the brand new Cenotaph.

Reclaiming, and giving a state burial to, an unknown soldier had been the idea of a young army padre, later a vicar in Margate, called David Railton. He passed the idea to the Dean of Westminster, who wrote to the King. George was initially against the notion, worrying that it was too morbid, but he was won round. As the writer Ronald Blythe later said, 'The affair *was* morbid, but grandly and supremely so.' It proved hugely popular and cathartic, partly because it was in its way democratic. Millions of bereaved parents, brothers and sisters could half-believe that the recovered body was theirs, and certainly that it represented their dead boy. There had been much argument about the different treatment of aristocratic or upper-class corpses, which might be returned for burial at home, and the great mass of the dead who were left near to where they fell. Overall, the funerary democrats – led by the poet Kipling – won the argument for all to be treated alike in death, officers and men lying alongside one another with similar headstones. This was not trivial. At a time of revolution abroad, democracy needed to be symbolized. These were the years of the memorials: the vast Commonwealth memorials in France, requiring their own large bureaucracy and the factory-scale cutting of headstones; the thousands of granite crosses, sculpted Tommies and gold-painted wooden boards in villages, schools, train stations and city squares. In every style from the mimicry of ancient Greek and Egyptian funerary art to the latest in angular modernism, the British raised up and then lived in a garden of death.

Though there was not, in statistical terms, a lost generation as is sometimes still claimed, the three-quarters of a million dead were a ghostly presence everywhere; faces staring out of school and sporting photographs, empty upstairs bedrooms in suburban houses, silent family meals, odd gaps in offices or village pubs between the old and the very young. In the ten years after the war 29,000 small country estates were sold off, often simply because there was no heir to inherit them. The wounded and maimed were also visible everywhere. They might be blind, gassed, distressingly unpredictable, hobbling with empty trouser-legs or pinned-up arms. The worst were still coping with open wounds which needed to be dressed daily to staunch infection. New plastic surgery techniques, still crude, could last until the late 1920s before patched-up faces were ready. Unsettling smells broke through the cigarette smoke. Park benches were sometimes painted blue to warn passers-by that they were reserved for badly wounded men from hospital, in their floppy serge uniforms and blue caps. The exuberance of blood – the erect spirit – of Edwardian times had been drained. Though in theory there were enough men for most women to marry, that was cold arithmetical nonsense for the hundreds of thousands who had lost the only one they loved, and who were still wearing black and would never wed. The current author is old enough, just, to remember great-aunts who did not marry 'because of the War' and lived single lives – albeit quite cheerful ones – focused on fruit cake and friendship.

Eventually, of course, the sadness was too much, the weight of public stoicism too heavy for living, breathing humans to bear. Those who had survived wanted some fun again. The brittle urban gaiety for which the twenties are known was an essential response to the muffled drums and the silences and the hat-doffing to piles of brick and bronze. Ponderous hymn tunes consoled many. Jazz replied. The war had dulled and shabbied the country, so there followed a time of paint and silliness. Upper-crust girls could shock their parents by aping the masses and using rouge and mascara and lipstick. Women began smoking in public. The Great War, like littler wars, had been an overwhelmingly masculine affair. Boys grew into men very fast, and died as men. Men dressed as modern warriors in thick polished belts, heavy boots, rough, bronze-decorated overcoats and peaked caps. In wartime, beards and long hair were symbols of dissidence which drew angry looks and loud comments. So after it was over the younger men who had just missed the war responded with colourful and, to their elders' eyes, effeminate clothing. Women, in turn, looked a little more like boys. Tubular dresses, bindings round the chest to disguise the bust and short haircuts, the bob and then the shingle, made girls seem unsettlingly androgynous. When the insolent-puppy writer Evelyn Waugh married a woman also called Evelyn, they were called He-Evelyn and She-Evelyn, and they gaze back from photos in identical trousers and shirts with similarly camp expressions. The upper classes and their arty hangers-on led the way, but thanks to the mass newspapers people across the country watched and in some ways mimicked them.

Though we think of the most riotous scenes of misbehaviour coming in the twenties, the years of the Bright Young Things, the pattern had been set during the war. A good case-study can be found in the diaries of Duff Cooper, for most of the war working at the Foreign Office and in love with Lady Diana Manners, who had been a great and well-connected Edwardian beauty. His diaries recount an astonishing amount of casual love-making and hard drinking. The affairs are probably mostly not fully physical, because of the dangers of pregnancy, but in variety and number his circle rivalled or outpaced the behaviour of people in supposedly laxer, later days. The fine wines and champagnes gurgled away through the war, as did the old brandies and whisky, and a fair amount of drug taking – morphia, mainly, injected. You could buy what was, in effect, cocaine and heroin quite legally – people sent it to the troops. At one level, it is a record of hedonism and self-indulgence on a scale that would have shattered the constitutions of most rock musicians sixty years later. Yet it is only when set together with the equally astonishing death-rate of their friends that it makes full sense. After yet another friend, an in-law of the Asquiths, has been killed, Cooper recalls Edwardian parties of which he was now the only male survivor and records a day of helpless crying. It ends with him dining in his club: 'I drank the best champagne – Pommery 1906 – because I felt that Edward would have wished it and would have done so had I been killed first.' He refuses to go out to eat 'simply because I was afraid that I might cry in the middle of dinner'. Cooper went on to serve towards the end of the war, with spectacular bravery.

This determination to drink deep and party while there was still time flowed unchecked into the post-war world. The nearest recent equivalent might be the drug-taking hedonism that flooded American youth during and after Vietnam. As then, in twenties Britain it pitted young and old against each other in an epic generational battle. The jittery, shallow, fancy-dressing army of upper-class children who smashed up bars, invented new cocktails, danced along the counters of department stores, learned to dance the camel-walk, the shimmy, the black-bottom and the notorious Charleston and stole policemen's hats contained plenty of ex-officers from the front, and many whose brothers, cousins and lovers had been killed. Among those who arrived in London and changed the city's taste were the first Harlem hot jazzmen, black musicians bringing the allure of early Hollywood pictures and stories of gangsters. Elders and betters looked on aghast; and, as ever, the media, in this case the fashionable new trade of newspaper gossip columnists, stoked up the story. Noël Coward, whose play *The Vortex* dealt with drugs, was able to pose to a popular newspaper in a silk dressing gown with an expression, it reported, of advanced degeneracy. He promised the London *Evening Standard* that 'I am never out of opium dens, cocaine dens, and other evil places. My mind is a mess of corruption.'[2] Gangs like the Sabinis and the Titanics (the latter apparently so named because they dressed up poshly, like passengers on the liner) fought across Soho, across the racetracks and for control of the new centres of vice in twenties Britain – the nightclubs. There you could find ex-officers, Sinn Fein men, gangsters, prostitutes, dancers and drug dealers like the famous opium supplier 'Brilliant' Chang. There were also homosexual clubs, crowded with men who had failed to heed their monarch: George V, told that an acquaintance was a 'bugger', replied with consternation: 'I thought men like that shot themselves.'

Falling from Grace: Nightclubs and Peers

The 'Queen of the Nightclubs' was a woman of the most respectable background, whose children were sent to Harrow and Roedean.[3] Kate Meyrick had been brought up in a house in Ireland called Fairyland, and when she and her doctor husband split up, faced with having to earn a living, she resolved to create some enchanted spaces of her own. She opened her first club in Leicester Square in 1919, where her guests ranged from the King of Denmark to Russian refugees, gangsters and Marie Lloyd. There were pistol shots and confrontations, attempted blackmailings and rows over the drinks licence. She was beaten up by a Soho gangster for refusing him entry, raided by the police and fined, but her little empire expanded. The Manhattan, the Little Club, the Silver Slipper and many more made Meyrick one of the most powerful entertainment figures in the capital. The most famous club she owned was known simply as the 43 after its address in Gerrard Street, Soho. It was a large building and photographs show a rather bare, even stark dance floor, with bentwood chairs of the kind you find in church halls, and white tablecloths. Yet the 43 was destined to become the most notorious nightclub in Britain. Its clientele included Rudolph Valentino, Charlie Chaplin, many peers, socialist and Tory MPs, a couple of infamous murderers, financiers and hundreds of ordinary middle-class people looking for fun. The Silver Slipper had a glass dance floor, lit from underneath by coloured lights and with a wave-effect: in the mid-twenties it was the most sophisticated club in Britain. Mostly the nightclubs catered for nothing more than late-night dancing, drinking and flirting, but they became a symbol of decadence and youth revolt.

If Kate Meyrick was the face of the fun-loving twenties, the face of authority throughout most of her career was the round, pink one of 'Jix' – as Sir William Joynson-Hicks was universally if unaffectionately known. A teetotal hard-line right winger who had fought and beaten Churchill at a famous Salford election before the war, Jix was famous for defending all the most conservative causes. He fought against reform of the Prayer Book, he defended General Dyer for massacring Indians at Amritsar, he would have supported rebellion and civil war to keep Ulster British and he had no time for Jews or foreigners. He first arrived as home secretary under Baldwin in 1924 and, when asked exactly what he did, replied with barely a twinkle in his eye, 'It is I who am ruler of England.' About the only moment of self-questioning in a life devoted to simple certainties was when he arrived one day at Buckingham Palace only to realize he was wearing brown shoes.[4] Luckily disaster was averted with a borrowed pair and the King, fine fellow, laughed heartily about it for days. Jix never faltered. He began a campaign against the 242,000 registered 'aliens' in Britain and fiercely toughened up the ports of entry against would-be immigrants. He ran vehement campaigns, too, against vice in public parks, supported prosecutions against 'indecent' poems (including privately printed ones by D. H. Lawrence) and pictures (getting into trouble when drawings by that louche contemporary figure William Blake were seized) and did his best to stamp out homosexual beastliness.

Jix also developed a near fixation with nightclubs. By 1928 he managed to have sixty-five clubs raided and prosecuted for infringements of their alcohol licence and sixty-two of them closed down: but Mrs Meyrick's 43 was strangely and infuriatingly immune. Finally, it was discovered that a member of the vice squad, a station sergeant at Soho called George Goddard, had been taking bribes. Mrs Meyrick was sentenced to fifteen months' hard labour – one of her five visits to Holloway before she died in 1933. For a conventionally minded middle-class woman this was a terrible ordeal: the hard-labour women, she recalled, had to do all the prison laundry, boot-repairing and oakum picking; the grave of a woman recently hanged, who had gone to her death screaming and kicking, was clearly visible as they were marched for exercise. From this world, time and again, Mrs Meyrick would return to hobnob with the leading society figures of the day. Then, when Jix, armed with DORA – the repressive wartime Defence of the Realm Act, which remained in force – pounced the next time, back she would go to jail. But she, perhaps, had the last laugh. She stares out of photographs boldly and proudly and never showed any shame about her periods of imprisonment. Of her daughters, two – equally direct and striking – married into the peerage, one becoming Lady Kinnoul and the other Lady de Clifford.

Mrs Meyrick's story helps unlock other aspects of post-war society. At one level, Edwardian 'society' was back. The nightclubs' magic required ancient, famous names to be there, mingling with the Americans and the new rich. The presentation of debutantes to the Queen in 'the Season', with parties for the aristocratic youth in grand London houses written up with grovelling attention by the press, was as important to a titled young woman or 'Hon' in 1922 as it had been in 1912. The country-house parties of Waugh's generation were not so different from those of their Edwardian parents. In politics, class continued to matter – in some ways more, as Lloyd George's government was replaced by a Conservative regime. Country-house politics seemed to be back. In 1922 a pro-

Lloyd George Tory MP, Arthur Lee, gave his own country house, Chequers, to the nation for the personal use of prime ministers, in case they did not have one. Grand old names predominated – Cecil, Derby, Devonshire, Balfour, Curzon. Even the rebels tended to be titled. The Irish revolutionary heroine Constance Gore-Booth, Countess Markiewicz, was of aristocratic stock and related to families such as the Westminsters, Zetlands and Scarboroughs. The socialists were supported by aristocratic renegades like Lord Strabogli, Lord Parmoor and Stafford Cripps. The imperial state seemed to require an endless supply of aristocratic proconsuls, while any respectable public company had a baronet or two on the notepaper. It was the great age of London's gentlemen's clubs; but not only London – every big city had its exclusive clubs. The novelists kept the notion of the grandees alive to the general middle-class reader. There was Waugh and Wodehouse, Brideshead and Blandings; but Compton Mackenzie had his ancient Highland lairds, barely touched by time, and the new fad for crime novels required murderous butlers as well as the 'big house' up the hill from the village. It is all a very long way from the devastation wreaked on the aristocrats of Russia, never mind the landed gentry of Germany or France.

Yet the fact that Mrs Meyrick could marry two daughters into the aristocracy shows how thin the veneer of high-born life had become. In the nightclubs, the titled youngsters were fawning on stars who had blown in from Hollywood and rich, talented outsiders, as much as the other way round. Agricultural depression would swiftly return to force a mass sell-off of estates and the destruction of many country houses. The London Season might continue, but many of its venues were going. The world of Galsworthy's Forsytes, in their huge Mayfair palaces, was giving way to the London of hotels and blocks of flats. In the first year after the war, the Cecils' grand house in Arlington Street was sold, as were Devonshire House and Lord Dartmouth's Mayfair mansion. No axes swung over the aristocrats, but the demolition balls were swinging through their homes. Dorchester House, Lansdowne House, Chesterfield House, Sunderland House and Brooke House would all go. In their place came entertainment venues and apartments: Mrs Meyrick's nightclubs were catering for a new urban scene which was moving from private ballrooms and dining rooms to public spaces, open to anyone with enough cash and a clean shirt front. The leaders of Edwardian high society were clear that 'society' as they had understood it before the war, with its strict codes, interconnected family circles and prestige, had at last gone, smashed by war and tax. The pre-war Liberals had begun to mine through its ancient privilege and it was now less a grand edifice than a sponge, full of holes into which democratic culture was seeping. We only speak about Brideshead, after all, because a suburban publisher's son got himself invited to very posh parties.

The war had shaken up the old order but had failed to impose anything else. 'Jix' represented a strong instinct for a return to Victorian values, or at least to an imaginary less turbulent pre-war England, where the bishops were taken seriously and the hangman's work was never done. But he was also much mocked, even by other ministers. He seems to have known that the spirit of the times was against him, or at least to have enough of a sense of humour to collect the numerous cartoons satirizing him. The truth was that the kind of authority he represented, Crown and State, had diminished. It had not collapsed, as in Russia or Germany. The older, more conservative sections of the country took it seriously. Church-going remained strong. Organizations such as the Scouts, the Boys Brigade and now the British Legion were at their zenith. But much of the rest of the country simply ignored the old authorities and went their own way. The pre-war question – how then shall we live? – came back with extra force and this time with a more personal edge. Mrs Meyrick, the entrepreneur of fun, deserves to be remembered as a truly emblematic figure, as significant in her way as T. S. Eliot or Edward VIII. An age of experiment in politics, drugs, sexual behaviour, art and writing had opened. The age when Westminster really dominated Britain had begun to ebb, just as women finally got the vote. For that, the politicians themselves were mostly to blame.

Sleaze in the Old Style

The years after the Great War offer some of the most dispiriting and third-rate politics in British history. Pudgy nonentities waddle across the stage. It often happens when a Titan falls. In this case the falling

Titan was Lloyd George. He was not yet an old man, just fifty-six at
the time of the Paris peace conference, though his chaotic yellow-
white moustache and untidy hair made him look like something
between a walrus and an elderly folk musician. Keynes, who came
to know him at Paris, called him 'this syren, this goat-footed bard,
this half-human visitor to our age from the hag-ridden magic and
enchanted woods of Celtic antiquity', which was perhaps going it a
bit. His Tory colleagues, with a nod to his propensities, called him
simply the Goat. And his feet were solid clay. In photographs,
surrounded by other leaders in their top hats and frock coats, he
somehow conveys the impression of taking none of it quite seriously.
In person he was as mesmeric as ever, still a good listener while
exercising near-dictatorial powers, his shockingly blue eyes full of
mockery and cheek. He worked hard and played hard. He was
undimmed. Yet politically his games were finally catching up with
him and, twist and turn as he might, he was a doomed leader almost
as soon as the guns had fallen silent.

In modern terms we would call him sleazy. He sold peerages and
knighthoods for cash. This was not new. Political parties have
rewarded their supporters (financial and otherwise) throughout history. Long before Lloyd George was in the position to offer any kind
of patronage, Alfred Harmsworth had turned down a minor title,
explaining 'when I want a peerage, I will buy one, like an honest
man'. Before the Liberal landslide victory of 1906 the Liberal chief
whip, Lord Murray of Elibank, was selling the promise of honours
to raise cash; after the Marconi scandal of 1911, which nearly brought
down Lloyd George, Murray was obliged to flee for a while to
Bogotá in Colombia to evade persistent journalists. Long after
Lloyd George had departed to the wilderness, the exchange of cod-
aristocratic handles and trappings for hard cash continued to be
almost routine at Westminster; it is still occasionally the subject of
angry debate now. What was so outrageous about Lloyd George?
Simply, he was blatant. Lloyd George had always taken a practical
approach. He admired businessmen, self-made people like himself.
Unlike most politicians of the age, he had never had money of his
own, and after he became coalition prime minister he had no
independent party machine of a truly national kind either. So he set
about selling honours to raise funds to keep himself in politics. A

tariff was quickly established – in today's terms it cost about £330,000 to become a knight, and £1.3 million to become a baronet. He was not too particular about whom he charged. And, fatally, he used the services of an old friend and fixer, a clergyman's son, former spy, blackmailer and rogue named Maundy (like the money) Gregory.

Maundy Gregory had been a theatre impresario, but it was his years as a secret agent, collecting dirt on half of powerful London, which gave him his true calling. Westminster has always attracted con artists and fantasists. Today, there is a whole industry which survives by convincing outsiders, mainly companies, that its sleek practitioners have fabulous access to power. Sometimes they do. Maundy Gregory, however, took it to extremes. His opulent offices, at 38 Parliament Street, were in sight of the Commons, had a useful back entrance and a curious system of coloured lights to summon taxis. Gregory employed his own 'messengers' in uniforms with gold crowns in braid on them, looking strikingly like official government messengers. He published a small-circulation, impressive-looking journal called the *Whitehall Gazette* with dull articles, information on appointments and patriotic advertisements which was easily mistaken for an official publication. He mixed and mingled with senior ministers, officials, foreign dignitaries and minor royals to the extent that many people assumed he was in some vague way a senior part of the administration himself. His Whitehall offices became a clearing-house for gossip, kickbacks, influence peddling and bribery. Among his friends he numbered the founder of MI5, the Security Service. His views, as expressed in the *Whitehall Gazette*, were extremely right-wing and anti-Jewish. He lived more or less openly with another man's wife, his mistress Edith Rosse, and there is circumstantial evidence that, bored, he later murdered her. He was emblematic of the estimated 340,000 profiteers who had done well out of the war, while other men were dying, and who emerged in the early twenties as unbearably and mysteriously powerful.

This was the man Lloyd George and his chief whip, Freddy Guest – a cousin of Churchill's – chose to act as the broker in his honours-selling business. Guest confided that he did not himself like to deal with 'grubby little men in brown bowler hats'.[5] Gregory sold anything. He sold OBEs, the more democratic awards created in a public spirited mood during the war, to the extent that they became known not as the Order of the British Empire but as the Order of the Bad Egg – 25,000 were awarded in just four years, from the arrival of Lloyd George as prime minister to his fall in 1922. He sold knighthoods. Some 1,500 of them were awarded in the same period and those in the know called London the city of dreadful knights. He sold peerages and Privy Councillorships, touting them around in an everything-must-go fashion. He sold them to war profiteers, to convicted criminals and to fraudsters. Not surprisingly, the King became increasingly worried and then angry. Lloyd George and Gregory seemed to be mocking the very foundations of sacrifice and honour with which the country comforted itself in the aftermath of war.

The King was not the only one. Here we have to reintroduce another mysterious and charismatic character who has appeared briefly already. We last met Victor Grayson when he had been elected as a socialist in a famous 1907 by-election and was about to succumb to alcoholism, which quickly terminated his parliamentary career. He recovered enough to fight in Flanders and the trenches cured him for a time of his whisky addiction. Back in Britain, wounded, Grayson lost his wife and daughter after a premature birth and tried to rebuild his political career, touring the shipyards and factories making pro-war speeches. He joined the vehemently anti-German and anti-Bolshevik British Workers United League, and here he met Gregory and the jingoistic bully and con man Horatio Bottomley. After the war was over he seemed strangely affluent, tried to return to Parliament and continued to make speeches around Britain defending the cause of returning soldiers.[6] There were stories that he was being spied on by MI5 or Gregory, suspected of being a Bolshevik or Irish Fenian agent. There were also stories that he was in the pay of MI5 or Gregory, or both. Who was Victor Grayson?

Whoever he was, in September 1920, he blew the whistle on Lloyd George and Maundy Gregory in a speech in Liverpool, reminding his audience that the prime minister had offered returning servicemen a land fit for heroes to live in:

And what do they get? A miserable pittance on which to start life anew, the permanent threat of unemployment and never a word of credit. What do they see? The war profiteers with so much money that they pay tens of thousands for a barony. I declare that this sale of honours is a national scandal. It can be traced right down from Number Ten Downing Street to a monocled dandy with offices in Whitehall, who organized the greatest piece of political chicanery this country has known since the days of the Rotten Boroughs. I know this man, and one day I will name him.

A few days later Grayson was beaten up in the Strand. Then, on the night of 28 September 1920, he had been drinking with some New Zealanders when he got a message to go to a hotel in Leicester Square. He assured them he would be back soon. He was spotted later that night by a painter called George Flemwell who was painting a night scene of the Thames near Hampton Court Palace. Flemwell knew Grayson because he had done his portrait and recognized him crossing the river to Ditton Island in a new-fangled electric canoe, clambering onto a jetty and going into a modest bungalow. Grayson was never seen for certain again. To all intents and purposes, he vanished. The bungalow was called Vanity Fair and it belonged to Maundy Gregory.

Was Grayson murdered? Was he merely paid off? There were sporadic claimed sightings of him right up to the fifties, in a London Underground train, in Spain, in a poor district of north London and in New Zealand. One journalist who was sure he had recognized him was shunted to a well-paid and obscure government job by the then prime minister Winston Churchill. There had been persistent rumours from Edwardian times that Grayson was a love-child of the Marlborough family (hence his wealth and self-confidence) and was thus Churchill's secret cousin. The trails seem to have gone cold long ago and this is a mystery unlikely ever to be cleared up. But we know, at least, what became of Maundy Gregory and the sale-of-honours business. Lloyd George carried on blithely. Privately he defended the trade as 'the cleanest way of raising money for a political party' even if it could not be defended in public. In his June 1922 honours list, four out of five nominations for peerages were claimed to be 'unrespectable'. One of them certainly was. A convicted South African fraudster called Robinson had his name published as a new peer. The outrage was such that Freddy Guest had to visit Robinson in his suite at the Savoy Hotel to explain that the deal was now off. Robinson, slightly deaf, thought he was being asked for more money and pulled out his chequebook. King George regarded it as an insult to the monarchy and Lloyd George's speech to the Commons in the ensuing debate was a disaster. Though the final cause of his fall from power was a cack-handed attempt to engineer a foreign-affairs crisis in Turkey, the Tory MPs who withdrew support from the out-of-tricks Welsh Wizard did so mainly because they were disgusted by his sleaze. He had lost his authority. A Royal Commission produced plans for reform, leading to the 1925 Honours (Prevention of Abuses) Act – though as we know today, the title of the legislation was optimistic.

And Gregory? He continued in business, simply transferring his trade and taking more precautions. He was finally trapped in a complicated sting operation run by a leading Tory, J. C. C. Davidson. He tried to charge a former naval officer £10,000 for a knighthood and was convicted under the new act, imprisoned and offered a deal to keep silent. As Davidson later revealed, he was told that if he said nothing about all those in high places who had bought their high places, 'we could bring pressure to bear upon the authorities to let him live in France after his sentence had been served . . . [getting] a quarterly pension'. He was offered £1,000 a year and, haggler to the last, managed to get it doubled. In Davidson's words, 'Maundy Gregory did keep his word . . . and we kept him until the end.' He changed his name and lived a life of apparent respectability in Paris until, when the Germans invaded France again, he was rounded up and sent to Drancy prison camp. He is said to have resisted German attempts to make him turn traitor and died there in 1941.

The Last of the Liberals

In the immediate aftermath of the war, Lloyd George's triumph and Britain's seemed intermingled. The Royal Navy was bigger than any navy had ever been, or has ever been since. Soon, surely, the pound would again dominate the world's trading system, and London once more hum as the capital of capital. For the rest, Lloyd George promised a new Jerusalem. Orgiastic scenes had followed the Armistice, with stories of drunkenness on buses and open copulation on the streets – a national tribute, perhaps, to the Goat – and a short boom followed the mirth. Employment rates, wages and prices all rose as the economy returned to peacetime demands and trade suddenly expanded. The industrial and social controls – on prices, on production, on travel and money – upon which Lloyd George had built his wartime state economy fell away.

Yet Lloyd George had run out of political road. He might have been a radical but his coalition was conservative. His 1918 promise to make Britain 'a fit land for heroes to live in' was contradicted by the surrender of almost every mechanism of government he would have needed for economic transformation. After a near-dictatorship in war, Britain abruptly returned to something close to laissez-faire. The railways were handed back to the railway owners and the coal mines, despite strikes and lock-outs, to their former owners. There were few controls over wages or prices, nor any major programme of social reform as after 1945. A flurry of house building did take place, but resulted in the resignation of the minister responsible when the cost was revealed. By 1923 the shortage of new homes, a gap of more than 800,000, was worse than at the end of the war. Many more workers were insured against short-term unemployment and illness after the extension of the pre-war Lloyd George reforms but there was no talk of a new national health system, or radical reform of education. The school-leaving age was raised, but only to fourteen, and promised new secondary schools for the working classes failed to materialize. Women would not get the same voting rights as men until 1928.

Given that Parliament was dominated by an anti-big-government party, it is hard to see how Lloyd George could ever have made good. He might talk the language of intervention and reconstruction, but he did not have the cash or the votes to make it happen. The war had cost a massive sum, most of it raised by borrowing. The national debt was fourteen times what it had been in 1914. Patriots were urged to help pay this off: Stanley Baldwin, then a relatively unknown MP and financial secretary to the Treasury, spent a fifth of his wealth on buying War Loan bonds and then handing them straight over to the Treasury to be burned. In a letter to *The Times* signed (for his job) 'F.S.T.' he explained what he had done, concluding: 'I give this portion of my estate as a thank-offering in the firm conviction that never again shall we have such a chance of giving our country that form of help which is so vital at the present time.'[7] Strange times: a Treasury minister had taken a personal stand, and taxed himself first and hardest. Barely anyone followed his lead.

Meanwhile, income tax stayed high – 33 per cent for well-off people, compared with 8 per cent before the war – and government spending was slashed, from £2.7 million at the height of the war, to around £1 million in 1920–21. When boom turned to bust that winter there was, therefore, no extra spending to cushion the effect, no make-work programmes or plans for industrial modernization. The recession was dire, described at the time as the worst year for the economy since the industrial revolution. British industry had been out of date before the war and was archaic now, except for a few bright spots in engineering. Around half of all exports had been coal and cotton, and cotton was now being produced by Asians, for Asians. Soon fears of foreign 'dumping' would revive the old argument about tariffs and even traditional free-trade centres such as the Yorkshire woollen industry would be calling for protection. Across Britain, in the old industries, employers reacted by cutting wages, or closing workshops. Modernization would come, but meanwhile the long agony of high unemployment that marked the inter-war years began, with the jobless total soon reaching a million. In 1920, not even Keynes was a Keynesian. As the newly formed Communist Party began to worry ministers, and industrial unrest spread, any thought that Lloyd George was the workers' natural friend was finally and permanently laid to rest. He himself became as much a figure of hatred among trade unionists and radicals as his own one-time aristocratic enemies had been.

Lloyd George quickly found he had limited power overseas, too. Britain might rule the waves, but she was ineffective on dry land. The interventions in Russia to aid 'White' forces against Lenin and Trotsky were utter failures. British troops in their thousands had been sent to shiver at Archangel, Murmansk and with Admiral Kolchak in Siberia. There, with Russian nationalists, Americans, French and Czechs trying despairingly to get home, they were to be pitted against the pitiless. The Red armies commanded the heart and nervous system of Russia; the Whites, using terror as enthusiastically as the Leninists, were hardly a democratic alternative; and the entire intervention would succeed only in confirming everything the Bolsheviks thought about the capitalist West. Churchill in the War Office had been the main enthusiast for a new war against the Bolsheviks, 'a Russia of armed hordes smiting not only with bayonet and cannon but accompanied and preceded by swarms of typhus-bearing vermin which slew the bodies of men, and political doctrines which destroyed the health and even the soul of nations'. The country was in no mood for this kind of talk. Lloyd George hated it. Churchill's old Westminster critics saw it as another example of his schoolboyish enthusiasm for bloodshed. In his left-leaning constituency of Dundee it went down so well that he was finally defeated by a Prohibitionist candidate. (And it takes something for Dundee to vote teetotal.)

Failure in Russia was not the only sign that Britain would not have things her own way. In the Mediterranean, the Turks under their new nationalist hero Mustapha Kemal ran rings round the British. In India, rising discontent was met with panic and repression. The worst incident of all, the Amritsar massacre in April 1919 when General Dyer ordered troops to fire on an unarmed demonstration and killed 379 people, caused great debate in Britain between those who saw him as a boneheaded killer and those who thought he was a great imperial hero. It would lead to Gandhi's campaigns of civil disobedience and the beginning of the end of the Indian Empire. This would be a long ending, delayed for many years by Churchill and other nostalgists, but the rot was apparent soon after the Great War ended. We have despaired already at the ignorant treachery of British policy in the Middle East, and observed how the German fleet water-cocked a snook in Scapa Flow. But the most serious evidence of Britain's waning ability to control the world around her came, almost inevitably, from Ireland.

It is rare for a country to take part in a general election and then ignore the parliament for which it was designed, but that is what happened in southern Ireland when Sinn Fein swept to victory in 1918 and formed the independent Dáil, boycotting Westminster. The blood of the Easter Rising leaders had fertilized revolt just as Pearse had dreamed before his execution. The Dáil declared the Republic, chose de Valera as its president, set up its own courts,

raised taxes and spent money just as if it was the legal parliament
of an independent state. This was, to put it lightly, a poser for
Westminster. Had things stopped there it is fascinating to speculate on what Lloyd George would have done; Britain was hardly
in the mood to fight a further war. There might have been a peaceful deal. But quickly the old Irish Volunteers were revived by
Michael Collins, as the Irish Republican Army. Armed with money
and guns from America and inside information from the British
administration, Collins and several thousand followers began their
own small war of ambushes and murders, targeting British troops,
police and anyone thought to be a collaborator. It was a classic
guerrilla operation, and very hard for a traditional army to deal
with. As the violence spread, Britain responded by outlawing the
Dáil and Sinn Fein and, before long, allowing the use of 'Black and
Tan' auxiliaries, mostly demobilized soldiers, to go to Ireland and
use IRA-style tactics on the population.

It was a bitter, brutal little war characterized by assassinations
and cold-blooded executions on both sides. A crowd watching
football at Dublin's Croke Park were fired at by armoured cars
sent onto the pitch, and a dozen killed – a British reprisal for the
killing of fourteen British officers earlier. As the violence worsened
and criticism grew at home, Lloyd George was told by the army
commanders that he should either pull out or go 'all out', waging
full-scale war, which would mean 100,000 men, blockhouses, blocked
roads and all the paraphernalia of full-scale repression. It sounded
like a greener version of the campaign against the Boers twenty years
earlier, and was not appealing. Asquith had already said that British
actions in Ireland rivalled 'the blackest annals of the lowest despot-
isms in Europe'. By now Lloyd George's original idea, of an Ireland
split between two home-rule parliaments connected by an Irish
Council and swearing ultimate loyalty to the Crown, was hopelessly
out of date. The relevant act had passed through Westminster,
however, and the Northern Irish Parliament was opened at Belfast
City Hall in June 1921 by King George V, who seems to have agreed
with Asquith about the bloody repression. The King had been advised
not to go because of the danger of assassination but insisted, and
made an eloquent appeal for all Irishmen 'to pause, to stretch out
the hand of forbearance and conciliation, to forgive and forget and

join in making for the land which they love a new era of peace, contentment and goodwill'. This was received by de Valera in Dublin as an olive branch, and plans began to send Michael Collins over to London to negotiate a peace treaty. The historian A. J. P. Taylor called King George's action 'perhaps the greatest service performed by a British monarch in modern times'.

The talks between the guerrilla leader and the cabinet ministers – prefiguring many later incidents when politicians ate their words about not negotiating with 'terrorists' – lasted from October to December 1921. They produced a compromise deal. Ireland would have dominion status within the Empire, on the same footing as Canada, governing itself. The six northern counties could opt to stay as part of the UK. Collins believed this was the start of a process which would lead inevitably to full independence for the Irish Free State; but he knew enough about the dark passions roused to predict that in signing the treaty, 'I have signed my death warrant.' Whether or not the wily de Valera had sent his rival over in order to destroy his republican credibility, Collins was quite right. The Dáil backed the treaty by seven votes, but the IRA leader was widely denounced as a traitor, the IRA itself split and a vicious civil war began – nastier, almost unbelievably, than the earlier fight against the British. The pro-Treaty and anti-Treaty factions slogged it out for nearly a year from the spring of 1922. The anti-Treaty IRA had more men but they were under-armed and badly led while Collins and the pro-Treaty forces soon acquired artillery, guns and tanks from the retiring British and were able to hold the main towns. The Four Courts buildings in Dublin were held by the anti-Treaty forces for months, and when finally taken by Collins's men, Ireland's national records were destroyed. So too were many great houses, symbols of the English ascendancy. The final stages of the war were stained by cold-blooded executions of prisoners. These included Erskine Childers, the intrepid author of *Riddle of the Sands*. He had been given a handgun for his own protection by Michael Collins, a friend to whom he was now opposed. In an early round-up by Collins's soldiers it was ordered that all who were found with guns should be shot. Childers's revolver was discovered and, despite its origin, a debate about whether he could be spared ended in the decision that there should be no special cases. Childers agreed that this was fair, and shook hands with the firing squad before they killed him. Collins himself was ambushed and gunned down on a quiet country road in County Cork in August 1922, one of around 4,000 who died.

For Britain, the lesson of the Irish revolt and war was simply that no empire can hold peoples down unless it is prepared to be ruthless and to ignore public opinion. Rightly or wrongly, Collins had suggested the IRA were close to being beaten before George V's intervention, but Britain could only have held Ireland at a very heavy cost, one that this growing democracy was not prepared to pay. India, Egypt and the sub-Saharan African colonies were, of course, much further away but the same would eventually apply to them. Britain did not bestride the world after the first German war in the same way that America did after the second. She had the appearance of world power but could not continue both as a vast imperium and as a democracy. Lloyd George and the many other senior politicians failed to understand that democracy and empire are opposing ideas and cannot live long together. Britain in 1920 was closer to being a democracy than ever before, and had experienced how an interventionist state could shake things up. She was on the way to being modern. But she remained in many ways an inefficient and old-fashioned country, yearning for some kind of Roman imperial past and confused about the future.

As for Lloyd George, his time was now over. He had hugely enjoyed the drama of the world stage which victory had brought him, and he was as full as ever of ruses and wheezes. But though he was Everything, he was also Nobody: he had no real national party to lead, and no agenda that would enthuse the Conservative MPs he didn't quite lead. When, in October 1922, the Tory backbenchers met at the Carlton Club and decided they wanted to fight the general election as Conservatives, chucking aside Lloyd George and the coalition, he could give them no reply. The meeting cast a long shadow: even today the Tory backbenchers' organization is called 'the 1922 committee', or just 'the twenty-two'. It was an extraordinary moment, when the ordinary MPs of a party founded on deference and order rose up against their grandees, Austen Chamberlain, F. E. Smith and the rest. Leading the revolt were Bonar Law, who had been outside government and was already ill, and Baldwin. Having burned some of his fortune, he had taken a further bold step by telling the rest of the Unionists in government he would not under any circumstances continue to serve under the Goat. Now, his speech was devastatingly simple. He merely pointed out that Lloyd George was 'a dynamic force . . . A dynamic force is a very terrible thing.' This one had smashed the Liberal Party to pieces and would smash the Tories to pieces too. By 185 votes to 88 they decided to ditch Lloyd George and return to independent Toryism. It was an act of defiance unmatched until the 'peasants' revolt' which installed Margaret Thatcher. The grandees were offended and sulked, though Lord Curzon came round soon enough.

The election which followed saw a slaughter of Lloyd George's supporters. He survived, almost alone of the leading National Liberals, left in very much the same position of humiliated impotence as Asquith had been a few years earlier. Time brings in its revenges. Lloyd George would continue to speak, write and plot, trying to answer his military critics in voluminous war memoirs, and would later propose a massive programme of state works and Keynesian spending to beat the Great Depression – a democratic version of the economics of the great dictators (and of Roosevelt's concurrent New Deal). He quickly made a kind of peace with Asquith and later became leader again of a more or less united Liberal Party, giving the larger Labour Party a few nasty shocks before withering. Then, with the formation of the National Government, he was once again in the wilderness. In his worst misjudgement of all he would go to fawn on Hitler, calling him, bizarrely, 'the George Washington of Germany'. He recanted and in the early stages of the Second World War helped destroy Chamberlain in the Commons, making way for Churchill's return. But once the war was fully engaged, he became defeatist. Had Hitler successfully invaded Britain, it is horribly possible that Lloyd George would have been used as our Pétain. He had been a great radical and a great wartime prime minister but he had smashed his party and never again found a way to count. A dynamic force is indeed a very terrible thing.

Britain would be spared another such force for years to come. After Bonar Law took over as Tory leader and then prime minister, winning a massive majority in 1922, he ran a brief and unmemorable administration. His admirers, notably Beaverbrook, had assumed he would bring in protection, or 'imperial preference', finally ushering in the paradise Joseph Chamberlain had conjured up twenty years earlier. But by now he was a caricature of his former self, and even his former self had never been inspiring. He was pallid, nervous, indecisive, tobacco-scented and increasingly frail. His voice disappeared. Baldwin had to sit beside him in the Commons and speak for him. Bonar Law was sent on a holiday to recuperate in the Mediterranean – it is a safe rule of thumb that all British politicians of the period are to be found in the South of France almost as often as they are in London. There he deteriorated further. The same doctor who had told him ten days earlier he just needed a rest was summoned to Paris, where he noticed that poor Bonar Law was suffering from inoperable throat cancer and would be dead within a few months. Bonar Law did not concern himself with who his successor should be. King George V, having intervened in Ireland, would now be called upon to intervene again.

The scene now shifts to Montacute House in Somerset, a honey-coloured gem of Elizabethan architecture. Best known today as the setting for one of the films of Jane Austen's *Pride and Prejudice*, it was one of the first grand houses bought and saved by the National Trust after it had been on sale 'for scrap'. In 1923 it was being rented by Lord Curzon, the insufferable grandee who had been making a good fist as foreign secretary and who had been writing little notes to Bonar Law expressing the hope that he was not about to have to leave public life, though if he was . . . well, Curzon was clear who must succeed him. In a cruel but amusing sequence of scenes we see Curzon placidly strolling through his garden waiting for the summons from the King. We see the arrival of the boy with the telegram – for Curzon was too grand to have a telephone – explaining that the King's private secretary Lord Stamfordham would visit him at Carlton House Terrace, Curzon's London home, the following day. We follow Lord Curzon and his wife on the train to Paddington, deciding not to live in Downing Street, discussing the new shape of his cabinet, and even getting down to the appointment of bishops. We wait with His Lordship at Carlton House Terrace, a little uneasily as the message comes from Buckingham Palace that Stamfordham will arrive later in the afternoon. Then we have the horrible denouement as the courtier arrives to explain that, er, actually it is not Lord Curzon whom the King is asking to be his first minister but (as Curzon put it) that 'man of the utmost insignificance' Stanley Baldwin.

Curzon, in his devastation, begged Stamfordham to get the King to think again but in fact Baldwin had already kissed hands. Various go-betweens have been blamed for telling George V that Baldwin was more favoured by Bonar Law than he really was. But, given that Baldwin had been Bonar Law's voice while Curzon had been openly suggesting he replace him, it seems unlikely that Curzon was ever the favourite. Though he was clever and well versed in foreign affairs, he was in the House of Lords and he was famously arrogant. In one of the memos sent to the King, George was asked to contemplate the idea of a delegation of miners' leaders, or dock workers, meeting Curzon. If that was enough to settle the King's mind, one can only say it was evidence of the same common sense he had shown in Belfast. So Britain got the leader who would dominate the inter-war years, an apparently stolid and thoroughly decent squire-like man who was, in fact, an ironmaster's son from Worcestershire. He cultivated the image of a bucolic philosopher, never surprised and rarely roused. Yet he was a nervy creature, really, a man whose eyes darted, whose face twitched, who cracked his finger joints and who was easily exhausted. He had been flogged for writing pornography at Harrow and his family included lush Victorian artists, as well as his cousin Kipling. He was no Lloyd George. But he was more interesting than he pretended.

Interlude at Garsington

Baldwin's Britain was a country where people went hungry. There were deep cracks in the pavements through which anyone could fall. Offend the codes of society and the punishment could be severe. It is as well to remember this when thinking about the great artistic revolutionaries who lit up British life after the Great War. Though he is unfashionable just now, David Herbert Lawrence, a child of the Nottinghamshire coalfields, was among the most significant. He was a seer who changed the country. Today's sexualized culture, even if it has become horribly commercialized and degraded in ways Lawrence would loathe, owes a lot to the frank gaze of the miner's son.

Without the education reforms of 1870 and then far-sighted scholar-
ships from Nottingham County Council, Lawrence would never
have escaped the life of a coal miner. Like many Edwardian men he
was sexually uneducated – at around the age of twenty he did not
believe women had pubic hair, for instance. What changed his life
was a chance meeting in March 1912 with a thirty-three-year-old
German, aristocratic Frieda Weekley of the von Richthofen family.
She had three children aged between twelve and eight and a highly
respectable extended family – a 'position', in other words.

For him it was a consummation of sexual joy beyond anything
he had experienced, and which lit up his writing. For her it was a
lifelong love affair, if a very difficult and often angry one. But it was
also a catastrophe. She barely saw her scandalized German family
again and her husband had no problem gaining custody of the
children. She was reduced to hanging round her son's west-London
school to try to catch a glimpse, and on one occasion breaking into
the children's nursery. The children were entirely against her and
she never saw them again until they were adult. As for Lawrence,
the suppression of his novel *The Rainbow* in 1915 torpedoed his
literary career. Too sickly to fight, he and Frieda took refuge in a
remote cottage in Cornwall. But her German identity stirred up local
feeling against them and when the submarine attacks and Flanders
slaughters of 1917 arrived, the coincidence of a German woman, a
bearded oddity and a house near the coast was too much. They were
banned from Cornwall or any coastal area under the Defence of the
Realm Act. Back in London, they were tracked by the police, spied
on and had their letters opened. After the war, the pair of them fled
abroad, to Italy, Sicily, Australia and New Mexico, not properly
returning to Britain until 1925.

Yet wherever he was, Lawrence was conducting a dialogue with
his homeland. He wrote about leaving England in 1919 and looking
back from the Channel steamer at a land which 'seemed to repudiate
the sunshine, to remain unilluminated, long and ash-grey and dead,
with streaks of snow like cerements'.[8] What might light the old land
up again? Lawrence insisted that a true revolution would have to
come from inside people's hearts, not through any of the fashionable
political nostrums. He was one of many, including the novelist John
Cowper Powys and the painter Stanley Spencer, mixing mystical

idealism and a frank interest in sex as they dreamed of mankind remade. They wanted to go back to basic, sensual realities, throwing aside the clothing of decorous post-Victorian society, and emerge afresh, feeling, sniffing, tasting, loving. It was a time when intellectuals gathered together to plot better futures, to think themselves into an alternative England, a green England, a radical escape from the scarred and industrial and half-broken country around them . . . and had the great good luck to be offered spectacularly pleasant places in which to do their plotting.

Nowhere more so than at Garsington Manor in Oxfordshire, home of the amazing Ottoline Morrell and a small paradise, variously compared to the set of a Mozart opera, a scene in a Shakespearean fantasy, an Italian villa or a painting by Watteau. Ottoline and her husband Philip had built a garden filled with flowers, ponds, peacocks and statues. The house was decorated with paintings by the best artists of the age, and a glittering scatter of beautiful pieces of furniture and ornamentation. Ottoline, clever and well born, was one of the first generation of women to get a higher education. Enraptured by her romantic ancestors, she took to draping herself in silks and dresses copied from Velázquez and Van Dyck. Nearly six feet tall, with cascades of red-gold hair and turquoise eyes, she had the long bony face of a Cavalier officer and was, inevitably, much admired by Asquith.[9] At Garsington she created a warm haven for poets, artists, philosophers and novelists. Lawrence, Virginia Woolf, Vanessa Bell, Augustus John, Mark Gertler, Carrington, T. S. Eliot, E. M. Forster, Aldous Huxley, Jacob Epstein, Stanley Spencer, Siegfried Sassoon, Wyndham Lewis, Yeats and her lover Bertrand Russell were just some of the guests. There they were rested and fed while they talked and worked. Lawrence and she were mutually mesmerized, walking for days in the Oxfordshire lanes, talking of love and art; for a while the radical working-class writer and the aristocratic world could go literally hand in hand.

In return for this, Ottoline has been remembered as a freak, an intimidating, yet silly woman, mocked in hundreds of letters and many books. D. H. Lawrence betrayed her in *Women in Love*, portraying her as the 'impressive but macabre' Hermione Roddice, remarkable but 'repulsive'. Virginia Woolf was more ambiguous. She genuinely loved and revelled in her trips to Garsington, her diary recalling all those clever 'people strewn about in a sealingwax coloured room'. Yet the index to the same diaries gives some indication of her feelings about Ottoline herself: 'old, languid, weary ... rebuffed ... will be enraged ... bitter ... defiling talk with ... despicableness of ... and ulterior motives'. Ottoline suspected that she was not loved as she had hoped but never quite knew the true venom of those she offered hospitality to. The old landed classes were failing and the new intellectuals rising, and the collision was not always a pretty sight. Yet without Ottoline and Garsington the story of English radical culture between the wars would have been different. She not only bought work from, fed, sheltered and sustained conscientious objectors and poor artists, but gave people from different backgrounds a place to meet and exchange ideas. She was not an artist or a painter, but Garsington made her a player in the world of radical chic.

Red Clydeside

There were worse worlds for revolutionaries, and more serious revolutionaries too. In the final days of a freezing November in 1923 in a grimy street in Pollockshaws, just outside Glasgow, a former schoolmaster gave his only overcoat to a destitute immigrant from Barbados. Soon afterwards, aged just forty-four, the teacher himself died from cold and hunger. More than 10,000 people marched behind his coffin. A stocky, self-certain Marxist agitator, John Maclean was reputedly described by Lloyd George as the most dangerous man in Britain. He had certainly been discussed by the cabinet and hailed across Russia. In Britain he is mostly forgotten, but his face was once on a Russian postage stamp. Lenin had appointed him the Soviet Union's consul in Glasgow and he had been made the honorary president of the Petrograd Soviet. From a fiercely religious Presbyterian family of Highlanders, seditious, openly hostile to the war against Germany and repeatedly imprisoned for his speeches, Maclean was the most charismatic revolutionary of the time. The important thing, however, is that he and his comrades were completely unsuccessful.

It had not always seemed that way. The war had meant heavy

demands on Clydeside ship workers. Housing was short, rents went up, hours were increased and food prices rose. Maclean and other socialists had their first big victory in November 1915 when a rent strike by tenants refusing to pay more for their foul tenement flats had landed up in the Glasgow courts. Thousands joined them to show their support, including munitions workers. Maclean called on the government to freeze rents for the rest of the war, or face a general strike: the Rent Restrictions Act which followed seemed like a climb-down. He went on making seditious speeches and was repeatedly arrested and finally imprisoned, leading to a nervous breakdown. Let out in 1917 because of his poor health, he was soon back setting up Marxist education classes in Glasgow. By May 1918 Maclean was on trial again, declaring to the judge: 'I come here not as the accused but as the accuser of capitalism, dripping with blood from head to foot.' He was duly sentenced to five years in prison, where he went on hunger strike and was finally released early when the war ended on 11 November. He then stood in the 1918 election but at a time of patriotic fervour was easily defeated.

Yet the aftermath of the war produced a more excited mood in the shipyards and the surrounding slums than before. Clyde workers wanted a shorter week, to spread the work around. The old worries about higher rents and vile housing were back with a vengeance. This, surely, was the revolutionaries' moment. The months ahead would bring the most dramatic confrontation in Glasgow's political history. But Maclean and other Marxists were barely involved. They squabbled about which parties should be formed to carry the communist flag, who should lead them and what could be done to help Russia. Less ideological men led the great 'forty hours strike' of January 1919. Using mass pickets, they soon had 70,000 men out and seemed threatening enough to the authorities. One, Manny Shinwell, promised to shut off Glasgow's power stations and close down the trams. Using groups of up to 10,000 pickets at a time, many of them recently demobilized soldiers, he intended 'to stop every tramcar, shut off every light, and generally paralyse the business of the city'. Ministers decided Britain was facing 'a Bolshevist uprising'. By the time the leaders of the strike had gathered in the city's main square, George Square, on Friday 31 January, to hear the government's response, six tanks and a hundred motor lorries of troops had been sent north from England. Believing that the crowd of around 25,000 people was about to stop the trams, the police baton-charged, driving the protestors up a steep side-street, where they came under a hail of lemonade bottles. The Riot Act was read, ringleaders were arrested, many heads were broken and running battles continued across the city for the rest of the day. The *Glasgow Herald* declared 'the battle of George Square' to have been 'the first step towards that squalid terrorism which the world now describes as Bolshevism'.

Cabinet fears about a communist revolution were equally hysterical, fed by alarmist tittle-tattle from Scotland Yard's director of intelligence, Sir Basil Thompson. On 2 February 1920 one cabinet observer reported that Churchill and Sir Henry Wilson, head of the Imperial General Staff (who would later be assassinated by the IRA), were painting 'a very lurid picture of the country's defenceless position' to the rest of the cabinet. Lloyd George turned to Sir Hugh Trenchard, in charge of the RAF, and asked: ' "How many airmen are there available for [repressing] the revolution?" Trenchard replied that there were 20,000 mechanics and 2,000 pilots but only 100 machines which could be kept going in the air . . . The pilots had no weapons for ground fighting. The PM presumed they could use machine guns and drop bombs.' It is a sobering thought that a British cabinet was seriously discussing plans to strafe the working classes not much more than a year after the Great War ended. By April 1921, when the miners were striking against wage cuts, the cabinet was debating how many battalions were available to fight the revolution. The answer was eighteen, but seven of them were Irish 'and we were not sure of their temper'. There was much discussion about whether troops should be brought back from Silesia, where they were enforcing the peace terms in Germany, and Egypt and Malta. Yeomanry were to be recalled. Troops should even be brought back from Ireland, herself on the edge of revolution. 'Yes', said Lloyd George, according to the hurried notes – 'if bigger trouble here . . . let Sinn Fein go'. How many battalions would be needed to hold London? F. E. Smith declared the cabinet 'ought not to be shot without a fight, anyway'. Such talk seems insane now. But with a slump, high unemployment, bad housing and some dedicated revolutionary leaders, it seemed sensible back then. There were numerous references to a 'revolutionary mood' sweeping the country. So why did no revolution come?

Unlike Russia, Britain had been victorious. There was still a strongly patriotic mood in the country, and its government was not blindly belligerent. Lloyd George's War Cabinet official Thomas Jones was advising a programme of cutting working hours, introducing minimum wage deals for key industries and energetic house building by city authorities, as 'the best antidote' to revolution. The government would fall far short of this, but in 1919 Lloyd George still had just enough of a radical reputation, plus some solid advances on health insurance, for his promises to be heard. The trade unions were in the hands of moderate and conservative leaders, except for a few areas where local radicals had taken charge – Clydeside being the best example. The revolutionaries were so busy fighting one another they had little energy left for any uprising. Though the Communist Party of Great Britain was finally formed in 1920, many comrades, including Maclean, had been struggling to set up other parties. The left's famous enthusiasm for splits and sects began from the very start. Finally, the Labour Party was on a rising curve, absorbing former revolutionaries as it went. Between 1918 and 1922 there was a sharp rise in the Labour vote, particularly in Glasgow, Sheffield and Manchester. Of the rebel leaders of 'Red Clydeside', Shinwell would end up as secretary of state for war, John Wheatley would become health minister in the first Labour government, responsible for a useful housing programme, Jimmy Maxton became an MP for the Independent Labour Party, much admired by Winston Churchill. William Gallacher remained a communist, though as MP for West Fife until 1950 he was never much threat to the British state. And John Maclean, with his Christlike readiness to give away his only coat, was on the way to romantic martyrdom as a postage stamp.

Will the Bloody Duck Swim? Churchill, Tories and Gold

If there is one man who symbolizes British capitalism in these years, it is the theatrical, bearded guru of high finance, Sir Montagu

Norman, whose governorship of the Bank of England ran from 1920 to 1944. Norman looked more like a raffish painter than a banker. He liked to wear a cloak, travel incognito and, interested in spiritualism, apparently told a colleague he could walk through walls. Superbly connected across the old City of families of merchant bankers and Old Etonian stockbrokers, Norman awed Britain's politicians (whom he detested). Described by other bankers as being charming, feminine, vain, unstable and prone to nervous breakdowns, Norman was, however, a steely and dominant figure. For much of this period he kept the Treasury at arm's length and boasted to parliamentarians who had the cheek to question his judgement that he operated by instinct, not facts. He matters above all because he was a devoted believer in the gold standard, the pre-war financial system. The long boom in world trade from the 1880s onwards had been underpinned by this system, led by Britain, with the United States (plus most European countries, Japan, and the British possessions) an enthusiastic member. By fixing the price of each currency to a set amount of gold, which was then freely tradeable, it made trade easier and allowed real price changes to be exported and imported. But it left little hiding room for governments whose economies were in trouble.

Gold-standard nations whose governments spent too much would be forced to raise interest rates, or see investors sell their currencies for gold. So the most successful countries accumulated the most gold. The shock of the Great War had destroyed the gold standard, and after it the United States, surging economically, had about 40 per cent of the world's stock of gold. Britain, having had to borrow huge sums to pay for the war, was in a very weak position. But Norman, like most City opinion, was determined that the pound should return to the gold standard, thus re-establishing Britain and her Bank as standing at the heart of the international capitalist system. For him it was a matter of morality, deterring inflation, as well as common sense and 'fidelity'. As we shall see, 'going back to gold' was one of the greatest controversies of the age and is generally reckoned now to have been economically catastrophic. It would entangle Churchill and damage his reputation permanently. This, however, was not the end of the Norman conquest, for the Bank also successfully championed a view of the economy that paid scant attention to British manufacturing. Critics complained that the City failed to back the country, one merchant banker finding himself 'constantly struck by the peculiar lack of contact between the chief financial centre of the world and the industry of its own country'.[10] This, it was argued, was why Germany was leaping ahead with new industrial techniques and why America's steel industries were so advanced, compared to the creaking British plants. So the City would have a double effect on Britain, pressing for a financial straitjacket the country was too weak to wear comfortably, and failing to provide the capital her ageing industries needed. When the economic storm finally arrived, Montagu Norman would find himself in the middle of it; neither his famous cloak nor his alleged propensity for walking through walls would provide any hiding place.

By the early 1920s in politics, the old battle line between protectionist Tories and free-trade Liberals was being replaced. Now it was pro-capitalist Conservatives against socialists. This would squeeze the Liberals into near oblivion. Before it did, Britain went through volatile three-party elections. After capitalizing on his war leadership in 1918 Lloyd George had been hammered in 1922. When Stanley Baldwin became Conservative prime minister, replacing the dying Bonar Law, he decided to call another general election for late 1923. Baldwin was trying to resurrect the old politics of imperial protection, partly because he had heard a rumour that Lloyd George was planning to do the same and, in Baldwin's words, he would 'dish the Goat'. Even traditionally strong industries such as the woollen manufacturers were calling for help, but the British public does not like unnecessary elections. So Baldwin got dished instead, allowing Labour its first brief chance in power as a minority. Then Baldwin brought Labour down and provoked yet another general election in 1924, which won the Tories a solid five years in power. Two great questions seemed to face the British political world: Could the Labour Party keep itself independent of Russia and of home-grown revolutionaries, to become a normal parliamentary governing force? And could the Conservatives govern properly in the interests of the whole country, rich and poor, in hard times? Baldwin might have been Conservative leader, but nobody would be more important in answering that second question than Winston Spencer Churchill.

An ill Churchill had lost his seat in the parliamentary rout of 1922, and failed again the following year in Leicester. He was still attached to the collapsing Liberal cause, enough so to attack Baldwin with some vigour. But he had a new favourite enemy in socialism. Though genuine, this was also shrewd since it would offer him a way back to the Conservatives, and therefore power. In March 1924 he fought a by-election at Westminster as an 'independent anti-Socialist candidate'. His main theme was Labour's loan for Russia: 'Our bread for the Bolshevist serpent; our aid for the foreigner of every country . . . but for our own daughter states across the oceans . . . only the cold stones of indifference, aversion and neglect.'[11] Backed by a colourful array of political chums, he turned the by-election into a carnival. As he later recalled: 'I began to receive all kinds of support. Dukes, jockeys, prize-fighters, courtiers, actors and business men all developed a keen partisanship. The chorus girls of Daly's theatre sat up all night addressing the envelopes and despatching the election address.' The Tories, suspicious and divided about Churchill, were equally divided about what to do in one of their safest seats. Around twenty-five MPs came out openly for him rather than their own man. In the end their candidate won by just forty-three votes, but Churchill had enjoyed a personal triumph. Later that year he formally rejoined the Tory Party, becoming Conservative MP for Epping in the general election of 1924. As he cheerfully put it, anyone could rat, but it took a special calibre to re-rat.

Yet if Churchill's twenty-year career as a Liberal was finally over, he had not lost his belief in social reform. From now until his great comeback in 1940, his politics were hamstrung. His views on social questions – insurance and the relief of unemployment – were particularly offensive to the very same diehard Tories with whom he most agreed when it came to the Empire and foreign policy. For mainstream Tories he was either too far to the left or too far to the right, an unsettling and flashy carnivore in the middle of the herd. That paradox would be resolved only after the rise of Hitler. Meanwhile, to his utter amazement, the new prime minister made him Chancellor of the Exchequer. Churchill had been mulling over which of the more minor appointments (if any) he would be offered and what he might accept. When Baldwin asked if he would go to the Treasury, 'I should like to have answered, "Will the bloody duck swim?" but as it was a formal and important conversation I replied, "That fulfils my ambition. I still have my father's robe as Chancellor. I shall be proud to serve you in this splendid office." '

As chancellor, Churchill immediately had to confront the ugly truths about British power which were still hidden under the imperial gloss. He desperately wanted to introduce better unemployment insurance and to revive industry by cutting taxes for the middle classes. But the sums did not, and would not, add up – unless he also managed to impose deep cuts on military spending, particularly the Royal Navy. Churchill has received a severe kicking from some historians in recent years over his own 'appeasement years' when he was urging the abandonment or delay of major warship and military-base programmes which might have avoided later military humiliations such as the fall of Singapore to the Japanese. As chancellor he upheld a 1919 principle that military spending should be based on the assumption that no major conflict would occur for ten years. This ten-year rule, rolled on by later chancellors, is one reason Britain was so badly militarily prepared in 1940. Churchill, clearly no pacifist, thought that air power and new scientific weapons, still uninvented, would transform warfare. His mind was mostly elsewhere. He was talking about appeasement – but, in his phrase, 'the appeasement of class bitterness'. Pensions for widows and orphans; earlier old-age pensions; health insurance – those were what he wanted much of the military savings to finance. Given that he believed socialism was the real enemy, that was hardly a foolish agenda.

So why has Churchill been remembered as a hard-faced anti-Labour ranter? His rhetoric against all socialism was flaming and inflammatory. But nothing did his reputation more harm in domestic politics than his decision as chancellor to return Britain in 1925 to the gold standard, with sterling valued at the pre-war rate to the US dollar. Not only Norman and the City grandees but almost all serious opinion-formers in Britain in 1925 supported this as a return to traditional, well-tried disciplines and to a clear, predictable system of world trade. As Churchill put it, Britain would be less shackling herself to gold than shackling herself to reality. The question was how much trouble the British economy was in; and therefore how painful the shackles would be. During the war New York had become the rising centre of world capitalism. Going back at the old rate would be a defiant assertion of British willpower and importance, but it would also make British goods more expensive and further damage the creaking, now old-fashioned heavy industries on which so much employment depended. What had been comfortable in 1880 would not be in 1930.

Churchill intuitively knew it. He challenged his Treasury advisers in long, detailed letters. On the one hand, he pointed out, there was a shortage of goods for British consumers, on the other hand a shortage of jobs: 'the community lacks goods and a million and a quarter people lack work'. Proper economics, surely, would bring both into alignment. Would not going back on gold sharply raise unemployment? As he put it, 'I would rather see Finance less proud and Industry more content.' He did more. He brought together the best two anti-gold-standard thinkers, the radical young economist John Maynard Keynes and the old former Liberal chancellor Reginald McKenna, along with the pro-gold-standard Treasury men, and got them to argue it out over dinner. At the end McKenna, recognizing the huge political pressure on Churchill, gave in and told him there was no escape and that he would have to go back, adding, 'but it will be hell'.

It was hell; or at least, some kind of economic purgatory followed. Keynes turned the attack back with a famous pamphlet later that year, 'The Economic Consequences of Mr Churchill'. But Keynes was a rare voice then. Britain was forced off the gold standard again in the economic crisis of 1931 and the experiment was blamed for causing slump and misery. It increased his reputation as a ruth-less anti-worker Tory. But at the time Churchill had gone as far in challenging the economic orthodoxy as any chancellor was likely to have done; and it is by no means clear that the gold standard was as decisive as was claimed. Britain had low-investment, poorly managed heavy industries, increasingly challenged by newly industrialized and larger nations. She was spending a disproportionate amount of money defending a vast empire that brought her little economic benefit. Those were fundamental problems, as much as a brief and ill-starred attempt to resurrect a world economic system which had greatly enriched the pre-war world but which ought to have been left for dead in Flanders.

Dog Stars, Tramps and Superheroes

In the early years of British cinema films were shown in travelling booths at fairgrounds, as brief interludes in variety performances and at the notorious 'penny gaffs' where a dozen or twenty people stood in a dark, smoky shack, sometimes seizing the chance of a squeeze and a snog. The country's first public film-show had probably been at the Indian Exhibition of 1895. By the time Queen Victoria died there were many short, single-shot films – mostly showing national ceremonies, sporting events and parades. For the Edwardians they were novelties, yet the national character quickly asserted itself. Cecil Hepworth, one of the great pioneers, based himself at Walton-on-Thames and scored a particular hit in 1905 when he introduced the world to its first named star of the screen, Blair. Being Britain, the film star was a dog, appearing in *Rescued by Rover*. Early films were used in restaurants for 'bioscope teas' and dropped into operatic performances. Rather as it was not clear in the early days of the internet just what it would be used for – a research tool or a kind of library, perhaps? – so the early film-makers were unsure what they were up to. Were films for instruction, education or entertainment? There were films showing the Delhi durbar, and Peak Freans biscuit factory, and mountaineers and coal miners, and the Scottish Highlands, and Blackpool holidaymakers and exotic foreign rulers, as well as schoolgirl high jinks and exciting chases of robbers. But by 1910 the 'penny gaffs' were disappearing and longer films with sentimental stories, funny stories, even classic Shakespeare and Dickens stories were being made.

Before Hollywood was more than orange groves, British film makers were developing comedies, chase sequences, jump-cuts and historical epics.[12] Tragically, of the thousands of films made, only a few hundred survive, preserved by the British Film Institute. There was a movie world before Hollywood, but it is mostly a lost one. Britain's first film-only picture theatre, the Balham Palace, opened in 1907 and the first purpose-built picture house, in Colne, Lancashire, let in customers the following year. They were quickly followed by Olympias, Bijous, Picturedromes and Palaceadiums around the country, initially small but soon growing larger and offering two sittings a night of a mix of long and short films, usually a couple of hours in total. By 1913 music-hall stars like Marie Lloyd, Albert Chevalier and George Robey were appearing on screen.

A year later, just before the outbreak of war, the British got their first chance to see an even bigger star. He too had emerged from music hall and variety theatre. As a child actor and teenage stage comedian, he had watched Marie Lloyd prepare herself behind the wings at the Tivoli theatre in London's Strand, had endured a hail of orange peel and coins when one of his acts bombed and had tramped the provincial towns of England in a clog-dancing show. His mother had been a 'soubrette', a stage singer. When she finally lost her voice, she was booed off the stage and her young son was pushed on to take her place; he recited a poem, mimicked her cracked singing and was showered with money. His father had been a well-known variety-hall baritone who lived on raw eggs and port wine, deserted his family early on and drank himself to death in his thirties. The boy's early life was so grim it rivals the early years of Charles Dickens. Living in Lambeth with his mother and elder brother, he had often gone hungry. When the family ran completely out of food they had been forced to endure the squalid humiliation of the workhouse; then the two boys had been sent to Hanwell School for Orphans and Destitute Children, a bleak place of whippings and bullying. His mother suffered increasingly distressing bouts of insanity and was taken into lunatic asylums, where she was separated from her younger son while she was given brutal cold-water treatments and long spells in a padded cell. Often her boy had to live on his wits on the streets without any adult supervision or company, sleeping out by braziers and befriending tramps and destitute workmen to beg food.

By astonishing perseverance and luck, he won some child-actor roles and then joined his brother in an unusual troupe of variety artists, the south London 'fun factory' of Fred Karno. And the structure of early Chaplin films – we are talking, of course, about Charlie Chaplin – owes a lot to the hugely popular sketches of Karno's troupes of actors, with slapstick, sentimentality and mime. Karno himself had been a famous acrobat and clown and drove his actors very hard, with frantic rehearsal schedules. If he didn't like a performance he would stand in the wings and blow raspberries.

Vaudeville criss-crossed the Atlantic, and Chaplin was finally spotted by the nascent American film industry during his second tour with a Karno troupe during 1910–12. His first film, *Making a Living*, was released in 1914 and the contract stipulated that he had to appear in three films – every week. In fact, in that year he made a mere thirty-five films. With no idea of the true significance of movies, Chaplin thought they would be just a good way to boost his image in variety. But by this stage even the British were going to films in their millions. By 1914, when *Making a Living* (by no means a masterpiece) was on show across the country, it is reckoned that up to 4,500 cinemas had opened. Some 75,000 people were working in Britain in the new industry, yet the anarchic Chaplin style was not what the fustier British film-makers thought their audiences wanted. Had he stayed behind, Charlie Chaplin would today be a name known only to enthusiasts. Or else, like so many of his age, he would have joined up in 1914 and been killed or maimed during the four years that followed.

And it was the Great War that boosted the film industry. There were films showing the King visiting troops, British soldiers in training, the fleet and military victories in the Middle East, along with some anti-German propaganda films, recruiting films and even a few documentary-style films from the front. This started to make the medium respectable and patriotic: film magazines of the time are full of earnest protestations about the young industry doing its bit. The breakthrough film was made by a plucky young director called Geoffrey Malins, whose 1916 *Battle of the Somme* was made partly on location and showed identifiable regiments – Bedfords, Suffolks, Gordon Highlanders – and dead bodies, wounded men and real fighting. The next year he followed it up with a film showing British tanks advancing. Both probably included faked material shot far from the action, but they astonished audiences at home and delighted both the King and Lloyd George, who urged everyone to see *The Somme*. The newspapers agreed. It was booked in 2,000 venues in the first two months but many people wanted to be distracted and entertained, and recoiled from war films. In Hammersmith, west London, one cinema hall had a poster reading: 'WE ARE NOT SHOWING THE BATTLE OF THE SOMME. THIS IS A PLACE OF AMUSEMENT, NOT A CHAMBER OF HORRORS'.[13]

Britain had lost Chaplin. But there were others, and they do not deserve to be forgotten. George Pearson was one. At about the same time as D. H. Lawrence gave up school teaching to write novels, Pearson, who looked rather like Lawrence, with hooded eyes and a full moustache, gave up teaching to devote himself to writing and making films – a crazy gamble. After working for tiny companies he became head of Gaumont's new British operation and in 1915 was asked to come up with a series of thrillers. He invented a daring adventurer, wreaking revenge on enemies who thought him dead, called Ultus. Played by an Australian actor called Aurele Sydney, described as 'a real he-man type', Ultus became a hugely popular wartime cult. First discovered left to die by a traitorous accomplice in the desert, Ultus the avenger returns to punish the traitor. He has been compared to an early version of Batman or Zorro, the avenger with a conscience. These films were chase-and-mystery plots but made with a subtle touch that was rare in early British cinema and won Pearson admirers ever afterwards. His work at new studios in Shepherd's Bush included experimenting with a more mobile camera, cleverer lighting and more realistic sets – which were needed because Sydney was such a he-man that when he came through a door and closed it either the handle or the door tended to come away in his hand.

Pearson's great post-war discovery was Betty Balfour, probably the most popular home-grown British film actor of the twenties, but he wanted film to do more. Now with his own company, he offered alternative happy and unhappy endings to the same film (*Love, Life and Laughter* of 1923) and tried to show how the war had affected a group of working-class people in the only vaguely plotted *Reveille* of the following year. In his way he was as idealistic as Lawrence, if more sentimental, and dreamed of films liberated from story-lines and built instead 'emotion by emotion'. He made more experimental films, including in 1926 *The Little People*, on the theme of everyone being puppets, pulled by invisible strings, and set among the puppet-eers of Milan. It was a popular failure. By then the 'talkies' were coming and, anyway, people wanted plot. Pearson would continue making films almost all his life, though reduced to shorter and documentary work. Like most of the rest of the industry in Britain, he had failed to realize that the world of film would depend on simple, fast stories and lots of laughs.

By the close of the Great War British film production was mostly scattered round London and the Home Counties, in steel sheds with large windows for lighting and piles of painted stage-set scenery. There was Barker Motion Photography at Ealing, the London Film Company studios at Twickenham, Master Films at Esher, the British and Colonial Kinematograph Company at Walthamstow, Broadwest, also at Walthamstow, Hepworth at Walton-on-Thames, plus the French-owned incomers Pathé and Gaumont. The twenties saw a flurry of mergers, new companies starting and old ones closing, and the industry growing fast. Small cinemas were steadily replaced by much bigger ones, the lavishly decorated dream palaces of cinema's golden age. Art-nouveau 'picture houses' and 'cinematographic theatres' closed and sleek, marbled Gaumont Palaces took their place, with the latest Otis lifts, sweeping staircases and raised seating. The newspapers now took films semi-seriously, and there were the first signs of interest in world cinema – Wells, Keynes, Shaw, Ivor Novello and John Gielgud were among the early members of the Film Society, founded in 1925 to raise its intellectual tone.

But if the war had made film more respectable, it had also starved the British film industry of capital. British films were made for a fraction – between a quarter and a tenth – of what American films cost, and British film actors earned paltry wages by Hollywood standards. Despite this, in the final years of the silent movies, British film-makers produced a slew of gripping, dramatic and highly imaginative films which are only now beginning to be rediscovered. The arrival of Hollywood stars such as Mary Pickford and Tallulah Bankhead caused massive press excitement. Hollywood quickly came to dominate. It was the bigger, brighter, brasher capital of cultural revolution just as surely as Moscow wanted to be the centre of political revolution. British film-makers protested about the endless supply of fast-moving American movies and particularly the Chaplin comedies. Londoner he might have been but now he was a symbol of American domination, the living Coca-Cola bottle of his day. British politicians and imperial prime ministers became increasingly worried that the Empire was being edged out. In 1927 a quota system was introduced: 7.5 per cent of films shown in British and imperial cinemas had to be empire-made, rising to 20 per cent by 1935. It was naked protectionism and it worked, at least in increasing the number of British films made. They included ripping imperial yarns and homely comedies which remained popular. But, swamped by the sheer volume of material from America, British film-making was always on the back foot.

The achievement of British film, particularly before the arrival of talkies in 1929, has been written out of the national story. It is a great pity so few modern Britons have seen or heard of the stars and stories that delighted their ancestors. Yet there is no getting away from the fact that British film culture was a little too deferential and backward looking compared with the surging energy of American film in its heyday. The tyranny of Respectable and Educated Opinion meant too many costume dramas: perhaps the fact that even the great film-maker Michael Balcon chose to call his company 'Gains-borough' says it all. The public wanted fun, cheerful escapism, thrills and chases – they wanted Ultus, and above all Chaplin. There would be some excellent British films to come, notably from a plump young Londoner called Alfred Hitchcock. But in film, as in factory tech-niques, music and celebrity culture, the Americanized world was already emerging from the plains and orange groves.

Anti-Modern

How modern did the British really want to be? To find where the heart lies, look at the home. Modernism was the dominant visual idea of the age, but you do not find it in the suburbs of Britain. Modernism is easy to recognize, harder to define. We know what it looks like – in buildings, it means sharp, harsh lines and angles, lots of white paint, metallic furniture, only the simplest brick decoration. But the spirit behind the buildings is where we need to start, because it influenced how people behaved, how they thought about their bodies, and how they saw the world. In essence, it was a sweep-clean movement. Away with the complication, the pomposity, the class divisions and the gloomy grandeur of the pre-war world – away with the discredited heaviness of the defeated Kaiser's Germany, the refined pleasures of the discredited Czar's Russia and the destroyed Habsburg Empire. In the place of stuffy rooms, heavy clothes and formality, let there be a new world of light, airy buildings, simple fashions – above all, youth and health. Modernism could take strongly political forms. The Italian futurists, celebrating speed and vigour, were early supporters of Mussolini while in Soviet Russia modernist architects and photographers would try to create a new aesthetic, until Stalin, whose tastes were far more traditional, put paid to them. In Holland and Austria modernism was the clean-limbed expression of social democracy. In Germany itself the Weimar Republic had a modernist flavour – the Bauhaus movement, with its stark and simple factories, its mass-produced, airy workers' apartment blocks, suggested a new world. To begin with the Nazis appropriated some of the feel of modernism, from the clean lines of the Volkswagen car and the stark simplicity of the Autobahns, to the Mies van der Rohe plans for vast glass, granite and marble monuments to the new regime. Then, like Stalin, Hitler made plain his preference for stodgy dictator-romanticism, and the modernists had to flee.

Many ended up in Britain, and the look of the country in the late twenties and early thirties was certainly affected by them. Berthold Lubetkin from Georgia had been an early enthusiast for the Russian Revolution; when he arrived in London in 1931 and set up his architectural practice Tecton, he gave the capital the famous Penguin Pool at London Zoo and those radical concrete-and-glass apartments known as Highpoint One and Highpoint Two, then the equally modernist Finsbury Health Centre. One of the other great buildings of the thirties is the De La Warr Seaside Pavilion at Bexhill in Sussex, a bright white and glass combination of theatre, bars, restaurant, café, sun terraces and bandstand that breathes optimism and ozone: it was designed by Erich Mendelsohn, who had fled from the Nazis, and by Serge Chermayeff. Other modernists were home-grown, such as Harry Beck, a young draughtsman working for the signalling department of London Transport, who in 1931 came up with the idea for the Underground map – a simple breakthrough which has been copied around the world and was voted Britain's second-favourite design of the twentieth century (after Concorde). Indeed, London Transport, under the leadership of Frank Pick, a nonconformist and teetotal idealist, became the flag-bearer for modernism in Britain. Stations like Arnos Grove, designed by Charles Holden, are directly influenced by Swedish and Dutch examples. The Scottish calligrapher Edward Johnston provided the clean and distinctive platform logos still used today.

Modernism at its best was meant to make the world brighter, lighter and healthier. Yet it failed to answer some strong instinct in the British – the love of privacy in a crowded island, a quiet suspicion that the past for all its faults might perhaps have been a nicer country. For the truly characteristic buildings of the period were not white or cubist but boxy, cosy, semi-detached bungalows stretched out on the new arterial roads. We know them because they are all around us, these homes with tiled roofs, brick decoration, Hobbit-friendly porches, gently curved front windows, walls or hedges at the front, crazy-paving paths, all the same and all subtly different. Hydrangea homes; homes fit for people who know their place; homes with potting sheds for pottering in. 'Metro-land' was the name invented before the Great War for that chunk of land north of London where the Metropolitan Railway extended and bought thousands of acres of land for speculative building. It became shorthand for the new suburbs everywhere, places connected to city centres but allowing the middle classes gardens, privacy, comparative quietness – not the countryside, but the sound of songbirds.

The most thought-through versions of this dream were the two pioneer garden cities, first Letchworth and then Welwyn. They were the creation of a cluster of idealists, led by an admirer of Ruskin and the back-to-nature reformers of Victorian Britain called Ebenezer Howard. His main job had been the gloomily repetitive one of parliamentary shorthand writer (he was responsible for several innovations in typewriting), but he had dreams of a better way of living, not just for himself but for every town dweller. He thought new towns must be built, with decent spaces between the houses, trees, avenues and the industrial zones far enough away to avoid pollution, while the nearby countryside would be used to provide food. It was, in sum, a vision of sustainable urban living which still seems radical and appropriate in the twenty-first century. Howard's vision was not about pretty housing estates but about a reshaping of how and where we live. With an energetic architect called Raymond Unwin, who had worked with Seebohm Rowntree, Howard's first garden city at

Letchworth began to take shape in 1904. Then, in the closing months of the war, the now-aged Ebenezer spotted a second site at the village of Welwyn, north of London, and raised cash to buy a shooting estate from its debt-laden owner. There, from 1921, Welwyn Garden City began to appear: among its backers was Harmsworth's *Daily Mail*, which had been sponsoring its Ideal Home Exhibition since 1908 and offered to build some cottages free of charge. There was even a Dailymail Village, though it is now dully called Meadow Green.

The garden-city movement did not transform Britain, as Ebenezer Howard, sitting in his parliamentary cubicle, had once hoped. It did influence garden suburbs all over the country, however, and had a big impact on the post-1945 new-town designers. More to the immediate point, Howard and his friends were the transmission system through which ideals about semi-rural or cottagey living were passed from high-minded Victorian dreamers to the rampant speculative builders of the inter-war period who covered this country with semis. Howard's architect follower, Unwin, was a member of the 1917 select committee of MPs which drew up new standards for public housing, or 'cottages' for the outer suburbs: the first wave of homes for heroes that Lloyd George had spoken of. And its recommendations were turned into a pattern book of housing designs in the *Housing Manual* of 1919, by the Ministry of Health. These, in turn, would be borrowed and used by the private speculative builders whose work dominates much of Britain today. The designs came not from architects but from guides almost as simple as those you would need to assemble a model aircraft kit or a complicated set of flat-pack furniture. It was hardly what Ruskin or William Morris would have expected to leave as their heritage.

Immediately after the war, the housing was mostly public, or local authority, under the leadership of Christopher Addison, a Liberal reformer who later joined Labour. But despite the high-flown hopes of the 1919 Addison Act, slum clearance was a great inter-war failure. To start with, there were nothing like enough qualified builders available after the culling of the trenches. It was reckoned that in 1920 only half the bricklayers and plasterers needed in London could be found. Nor was there enough money. Addison himself was sacked when it emerged that his houses would cost twice the original estimate. Despite much campaigning by church leaders and rising journalists such as George Orwell, not nearly enough new homes were built to begin to rid urban working-class Britain of stinking, insanitary and overcrowded Victorian dwellings, generally without such amenities as damp courses. Where politicians were ambitious, as the Clydeside Catholic John Wheatley was during the second Labour government, the constrictions imposed by hard times frustrated them. Apart from a short time immediately after the Great War, private building outstripped public housing easily – by 1939, nine out of ten new-built homes were private, and three-quarters of them were built by speculative building firms.

It was a vast housing boom, only equalled by the boom in high-rises in the late sixties and seventies, producing nearly 4 million new houses. It was based on lax planning laws, cheap land, vigorously aggressive building societies and speculative builders working to simple, repetitive designs. One example of the new housing entrepreneurs was a sixteen-year-old boy who taught himself brick-laying, glazing, woodwork and plumbing so he could erect a pair of houses for his family in Blackpool. Passers-by offered to buy them before the roofs were on. He made a handsome profit and never looked back. In 1921 his uncle came into the business – the boy's name was Frank Taylor; his uncle's Jack Woodrow. Their firm became the giant Taylor Woodrow. All over Britain, rows of so-called Mock Tudor, Brewer's Tudor or Tudorbethan houses that ripple out of almost every major city in Britain were clustered on the arterial roads because land beside the new roads was blighted and cheap. Names such as Taylor Woodrow, Wimpey and Laing were among the firms already producing prefabricated joinery details, a mix-and-match variety of bay windows, half-timbered frontages, gable details and porches, the whole covered with pebbledash, hanging tiles or concrete render to hide sometimes slapdash bricklaying. Architects, as such, were rarely involved. One builders' magazine commented that 'it is undeniable that a sound well-planned house can be erected almost equally well from a series of sketches on the back of an old envelope as from a neatly executed and carefully coloured working drawing'.[14]

The result was a bottom-up native rebuke to modernism which has far more impact on how Britain looks than any immigrant modernist. This is what we have been left with: an architecture which, instead of stripping back unnecessary detail, piled it on; which preferred sloping roofs to flat and rough surfaces to smooth; which painted on wood beams and added twiddly bits; which sprawled a little, rather than kept its toes in; and which instituted the kitchen as the cosiest and most often-used room in the house. Compared to the terraced houses of earlier speculative building booms, it proved a handy place, with fewer floors and far fewer stairs. Because these millions of houses took up space in the south-east of England, and between urban villages where there had recently still been fields or copses, and because they seemed to cringe a little, looking upwards architecturally at their betters, they were cordially despised by intellectuals. It is the England where Orwell's aspidistras are always flying. These were not homes for struggling factory workers, still less the unemployed. They were homes for teachers, clerks, skilled workers, policemen and the like, people who suddenly found themselves able to borrow money for mortgages with which to buy quite cheap houses. They express the conservatism of British society, the small dreams easy to sneer at, particularly in an age of big ideas. One recent architectural historian points out that they were built after a horrific world war: 'For many, a mythological Elizabethan age and the Tudor past represented an age of stability and secure living . . . [producing] a house that at least gave an outward impression of unshakeable stability.'[15] There is much in that. They were also, of course, the places where many of the next generation of intellectuals, to their retrospective fury, would be born and raised.

There were modernist housing projects by local authority builders and planners, who copied their rounded corners, steel-framed windows and flat roofs from architectural magazines and exhibitions, and they offered some working-class families a better way of living, with gas heating, separate bathrooms and more natural light. The classic modern buildings of the age reflected – not surprisingly – the new enthusiasms and industries. They were public, not private. There were strikingly modern airport buildings at Gatwick, Heston, Shoreham and Jersey, the earlier and jaw-droppingly large airship hangars at Cardington, and light-engineering factories such as the famous Hoover Building of 1932–5 in west London. Road building was minimal by German standards, but the fashion for 'roadhouses' – airy places to stop, with bars and restaurants – brought art deco to the suburbs and countryside along the new roads. It was an age of sun-worship and thus of the open-air lidos. Transport projects included the massive Liverpool Mersey Tunnel of 1925, with new-fangled catseyes, a great British invention, and the skyscraper-like St George's ventilation tower. Garages were new-fangled too, of course: the Bluebird Garage of 1924 in London's Kings Road was the largest in Europe when it opened, with space for 300 cars. By 1937, when the Olympia Garage opened nearby, it had eleven concrete floors, the curving ramps familiar to everyone now, and space for 1,000 cars.

We are not yet really in the car age. Photographs of those Tudor semis from the thirties show a few cars parked in the driveways, not hundreds of them. There were around 100,000 cars on British roads at the time of the Armistice and 2 million by the time Chamberlain had failed to appease Hitler. But the Fordist mass-production techniques had arrived. Cheap, popular cars of the twenties such as the Bullnose Morris and the Austin Seven, small and quirky and some-how essentially English, had been built by hand. Soon those companies, but also Alvis, Wolseley, Triumph, Sunbeam and Rover, were producing metal-pressed and mass-made vehicles and the small, winding roads of Britain were filling up. The narrowness of ancient British city streets and of most old roads meant that, apart from a small number of highly expensive vehicles, the British car already seemed pinched, boxy and mildly apologetic compared with the more expansive, show-off, exhibitionist automobiles of America, Germany and Italy. Even here, modernism had its limits.

Outside Britain, modernism meant sun-worship, often nudism, and mass gymnastics: some of the earliest modernist buildings were Swiss sanatoria. Health meant being free and being active. It could mean new, energetic rhythmic dances, brought by gurus such as Rudolf Laban in Germany. Though the British climate and the smoky air of British cities meant most people kept their kit firmly on, even in this country the fresh-air fad took sporadic hold. Sunbathing became popular, even if it was treated with an endearing earnestness – one guide published in 1931 suggested various ways of 'exposing the naked body to the solar rays', but particularly recom-mended a sun-box, which protected the bather from the wind, or 'reclining on a bed in a ventilated glass solarium . . . a cold wet cloth over the head'. Beach holidays were hugely popular, though in most parts of Britain a strict dress code limited too much exposure of the body until the mid-thirties: for instance men were not permitted to wear bathing costumes that let their chests be seen – except on Brighton beach, which has always been a law unto itself. Sunlamps and sun lounges were widely used and the first sunglasses sold. Flouncy Edwardian bathing dresses were replaced by one-piece woollen costumes and eventually, for men, trunks. Rubber bathing caps arrived, then figure-hugging swimwear, bra-and-pants combinations and cork sandals. In general, the British seaside at the beginning of the twenties featured people who might have been mistaken for Victorians. By the end of the thirties they looked much like us. In our holiday moods, if not our houses or cars, we were leaving the good old days behind.

Downhill all the Way

For the British, as for the French, Italians, Germans and Americans, the inter-war period was the time when the thrill of speed caught on. Until then, apart from a handful of pioneer aviators, motor-car enthusiasts and yachtsmen, the only way you could go fast by yourself and take risks was on the back of a horse. But after the Great War, speeding became an obsession, linked to notions of freedom, national destiny and modernism. It was the age of the first British Grand Prix, the time of the Schneider Trophy, which saw seaplanes roaring round Bournemouth and Cowes, watched by hundreds of thousands of spectators. It was the era of rich young things flying themselves across Europe and of flying circuses which allowed ordinary people to clamber into the back of a biplane and experience, for a fee, the thrill of looping the loop for themselves. And it was the golden age of skiing, the birth of what has become a mass sport, utterly transforming the Alps and many other mountain ranges in the pursuit of the simple thrill of sliding down hills at speed.

A shrewd and pious Edwardian Liberal called Sir Henry Lunn was first at the top of the slope – though only metaphorically, since he did not ski himself. The son of a Lincolnshire greengrocer, he had two religious experiences at the ages of nine and seventeen, and became a missionary and preacher. Convinced that his great calling was to bind the fractured Christian churches of the West, he organized conferences to bring together Anglicans, Methodists, Baptists, Presbyterians and some Catholics. He chose Switzerland. Its valleys had become a favourite winter destination for rich travellers ever since 1864, when an entrepreneurially minded hotel-keeper in a remote mountain village bet some British guests that they would find the Alpine winter delightful, rather than horrifying, which was the accepted view of high, cold snowy places at the time. It worked. They stayed, they paid, and they brought all their friends. His village was called St Moritz and Switzerland, not to mention Alpine France and parts of Austria, has never been the same since. Lunn began organizing his Christian unity conferences, with a lot of high-altitude praying. The churches never unified but he proved to have as shrewd a nose for business as that first Swiss hotelier and began organizing winter sports holidays for the better-off Edwardians. His name survives as half of Lunn-Poly, the package tour operator.

Winter sports, in those days, mostly meant skating and tobogganing. Skiing, which had been a provincially obscure way of getting from one place to another, was a poor relation. As a sport, it had started in Norway and Sweden with peasants teaching urbanites their techniques, and was only slowly spreading to the Alps. It involved very long wooden skis, ordinary leather boots and a single pole, used for balance and braking. It also involved endless rows about technique – literally, how to get down a slope without breaking bones and maintaining some kind of control. It was uncomfortable, dangerous and very, very cold. Skiing was as much about getting up the hills, using sealskins to grip the snow, as it was about sliding down them again. Various Austrian, German and Swiss pioneers were soon devising the snowplough and parallel-turn techniques familiar to any modern skier, but there was one Briton whose contribution was so huge that he is still remembered throughout the skiing world.

He was another Lunn, Sir Henry's son Arnold, who after flunking Oxford and setting up university skiing clubs, went on to invent the slalom race. At the time, skiing was rather like orienteering in the snow. When Lunn devised a fast downhill race with lots of turns, Norwegians protested: what would the English think if they tried to change the rules of cricket? It would probably result in better cricket, Lunn retorted. Anyway, 'It has never been the habit of the British to follow blindly where others lead.' The initial British skiing race had taken place as early as 1903, when the first British club, the Davos Ski Club, was formed, and in 1911 the imperial war hero Lord Roberts of Kandahar sponsored a skiing cup for the Public Schools Alpine Sports Club. What was skiing like then? Lunn recalled that race as 'a climb of seven and a half hours to the starting point, a night in an Alpine hut and a racing course which included three miles across a glacier, a short climb, a descent of 5,000 feet, including 1,500 feet of difficult windswept crust and 1,000 feet of very tricky running through a wood. This was a course for heroes.'

The Great War, unsurprisingly, halted the growing British skiing obsession, though interned soldiers made the most of Swiss mountainsides. But after it Arnold Lunn returned to the slopes. 'At the end of 1919 I found myself the owner of a small silver cup which had been purchased before the war for a prize in a golf competition which was never held. I decided to give the cup for a new type of skiing competition.' Lunn was himself a skier and mountaineer of heroic accomplishments and great personal bravery: he had shattered one leg in a Welsh climbing accident before the war and was in great lifelong pain. One leg being shorter than the other, he had to devise different bindings for his skis, which did not seem to hold him back. In 1922 the first slalom race was held under his guidance: most fast skiing derives from that breakthrough experiment. The (British) Kandahar Ski Club, with its distinctive K badge, led the charge for the new sport of fast-turning skiing, followed by the Downhill Only Club and many more. By the end of the decade the British rules for downhill and slalom skiing had been internationally accepted, and skiing was an Olympic sport. From the mid-twenties through to the early thirties, British skiers were rivalled only by the Swiss for speed and technique, and brought to Switzerland the hard-partying, mildly glamorous atmosphere the great Swiss resorts enjoyed between the wars. The golden age would end only with the rise of fascism.

It remained a tough sport. It involved huge amounts of slogging uphill to find the runs, and the few 'hard snow' pistes were flattened only by scores of helpers using their boots to stamp it down – on one occasion employing the services of Alpine troops for mass stamping. Though a primitive ski lift was reported from the Black Forest in 1906, the first engine-driven lifts did not appear in the central Alps until 1935–6, and chair lifts, invented in America, did not arrive until after the Second World War. A competent skier had to understand many different types of snow, and find his or her route through the mountains, sometimes squinting through home-made wooden slats with eyeholes to prevent snow-blindness. Lunn later recalled: 'The pioneers of Alpine skiing . . . loved the mountains. They enjoyed skiing but they regarded the long descent as a glorious extra, a bonus.' Yet the sheer thrill, which he had done so much to encourage, was what brought ever larger numbers of adventurous holidaymakers to the Swiss and French Alps between the wars. The boat train into Victoria became crammed with sunburned men and women in tweeds and plus-fours, often sporting broken arms and legs as they returned to tell stories of heroism and haplessness. It seems that the essence of skiing was not so very different from today. In the late 1920s Lunn himself asked: 'Do we ever enjoy skiing, I wonder? For we are always either skiing too fast and frightened, or too slow and ashamed.' By then, plenty of other people knew what he meant.

Off in a Flying Boat

For those lucky enough to afford the fares, these were the golden early years of air travel. Few journeys can have started as romantic-ally as a flight to somewhere in Africa or India on an Imperial Airways flying boat in the mid-thirties. You would check in at the cleanly modernistic new terminal near Buckingham Palace, where after presenting your ticket you would be surreptitiously weighed – in early aircraft every pound counted, but the nice people at Imperial did not want fat passengers to feel embarrassed. You would pass over your luggage, maximum 33lb, board a special Pullman carriage at nearby Victoria station and be whisked to Southampton, to the luxury South Western Hotel. At 5 a.m. the following day you would be woken and taken to Berth 101. There you would cross a floating gangway to a raft, and then climb into the side of a Short Imperial Flying Boat, an 18-ton, 88-foot monster built along the coast at

Rochester. Settling into its 'promenade saloon' with your fellow dozen passengers, you would notice the soft luxury leather arm-chairs, the carpets, the smell of breakfast being prepared. As the craft roared across Southampton water, sending plumes of spray over the window, you would settle down to read your free guidebook, and follow a map showing the journey down to the Mediterranean, then the great British airport at Alexandria, and thence perhaps to India or central Africa. In the air, making a good 200 m.p.h., you would enjoy the huge picture windows and sit back. One guide to world airlines reckoned that 'voyage by Imperial Flying Boat is the most comfortable air travel in the world . . . Plenty of space, fresh air and good ventilation, heating, excellent catering, attentive stewards.'[16]

Even for those undertaking a shorter plane trip to Paris, Amsterdam or Berlin, the experience was far more like that enjoyed by a private jet owner now than by most of the air-travelling public of today. You would be a rare and lucky traveller, but by 1935 hardly a unique one: Imperial alone was carrying 68,000 people that year. The first glimpse of the modern air-travel economy was visible. It had been a bumpy flight to reach this semi-modern industry, however. In strict terms the first regular air service in Britain dated back to 1910 and a Hendon-to-Windsor mail run, but this was little more than a gimmick. In the same year an act of Parliament had asserted that the air over Britain and her dominions was inviolable by outsiders, intended with heroic optimism 'to protect the nation against aviation'.[17] The war, of course, had accelerated the technical advances in aviation so that by 1918 British aircraft were easily able to reach Berlin. The following year Alcock and Brown completed the first non-stop transatlantic flight and it was obvious to everyone that a new age of air travel was not far away. Even as the fighting drew to a close, RAF and freelance operators were flying mail to the continent. The first commercial passenger flight seems to have been between Heston and Le Bourget in France on 15 July 1919: there was one passenger behind the pilot who, meant to land at Hounslow to clear Customs, simply could not be bothered. By now it had become clear to the British government that its old hostility to allowing free access to national airspace was horribly misplaced. Aircraft still could not fly very far, and any British machines wishing to get anywhere else would have to cross over France, Belgium,

Germany and other neighbouring countries. Yet although an agreement was signed at the Paris peace conference, rows about airspace
erupted again and again, slowing down the possibilities of genuinely
popular air travel.

It was not just legal difficulties. The first commercial air services
were manned by brave pilots struggling to keep to routines despite
cloud and fog and with limited instruments. At least one early near
miss over London came close to knocking a hole in St Paul's
Cathedral. Nevertheless, several companies did their best to encourage this new business. Frederick Handley Page, whose bombers had
already become a mainstay of the RAF, converted some of them to
passenger planes. By October 1919 passengers for Paris and Brussels
were arriving at his Cricklewood aerodrome, where they could buy
for three shillings a lunch box of six sandwiches, fruit and chocolate,
before clambering into an unheated plane, ten at a time. The aircraft
were noisy and slow but, guided by Marconi radio telephony,
relatively safe. Other early passenger services included those of
Instone, a colliery and shipping company whose planes took off from
Croydon trimmed with silver wings and a royal-blue fuselage and
whose pilots (because of the firm's nautical history) dressed in sailor-
like uniforms, perhaps influencing pilots' and stewards' dress even
today. Then there were the red-and-white painted planes of Daimler
Hire, flying to Berlin and Amsterdam, and, down at Southampton,
the seaplanes, Supermarine Sea Eagles, owned by the British Marine
Air Navigation Company, which flew to the Channel Islands. It was
clear that the British private firms would struggle against rivals from
the continent who were being subsidized by their governments. But
Churchill, as air minister, told the Commons in March 1920: 'Civil
aviation must fly by itself: the government cannot possibly hold it
up in the air.'

Churchill turned out to be wrong. The new form of travel had
captured the imagination of the country. It proved surprisingly safe:
in the five years to 1924 the little airlines with their biplanes and
converted military bombers managed to transport 34,600 passengers
while killing only five of them. But it was not, and could not be,
profitable. The cost of the aircraft and the primitive arrangements
for passengers, never mind arguments about airspace, meant that
every one of the companies was broke. By 1922 the government was

beginning to accept the need for subsidies. The following year a new air minister was given cabinet rank and a year later came the agreed merger of all the small private companies into a single national air-passenger outfit – Imperial Airways, now subsidized by the taxpayer and given a virtual monopoly on overseas flights. As legal problems continued to dog continental routes, it lived up to its name and to the obsessions of twenties Britain: it turned towards the Empire, not to Europe. The early routes included Basra, Baghdad and Cairo. By 1929 Imperial was flying in hops to Karachi, reaching Delhi the following year. In 1931 its long-range airliners were landing in central Africa, and by 1932 Cape Town. In 1933 the Imperial Airways service to Singapore began and after that, in 1934, it was flying a regular passenger route to Australia. These could be trips of many days, with stopovers at hotels for the night. But they were already shrinking the world.

The government had ulterior motives. It was not only interested in linking the Empire more closely together, it also knew that defence in the future would require a strong aircraft industry. In the early years Imperial was not making anything like enough money to sustain a major building programme: many of its early airliners were literally hand built. Yet Imperial, alongside the RAF, did keep enough aircraft manufacturers going to ensure that, when war came again, Britain would be able to churn out fighters and bombers in large numbers. De Havilland, whose DH4 bomber had been one of the flying successes of the war, used a new plywood-based aircraft – the Comet – for the 1934 London to Melbourne race, beating American competition; the construction techniques later reappeared in the wartime fighter-bomber Mosquito. Handley Page built large all-metal biplanes for the Imperial Airways routes; they quite easily moved back to building bombers, most famously the Halifax, during the next war. As with many of the new industries, these firms tended to be clustered in the south of England. A. V. Roe was the main exception, with its Manchester factory, and Armstrong-Whitworth was in Coventry. Handley-Page, as we have seen, was in Crickle-wood, De Havilland was at Hatfield, and Short Brothers, who built those fantastic flying boats, were in Bedford and Rochester. The long imperial routes meant an emphasis on large planes: the Armstrong Ensign looked relatively modern, with a sleek metallic finish, but the

DH Frobisher's and Dianas were lumbering beasts; and the famous Short-Mayo Composite was downright weird. It piggy-backed a seaplane onto a flying boat: with the eight engines of the two planes working together it would become airborne, then they would break apart and the seaplane, more heavily loaded than it could have managed if taking off alone, flew on by itself. The emphasis on flying boats and seaplanes may seem strange to modern eyes, but in the context of the thirties it made perfect sense. There were few proper airfields, but they could land on any decent-sized piece of water. Air already seemed the new highway and also the coming battleground.

The Failure of the Clever

Should not a new world, born in the pain of world war, look different? Though Britain boasted some fine painters and sculptors in these years, nobody could say it was a great age for art. Conservative painters at the Royal Academy, offering aristocratic-style portraits, hunting or nature scenes and quiet still lifes, dominated public taste. In music, for once, England had a sound of her own, with composers such as Ralph Vaughan Williams, Arnold Bax and William Walton. It was new, but hardly surprising compared with the music being written in France or Russia, or the jazz of America. For real radicalism we turn to literature. James Joyce, T. S. Eliot, Ezra Pound – an Irishman and two American exiles – broke up and reassembled the very language of the English-speaking world. They would have a major influence on intellectuals and university students but almost none on the wider public. The next generation of poets, politically engaged by the threats of the thirties, turned back to simpler and more direct words. The real question is why literary modernism, bursting with genius and ambition before 1914, had so little impact on the thinking or attitudes of inter-war Britain. Where were the home-grown British modernists?

There was one man who had fought in the Great War, painted it and was regarded as a serious literary rival by Joyce, Pound and Eliot. The war, said Percy Wyndham Lewis, had been 'a black solid mass, cutting off all that went before it'. His short-lived Edwardian movement, vorticism, had been a British response to French cubism and Italian futurism. His angry little magazine *Blast*, a kind of manifesto for his Rebel Art Group, had fizzed. His whippy, sneering drawing was equally fresh. Wyndham Lewis was not wholly British. He had been born on a yacht off Nova Scotia and his father was an American who had fought in the Civil War. But he had been brought up in England, ending up at Rugby School. Equally at home with a fountain pen or a paintbrush, he was not a modest man. He wrote satirical novels which caused much offence, including to his some-time hostess Ottoline Morrell, but he was a genuinely original artist. If you have in your head a drawn or painted image of Joyce, Eliot, Pound or the Sitwells, it is almost certainly one of his. Wyndham Lewis's theory was that the 'men of 1914' – the original radicals – had tried to break away from romantic art and propaganda to a purer art, 'the detachment of true literature', but were defeated by the war: 'We are the first men of a Future that has not materialized. We belong to a "great age" that has not "come off".'

So serious art in Britain had been aborted? The great slaughter had turned the country back to the pretty-pretty and the reassuring? Up to a point. But there was another problem with modernism which Wyndham Lewis personifies: the overwhelming tenor of the movement was right-wing, aristocratic and anti-Semitic. T. S. Eliot's anti-Semitism, which was not a minor affectation, has been much discussed in recent years, while Ezra Pound became a wholehearted admirer of Mussolini and broadcast for the fascists during the war. W. B. Yeats became disillusioned with democracy and wrote march-ing songs for the Irish semi-fascist Blueshirts organization. And why, given his undoubted talents, energy and wartime courage, is Wynd-ham Lewis himself not so well known these days? Why is there some hesitation about him? Perhaps it is something to do with a book called simply *Hitler* and attractively decorated with swastikas in which Lewis lauds the rising Nazi movement and contrasts it with the decadence and minor bullying of Weimar Germany. The first work in English about Hitler, it seethes with dislike for the 'perverts' paradise' of Weimar Berlin, a place of 'night circuses, *Negertanz* [nigger-dance] palaces ... flagellation bars, and the sad wells of super-masculine loneliness, shining dives for the sleek, stock-jobbing, sleuths relaxing'.[18] It is not so far removed from Eliot's visions of modern corruption. *Hitler* is full of wild misjudgements ('Today Paul

Gauguin is totally discredited as an artist . . . It is very unlikely that there will be any swing of the pendulum, either, in favour of such pictures'), but the most astonishing of all are that Hitler himself is 'a Man of Peace' who would in power 'show increasing moderation and tolerance', while his admittedly drastic proposals against Jews are 'a preliminary snag' and 'a mere bagatelle' which should not sway British people against the Nazis. To be fair to Wyndham Lewis, he later renounced Hitlerism, just before the Second World War (which he spent in America). But he was enough of a serious and early admirer to be applauded in the Nazi press and he made repeated private visits to the British fascist Oswald Mosley, whom he greatly admired.

Eliot was a man of very different temper, whose cultured, pessimistic and intellectual form of modernism turned into a devotion to High Anglican Englishness. He would call himself a royalist in politics (quite something for an American; he also took British citizenship in 1927), was an Anglo-Catholic in religion and a classicist in literary taste. His 1922 *The Wasteland* is a brilliant technical achievement, a lament for a civilization engulfed by barbarism and commercialism, but it is also supercilious in tone, sexually cold and requires a lot of work to fully appreciate. His friend Ezra Pound would take obscure referential tactics to absurd levels later in his *Cantos*. Eliot, a genuinely great poet, was saved from the full impact of his political views by his conservative caution. Later he would help Jewish émigrés and support the state of Israel, but he is another example of the tendency of British modernism to define itself by disdaining the common reader. Virginia Woolf too found the working classes squalid, greedy and confusing. Consider her reaction to a perfectly ordinary restaurant at Richmond railway station where she 'looked into the lowest pit of human nature; saw flesh still unmoulded to the shape of humanity – whether it is the act of eating & drinking that degrades, or whether people who lunch at restaurants are naturally degraded, one can certainly hardly face one's own humanity again afterwards'. Modernism, by breaking down the traditional forms of art which had evolved over centuries, had its moments of exhilarating energy. But it then shuffled the hoarded fragments of elite culture, despaired at democracy and fell for the cult of the Great Man. That is why it failed; and this happened just

From frolicking to marching: the original Kindred of the Kibbo Kift; and John Hargrave addressing a rally of his Greenshirts.

Lady Ottoline Morrell: flamboyant, big-hearted – and betrayed.

Garsington Manor, Ottoline's paradise.

The Red Clydeside riots: police keeping the road clear during the Battle of George Square.

The studied personification of English calm; but Stanley Baldwin was slightly more interesting than he looked.

The King-Emperor who saw disaster ahead: George V at the helm, 1924.

The Queen of the Night: Kate Meyrick, centre, with friends at her Silver Slipper club after yet another spell in Holloway Prison, 1928.

Left Anorexic models, androgynous fashions: the twenties were not a different country.

Below left Those small enough for you? Eric Gill, scandalous sculptor, and a modestly endowed Ariel in front of the new BBC headquarters, 1925.

Below A radical hero in his youth, remembered as a ninny later: Ramsay MacDonald in his prime, 1926.

'The King was wearing enough for both of us': Gandhi being cheered by Lancashire mill workers during his 1931 visit to Britain.

The voice of left-wing Britain and almost as popular a broadcaster as Winston himself: J. B. Priestley.

Scotland's wildest son: Hugh MacDiarmid, poet and revolutionary.

Dreaming of better ways of living: an early advert for the
newly mortgage-intoxicated society.

BUTLIN'S HOLIDAY CAMP
CLACTON-ON-SEA
IT'S QUICKER BY RAIL
ILLUSTRATED BOOKLET FREE FROM R. P. BUTLIN'S PUBLICITY DEPARTMENT, SKEGNESS, OR ANY L·N·E·R OFFICE OR AGENCY

Paid holidays arrive at last in the 1930s. Billy Butlin offered a week's holiday for a week's wages.

Heels for the masses: the thirties were, for much of the country, the first years of mass consumerism.

Those extraordinary Mitfords (clockwise from bottom left): Nancy, Unity, Jessica, Diana; novelist, Nazi, Red and fascist pin-up.

Wallis with Edward: despite the trauma of the abdication crisis, she did Britain a favour by removing a worryingly pro-German King.

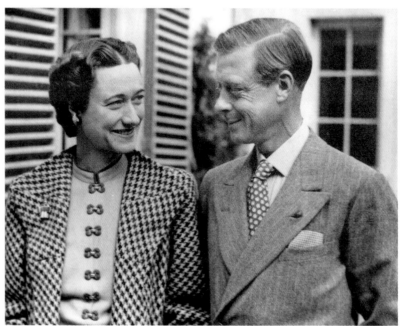

as British society in other ways was becoming more democratic, more consumerist and a little more open.

The Lost Hero

British socialism between the wars had no gods, and precious few heroes. If only, people say, Labour had produced a great early speaker who could have dominated Parliament and electrified large crowds. If only there had been one truly brave and effective leader – how different the politics of the twenties might have been. Someone, perhaps, who had shown the colour of his principles by suffering for them, who had come from the bottom of the social heap, who understood international issues, and who could rouse crowds to the highest pitch of feeling. In fact, there was one such man. But he has been dismissed, written out of the story. He was the bastard son of a hard-working mother, who had clawed his way up to a junior white-collar job, never losing sight of his socialist principles. He had spoken out against the Great War when it was dangerous as well as politically inconvenient to do so. He had been abused, physically attacked, had lost many of his friends and been so viciously assaulted in by-elections that he nearly lost the will to keep fighting. Later, he remembered, 'the haunting memory of the women – bloodthirsty, cursing their hate, issuing from the courts and alleys crowded with children – the sad flotsam and jetsam of wild emotion'. He was for years the most hated and feared radical politician in Britain, a semi-official position later held by Nye Bevan and Tony Benn. Newspapers revealed his illegitimacy and suggested he should be taken to the Tower of London and shot. He was a founder of the Independent Labour Party (ILP), to which most of the 'Red Clydesiders' belonged, and a member of it for nearly forty years. When he stood for Woolwich, the London trams carried posters on the side asking blankly: 'A Traitor for Parliament?'

As an orator, though no film exists of his great days, he was clearly spellbinding. He was an important political theorist, too. While many socialists were falling for the spell of the Bolsheviks and their idea of a revolutionary vanguard, this was the man who saw very early that Bolshevism had to lead to tyranny: the 'dictatorship of the proletariat' would become mere dictatorship. He did more than anyone to keep Labour radicals, mainly in the ILP, out of the clutches of Moscow's Third International. He told them that, under Lenin, Russia would develop a bureaucracy of repression 'so the revolution changes from being a movement of ideas to becoming a series of bloody events; repression finally develops into a complete policy of extermination'. This was said before the rise of Stalin. It was long before Orwell. It was genuine prophecy. And he was a genuine socialist, whose attacks on capitalism's use of 'the whip of starvation' made him a hero to party members during his years in the wilderness. Finally back in Parliament, he was abruptly thrown into national leadership by Baldwin's strange decision to hold a general election in the winter of 1923 so that he could repudiate free trade. Some idea of his popularity then comes from reports of his campaigning in Wales, where he was hailed as 'the Messiah' and had his car dragged by supporters through the streets with a brass band in front of it. A Labour newspaper reported on his last rally, held by moonlight, that 'the crowd bore down on the car like an avalanche. What mattered it that the windows were smashed? – the eager men whose arms went through could not help themselves in the impetuous rush of the hundreds ... It took the car nearly two hours to travel a mile. That speaks for itself ... rarely, if ever, in English political history has such a scene been witnessed.'[19]

So who was this far-sighted and popular radical hero? He was Ramsay MacDonald, who, in 1924, became the first Labour prime minister of Britain. MacDonald, from the small Scottish east-coast town of Lossiemouth, is remembered today as Labour's traitor, because he split the party and accepted office in the National Government of 1931. One biographer argues that no British political leader in the century has been so reviled.[20] He became the ultimate symbol of lickspittle turncoat politics, fawning on duchesses and selling out the workers. For a while he so embarrassed Labour that he was airbrushed out of the party's history. Yet MacDonald was a strikingly brave, patriotic and radical politician who was seen in his day as the great hope of the left. He is hardly the first person to have crossed the political divide during a time of crisis – Churchill and Lloyd George both did the same, and the latter also smashed his party while doing so. Yet because the National Government has been so unhappily remembered, the men who brought us mass unemployment and appeasement, and was followed by the country-changing 1945 Labour government (by which time MacDonald was long dead), his reputation has been trashed. His personal courage has been forgotten – he lost both wife and son very quickly, and worked himself almost to death. Surrounded by waspish and snooty intellectuals, his achievement in setting out what a non-revolutionary socialist party might achieve has been ignored. He was long-winded, self-pitying and arrogant. But again, that puts him in busy political company.

MacDonald's great failure was that he was unable to chart a democratic socialist course in Britain between the wars. Along with Philip Snowden – the weavers' son from the Pennines, who also helped found the ILP and whose anti-war stance was similar to MacDonald's – he was in his economics a traditional Liberal, even a Victorian. This meant that he believed in free trade, balanced budgets and government economy, all paid lip service to by today's politicians but an inadequate response to the mass unemployment and slump of the inter-war years. It meant limiting socialist reforms to good times; but these were bad times. In 1924 the alternative, Keynes's advocacy of high spending to kick-start growth, was only beginning to be debated among intellectuals. More generally, MacDonald's insistence that Labour must be respectable was a reasonable response to what was still an essentially conservative country, so recently and violently hostile to socialists. His first government lasted only ten months, always dependent on the other parties to let it continue in office. Despite some useful housing reforms, it achieved little before being beaten in the 1924 election, partly thanks to the 'Red scare' of the forged Zinoviev letter purporting to be secret instructions from the Russian communists to their British comrades, and published in the *Daily Mail* the day before the election. Between the iron certainties of the revolutionary states abroad, and those of traditional liberals at home, there was almost no ground at all. And if anyone doubted that, the General Strike of 1926 rammed the message home.

A Very British Revolt

Britain's million-plus miners had a very good case. They were paid atrocious wages and treated little better than medieval serfs. The industry was badly run, out of date and archaic in its structure. This meant that, when the German coal of the Ruhr returned to the international market at below British prices, owners could only think of cutting wages and lengthening hours to stay in business. The government had long since handed the mines back to their private owners and was trying to keep out of the dispute. This was ludicrous: Britain ran on coal, and with the TUC involved in stopping all movements of coal to help the miners, the country would soon judder to a halt. Faced with the obvious, in July 1925 the Baldwin government gave in. A nine-month subsidy and a Royal Commission to investigate the industry bought time. But when it reported in March 1926 insisting that wages must be cut, there was nothing for the TUC to do but support the miners as had been promised. 'Not a penny off the pay, not a minute on the day,' said the miners' leaders. The owners replied that wages would be cut and, if this was not accepted, the miners would be locked out from 1 May 1926. The TUC responded by calling a General Strike two days later. And how, this time, could the government pretend not to be involved?

The fight between the miners and the mine owners had become one between the TUC and Baldwin's government. Matters of pennies, shillings, pithead baths and company amalgamations became issues of power and the authority of the state. It was not a revolutionary strike, or meant as one. It was not meant to bring down the elected government, or to depose Parliament as the source of all political power. Yet it could not possibly succeed unless the elected government was humiliated; unless Parliament bowed to strike action; unless, in short, there was a revolutionary situation. Since the strikers' leaders did not want that, they were bound to fail. The last chance for a peaceful resolution was ended by printers, who refused to allow the national edition of the *Daily Mail* to be published. Its editorial, headed 'For King and Country', contained the sentiment 'A General Strike is not an industrial dispute. It is a revolutionary movement which can only succeed by destroying the Government and subverting the rights and liberties of the people.' Since one of those liberties has been taken to be freedom of the press, it might be thought that the printers had shot themselves in the foot, or at least confirmed the *Mail* leader-writer's point. At any rate, this led to the Baldwin government, with Churchill in the vanguard, breaking off negotiations. Baldwin's private secretary excitedly telephoned the King's private secretary at Windsor Castle late at night to say: 'The *Daily Mail* has ceased to function. Tell his Majesty so that he should not go off at the deep end,' only to be rebuked: 'We don't take the *Daily Mail*.'[21] The TUC manifesto said: 'The trade unions disclaim all responsibility for the calamity which now threatens.' Action was directed not at the public but at the mine owners and the ministers. Baldwin responded in the Commons by saying the trade unions were imperilling 'the freedom of our very constitution' while Churchill, more briskly, accused them of trying to overthrow the government.

Behind the scenes there were already tensions in the cabinet. Churchill was forging ahead with his own newspaper, the government's mouthpiece, to be called the *British Gazette*. Since he was Chancellor of the Exchequer at the time, this was hardly in his remit. In fact, the job of dealing with propaganda was in the hands of J. C. C. Davidson, a Tory close to Baldwin, who recorded that the prime minister wanted Churchill to turn editor to 'keep him busy, stop him doing worse things'. Baldwin added: 'I'm terrified of what Winston is going to be like.' Davidson responded that if 'Winston tries to turn the men into an army of Bolsheviks [roughly speaking, Churchill's view] I shall resist that' – to which Baldwin replied, 'That's absolutely right, of course you will.'[22] Churchill, though kept vaguely in check by Davidson, had a lovely time. He commandeered the newsprint of all the main papers, and the presses of the right-wing *Morning Post*, where he charged about changing commas. The *British Gazette* demanded unconditional surrender and Churchill provocatively insisted on food supplies into London being escorted by tanks and soldiers with machine guns. Davidson plaintively complained to Baldwin that Churchill now thought he was Napoleon.

The government's preparations were effective and fast. Around 1.75 million workers came out on strike in support of the million miners. With the buses mainly stopped, the railways silent and the Underground closed, those not striking walked to work: there were confrontations with pickets and some violence, mostly in east London. Using the old wartime emergency powers, the government recruited middle-class volunteers to run buses and even trains, to patrol as special constables and to carry food supplies round the country using that new technology, the lorry. Thousands volunteered, including around 450 Cambridge undergraduates who came to London and Dover to break the strike in the docks in the spirit of what one called 'hurrah-patriotismus'. Sailors were pressed into service unloading ships and City gents worked to shovel coal at gasworks. Submarines were moored with their engines running to keep warehouses refrigerated. The Ranelagh Polo Club patrolled central London on their polo ponies and titled ladies turned up in leather greatcoats to organize food supplies. Within three days there were half a million volunteers available: something like the spirit of August 1914, though without the danger, had infected the middle classes. There was sporadic violence. Buses and trams were stopped by pickets, overturned and burned. To protect their amateur drivers, some were cocooned in barbed wire. A train was derailed. In Aberdeen, Middlesbrough, Glasgow and Edinburgh there were confrontations and stone-throwing, baton charges and arrests. There were also small signs of revolutionary agitation. It is reckoned that at least half of the British Communist Party's 5,000 members were arrested, including the Indian Communist MP for Battersea, Shapurji Saklatava, who was charged for saying the Union Jack had only protected fools and rogues, and for telling the army not to fire on strikers. Britain's small band of fascists responded with hysterical racist abuse.

On the fifth day of the strike the government made its decisive move. London was going short of flour and bread: at 4 o'clock on the morning of 8 May a convoy of more than a hundred lorries, escorted by twenty armoured cars, went to the docks, to where strike-breakers had been quietly ferried on the Thames to avoid the pickets. Food was loaded and returned to a new depot in Hyde Park; the crowds watched but did not interfere. This was probably the psychological turning point, though the TUC and government continued to trade propaganda blows, and reports began piling up of accidents caused by volunteer drivers. Almost inevitably, and with echoes of the first winter on the Western Front, strikers and police were soon playing football matches. There were some dangerous incidents still to come, including the derailing of the *Flying Scotsman* and further disturbances in Plymouth, Hull, Doncaster, Cardiff and Newcastle. But with food being effectively moved around the country, and increasing rail and tram services, the TUC general council began to lose heart. The strikers had been disciplined and peaceful, and perhaps that was the problem: it quickly became a competition about organization, one the government was bound to win. Baldwin, who was being relentlessly reasonable in tone, finally heard from Arthur Pugh, a steel miller who chaired the general council, just after noon on 12 May that the strike was to be 'terminated forthwith'. Receiving the TUC men in Downing Street he checked: 'That is, the strike is to be called off forthwith?' Pugh replied in almost Monty Pythonesque terms: 'Forthwith. That means immediately,' and Baldwin exclaimed, 'I thank God for your decision.'

Despite brave words from the TUC's answer to Churchill's paper, the *British Worker*, this was a straightforward, unequivocal and humiliating defeat for the trade unions. They had done their worst but, being essentially law-abiding and respectable democrats, their worst was not very scary. Middle-class paranoia about Bolshevism at home now had its answer. Many thousands of men who had obeyed instructions to strike were victimized, being demoted or even losing their jobs. The TUC's leadership was badly damaged for years to come. Above all it was a terrible blow for the miners, whose dispute would go on for another six months until they were effectively starved back to work in November 1926. Longer hours and smaller wages were imposed in south Wales, Scotland and the north-east of England. However, the union movement, which lost members, but not in dramatic numbers, and faced some new legal curbs rather than a full repressive crackdown, survived and grew again. Churchill, having been a leading hawk, tried hard to get compromises from the mine owners, entertaining them and leading Labour figures, including MacDonald, to endless lunches and dinners where the champagne flowed and the oyster shells were emptied. The miners' leaders, to their credit, refused to have anything to do with champagne diplomacy and in the end the owners were as unmoved by Churchill's hospitality as they had been by the miners' strike.

Britain did not have a revolutionary temper, despite the harshness with which the miners had been treated. Moderation frustrated real reform in the inter-war years, and meant that Britain would fight the next war as very much the same unfair, class-divided, economically and politically old-fashioned country she had been in 1914. But moderation also meant that Britain never experienced the violent politics, street-gang murders and coups that ravaged the continent. Was MacDonald's timidity, one shared by most Labour people, a failure or a blessing? For him, the answer was clear. Unlike other crisis prime ministers he was leading a minority government, depending on the wary Liberals for daily support. He had by then undoubtedly been seduced by the delights of high-society life and in his loneliness had been patronized and flattered. As we shall see, when he took the decision to join hands with Tories and Liberals to form the anti-socialist National Government he came close to destroying the party he had once built. For his pains he would be largely forgotten (except by Labour people, who would use his name as a kind of swear word). And in truth, by the time he finally left public life, he had become an embarrassing figure. Yet it should never be forgotten that after 1926 he was leading a movement that had had its unity and self-confidence shattered, with no clear agenda for parliamentary power.

Air Magic

Long before it was technically possible to throw and catch sound with radio waves, broadcasting had been fantasized about. When the telephone first became popular, many people assumed it would be used to play live music, and drama, and that 'using the telephone' would mean sitting with headphones and enjoying a dance band. After the turn of the century the British government decided broadcasting might be useful in war to hold together the Empire, and it took control of wireless telegraphy. The real originating genius of broadcasting was a half-Italian, half-Irish gentleman scientist, Guglielmo Marconi, who had been granted in Britain the world's first patent for wireless telegraphy in 1896. He had demonstrated the new system, still used to send code rather than words or sounds, at Salisbury Plain and by 1899 had achieved wireless communications between France and England before building permanent stations along the south coast. Though he built on the work of many others, Marconi's rate of invention and his entrepreneurial enthusiasm set him apart. Had the BBC never been formed, in all probability the most famous name in British broadcasting would have been Marconi's. Soon broadcasting became a sport for eccentrics and home-taught boffins, with hundreds of licence-holding amateurs broadcasting or receiving in small areas, every man his own BBC. As soon as the Great War started, they were all closed down, while technical developments leapt ahead as the armies developed wireless communications. When it ended, licences were issued again.

Britain's first regular broadcasts were planned and prepared in the Cock and Bell public house in Writtle, a pretty little village near Chelmsford, the county town of Essex, some thirty miles north of London. The broadcasts aired each Tuesday lunchtime from 1922 under the enthusiastic guidance of an ex-RAF engineer and natural show-off called Peter Eckersley, who on one occasion offered radio listeners a 'night of grand opera' – sung entirely by himself. Down the road from the pub was a long, low wooden ex-army hut owned by the Marconi Company, which had just received permission to make regular broadcasts again, though only for half an hour a week, and interrupted every seven minutes by three minutes' silence when the engineers were supposed to listen out for military signals. In June 1920 Marconi had already broadcast a limited one-off entertainment from their Chelmsford offices, encouraged by Harmsworth's *Daily Mail*, when the great opera star Dame Nellie Melba had arrived in a makeshift studio and warbled 'Home Sweet Home' and other saccharine hits into a microphone cobbled together from a telephone mouthpiece and a cigar-box. Dame Nellie had done the same thing in Paris, and even in Newfoundland. But it was the Cock and Bell boys of Writtle who introduced regular broadcasts to this country.

Their call-sign 'Two-Emma-Toc' (for 2MT, the station identifier) became quite well-known during 1922–3 as Eckersley and his small band chose records, read out plays and sang their own satirical theme-tune. They were followed by another Marconi station in the centre of London, 2LO, which began with a live commentary of a boxing match and had an audience in 1922 of about 50,000, and then by Metropolitan-Vickers' 2ZY station in Manchester and Western Electric's 5IT in Birmingham. The companies were all backed by money from America, where a vibrant if chaotic 'radio boom' was already in progress. So why did British broadcasting not develop into a vigorous competition between rival firms, raucous and free? There were two reasons. The American radio boom had produced so many struggling competitors that the quality of the broadcast sound was often terrible; it was also funded by advertising. British politicians and civil servants thought that, in a much smaller country, the problem would be much worse. They also wondered whether broadcasting was not too important, too grand, to be funded by sponsorship.

The government committee overseeing wireless was dominated by military chiefs, the Treasury, the Foreign Office, the Board of Trade and other nervous, unimaginative patriots. But MPs quickly realized that nothing would happen without the support of the wireless amateurs and the companies making the sets they were using. A British compromise was agreed. The rival commercial enterprises making wireless sets would get together and form one company, working under the Post Office. The new company would not be allowed to broadcast advertising, but would get a share of the licence fee paid to the Post Office by everyone buying a set. The companies knew a tempting-looking monopoly when they saw one, and duly gathered together to form the new broadcaster, which came out of government regulation but would not itself be part of government. Based at the electrical engineers' headquarters at Savoy Hill, off London's Strand, it would be called simply the British Broadcasting Company, or BBC. Its first broadcast took place at 6 p.m. on 14 November 1922 – a news summary, followed the next day by the first election results. The short age of commercial-only broadcasting was over.

Enter, stage right, a tall, balding Scot with a long scar running down one cheek and a most alarming manner. To call John Reith, who was the real founder of the BBC, odd would be a wild understatement. The youngest son of a charismatic Presbyterian minister in Glasgow, he had grown up in a family whose siblings tended to dislike one another and were shaken by terrible rages. Reith himself was almost perpetually furious with someone, one of

the great haters of modern British history. An engineer, he became a
transport officer in the war, famous for picking even more fights
with his superiors than with the Germans. Badly wounded in the
face, he went to America to supervise arms contracts before returning
to find himself, after the Armistice, very bored and quite sure that
the Almighty had special plans for him. Through most of his early
adult life, Reith had been deeply in love. The object of his affections
was a schoolboy, Charlie Bowser, whose picture he carried next to
him in the trenches and whom he bombarded with ardent daily
letters, pressed flowers and presents. As Charles grew to adulthood,
he and Reith went on holidays together, liked to sleep together,
enjoyed naked swimming and even bought a home together. Yet he
was entirely open about the relationship, including to his intensely
religious and conservative-minded parents. This was probably a
relationship which was not sexually consummated but was perhaps
even more intense because of that, a kind of love which our more
genitally fixated culture has obliterated; a way of living killed off
by Sigmund Freud. Reith married; but when Charlie did the same
Reith's jealousy was so extreme it kept him in a semi-constant rage
for a decade or more. This was the man in whose hands broadcasting
was now to be placed.

Here is how it happened. The thirty-two-year-old engineer was
unemployed, living in a London club while he wondered what to do
with his life – perhaps a job in Bombay, or working for a South
American railway, or even going into politics? One evening he visited
his local London church in Regent Square, where he heard the
minister preaching from the Book of Ezekiel about the corruption of
Jerusalem. The preacher told the congregation that there might be,
that very evening, some person in the church who would save this
country from heathendom, immorality and love of money. Reith
went back to his club in a very excited mood, hoping that 'the blood
of Christ' would help him, writing in his diary that 'I still believe
there is some high work for me in the world'.[23] The following day
he saw an advert for the job of general manager for the new British
Broadcasting Company. Despite the amateur world of wireless taking
shape around him, Reith did not actually know what broadcasting
was. Nevertheless, he wrote off for the job, fishing the letter back
and changing it when he realized the chairman was from Aberdeen,

and asserting that he was too. Two months of silence passed. Reith spent the time dabbling in coalition Liberal and Tory politics. When he was finally called for an interview, he admitted later, he still 'hadn't the remotest idea as to what broadcasting was. I hadn't troubled to find out.' He was offered the job. He wrote in his diary that he was 'properly grateful to God' for arranging it. At the offices of the new company he installed himself in a cubbyhole, appointing Eckersley of the Cock and Bell as his chief engineer, and set to work.

At Savoy Hill, Reith grew his staff from four to 350 in a single year, ordering them to work twelve-hour days and demonstrating the energy and drive that was always his redeeming feature. New broadcasting stations began to open round the country. Studios were built, concerts broadcast and famous writers welcomed to the coal fire-heated, tobacco-scented offices, close to Westminster. But how close? Reith was taking over a new company with many enemies, including those who thought it should be run directly by the government. The press barons were mostly against it, even though the BBC was banned from saying anything controversial or from gathering news itself – it had to rely on news agencies to provide summaries, which would be broadcast late enough not to rival newspaper sales. The Post Office, though it was one of the sponsors of the new outfit, wanted to snaffle as much of the licence fee as possible. More generally, everyone was wrestling with two questions: what was broadcasting for, and who should control it? From the first, Reith had a clear answer to each. It was for education, culture, information and the higher arts; it was, therefore, a public service, not mere commercial entertainment.

Reith was firmly against giving people what they wanted. For one thing, they didn't know what they wanted. For another, they certainly did not know what they needed. Get broadcasting right, though, and it would produce a 'more intelligent and enlightened electorate' and strengthen democracy. When it came to the second question – who should control broadcasting? – Reith's enthusiasm for democracy faltered. That was easy: John Reith should control it. When the government decided a powerful new committee should be formed to investigate the future of broadcasting, Reith got himself onto it. He wooed and won over politicians, the Archbishop of Canterbury, newspaper owners and others. He tried and failed to get the Budget and other political speeches broadcast, but he did get election broadcasts from the party leaders in 1924 on air, and he broadcast George V's opening speech at the Wembley British Empire Exhibition the same year – 10 million people are supposed to have heard it.

Remarkably quickly, the commercial owners of the BBC were fading into the background and Reith was seizing the stage, a national figure already. He understood early on that if broadcasting was special, he would need to oust the previous owners and get the BBC established as a new kind of body, a national corporation. The BBC would thus be completely different from the maelstrom of American broadcasters, with their adverts and cheap music, and from the government-run stations of Europe. The physical expressions of this new power were the broadcasting stations being built everywhere, to bring good reception to the main cities of Britain. The BBC broadcast more music than anything else: there was great argument about whether it should be mostly opera, classical, jazz or dance. There were talks, too. Told he was not allowed to be controversial on the airwaves and that politics and religion were banned subjects, George Bernard Shaw sensibly replied that they were the only things worth talking about. *Women's Hour* and *Children's Hour* were early programmes that lasted. There were gentle comic turns. Sport was mostly kept off the air to calm the newspaper owners, but there were outside broadcasts from factories, nightingale-filled woods and Covent Garden opera house.

As important as any early decision was the tone of voice. It is entirely true that early BBC announcers were obliged to wear a dinner jacket and bow tie, though this was partly because they would also be announcing concerts in which the musicians would be similarly dressed. But Reith chose public-school and university-educated men to set his tone. He set up a committee under the Poet Laureate to advise on what he firmly called 'the correct pronunciation of the English tongue'. Though regional accents were acceptable in comedy performances, Reith wanted a single, standard English to be heard, and thus copied everywhere. About the only regular soft Scottish voice heard was his own, when he commandeered the microphone himself. Thus there spread across Britain what was first called 'public-school English' and later 'received pronunciation', or simply 'BBC English'. A country rich in accent and dialect, now listening in its millions every night to the voices of the metropolitan elite, would quickly become blander and duller, its variety smoothed out. Everywhere people must have listened to their own voices and asked anew, 'Am I speaking proper?' Samuel Johnson would have been delighted.

Eckersley, always the freer spirit, suggested that broadcasting should also mean regional variation, and different radio stations, as well as very local radio, broadcasting from schools, local news and local speeches. In this he was far ahead of his time. In the 1920s, local broadcasting was virtually snuffed out, and Reith's local stations became mere hubs for London, where another inquiry into broadcasting was set up. This time, Reith was so powerful and confident he did not even need to be on it; a British Broadcasting Corporation, with an effective monopoly, was duly recommended. The BBC received its first Royal Charter for the beginning of 1927, a year or so off, with the government keeping tight powers of control. But first it had to weather a storm big enough to sink the whole project, the General Strike of 1926. And this revealed much about the limitations, as well as the strengths, of the BBC.

The strike could hardly have come at a more sensitive time for the new institution, whose revised status had been agreed but not implemented. The government had the legal power simply to take the BBC over and order it to broadcast straightforward propaganda. Churchill, who first met Reith during the strike, wanted just that. With the newspapers silenced by the strikers and only Churchill's *British Gazette* putting the government view, one can see why. Radio was in a position of influence far beyond anything imaginable a few years earlier. It was only after a tense cabinet committee meeting, to which Reith had been invited, that the idea was dropped. Luckily for Reith, he was close to Baldwin, who turned out to be an early and talented political broadcaster. Reith's own politics, if judged through his diaries, could be wild. Like so many assertive public figures at the time he admired Mussolini and occasionally despaired of democracy. Later he expressed savage admiration for Hitler too. Yet his political behaviour during the strike was subtle. He helped Baldwin in his broadcasting, actually inserting words for the prime minister about being a man of peace – 'I am longing and working and praying for peace, but I will not surrender the safety and security of the British Constitution.' Yet he was no friend of the coal-mine owners. He did not allow Labour politicians and strike leaders to broadcast but managed to keep propaganda attacks on them off the air too. The BBC during the strike was pro-Parliament but never hawkish, and it reported trade union claims in its news. It soon had five daily bulletins, considered by wary newspapermen to be, by the end of the dispute, worryingly professional and generally fair. Reith succumbed to government pressure only when the Archbishop of Canterbury wanted to broadcast an appeal for a compromise deal and a peace plan. Baldwin thought this was a bad idea, and Reith buckled. He kept the Archbishop away from the microphone until the strike was over – which was pretty craven.

The strike tells us a lot about Reith's BBC, and thus 'Reithian values'. Trade unionists and some leading Labour people were angry that it had not given them a proper voice. Nor had it. On the other hand, Reith had managed to stop a straightforward takeover by panicky or gung-ho politicians. By ensuring that the BBC sounded reassuring, and somehow part of the establishment, he stopped it becoming Churchill's mouthpiece, which would have ruined its reputation in the twenties just as surely as being Churchill's loud-hailer helped raise its reputation in the forties. Meanwhile, for the first time, everyone was turning to the radio to find out what was happening.

The shape of broadcasting was now clear, and would remain so until the shake-up of commercial television after the Second World War. The BBC would be wholly dominant, part of the establishment though not part of government. It would be rather dull, highly respectable, cultured but not excessively so, and intensely centralist – rather like Britain itself. Right from the start, some hated it for being too conservative, for being too snooty, for being too 'London'. But most took to it, willingly paying for a licence even though there was no realistic chance of being caught and prosecuted for not doing so, and following the new programmes night after night. Radio in turn began to shape the tone of the country, even its sense of itself. At the end of 1926 the Archbishop, turning the other cheek, reflected that millions of people were listening constantly to the BBC: 'I hear of loud speakers now in constant use all over England – in hospital

wards, in union workhouses, in factory dining-rooms, in clubs, in the
servants' halls of the great houses, and even among the workers in
the fields.'[24] The sound of the country had changed. And Eckersley,
the exuberant pioneer, the boyish singer and engineer from that
Essex hut? He was fired by Reith for getting divorced.

Dreaming of an Old Britain

The desire to escape into an earlier England has been a theme of the
country's literary history but it seems to have been particularly
intense in the twenty years after the First World War. The great
outpouring of anti-war literature did not happen until the late
twenties and early thirties, when the immediate effects of the trauma
were beginning to wear off. When it came, books like Sassoon's
'Fox-Hunting Man' and 'Infantry Officer' memoirs, or Robert
Graves's *Goodbye to All That*, were not only records of the horror of
the trenches, but also love letters to Olde England, 'Olde' in this
respect meaning pre-1914 and largely rural. There were nostalgia-
soaked travel writers such as E. V. Morton, who was hugely popular
at this time, so that the hunt for a lost past could become the hunt
for lost paths and forgotten villages – a hunt fed from the thirties by
the finely illustrated Shell guides and a glorious period of richly
coloured travel posters published by the railway companies and
seaside councils. Across much of bestselling literature an aching rural
nostalgia is visible, flavoured or sauced in different ways. So, for
instance, in the country-house novels of Evelyn Waugh, the sauce
was satire; in the hugely popular crime novels of Agatha Christie or
Dorothy L. Sayers, the spice is human darkness, a traditional interest
in evil lurking behind the clipped yew hedges; in the English novels
of P. G. Wodehouse the flavouring is addictive farce; and in Barbara
Cartland it was sugar. In each case, though, the default setting was a
dense, leafy greenness in which the disappearing hierarchy of squires,
curates and yokels remained intact. When, at the end of the thirties,
war broke out again, government propagandists and BBC talk-writers
would be able to turn instantly to this manufactured and well-
understood notion of what 'Britain' – in reality, mostly England –
was all about.

D. H. Lawrence was hardly alone in identifying the move from natural life to urban falseness as a central dilemma for modern mankind, and in serious literature it was a general theme in these years. Among the great novelists of the time was John Cowper Powys, whose tales of Dorset, particularly *Wolf Solent* of 1929 and *A Glastonbury Romance* of 1933, are epic in scope and brim with mysticism and nature-worship verging on animism. Scotland produced in Lewis Grassic Gibbon her finest twentieth-century novelist: his trilogy 'A Scots Quair' is suffused with a love of the soil and history. For the poet Edwin Muir, brought up in Orkney, the jolt from natural Eden to urban Hell was as sharp as any of the industrial contrasts in D. H. Lawrence's life (he, of course, going in the opposite direction insofar as he could). Muir, later a savage critic of the spew and squalor and unfairness of industrialism, famously explained that he had been born before the industrial revolution: 'and am now about two hundred years old. But I have skipped a hundred and fifty of them. I was really born in 1737, and till I was fourteen no time-accidents happened to me. Then in 1751 I set out from Orkney for Glasgow. When I arrived I found that it was not 1751, but 1901.'

For the first time in British history it is reasonable to link 'high' or literary writers with popular bestselling novelists. It was the great age of the lending libraries and the first age of the paperback. And it is through the success of this simple technology that the British common reader begins to escape rural nostalgia and plunge into the politics of the modern world. Paperbacks had been around for decades, as 'railway novels' and penny dreadfuls in Britain, or 'dime novels' in the United States, universally regarded as low, lurid and trashy – not 'proper books'. The first, albeit brief, experiment in bringing out good books in paperback format happened in Germany in 1931 with Albatross Books. But the first successful experiment occurred in Britain thanks to a young publisher, Allen Lane, who had been working at his uncle's old company, the staid Bodley Head. He said later that he had been visiting Agatha Christie's country home in 1934 and, on the way back by train, found nothing worthwhile reading at the station. So he decided to print high-quality books in a uniform way, with sober covers, priced at 6d – (two and a half pence in today's degraded currency). Whether consciously or not referring back to the dead Albatross, he called his books Penguins. A Bodley Head artist, an amateur, drew the cheerful waddling penguin picture and a publishing revolution began. The experiment was hanging in the balance until Woolworth's placed an order for 63,000 copies, leading in 1936 to the setting up of Penguin Books.

There were many revolutionary things about Penguins: they were cheap, well printed and little larger than a cigarette packet. And Lane deliberately mingled the categories of serious and popular writing: his first authors included such noted highbrows as André Maurois and George Bernard Shaw; but also Agatha Christie and Dorothy Sayers. A mental barrier was broken down. Without him, the notion of the high-quality fictional bestseller, celebrated today in endless literary prizes and the books pages of newspapers, might never have taken off in quite the same way. As the war approached, Penguin Specials began to warn of the rising German threat and during the war Penguins were sent across the world to wherever British soldiers were fighting. Lane's success was followed by a spate of book clubs, including Victor Gollancz's communist-influenced Left Book Club, which published many of the most famous political tracts of the time, such as the work of Orwell and Ellen Wilkinson. Much of the mental climate of the British before the Second World War was formed through the paperback revolution, including the high-minded leftism which would break through politically in 1945. Yet we should not forget that paperback books, and all the pamphlets of the age, were only a small part of the written-word culture: this was also a great newspaper period, when serious writers were being used as regular commentators and when the violent political disputes of the era were fought out in angry editorials. Politicians, notably Churchill himself, earned large sums for regular articles in publications ranging from the *Daily Mail* to the *News of the World*, while the *Daily Mirror* was undergoing the transformation into an easy-to-read left-of-centre paper which would give it such unparalleled influence during the war. In short, this was so long ago that writers still mattered to the general public.

The Great Outdoors

If in the early twenties you happened to be mingling with the crowds at Speakers' Corner in London's Hyde Park, listening to the 'British fascisti' or the communists, or the religious cranks, you might have noticed a tall man with a high domed head, dramatically swathed in the black-and-white habit of a Dominican friar, a pair of clumpy big boots on his feet and a very arresting Irish voice reaching through the hubbub. Father Vincent McNabb had an alarmingly direct manner. If you fed or entertained him, he would throw himself down and kiss your feet. Week after week he turned up at Speakers' Corner, or anywhere else he could get a hearing, to explain to the crowds that they must give up their insane lives in the city and return to live simply with nature in communes and holiness. He was preaching a version of the 'good life', which in the twenties had its own name, organization and celebrities. 'Distributism' had originated with influential Catholic writers such as Hilaire Belloc, who had published *The Servile State* before the war, and G. K. Chesterton, the obese short-story writer, novelist and essayist to be found stamping round the watering holes of Fleet Street in a cape and flamboyantly large hat, pretending to be a latter-day Dr Johnson. In 1926 the pair founded the Distributist League. Their creed might have been outlandish (perhaps just landish) but its earthy belief in a return to the soil, opposing the grand theories of communism, was popular for a while. The twenties are the years not only of flappers, cocktails and angry veterans, but also of 'let's build a new world', a great boiling vat of optimism, dottiness and fearless rethinking.

Distributists certainly looked different. They often wore hand-woven clothes, shapeless and woolly and coloured with muddy vegetable dyes, and sported hand-made sandals. Their spiritual homes were in the new 'garden cities' and their caricature enthusiasm was pottery. McNabb and his followers hoped for a full-scale revival of Catholic England, a repudiation of the Reformation and the industrial age. The most famous commune-founding Distributist was Eric Gill. One of the best-known public artists of the time, he was responsible for the sculptures of Prospero and Ariel above the BBC's new Broadcasting House in Langham Place. The BBC governors, viewing the naked Ariel from behind a tarpaulin as Gill was working, insisted he make the penis and testicles smaller. He was also the creator of the 'Stations of the Cross' in Westminster Cathedral, the famous Leeds University War Memorial, and typefaces still used by a huge number of organizations, from newspapers to shops. Gill wore a roughly belted smock and stockings and lived in a series of communes, at Ditchling Common in Sussex, in the Welsh mountains above Abergavenny and in the Chilterns. With his beard, spectacles, flow of drawings and writings attacking industrialism and city life, he was a well-known figure, something of a sage. He was also, however, sexually omnivorous, engaging in endless affairs, committing incest with his daughters and even assaulting a dog. If we play the Virginia Woolf game with the index to Fiona MacCarthy's biography of Gill, we find listed under sexual tendencies references to his 'bestiality, casual liaisons, *droit de seigneurism*, homosexuality, incest, *ménage a trois*, New Women (attraction to), phallic fixation, pubescent girls (attraction to), uxoriousness, voyeurism and women in uniform (attraction to)'. He was a busy fellow. Gill's frankness about sex, his innocent wide-eyed attitude to religion, and his homeliness can all be found too in D. H. Lawrence. The novelist was, by comparison with Gill, repressed about sex, but there is in Gill's writings, if not his scandalous life, a thorough questioning and rejecting of material bourgeois culture which parallels Lawrence. The urge to return to basic instincts, to strip away the clothing of urban civilization, can be found time and again in the Britain of the twenties. Gill continued throughout his life as an important emblem of Catholic living in Britain, accepted as a spokesman for holy simplicity by senior priests, including the original role-model for Chesterton's Father Brown; he lived long enough to back the Republicans in Spain against Franco.

At a less extreme level, the fresh-air tendency had its hikers, cyclists and, of course, Britain's vast new youth movement, the Boy Scouts. Sir Robert Baden-Powell's first experiment with a Scout camp happened in 1907, on Brownsea Island in Dorset, and his book *Scouting for Boys*, which is said to be the fourth most popular in the world (after the Bible, the Quran and Mao's Little Red Book) came out the following year. But it was in the twenties that Scouting reached the zenith of its prestige. Its original mixture of patriotism, a whiff of the military and outdoor adventures for urban children made this a 'how shall we live?' movement shorn of the sexual and political issues of adult back-to-the-landers. In these years, clusters of small ex-army tents full of working-class boys ruled over by wiry ex-military Scoutmasters could be found in woods across Britain, a Union Jack hanging from a nearby tree. In city streets, small boys carrying whistles and sticks, dressed in the khaki shirt, shorts and floppy hats which Baden-Powell had copied from the South African police force, marched around looking for opportunities to carry out good deeds.

The first international Scout Jamboree took place in 1920 and afterwards Baden-Powell was solemnly declared Chief Scout of the World. A year later he was created a baronet. Scouting was a rare British cultural export. The imperialism and jingoism of the pre-war movement was replaced by a new emphasis on internationalism and brotherhood, and by 1922 there were 3 million Scouts in thirty-two countries. One early convert was a young Lake District artist called John Hargrave, who supplied the drawings for John Buchan's novels. Impoverished and a Quaker, Hargrave moved to London, where he became a newspaper cartoonist and writer on Scouting under the name White Fox. He rose fast through the Scouting movement and was seen as an obvious successor to Baden-Powell. But Hargrave, a pacifist, fell out with the military hero and in 1920 was expelled from the Scouts. Hargrave was at least as naturally autocratic and charismatic as B-P himself and immediately set up a rival organization, the Kindred of the Kibbo Kift, taking the name from the Old Kentish for 'great strength'. They were organized in clans, tribes and 'rooftrees' and expected to make their own clothes, including Saxon cloaks, jerkins, shorts and hoods. They mingled the Nordic and the Red Indian yet have also been described as the only genuinely English national movement of modern times. Like the Scouts, they camped, using Hargrave's original design of a lightweight, one-person tent. On ceremonial occasions such as their annual Whitsun gathering, the Althing, they wore luridly coloured robes and carried freakish totem poles with carved skulls, animals and eagles. Though we have learned to distrust organizations with too many K's in their name, Kibbo Kift were for world peace, handcrafts and ritual. Open-air living would redeem the spirit, broken by war and industrialism. Hargrave expected more war and the eventual collapse of civilization

– just like many Marxists and Christians – and saw the Kibbo Kift as an elite group who would survive to pick up the pieces and create a new civilization.

They were part of a wider post-war movement which was particularly strong in Weimar Germany, where the *Wandervogel* youth groups set off for the mountains and forests to recover a sense of themselves they felt had been lost in the cities and the detritus of defeat. There was much interest in folklore, folk dancing, 'pure' local food and nudism and the groups in turn influenced early Nazi youth culture, the so-called blood-and-soil national socialism. The pre-war German *Wandervogel* had been visited by an Englishman with Austrian and Scandinavian blood in his veins. Rolf Gardiner had been brought up in Berlin and later at the progressive boarding school Bedales and Cambridge. He shared the *Wandervogel* interest in folk music and folk dancing. Today folk dancing has a bland, often derided image best summed up in the remark by the composer Arnold Bax that you should try everything once, 'always excepting incest and folk dancing'. But for idealistic radicals in the early decades of the twentieth century, the people needed to go back to their rural origins, re-learn the old songs and the old dances and get away from the imported dance bands and the entertainment industry. Gardiner's dancing was wild and even angry, and he championed sword-dancing against the gentler dances favoured by the folk revivalists of Edwardian England. For Gardiner, dancing was a cult, and cleansed the soul.

After the Great War, Gardiner fell in with Kibbo Kift. By now his political vision had expanded. He believed in a union between the German, British and Scandinavian peoples, a Northern Federation, to replace the dirty business of empire and the influence of American consumer culture. He also thought it was essential to return to the soil, and for Britain to become self-sufficient in food again, reversing the decline of the countryside. Going his own way, he fell out with Hargrave and left Kibbo Kift, protesting that it failed to fully believe 'in blood contact with the living past of the English earth'.[25] At the same time he had become friendly with D. H. Lawrence, visiting him in France and exchanging long letters. Lawrence wanted Gardiner to create a community which could express some of his own ideas; and Gardiner established himself in some mill buildings by a farm on the edge of Cranbourne Chase in Dorset. A skilled farmer and forester, he reclaimed much ravaged land. In the thirties he ran regular voluntary work-camps as the centrepiece of his 'Springhead Kinship', with ritual dances for unemployed people, local farm workers and urban youth, gongs to mark the times of day, and flapping overhead the Cross of St George with a Wessex dragon on it. Gardiner was a serious man, involved in the Country Landowners Association and a county councillor. But frequent visits by Germans were leading him towards dark and treacherous waters. He wrote an admiring letter to Goebbels in 1933 and as late as 1939 was teaching 'ceremonial dances' to storm troopers and SS men. Yet he was himself partly Jewish and argued at the same time that the Nazi regime was itself corruptly corporate and aggressive. He seemed unable to disentangle his life-long love of Germany from its new regime. Gardiner's deepest interest, however, was in the soil and farming. Planting forests and pursuing organic ideas, he was far ahead of his time in that at least. He went on to found Kinship in Husbandry during the war, an organization dedicated to reclaiming the countryside for traditional farming, which in turn founded the Soil Association after the war. Gardiner later became one of the earliest campaigners against factory farming and the European quota system, and in favour of sustainable development. Every time a British shopper picks up a bag of potatoes or a loaf with the distinctive Soil Association symbol on it, they are unwittingly connecting to a line of thinking that includes boys leaping around doing sword dances, and even prancing storm troopers.

For millions who had no interest in creating a new world civilization, this was also a great age of going tramping and camping. For every cult and home-made messiah there were hundreds of groups interested only in fresh air and rediscovering their own country. Partly this was thanks to that unbucolic invention, the motor car, which allowed people to reach parts of the country they had never seen before, and then camp on them – something which delighted hard-up farmers and infuriated landowners. In 1919 Baden-Powell became president of the Camping Club of Great Britain and Ireland, which held its first Club Feast of Lanterns at Deep Dene in Dorking in 1921 – Chinese lanterns rather than Indian tents and Nordic headdresses, but yet a more bosky ritual. The first non-gypsy caravans were soon taking to the road, often hand-made out of ash wood and the salvaged remains of old cars. The wandering gypsy life had been much romanticized; now the open road was available to middle-class adventurers. Motorized charabancs, early open-topped buses (the word is French for carriage-with-benches; the first charabancs were horse-drawn), brought poorer city-dwellers to the countryside for a day out. For the more active working-class enthusiasts there were the ramblers' and hikers' groups – and these were also more political.

Bennie Rothman had been a scholarship boy at Manchester's Central High School, having arrived in the city from the United States with his Jewish-Romanian parents. At the city's Clarion Café, he met socialists of all kinds and soon joined the Young Communist League and then its offshoot, the British Workers' Sports Federation. Weekend camps in Derbyshire followed, with Marx and socialist sing-songs around these campfires. During one, Rothman was aggressively ordered off the land by a gamekeeper. He began to plot a mass trespass in protest. By this stage it was estimated that, every weekend, some 35,000 people were leaving Manchester with boots, mackintoshes and haversacks to spend their free time rambling. Though rambling or hiking had begun in late-Victorian times, it was only after the war that big ramblers' federations were formed in the main cities – Manchester in 1919, Liverpool in 1922, Sheffield in 1926 – to help working-class people reach the open spaces. The national ramblers' organization arrived in 1931, the year before Rothman's rebellion. Around 500 people gathered at a quarry, accompanied by many local police, and began to set off across the grouse moors to the Peak District's highest point, Kinder Scout. There were scuffles and 'riotous assembly' was deemed to have been caused. The twenty-year-old Bennie Rothman and five others were arrested, tried at Derby assizes by juries including two brigadier generals, three colonels, two majors, three captains, two aldermen and eleven country gentlemen, and sent to prison. Another man on the trespass was a teenage Salford communist who would later become famous as the folk singer Ewan MacColl: his song 'The Manchester Rambler' gives some of the spirit of the time. Its chorus celebrates the 'wage slave on Monday' who is a 'free man on Sunday' but who is confronted by a furious gamekeeper:

He called me a louse and said 'Think of the grouse'.
Well I thought, but I still couldn't see
Why old Kinder Scout and the moors round about
Couldn't take both the poor grouse and me.
He said 'All this land is my master's'.
At that I stood shaking my head,
No man has the right to own mountains
Any more than the deep ocean bed.

Bennie Rothman, it should be added, left prison to continue a life of political activism, including serving with the International Brigade in the Spanish Civil War and campaigning against Conservative policies on the countryside in the Thatcher years. Still rambling into late old age, he lived until 2002.

So it was possible to be a ruralist fascist or a ruralist communist or anything in between. We should beware of connecting the huge back-to-nature movement of the inter-war years too closely to the dislocating impact of the Great War. It clearly had some effect in persuading would-be leaders and mystics that civilization was smashed and had to be redeemed far from the cities. But Britain was also then, as it is now, a small and crowded country. Its population was almost 30 million fewer but most people were crowded more hotly, smokily and intensely into city centres; fresh air and space were just as alluring as they are now. As the world's first industrial-ized nation, Britain had lost much of herself in the previous hundred years – the intimate sense of place, the old skills, crafts, dances, songs and dialect. Many of those who pulled on old army shorts and set off to rediscover themselves were certainly eccentric. Part of the background noise of the twenties is chanting in forests and the clatter of sword dances. But they were not all mad and they were not always wrong.

Heroes of Speed

Britain might have been struggling economically and worried already about her future as a great power, but in answering the charge that she had become 'effete' many pointed to her heroes of speed. For quite a few of the inter-war years Britons held the world speed records in the air, on land and on water – and Britain had the speed record for trains, too. This mattered not only as a source of national pride, at least at a magazine-reading, cigarette card-collecting level, but also because it demonstrated that British engineering remained world class, if not in mass manufacturing then certainly at the adventurous tip. And the heroes were indeed a little larger than life. Through the twenties, for instance, the world land and water speed records were fought for, and dominated by, two former Royal Flying Corps pilots, Malcolm Campbell and Sir Henry O'Neal de Hane Segrave. Campbell was a gung-ho character, the son of a Hatton Garden diamond merchant who progressed from bikes to motor-bikes, from them to fast cars and from cars to flying. After a wartime career as a fighter pilot he returned to his speed obsession. He was not, by and large, a culture vulture but as a young man he did go to see Maurice Maeterlinck's tedious symbolist play *The Blue Bird* and was impressed enough to call all his subsequent cars *Blue Bird*, handing the name on to his son Donald, famously killed trying for another water speed record in 1967. The older Campbell has been a little eclipsed by the younger, more by the hypnotic quality of the film of that final crash than from any fair assessment. Malcolm Campbell was a huge hero between the wars, his chiselled, long-chinned face familiar across Europe and America, appearing on German postcards, recorded in *Tintin* drawings and advertising everything from motor oil to American cigarettes. He took the world land speed record for the first time in 1924 on Pendine Sands in Wales driving a Sunbeam, then partly designed his own Campbell-Napier *Blue Bird*, winning it again in 1927.

Enter, on a Florida beach, his great rival Henry Segrave, another boy's own heroic type, an Etonian who had fought in the war as a machine gunner and then a fighter pilot, being badly wounded twice. The first Briton to win a Grand Prix race in a British car, Segrave had decided to also become the first man to travel on land at more than 200 m.p.h. Much mocked for boasting about the impossible, he achieved it in March 1927 in his *Mystery Sunbeam*. Campbell responded by moving to Daytona Beach too, and reaching 206 m.p.h.; but Segrave was soon back in his *Golden Arrow*, which used the latest Napier aircraft engine, getting to 230 m.p.h. in 1929. Then, with Britons holding both the air and land speed records, Segrave mounted a huge new Rolls-Royce aero engine in a specially designed boat to take the world water speed record. On Friday 13 June 1930, on Lake Windermere, he duly achieved that too, before hitting a log and crashing. Dragged from the water and rushed to hospital, he asked his wife whether he had set a world record and, told that he had, promptly died in her arms. Campbell's great rival had gone, but he kept going with ever faster cars and boats. Moving to the Bonneville Salt Flats in Utah, in 1935 he became the first man to drive at more than 300 m.p.h. Then, like Segrave, Campbell turned his attention to water speed records, getting the world record in 1937 and again, just weeks before the next war broke out, in 1939 too. He died of cancer shortly after the war, an undramatic ending, though his son's spectacular crash in the last Campbell *Blue Bird* made up for that.

Campbell was claimed by the fascists as a supporter of the BUF and Mosley, but Campbell was also an early Cassandra about the coming war with Nazi Germany, fiercely hostile to Hitler and a propagandist for good air-raid preparations. What is certainly true is that there was a strong connection between pilots and right-wing politics, too strong to be entirely coincidental, and presumably to do with a sense of destiny felt by early fliers looking down on the smudged and smoky lands below. In the Schneider Trophy races of the twenties and early thirties, national speed competition also led directly to some of the key fighter planes of the next war. The trophy, for seaplanes and with complicated rules, had been established by a Frenchman before the Great War but the most spectacular races were run after it, and dominated by Mussolini's Italy, the United States and Britain. After a badly run race at Bournemouth, many of the contests took place off Venice and Baltimore, with the national air forces of all the countries struggling for superiority. Britain's first Supermarine victory came in 1921, but it was really in three races – 1927, 1929 and 1931 – that sleek Supermarine seaplanes, designed by R. J. Mitchell and using new engines by our old friend Royce, finally stamped British victory. Three consecutive wins – the race was run every second year – meant that under the rules the trophy went permanently to Britain. More important, Reginald Mitchell went on to design the Spitfire, using what he had learned from the Schneider winners, before he died of cancer in 1935.

So the speed maniacs mattered, in the direct sense that their enthusiasms kept national designers and engineers working at a pitch of development which would affect the war to come. They also mattered for national morale. Even something so unwarlike as the achievement of the London and North-Eastern Railway Company's *Mallard* locomotive, which in 1938 became (and remains) the fastest steam train ever, had an impact on how people felt about being British. For *Mallard*, designed by LNER's chief Sir Nigel Gresley, not only had the sleek, striking look of the era – not so different from a Supermarine seaplane, in a way, nor one of the Campbell *Blue Birds* – but also seized the record from a rival express locomotive made in Nazi Germany. Did the boys collecting pictures of *Mallard* on cigarette cards or jigsaw puzzles know this? Naturally. It was a time when politics saturated even the world of the trainspotters. The thirties are sometimes painted as the decade of pacifist Oxford intellectuals and communist fellow-travellers, which is true, but they were also the time of right-wing speed maniacs, far better known in their day, who were planning for the next big fight.

From Rambling to Marching

There is no reasonable way of marking the borderline between the frantic, sometimes silly political searching of the twenties and the darker mood of the thirties. But it could be said that the rambling stopped and the marching began. Instead of the home-made clothes and sexual libertinism of the commune-dwellers, we enter a time when the streets of Britain are suddenly crowded with lines of marching men, often in uniform. There are the communists, either in their own right or as Unemployed Workers. There are Mosley's Blackshirts, and other rival fascist organizations, all with their drums, banners and placards. And then there are the most disciplined marchers of all, heckling at meetings, throwing bricks through the chancellor's window, tramping through the streets under their distinctive flags, running demonstrations and 'street patrols', handing out their tabloid newspaper . . . the Greenshirts. The who? The what? The Greenshirts were considered among the most effective street performers in the turbulent politics of the thirties. They were determined and enjoyed considerable intellectual support. Since then they have been almost entirely forgotten. This is possibly because they do not fit easily into the left–right politics that history remembers, and probably because they have left behind no successor organization at all. They were in fact our old friends the Kindred of the Kibbo Kift, still run by John Hargrave, but now mutated into a paramilitary movement dedicated to the cause of Social Credit.

Social Credit was also known as 'Douglasism' after its creator, a rather mysterious electrical engineer from Stockport called Clifford Douglas. A draper's son, he had worked on aircraft manufacturing in the war and had come to believe he had an answer to the post-war slump that did not involve the tyranny of Bolshevik communism but was, in its way, just as radical. Major C. H. Douglas, as he liked to be known, believed the real economic problem was lack of purchasing power. Rather than wages or the banking system, he thought that as wealth grew through technological advance, it should simply be divided each year among everyone, whether they worked or not, and passed to them as their share of the national dividend. Power would be removed from the Bank of England because 'the Credit of a community belongs to the community as a whole'. Eventually, as societies grew richer through technical progress, unemployment would disappear and people would have to work far less: the 'leisure society' would be born. Douglas was taken seriously by many and his third way, between totalitarian tyranny and capitalist anarchy, seemed highly attractive. Hargrave saw it as the economic ideology his movement had always lacked, and converted to Social Credit. He formed a 'Legion of the Unemployed' in Coventry in 1930 and then adopted a paramilitary uniform of green shirt and beret, folding the Kibbo Kift into the new movement.

Away went the totem poles and Apache-decorated tents and in came square-bashing, massed drums and flags – Hargrave was a talented artist and his Greenshirt insignia with two back-to-back Ks is as distinctive as a Nazi swastika. Yet though Douglas had the taint of anti-Semitism in his writings on the banking swindle, the Greenshirts were not anti-Jewish at all. They heckled both communists and fascists, but reserved their real hostility for the Treasury and the Bank of England. The Greenshirts lacked a big overseas sponsor, had very little money and eventually fizzled out, the final blow coming when the Public Order Act of 1937 banned the wearing of political uniforms. In a response straight out of P. G. Wodehouse, the Greenshirts for a while expressed defiance by marching with their shirts carried aloft on coat hangers. The movement had a curious afterlife in Canada, where the province of Alberta voted in a Social Credit government which soon ditched the pure milk of Douglas's ideas but stayed in power for thirty years. Hargrave himself went on to design the world's first moving optical map for aircraft – used much later in Concorde after his idea was filched – and continued to write novels and sell drawings. He tried to revive the Social Credit Party after the war, but without any success. He died in 1982. Though it has been forgotten, the mutation of the mildly batty and thoroughly idealist Kibbo Kift of the twenties into the paramilitary Greenshirt movement of the thirties seems a near-perfect parable of the age.

We have noted the acrid smell of anti-Semitism in some of these movements already, and the lure of blood-and-soil race politics. The rise of the Nazis, and the rise of anti-Jewish right-wing parties in France and other continental countries, has put inter-war Britain in a benign light. This was the country to which persecuted or worried Jews fled, after all. But the picture is too simple. For Britain had some ferociously anti-Semitic groups too. The British fascist groups were mostly small and inclined to fight one another. They emerged out of the Great War alongside anti-communist organizations – the Middle Classes Union, for instance, and the British Empire Union – and angry groups such as the Silver Badge Party of ex-servicemen, run by the eccentric aviator Pemberton Billings, who during the Great War had caused a sensation by claiming the Germans had a 'Black Book' containing the names of 47,000 highly placed perverts, and that the Kaiser's men were undermining Britain by luring her men into homosexual acts. Such people tended to see Lloyd George's government as a corrupt sell-out, and possibly under the influence of German Jews, much as the extreme right had seen things before the outbreak of war in 1914.

Henry Hamilton Beamish, a rear admiral's son who had fought

in the war, set up an anti-Semitic group called the Britons and campaigned for Jews to be resettled in Madagascar. By the late thirties he was publicly prophesying that Germany would have to invade Russia and place half the population in the lethal chamber: all Jews must be sterilized, killed or segregated. After losing a libel case he had to flee the country and eventually settled in Rhodesia. Arnold Leese, a retired vet from Stamford in Lincolnshire and a world authority on camel diseases, took control of the International Fascist League in 1928 and turned it into a fanatically anti-Jewish group; though never big, the IFL marched under its own uniform, including a black shirt, khaki breeches and puttees, a black beret and a Union Jack armband with a swastika on it. On Empire Day 1934 it raised a Union Jack with swastika over London's County Hall.[26] Then there were secret groups like the Nordics, and the Right Club, run by a well-known Conservative MP, Archibald Maule Ramsay; there was even a Nazi British version of the Ku Klux Klan, called the White Knights of Britain or the Hooded Men.

These groups were quickly penetrated by British intelligence and their extreme language kept them far from mainstream politics, but they should not be entirely dismissed. The Brownshirts and other fascist groups in Weimar Germany had also been small, apparently ridiculous, and fought vigorously among themselves. Had Britain been beaten in 1940, in the conditions of national collapse and a search for scapegoats, she had her proto-Hitlers waiting in the wings, ready to call on an underground tradition of anti-Semitism that ran from aristocrats to dockers. This will take us to Oswald Mosley, the man who dominated the British far right. He was vilified by the more extreme anti-Semites as a 'kosher fascist' and in return his party simply beat up its rivals, breaking up one of Leese's fascist gatherings so effectively in 1933 that the IFL virtually disappeared. Now, he would be brought to public prominence, if never to power, by the great world crash that upended half the world.

Crash!

If there is one thing we can learn from history it is that we rarely learn from history. In the United States of the 1920s, as eighty years later, there was a long stock-market boom. It was not all based on froth but on new goods and services pouring out to a hungry people; new cars being registered at the rate of a million a year; the entertainment boom of the radio age; nylons and cosmetics; soap powder and canned fruits. These were the flat-screen televisions and global coffee franchises of our grandparents' and great-grandparents' time. Yet much of the spending had been based on borrowing, albeit via the new hire-purchase deals rather than credit cards. There were property bubbles, notably a hysterical and fraudulent one in Florida devised by an Italian immigrant called Charles Ponzi, who sold tiny blocks of land for development, some of them actually underwater. Ponzi gave his name to a financial scam which again hit the headlines in 2008–9 with the arrest of the New York financier and former stock exchange chairman Bernard Madoff, who had modelled his investment con on the original 1920s model. Ponzi's Florida scheme was an early indication of the US economy running out of control but the warning signs were largely ignored in Washington, just as later 'sub-prime' mortgage assets took a while to become notorious as 'toxic debts'. Both Ponzi and Madoff ruined many, rich and poor.

The US president Calvin Coolidge, speaking just before the crash, had not promised there would be no boom and bust, but he had boasted of 'the highest record of years of prosperity' in US history, and promised a sunny future. There were no hedge funds or super-complicated financial instruments in the 1920s, but there were innovative and dangerous financial schemes, notably the pyramid arrangement of new investment trusts, borrowing and investing in each other. In the twenty-first century the spectacular fall of investment banks like Lehman Brothers and British mortgage lenders began a wider seizure of the banking system. In the early 1930s in America, which admittedly had a much more diverse and localized banking culture, around 10,000 banks failed following the first crashes of share values in Wall Street. That happened in October 1929 and over the next three years the US stock market lost nearly 90 per cent of its value. Eventually nearly a third of the working population would lose their jobs.

Some lessons would be learned. Economic historians mostly believe the US crash was provoked by a lack of liquidity, made far worse by tight monetary policies followed by the Federal Reserve. Around the world, as trade contracted by an extraordinary two-thirds, countries put up tariff barriers to try to protect their own industries, pushing recession into depression and slump. It is also widely believed that the gold standard, which Churchill and Norman had returned to the centre of British financial life, made the world crisis worse by transmitting the problems across the oceans. When today politicians speak of the need for radical action and international agreements they are remembering some of the after-the-event lessons of the Great Crash of 1929. Back then, the Wall Street disaster took longer to affect London and other world financial centres. Images of bankers throwing themselves from high buildings were not repeated in the Square Mile, perhaps partly because in the inter-war period it had no high buildings. But many City high-fliers were ruined and many cautious investors, older people living on their savings, lost almost everything.

Politicians sometimes talk of governments arriving in power at the wrong moment, receiving (in rugby terminology) a 'hospital pass'. In May 1929 it was a second minority Labour government which found itself in this unhappy position, winning the formalities of power less than six months before the crash. These were dark days for the world economy. Unemployment was already at nearly a tenth of the registered working population, 1.16 million. By June 1930 British unemployment had reached 1.9 million and by the end of that year 2.5 million. This was not unemployment as it is known today, with a large welfare state, free health care and free education. It was unemployment which kept families on the edge of starvation, in underheated and almost bare homes, with the cosh of the means test waiting for any family which might show the least sign, with decent sticks of furniture, warm coats or clean shirts, of living much above the breadline.

It was obvious that the old financial order represented by Sir Montagu Norman would be challenged. Norman himself greeted the arrival of Ramsay MacDonald and his chancellor Philip Snowden as 'the beginning of the end of all the work we have been doing'. In 1930, to his chagrin and public embarrassment, Norman was obliged to defend his policies publicly before a government committee of inquiry, goaded by the young Ernie Bevin to admit the impact of his 'sound finance' on industry. Sir Montagu, so sure of himself in clubland and the City, made a poor fist of it; bankers were no better as witnesses then than today. But by the summer of 1931, as gold flowed out of London, the Bank was forced to scurry around looking for support in the USA and, paradoxically, the balance of power shifted. Now it would be the same bankers blamed for causing the crisis who would dictate to the newly elected socialist politicians. Interest rates were frantically raised. The City became unpopular in the rest of the country. People spoke of Britain paying the price for choosing to be a nation of moneylenders rather than of manufacturers. And now, when the terms of an American loan arrived, it would be Norman – struggling with one nervous breakdown after another, so great was the strain – who forced MacDonald and Snowden to confront the cost of staving off bankruptcy. It meant drastic cuts in public spending, including a brutal cut in unemployment benefit, which half the cabinet would not swallow. This led directly to a split in the Labour government and the formation of a Tory-dominated National (coalition) Government to push through the cuts.

Even this, however, would not be enough to keep sterling backed by gold and in September 1931, after a failed emergency Budget, Britain 'temporarily' left the gold standard. Sir Montagu Norman was aboard a liner returning from Canada and was sent a telegram so cryptic he failed to understand what was happening – 'Sorry we have to go off tomorrow and cannot wait to see you before doing so'. The politicians would never be forgiven, either for their original belief in gold, or for the national humiliation of being forced off gold. Montagu Norman, on the other hand, recovered himself and sailed serenely on, advising against public works programmes on the Roosevelt 'New Deal' model, because Britain could not afford them, and surviving as governor of the Bank until 1944. But perhaps that is how things must be. As one historian of the City wisely put it: 'If politicians fail to challenge the assumptions of bankers, that ultimately – then as later – is their responsibility.'[27] Norman's simple vision of virtue, based on gold and free trade, had been broken, but not by the challenge of politicians or by marchers on the streets. The old world of the City had collapsed from the whiplash impact of the American crash and the judder of protectionism which swept the world. Then, as later, hardly anyone had seen it coming; the booming stock market party had been just too exhilarating to walk home from early.

The human consequences of Britain being forced off gold in the 1930s were complicated, rather as when Britain was forced to leave the European exchange-rate mechanism in the 1990s. After the 1931 election had effectively destroyed Labour and set in place the Tory-dominated National Government, policy was rather less unimaginative and tough than might have been expected. The devalued pound and lower prices meant the large majority of people who were in work were actually better off than ever before. Though protectionism in the form of tariffs on some goods did arrive, it did not have a decisive impact in a world where trade had already shrunk drastically. A housing boom helped move the economy forward again, and the policy of cheap money, partly influenced by Keynes, was relatively successful. By 1936 world rearmament finally laid the Depression to rest. The recovery was geographically biased, as we shall see: the north of England and much of Scotland and Wales, starved of capital by the high priests of the City, continued to moulder. Britain had ambled away from the slump rather than turning to sharp and radical measures when the crisis happened – something people with sharp and radical minds found intolerable. And this explains the appeal of the half comic demon-king of inter-war British politics.

The Pantomime Villain

Oswald Mosley is remembered as a full-blown villain, the nearest Britain came to siring a Hitler. But for the first half of his life he was a thoroughly mainstream figure, moving in high society and welcomed in the best political salons of London. When he first married, it was to the daughter of the Tory grandee Lord Curzon, and the King and Queen were among his wedding guests. From a wealthy landed family, he was brought up in a seemingly unchanged semi-feudal society in which everyone knew their place. He was sent to Winchester, a grand school which produced grand, self-certain and annoying adults, such as Stafford Cripps, who, in the thirties, was seen as the potential dictator of the left. Mosley joined the Royal Flying Corps – incubator of so many right-wing thinkers – and was wounded in a crash, making him the model of the dashing war-hero squire by the Armistice. In 1918 he was elected as a Tory in the landslide general election victory. His earliest political hero was Lloyd George, for his creation through the Ministry of Munitions of a really effective state reform system, though he also admired the 'social imperialists' who wanted to protect and strengthen the Empire in order to give the British working classes better lives. Though the family estate was one of those sold and broken up in the twenties, he was by any sensible standard very rich. Yet his first act of political heresy was moving to the left. He broke with Lloyd George over the repression of Ireland and turned more and more to study the problem of unemployment, as the post-war boom ended and the slump arrived. To start with, while people such as Churchill were inclined to admire Mussolini, Mosley was bitterly critical. Instead he became fascinated by Douglas and Social Credit, and began to admire those socialists who were also Social Credit enthusiasts, particularly the energetic Clydesider John Wheatley.

The young Mosley was not only dashing and cut a swathe through well-born British womanhood, he also had a raging thirst for ideas. He was an early and intelligent reader of Keynes. He went over to the United States and learned about the social ideas of F. D. Roosevelt and the organizational achievements of Henry Ford. That Keynes would end up as the guru of the British parliamentary left while Ford was a right-wing anti-Semite should not confuse us. The great division in the twenties seemed to be between those who wanted a more organized, efficient world in which unemployment and war could be banished, and those who stuck with the old ideas of the Edwardians. (The Bolsheviks were way out on the margins, regarded by all except a few clever billy-goats as barbarians.) In this division, the corporatism of fascists and advanced socialists did not look so different. The ruthless efficiency of Lloyd George in wartime, the direction and ordering-about of the parliamentary dictator, bore some relationship to Mussolini's public works programme. Political impatience was a virtue. Vice was to be timid, conventional, cautious about state power – the fallback position of Tories like Bonar Law and Baldwin, traditional Liberals like Asquith and soon of Victorian-era Labour leaders like MacDonald and Snowden. This was the political version of the war between the urgent young and the flaccid old we have already seen in the nightclubs and in culture. Unless one understands this urgent search for answers, and the way it darted across old party boundaries, one has no hope of seeing the Mosley story clearly.

When Mosley first moved over from the Tories to Labour, horrifying most of his friends, he had been impressed by MacDonald. He sucked up to the older, widowed man, paying for his car and helping with travel arrangements and hotels. Snowden and many other ordinary Labour people were jealous and suspicious. And indeed, Mosley was hardly living the life of a socialist, relaxing in Venice or on the French Riviera, enjoying comfortable country-house weekends and pursuing his private motto of the time, 'Vote Labour, sleep Tory'. In a grey political age, his plumage made ordinary MPs gasp. One of the seemingly hundreds of women who found him irresistible talked of his 'unparliamentary' good looks, those of a 'dark, passionate, Byronic gentleman-villain of the melo-drama, in whose presence young ladies develop unaccountable palpitations and sedate husbands itch for their riding-whips'.[28] Mosley was moving in the 'Bright Young Things' set of junkie-debutantes, cross-dressing peers' sons and rich lesbians, yet he studied hard, and seemed to take his politics very seriously. He ridiculed fascists and he and his wife did the round of political meetings as keenly as any more conventional socialist figures. When MacDonald was returned to power in the second minority government of 1929, Mosley was already being talked about as the man who would follow him as Labour leader. Surrounded by some of the brightest and most impatient young minds in the party, he seemed primed for greatness – though Baldwin muttered that he was a wrong 'un and Labour would find that out for themselves.

As it happened, MacDonald kept Mosley outside the cabinet, working on unemployment issues under a former leader of the railway workers called Jimmy Thomas, who was drunk, corrupt, lazy and unimaginative. New ideas were whirling about. Advised by Keynes, Lloyd George returned to the fray with his Orange Book, promising 'We Can Conquer Unemployment'. He called for high public borrowing to fund more house building and road construction. Some of the younger Tories, backed by the press barons Beaverbrook and Rothermere, returned to imperial preference, with a nationwide campaign for tariff walls, inside which the Bank of England could pursue deficit financing to boost the economy. There was excited talk of a new 'Young Party' which might bring together Churchill, radical Tories, Liberals and Labour people, including Mosley, who was bombarding the cabinet with his own plans for expansion. He wanted large-scale public borrowing, children to be kept longer at school, the retirement age to be cut and public works, including criss-crossing the country with a dozen 'speedways' – what we would call motorways.

In later decades, all these would happen, the hardly controversial reforms of mainstream Tory and Labour governments. But in 1930 the drunken Thomas was uninterested and the free-trade, balanced-budget Chancellor Snowden was openly hostile. Churchill had put it well when he said that, when Snowden returned to office, 'the Treasury mind and the Snowden mind embraced each other with the fervour of two long-separated kindred lizards'. Snowden blocked everything Mosley suggested. MacDonald, more sympathetic, dithered. Mosley worked up more detailed ideas. Again, they were brutally turned down. Herbert Morrison, later one of the most creative Labour figures when he ruled London, mocked Mosley for his Lloyd George 'roads complex' and when Mosley resigned, Snowden called him a traitor to Labour and a 'pocket-Mussolini'. A very obscure figure called Clement Attlee was appointed to Mosley's old job, and the government continued to do nothing very much. Eventually Snowden's solutions, a rise in income taxes (which he then flinched away from) and cuts in unemployment benefit, caused a mutiny in the cabinet and the collapse of the government. MacDonald and Snowden would jump ship and become part of the Tory-dominated National Government while Mosley would convert Snowden's jeer about Mussolini into hard historical fact.

Mosley's first venture, the New Party, still seemed more socialist than fascist. But it was a curious mix. It had left-wing thinkers in it.

It tried to attract up-and-coming Labour MPs, including the young Aneurin Bevan who refused, wondering where the money would come from (as we shall see, an important question) and predicting that it would end up as a fascist party. But other parts of the Independent Labour Party allowed joint membership and Mosley spoke eloquently, endlessly about unemployment, just as he had when a Labour minister. On the other hand, he set up a protection squad against socialist disruption, led by an England rugby player and called the 'biff boys'; he attracted the private support of right-leaning mavericks like the Prince of Wales, the car maker William Morris and the BBC boss John Reith; and some of his adherents quietly slipped off to Munich to see how the Nazis ran their party from the Brown House. Mosley's wonderful wife Cimmie, who had been a victorious Labour candidate and a highly effective MP, despaired of the drift towards fascism. But after a rough meeting in Glasgow, Mosley began to talk openly of the need for fascist methods: his rhetoric became wilder, as he enthused about 'riding rough-shod' over normal peacetime thinking. He was seen as a fascinating maverick himself who, if the crisis deepened, might soon be king-maker if not king. Churchill was among the politicians careful to stay friendly with him.

Stanley, the Empire and the Harlots

Unemployment kept rising, now to 3 million. In normal times this would be the Tories' hour. But the Conservatives had problems of their own. Stanley Baldwin had been fighting his own battle with the newspaper barons Rothermere and Beaverbrook who, still on their old hobby-horse of imperial protection, had been savaging the Tory leader and threatening him with their own rival party. Protectionism was still hugely popular. Mosley's New Party, for instance, had attracted around 5,000 members – but Beaverbrook and Rothermere's United Empire Party, now forgotten, had twenty times as many supporters as soon as it was launched. Baldwin told a friend he was fighting with beasts, 'and I hope to see their teeth drawn and their claws broken'. In fact he was compromising and making moves towards protection as he struggled to stay in the saddle. In a series of magnificent speeches Baldwin took on the newspaper barons, revealing Rothermere's 'preposterous' and 'insolent' demand to have oversight of a future Tory cabinet. But he moved far enough towards the protectionist argument to risk losing old free-traders like Churchill.

He, meanwhile, however, was on his way into that wilderness where he would famously spend the thirties, because of another policy entirely. Churchill was as much responsible as anybody for the cruel grip of nostalgia economics. But in his restless search for the next crusade, Churchill now moved away from domestic issues and towards a cause that would nearly destroy him, and rightly so. India's long march towards independence still had years to travel, but in the early thirties there seemed a chance of an interim compromise settlement allowing substantial home rule inside the Empire while a new Indian administrative and political class grew in confidence and experience. This was above all the achievement of Mohandas Gandhi, who rose from relative obscurity to become a world icon in these years. He had led the Indian National Congress from 1921 and won huge support for his first non-violent campaigns of boycott and home-spinning of cloth in protest at British rule, but had spent much of the decade either in prison or trying to unite disparate factions. In 1928, however, the arrival of a commission on India's future featuring not a single Indian encouraged him back to the front line with a resolution calling for a new campaign aimed at full independence. The Indian flag was raised and an Indian national day proclaimed.

Then, in March 1930, Gandhi began his new boycott, this time against the salt tax, marching thousands of his followers nearly 250 miles to a small coastal village in Gujerat, where he would pick up his own untaxed salt and carry it back. It was a symbol, a piece of brilliant political theatre. One writer on India, Jan Morris, compared it to the Boston Tea Party. The tax on salt affected everyone. Gandhi was inviting India to ignore it. The world's media followed him and he was celebrated, even sanctified, around the globe. Huge numbers took up his challenge and a widespread, good-humoured protest swept the country, humiliating the British Raj. Some 100,000 Indian nationalists were arrested and imprisoned, including Gandhi himself, under an act of 1827. Things were becoming ridiculous – the

Empire was becoming ridiculous, a worldwide laughing stock – and Gandhi was soon let out by the Viceroy, Lord Irwin. Later, as Lord Halifax and foreign secretary in Chamberlain's government, Halifax would have his reputation ruined as an appeaser, but in India a decade earlier this long, lean, devout and pessimistic man was something of a reformer. He believed self-government would come. In a further episode of unforgettable theatre, Irwin invited Gandhi to come and talk to him in his newly completed Lutyens-designed and very palatial New Delhi house. Gandhi arrived with his willow stick and shawl and entered the palace for eight discussions with Irwin, which apparently involved much laughter and a lot of non-alcoholic drinks, but which failed to produce a political breakthrough. Back in London, MacDonald's Labour government was now in favour of self-government for India, as was Irwin. British opinion, however, was still split. And Churchill ranged himself on the other side.

Perhaps nothing Churchill said has worn as badly as his infuriated description of Gandhi's visit to the Viceroy. He told his constituency association in London that he found it 'alarming and nauseating to see Mr Gandhi, a seditious Middle Temple lawyer, now posing as a fakir of a type well known in the East, striding half-naked up the steps of the viceregal palace . . . to negotiate and parley on equal terms with the representative of the King-Emperor'. Later, he is said to have added that he'd like to see Gandhi bound, laid in the dust outside Delhi and trampled upon by the Viceroy, riding an elephant. Joke or not, the comments ooze an almost physical loathing of Gandhi which betray Churchill's emotional failure of imagination. Irwin was much nearer the mark when he compared Gandhi to Christ: invited to admit his irritating character, he replied that 'some people found our Lord very tiresome'.[29] When in March 1931 MacDonald's government invited Gandhi to London to be the Indian National Congress's sole representative at round-table talks, he arrived in his loincloth and became a huge popular hero. He was mobbed in the streets, met celebrities such as Charlie Chaplin, was cheered by huge crowds when he visited Lancashire cotton workers to explain his Indian cotton policies, and was even invited (somewhat against George V's better judgement) to tea at Buckingham Palace. Memorably, when he left the encounter and was asked by journalists whether he really felt properly dressed for such an encounter,

Gandhi replied that it had been fine: 'The King had on enough for both of us.'

For the next four years the Empire dominated Churchill's political life and much of the newspapers' political coverage. In 1924 the country had been briefly transfixed by the British Empire Exhibition at Wembley. Britain celebrated Empire Day, when streets were bedecked with Union Jacks; the monarch was still officially the King-Emperor; there was a scheme to link the Empire with a fleet of airships. (This ended in March 1930 when, on her maiden cruise from Bedfordshire to Karachi, the airship *R101*, the largest flying craft ever built in Britain, crashed in northern France killing all but six of her fifty-four crew and passengers.) The world was already moving on from European empires. The rising powers were the red and black dictatorships and the vibrant democracy of America. By entering the struggle to keep India British, Churchill was throwing himself into years of wearisome, pointless and often very boring politics in which he acted as the champion of pampered Indian princelings and foaming Home Counties racialists. Churchill never drank as much as he liked to pretend, but nostalgia was for him a far more dangerous and addictive intoxicant than anything bottled.

On this, Baldwin was a better guide to reality than Churchill. He had the courage to set himself against the Indian nostalgists, just as he stood against the worst excesses of newspaper-magnate self-importance. 'Empire' – whether as diehard opposition to Indian self-government or the good old cause of protection – was the banner under which Beaverbrook and Rothermere tried to upend the Conservative Party. The spirit behind this attempted newspaper putsch was perhaps Northcliffe's, even though that great, self-tortured genius was long dead. He had died in 1922, quite mad, possibly the result of a blood infection, in a specially built hut on top of the Duke of Devonshire's house in London's grand Carlton Gardens. He could not bear being inside and the roof of his own house next door was thought too weak for the hut. There, with a revolver to ward off possible assassins and filled with religious manias (though concerned that God might be a homosexual), the original great press magnate had experienced a terrible last few days. At one point, newspaperman to the last, he had telephoned the duty night editor at the *Daily Mail* to whisper, 'They say that I am mad: send your best man to cover the story.' Yet Northcliffe's spirit long survived his physical death. There was the popular, aggressive, take-no-prisoners journalism, of course. But there was also his belief that as a press lord he could run the country at least as effectively as any politician – and that in some sense, he had the right to. He had challenged the wartime government, twice, and believed he had put in Lloyd George as prime minister. He had loomed over the *Express* owner Beaverbrook in the Canadian's most impressionable early years in London, giving him a sense of how press tyrants could behave. He had loomed, too, over his brother Harold, now Lord Rothermere and back in charge of the *Mail* and most of the Northcliffe empire (though not *The Times*). But what mattered most was that the pair of them had embraced in old Northcliffe's cold shadow. Rothermere, having lost two sons in the war, lonely and gloomy, had become thick with silver-tongued Max Beaverbrook. They exchanged thoughts and, what was worse, shares too; so that the two great rival empires of popular newspaper were tightly interlinked, a most dangerous thing.

Baldwin was up against two men who despised him and who were casting around for alternative national leaders. One would alight on Churchill, the other on Mosley. Rothermere had already intervened in British politics with the publication of the 1924 faked Zinoviev letter which had helped turn out Ramsay MacDonald first time round. Now he blamed Baldwin for letting in Labour a second time. He had a deep fear of communism and had invested both rhetorical support and some money in Hungary, perhaps as a bulwark (not a good judgement, given what was to come) – enough so to be invited to become Hungary's king. He was wise enough to decline that, though as we shall see his political judgement generally was as bad as it is possible to be. Beaverbrook, the unreliable and irrepressible imperialist, threw his *Daily Express* wholly into the campaign to destroy Baldwin. The paper's famous Crusader figure dates from this time. At by-elections and day by day it savaged Baldwin with something of Northcliffe's old fire, though with none of his wit. Rothermere for his part created much mirth by openly declaring that Beaverbrook was the man to lead the Tory Party and then the nation in Baldwin's stead.

Churchill's resignation over India in January 1931 made Baldwin's position even shakier and Beaverbrook and Rothermere came remarkably close to toppling the prime minister. Their United Empire Party had two good by-election performances. At the second, in Islington, Labour was able to seize the seat from the divided Conservatives. Tory morale began to shiver and shake. There was another by-election pending, this time in the St George's Division of Westminster, a constituency which covered some of the richest property in Britain. The Empire Crusaders were standing again. The official Tory candidate panicked and withdrew, saying he could not honestly make the case for Baldwin. The party's chief agent suggested Baldwin should stand down. Neville Chamberlain, whose father had started the imperial preference campaign thirty years before and who was now eyeing the leadership for himself, took this proposal to Baldwin with Uriah Heep apologies. Over a Sunday afternoon, the Tory leader seemed to have reconciled himself to going. But with the encouragement of friends his mood turned and he resolved to fight. Perhaps he himself would fight the Mayfair by-election? He told Chamberlain, who was horrified and blurted out that he should think of the effect on his successor. Baldwin eyed him coldly: 'I don't give a damn about my successor, Neville.'

In fact it was another MP, the socialite ex-diplomat and diarist Duff Cooper, who fought the by-election for Baldwin. Before he did, however, Baldwin delivered the only speech for which he is really famous – one so powerful and pointed that even people who do not follow politics have vaguely heard of it. He was responding to yet another attack in the *Daily Mail* signed by 'the editor' which alleged that Baldwin had squandered his father's fortune and was therefore not fit to lead the country. At London's Queen's Hall Baldwin directly turned on his tormentors. 'The papers conducted by Lord Rothermere and Lord Beaverbrook are not newspapers in the ordinary acceptance of the term. They are engines of propaganda for the constantly changing policies, desires, personal wishes, personal likes and dislikes of two men,' he said. Then he turned to the anonymous article about his father's fortune and his incapacity: 'The first part of the statement is a lie and the second part of the statement by its implications is untrue. The paragraph could only have been written by a cad.' He could sue for libel but he would not. 'I should get an apology and heavy damages. The first is of no value, and the second

I would not touch with a bargepole.' His cousin Rudyard Kipling is thought to have composed the final, famous shot: 'What the proprietorship of these papers is aiming at is power, and power without responsibility – the prerogative of the harlot throughout the ages.' There was a tremendous ovation. Against all predictions, Cooper beat the Empire Crusader by 6,000 votes and Baldwin's position was secure. The press putsch had failed. Newspaper owners would mount ferocious campaigns against politicians in the future, again and again. But they would never again try to become players as Beaverbrook and Rothermere had in 1931. It was an important moment for British parliamentary democracy.

Now that Baldwin was secure, he could play his part in the final collapse of Ramsay MacDonald's Labour government and the creation of the National Government that ruled Britain until 1940 and is remembered now without affection. MacDonald had already become notorious for his hobnobbing with duchesses and his increasingly grand, self-regarding, self-pitying air. He was hardly alone in having no answers to the economic crisis. The cabinet split over cutting unemployment benefits had seemed to be the end for a Labour government. The obvious step would have been to call a general election and see, presumably, the return of a Tory government under Baldwin. That is certainly what Baldwin wanted. But he was away that summer, as usual, on holiday in the South of France, leaving the negotiations to Neville Chamberlain, the Liberal leader John Simon and the King. The sense of crisis was acute. Chamberlain's role was important, since he rammed home to MacDonald, Snowden and their few supporters that economies would have to mean harsh cuts for the unemployed. A large part of the case for a MacDonald-led coalition was the understanding that its medicine would be bitter, particularly in the poorer parts of the country. MacDonald was to be the Labour fig leaf for Tory measures. Telling Chamberlain privately and rightly that he would be signing his political death warrant, and that if he joined the new government he would be 'a ridiculous figure unable to command support and bring odium on us as well as himself', MacDonald nevertheless agreed.

In the election that followed, the National Government candidates won a victory so overwhelming that it effectively liquidated parliamentary politics until the fall of France in 1940. It had 556 MPs, of whom 472 were Conservatives, the largest Tory contingent the Commons has ever seen. Just thirteen pro-MacDonald 'National Labour' candidates were returned. Labour itself was shattered, winning only fifty-two seats. MacDonald was therefore in something of the same position as Lloyd George had once been, a non-Tory prime minister entirely dependent on the votes and support of Tory MPs. But in reality his position was far weaker. Lloyd George had a plan, a good reputation, fire and fight. MacDonald was a broken figure, really, who, once he conceded Tory demands for some imperial tariffs, was merely a limpet and knew it. He had Chequers and his increasingly colossal vanity, but not much more. The iron economic measures run from the Treasury, first by Snowden and then soon by Neville Chamberlain, helped impose the 'hungry thirties' on much of industrial Britain. They helped breed the extra-parliamentary extremism the decade is known for too. And, most notoriously, they left Churchill and a few allies in the wilderness to warn with increasing vehemence about the Nazi threat, while doing too little, too late to prepare Britain's defences for what was surely to come. The reader, however, may have noticed something slightly odd about this familiar litany of failure. We can't quite get away from those figures. In 1931 and then again in 1935, the National Government was tremendously popular with the voters. It might have been stodgy, unimaginative, timid and even cowardly, but it seemed to be what the British, now armed with a full male and female suffrage, actually wanted.

Truth and Hype: Orwell's Englands

Throughout the thirties, there was a vast slab of the country left in despair, whose industries were declining and whose levels of unemployment were, with the low-welfare standards of the time, hideous. The northern industrial cities, which had depended on textiles, pottery, coal mining and heavy engineering, would never recover the self-confidence they had enjoyed in Edwardian times. Undercapitalized industries, including shipbuilding, their old markets devastated by protectionism and slump, were employing labour patterns, equipment and open-air working that had been left behind decades earlier in Japan, Germany and America. From south Wales to industrial Scotland major migrations began as men got on their bicycles, often literally, and looked for work. The Welsh moved towards London and the new light-industrial areas near the capital; Scots moved south too, or emigrated. Left behind in Victorian slums, surrounded by half-built ocean liners or smokeless chimneys, were millions of despairing people. Life was eked out with means-tested and meagre benefits, dreary food, outbreaks of domestic violence and a few cigarettes. Writers such as J. B. Priestley and George Orwell made journeys to the dead lands of failing industry and brought back angry epistles to the comfortable and employed. Yet the truth is that the unemployed and hungry of the north were remarkably ineffective in politics. In France, Germany and Italy the plight of industrial workers had caused turmoil, but in Britain it caused only unease. It was as if the north of England, never mind the Celtic nations, was considered not wholly British. The Labour Party might have shaved and mitigated some of the harshest financial penalties suffered by the unemployed, though after the split of 1931 it was entirely ineffective; meanwhile no other radical force emerged.

The communists, as we have seen, were a publicity-conscious fringe group, not a major force. They did achieve recognition through their sponsorship of the National Unemployed Workers Movement (NUWM), founded in 1921 by Wal Hannington in England and Harry McShane in Scotland. The NUWM organized a series of hunger marches in 1932, 1934 and 1936 on London, with thousands of men taking part, and at one point a million-strong petition. The image of proud, gaunt men in heavy boots and ragged jackets marching south, living on handouts from churches and supporters on the way, sleeping in halls and asking for nothing more than work, etched its way into the national mind. Yet again and again, after ritual meetings with politicians, they returned empty-handed. There is no doubt that the NUWM had a revolutionary tinge to its thinking. A fair example of its rhetoric comes from a 1932 pamphlet against the 'National Hunger Government', which complains that the austerity measures are

directly responsible for the appalling poverty conditions which millions of our class find themselves in today. The Government

no longer even pretends to be considerate to the needs of the
workers and their families. In the interests of capitalism it drives
forward with its murderous policy, ruthlessly grinding down the
workers and their families to depths of misery and poverty
beyond description. Despair creeps ever deeper into the homes
of our class. Mothers are reduced to nervous wrecks through
anxiety and worry. Children are being broken in health and
robbed of the chance of growing up healthy men and women.
Crime, disease and suicides increase through the increasing
poverty and destitution of our class.

Yet there was no political revolt to go alongside the message, which
left it plaintive rather than threatening. When Orwell conducted his
tour of Lancashire and Yorkshire early in 1936, he did not find it
hard to produce shocking journalistic prose about the stink, the vile
food, the despairing people and the squalid streets. He meticulously
noted the living conditions in makeshift caravans and slums that
had barely changed since Rowntree's investigations of 1900 and
the abominable working conditions of coal miners. He rubbed the
reader's nose in the stench of poverty. But he did not find a trace of
politically organized resistance. Indeed, he contrasted the atmosphere
with the briefly revolutionary mood of the immediate post-war
country, when even at Eton the name of Lenin was admired. Now,
he felt, the spread of gambling on horses, dogs and football – the
pools had become popular, starting in Liverpool, from the early
twenties – and the growth of consumerism, had somehow quietened
the anger. In his 1937 book of the journey, *The Road to Wigan Pier*,
he noted far more anger over an attempt to scupper the football
pools than over Hitler. Gambling and cheap luxuries had been very
fortunate for Britain's bone-headed rulers: 'It is quite likely that fish
and chips, art-silk stockings, tinned salmon, cut-price chocolate . . .
the movies, the radio, strong tea and the Football Pools have
between them averted revolution.' Despite years of mass unemployment and industrial decline, 'the working class are submissive where
they used to be openly hostile'. Orwell's book was loathed by many
orthodox socialists and communists, who preferred to idealize the
workers, and Orwell gave plenty of ammunition to those who
thought he had anyway turned against socialist cranks: 'If only the

sandals and the pistachio-coloured shirts could be put in a pile and burnt, and every vegetarian, teetotaller and creeping Jesus sent home to Welwyn Garden City to do his yoga exercises quietly!' No wonder they hated him.

Orwell was a strange fish, but he was right about the big things, and his assertion that the workers of Britain were more likely to carry on dreaming of horses coming in at twenty to one, and moan over their tea, than revolt was proved spot on. He had lived with tramps, understood his own prejudices, and would soon be off to fight for Republican Spain. There he joined the anarchist POUM militia, getting a bullet in the throat and seeing at first hand the brutal tactics of the Stalinist communists as they turned on their fellow leftists at Stalin's behest. Yet again, even as he told the tragic story of what was happening in Spain in his *Homage to Catalonia*, he was trashing some of the favourite myths of left-wing propaganda. It is quite true that more than 2,000 young British and Irish men left to fight against fascism in Spain; more than 500 of them were killed. Yet this was hardly a flood. Some 80 per cent of those who went to fight were communists, signing up for a force organized and directed by Moscow. Potential recruits were interrogated on their political views and general suitability by leading communist officials at a Party-owned house, once they had made their way to London; only then were they allowed to leave, on tourist visas, for Paris and the trains south to Spain. Those who, like Orwell, were going to fight without being CP members were in a small and much-mistrusted minority. Labour politicians backed the International Brigade, of course, and Clement Attlee even had a unit named after him following his visit to Spain. But this was not a spontaneous rising up of idealistic young poets and workers. Once again, Orwell drilled through to the truth behind the propaganda.

The left lost every significant battle in the Britain of the thirties, with the sole exception of the Battle of Cable Street, which denied Mosley's Blackshirts the right to march through the East End of London. Yet the left has won the battle for public memory. It is still the heroic young poets and workers dying to defend Madrid who are remembered when the Spanish Civil War is talked about in Britain. It is still the hunger marches which stamp their imprint on how we recall the thirties. None is more often referred to than the Jarrow

Crusade of 1936. Jarrow was a shipbuilding town, and the closure of its yard in 1935 had caused unemployment to soar. Some 11,000 people signed a petition demanding the opening of a steelworks to bring jobs, and 200 carefully chosen men carried it, in an oak box, south to London. They marched with blue and white banners, and a mouth-organ band, led for at least some of the way by their MP, the pint-sized, red-headed left-wing orator Ellen Wilkinson, and by a stray dog called Paddy. No drinking was allowed and there were no communists either; indeed, the crusade had begun with a church service. Everything that could be done to ensure the march was respectable and not threatening, appealing to the conscience of the nation, was done. And at the end of the nearly 300 miles of tramping and singing, the nation pretty much ignored the marchers. They were met with sympathy but only small crowds and in London achieved nothing at all. A small steel company opened later on, employing just a couple of hundred men; but even that was the result of a private initiative, not a government one.

Broken History: Scotland

History has many apparent dead ends. People and movements who seemed interesting at the time vanish from view because they fail to connect with historians and readers in later years. Then something changes, and we remember them again. The political history of Scotland between the wars is a classic case. It has been almost entirely wiped out of the story of modern Britain. Yet if this period gave us the beginnings of the great car society, and suburban spread, downhill skiing and nightclubs, the grip of Hollywood and the origins of the organic food movement, it also provides clues to the shape of today's Disunited Kingdom, in which Scotland and England are drifting apart. To understand today, we have to go back to some broken history, arguments which flared up in the twenties and thirties, when poets in kilts and newspaper barons thought Scotland would soon become independent.

In many ways Scotland mimicked the quirks and folly of what was happening at the same time in England and many other

European countries – the marchers, the secret societies, the fascination with Mussolini and race. What was different was that after the
great blade of the Second World War came down and sliced through
it all, so that post-war people decided to forget embarrassing parts of
their recent past, Scotland kept some connections. The Scottish
National Party, which at the time of writing runs a Scottish government in Edinburgh, emerged from the same angry but optimistic
political ferment described earlier. Unlike the fascists or the Communist Party, Kibbo Kift or the ILP, it survived and came to wield
real power. The post-war British decided that the early years of the
Scottish Nationalists and their enemies were irrelevant; this was
meaningless history, to be more or less consciously forgotten. Now
it seems that this forgetting was itself a mistake.

There were reasons for the Scottish story to be different. Scotland
had lost a higher proportion of her men in the Great War than had
any other part of the British Empire – around a fifth of all British
losses, and a tenth of all men of serving age. After the immediate
post-war boom, Scotland's economic decline was sharper than anywhere else in Britain. In the last full year before the war, 1913, the
Clyde alone produced more new shipping than the tonnage of either
the United States or the Kaiser's Germany. In the twenties the Clyde
began to decline fast, as did the heavy-engineering combines, the
coal mines and the textile industries on which smoky, crammed
central Scotland depended. By 1933 seven in ten Clyde shipyard
workers were unemployed and great ocean liners such as the *Queen
Mary* lay silent and unfinished in dry docks. Stagnation and decline
meant many Scots fled abroad, looking for a better life. During the
twenties Scotland's population began to fall. For every thousand
Scots, eighty emigrated. (For comparison, the figure for England was
five in a thousand.) Overall, between the wars, some 600,000 people
left a country of only 5 million. The Scottish middle classes lost their
confidence and their leadership role. Scotland did not develop the
new industries that began to revive the English south and Midlands.
From 1932 to 1937, 3,200 new factories were built in Britain, turning
out everything from aircraft to radios and light bulbs. Scotland,
however, had fewer factories. Scotland's old dominant party, the
Liberals, which had become an easy berth for English politicians such

as Asquith and Churchill, was split and fast declining. Something was obviously badly wrong, and in the politics-drunk atmosphere of the age, it was hardly surprising that radical answers were proposed.

As we have seen, this was a time when writing mattered. In the aftermath of the war, when the claims of smaller nations, both across central Europe and in Asia, were being urgently debated by diplomats, young Scots turned their attention to their country's plight; many concluded she too needed independence to deal with her poverty and backwardness. Their writings and answers have stuck in the memory as the work of full-time politicians has not. Edwin Muir, the poet and translator of Kafka, who had been born in Orkney and spent part of the inter-war period travelling in central Europe, became a socialist with nationalist tinges. So did Neil Gunn from Caithness, a fine and subtle novelist who worked as an excise man and became an early Scottish Nationalist supporter. So too did Lewis Grassic Gibbon, who died horribly young just as his genius was flowering. Not all the writers who began to change the atmosphere of Scottish life were on the left, of course. Compton Mackenzie, English born but a hugely influential satirical novelist in Scotland, had served with British intelligence during the Great War, and was a friend of both John Buchan and D. H. Lawrence. He was a romantic Jacobite more than a socialist, and he too helped found the Scottish Nationalist movement.

There were many more. No man, however, had a bigger impact on Scotland's sense of herself at the time than a postman's son from the Borders called Christopher Murray Grieve. After serving in the ambulance corps in the war and working as a journalist after it, he reinvented himself as the poet and polemicist Hugh MacDiarmid. For him, nothing less than a revolution in the Scottish soul, including a return to earlier Scots language, would begin to deal with the depths to which Scotland had fallen. He divides people even today. Many Scots are embarrassed by MacDiarmid. Some of his poetry is terrible. He lurched and weaved across the political spectrum, calling at one point for a species of Scottish fascism, then going on to express adulation for Lenin and even Stalin. He was kicked out of the Nationalists for his communism, and the Communist Party for his nationalism. Much of his prose is now virtually unreadable and he had a nasty line in literary feuds. Some wonder whether he almost literally lost his head one night in London when, drunk, he fell out of the top deck of a bus and was saved from being brained only by his huge shock of hair. His poetry, it is said, was never quite the same afterwards.

Yet much of MacDiarmid's earlier poetry and stretches of his later work are among the finest things written in Britain in this period. Like T. S. Eliot, James Joyce and Ezra Pound, he was struggling with how to reinvent a language that seemed to have become stale and incapable of expressing the ideas and complexities of modern life. While Pound reached out for snatches of Italian or Chinese ideograms, Eliot went for quotation, collage and incantation, and Joyce broke the very words apart, MacDiarmid used obsolete Scots, abstruse scientific phrases and political ranting. Amazingly, it quite often worked. He could be an infuriating man and moderate politicians regarded him as a menace, yet he was also electrifyingly energetic and optimistic, and the dominant publicist for Scottish independence. His extremism was a reflection of the mood of the age. He defended political murder by Leninists – but so too did Auden. He saw things to admire in the early Mussolini – but so too did Churchill. He wanted a nationalist revolution, and he talked about the Scottish 'race', which seems downright weird now – but before Hitler had come and gone, so too did many writers and politicians. He is picked out here because sooner or later modern Scotland is going to have to come to terms with him, as much as the English need to remember the full Kipling, or the Russians Solzhenitsyn.

The odd thing was that the Scottish left proved so ineffective in grappling with the growing demands for home rule, and left it to a wide coalition of outsiders and mavericks instead. Though 'Red Clydeside' was overblown, socialism in Scotland had caught on strongly and early. The Independent Labour Party was a predominantly Scottish creation, and Glasgow sent a stream of radical Labour MPs to Westminster. James Maxton, whose biography was written by the later prime minister Gordon Brown, left the railway station in Glasgow promising 'a Scottish Socialist Commonwealth' including a Scottish Parliament. He wanted it because, according to another Scottish Labour MP who put down a motion for a Scottish Parliament in the Commons, child poverty and other social problems in Scotland could only be dealt with by a Parliament which understood Scottish problems. Again and again motions for 'home rule all round', linking Scottish self-determination to Irish (and English), had been put to the Westminster Parliament. Indeed, one of the key pieces of legislation that was stillborn in 1914 was for a Scottish Parliament. Yet the post-war efforts of the Scottish Labour MPs to get Westminster to take home rule seriously were brushed aside very easily. And quite soon, as unemployment and then the international threat of fascism became dominant issues, even the Labour Party decided that Scottish self-government would have to wait. When eventually Clement Attlee became leader in the thirties it disappeared from the Labour agenda all together. This left a vacuum.

There had been pro-independence organizations before the ILP. The Liberals were, in theory, in favour of home rule. There was a Scottish Home Rule Association, with thousands of active members. There was a Scots National League, which wanted Scotland to separate entirely from England and which was dominated by romantic Jacobites, often living in London. But the man who began to draw the strands together was a twenty-two-year-old former Labour supporter called John MacCormick who founded a Glasgow University Scottish Nationalist Association and then in 1928, helped by the financial support of a tannery owner, created the National Party of Scotland. Scotland's older universities have the quaintly democratic habit of allowing the students to elect their titular leader, or rector. In 1928, in Glasgow, the prime minister Stanley Baldwin was chosen as candidate and the newly formed nationalists put up our old friend 'Don Roberto' Cunninghame Graham against him. To general shock, he came within sixty-odd votes of beating Baldwin. Bringing together all the very different groups who dreamed of an independent Scotland had, however, come at a price. The new party was not socialist and quickly fell out with the pro-home-rule people left in the Labour Party. It courted Scottish aristocrats and when in 1933 it merged with the right-wing Scottish Party to form the SNP, the break from radical politics seemed complete. Scottish public life was in those days rank with sectarianism – the Church of Scotland was particularly guilty of warning about the dangers of Irish Catholic immigration swamping the pure Protestant heritage, or what was called simply the 'green terror'. The nationalists played along.

Meanwhile, a bewildering number of small splinter groups, dedicated to 'Sinn Fein' tactics, private armies and secret plots, proliferated on the fringes of Scottish politics, sometimes cheered on by MacDiarmid and his friends. MacCormick was trying hard to make the SNP respectable, raising cash from wealthy supporters and proposing some kind of fusion with the Liberals; but by the later thirties, the new party was divided over the issue of national service. Radicals in the SNP thought Scots should have no part in a war between the British Empire and Nazi Germany and by 1936 all of its male members were committed to refusing military service in the British forces. The SNP began to attract the attention of MI5 and, though during 1938–9 the party reluctantly accepted the need for conscription in a coming war against Hitler, it would split itself apart in 1942 over the issue. History remembers the Oxford Union's 1933 debate when students voted heavily in favour of the motion 'that this house will in no circumstances fight for its King and Country', but the Scottish movement to refuse to fight which came later was rather more serious. Most Scots, of course, were not nationalists or home-rulers. They continued to vote for the mainstream Unionist, Labour and Liberal parties, just as the English and Welsh did. The next war would bind the peoples of Britain together strongly in sentiment, shared suffering and achievement, and usher in decades of intensely unionist politics. Yet from the perspective of a new century, the nationalist rumblings that grew out of the Great War seem at least as significant – part of the broken history still waiting to be resolved.

From the Black House to Pentonville

We last left Oswald Mosley still vaguely associated with the left, and yet showing clear leader-cult tendencies, attended by his 'biff boys' and more under the influence of Mussolini than of Hitler. He was not beyond the pale, not in the eyes of the Prince of Wales, or Churchill, or even idealistic Tory radicals like Harold Macmillan.

Mosley needed to start again because his New Party had been humiliated in the general election of 1931. He was confused enough to be seeking funds from such well-known Jewish businessmen as Israel Sieff, chairman of Marks and Spencer. In what must be one of the most cack-handed attempts at political fundraising in British history, Mosley told Sieff, in a bluff man-to-man way, that new movements 'must find somebody or something to hate. In this case it should be the Jews.' Realizing he might have been tactless, Mosley quickly added that it did not apply 'to Jews like you, Israel', but it was too late: Sieff told him to get out. The Nazis thought Mosley was nothing like anti-Semitic enough but Mosley's problem was that he was getting so much of his funding secretly from Mussolini, and Mussolini thought the Germans were far too anti-Jewish. So he hedged. Though he was waiting for the great economic crash to sweep him into power, Mosley was meanwhile dependent on the foreign powers that were prepared to fund him.

When Mosley launched his British Union of Fascists in October 1932, the Mussolini money became vital. It seems to have flowed in, brought in suitcases and deposited carefully to avoid official notice. It allowed Mosley to open up his own headquarters, a former teachers' training college, the 'Black House' at 232 Battersea Park Road, from where his Blackshirt army was organized and disciplined. Dark work was supposed to take place in the basement, including punishment beatings, but the supply of men and women who were ready to wear the militaristic uniform was steady. Mosley's capacity for work was huge and his aggression barely in control; once he leapt into an audience and beat three hecklers senseless, and another time knocked down one of his own officers who he thought had insulted him. He was soon soliciting support from right-wing aristocrats, intelligence officers, ex-military people and the fragmentary fascist groups that Britain already had. The most important event of the following months was, of course, Hitler's arrival in power as German chancellor, quickly followed by admiring profiles from Rothermere's *Daily Mail*. Launching its domestic campaign, the paper cheered: 'Hurrah for the Blackshirts!' and for six months in 1934 the Rothermere group was as frantic in its support for the British Union of Fascists as it had been a few years earlier for the Empire Crusade. It bought up hundreds of seats at Blackshirt rallies. Rothermere tried to start a cigarette-making company with Blackshirts to distribute them. He tried to run a beauty contest for Blackshirt women.

But then came Mosley's biggest rally, at London's Olympia on 7 June 1934, when 15,000 gathered to hear him, and a couple of thousand communist infiltrators heckled to the point where open and exceedingly violent confrontations with Blackshirt stewards erupted all over the hall and on the streets outside. In the Communist Party of Great Britain, Mosley was up against another group quite happy to use violence and which, indeed, thought that bloody public confrontations were a good way of radicalizing British workers. Rothermere at last seemed to understand what he was getting into. Public revulsion about the Olympia riot was widespread, a turning-away which showed just how far Britain was from Germany or Italy. In that year the BUF, with its press backing, had managed a peak of about 50,000 members, but in 1935 numbers crashed to about a tenth of that. Mosley's explanation for the defection of his main-stream newspaper support was that Rothermere had been leant on by his Jewish advertisers. Under the influence of Hitler, he was moving further in an anti-Semitic and violent direction. Searching for a new strategy, he decided to target one small part of Britain where, because it contained a third of British Jews and much poverty, the prospects for stirring up fascist feeling seemed particularly strong. He decided to make the East End of London his battleground. This would prove just as disastrous as his Olympia rally. Blackshirt speakers began to whip up anti-Jewish feeling in Rotherhithe, Bethnal Green, Stepney and Shoreditch. Blackshirt thugs, often very young, began daubing anti-Semitic slogans on walls, desecrating Jewish cemeteries and attacking synagogues and Jewish shops. From vague accusations of international Jewish financial control, the BUF had stooped to just the same attacks on individual, often poor Jews that the Nazis had initiated in Germany.

The East End, however, was also a Labour and communist stronghold, and a series of front organizations were quickly formed under Jewish communist leadership. The fascists were, in turn, attacked with razors and truncheons. Mosley decided on straight-forward mass confrontation. On 4 October 1936 he led around 2,000 BUF members in uniform in a march through the East End designed to intimidate local Jews and rally fascists. From his point of view it was a catastrophic mistake from which his organization would never recover. Waiting for him in Cable Street, under the banner of the Jewish People's Council against Fascism, were around 100,000 counter-demonstrators who had overturned a lorry and piled up bricks as a barricade. The police, seeing what was about to happen, ordered Mosley and his men to turn away. They did. The police then turned on the anti-fascist demonstrators and in the ensuing fracas more than a hundred people were injured and eighty arrested. There was a brief rise in BUF membership in the East End but, once again, the overwhelming public reaction was one of disgust. The Home Office and the Metropolitan Police had been debating the merits of banning fascist parties and continued to hold back, on civil-liberty grounds. Instead the government passed the Public Order Act which banned the use of paramilitary uniforms on British streets and the 'stewards' used by political parties, as well as giving the police new powers to ban marches all together. Insulting words likely to cause a breach of the peace were also outlawed.

This was repressive legislation, strongly protested against not just by the British Union of Fascists but by the communists and the Greenshirts too. But it worked. Mosley continued to hold his rallies, turning his theme to a campaign against any war with Hitler's Germany, but it had a limited impact. One writer on British fascism said that Mosley's 'dream of a fascist nation was reduced to the reality of a minority anti-Semitic sub-culture in some areas of the East End of London'. The extraordinary truth is that through all the battles between fascists, communists and others in Britain, not a single person was killed. Unfashionably, much of the credit must go to the Home Office and the police, who reacted moderately, refusing to take Mosley too seriously and relying on public ridicule. When war came, the fascists, including Mosley and his second wife, would be rounded up and imprisoned. His long-suffering first wife, Cimmie, had died from peritonitis in May 1933 and he had become infatuated with a woman called Diana Guinness, a great society beauty. Her original family name is even better known to students of these times, however. The story of the Mitford girls remains one of the essential essays in how extreme politics overturned the common sense of a small but vocal and vivid minority. It is an exotic,

almost unbelievable upper-class family saga; but our appreciation of
the texture of the times would be incomplete without it.

The Tragi-comedy of the Mitfords' England

They were famous then. They are still famous now, their lives
slimmed down by time to jokes and scenes that still have the power
to shock.

Scene one: Near High Wycombe in the Chilterns, a stream and
some rough-looking fields, just before the First World War. Three
girls and a boy are running, screaming with apparent terror, darting
past startled sheep, in and out of the running water until they
collapse with exhaustion and wait. Behind them, some way behind,
runs a lean, wiry, tall, rather handsome man in rough country
clothes carrying a whip, who is in turn chasing a bloodhound. The
man is the second son of a minor peer, wounded in the Boer War,
now working in the unlikely surroundings of the *Lady* magazine,
engaging in one of his favourite recreations, the child hunt. It is a
game; and the hound will slobber on the children eventually, rather
than tear them to pieces, but it seems alarming enough.

Scene two: Gloucestershire, 1926. The same man, just as
impressive-looking but now angrier, has been standing outside a
Jacobean country house, swearing about 'damned sewers' and cracking a long stock-whip to express his feelings. Inside a collection of
young Oxford aesthetes, with their flapping wide trousers, luridly
coloured Fair Isle sweaters and silk ties, has been staying the night,
friends of his eldest daughter, Nancy. One of the effeminate creatures, Mark Ogilvie-Grant, totters down for breakfast, much the
worse for wear. The whip-cracker, now Lord Redesdale after the
death of his eldest brother in the war, sees his chance. He welcomes
the young man by snatching off the cover of a tureen: 'Brains for
breakfast, Mark! Pig's thinkers.' Seeing the mess of boiled brains,
Ogilvie-Grant turns bright green and staggers out to be violently sick.
A brief flicker of something like satisfaction is seen on the peer's face.

Scene three: By now, it is 1931 and the aesthetes and flappers of
the Roaring Twenties are already history. We are in the upper floor

of a newly built house, Swinbrook, on a hill above the river
Windrush in the Cotswolds. Lord Redesdale has built it to his own
design near the earlier country house and his family regard 'Swine-
brook' as hideous. Two girls, aged fourteen and seventeen, are
glaring at one another across a room which they share. On one side
is 'Boud', or Unity Valkyrie Mitford, and on the other her younger
sister Jessica. Let her take up the story:

> We divided it down the middle, and Boud decorated her side
> with Fascist insignia of all kinds – the Italian 'fasces', a bundle
> of sticks bound with rope; photographs of Mussolini . . . photo-
> graphs of Mosley trying to look like Mussolini; the new German
> swastika, a record collection of Nazi and Italian youth songs.
> My side was fixed up with my Communist library, a small bust
> of Lenin purchased for a shilling in a second-hand shop, a file of
> *Daily Workers*. Sometimes we would barricade with chairs and
> stage pitched battles, throwing books and records until Nanny
> came to tell us to stop the noise.[30]

Later Unity would say she was going to Germany when she was
older to meet Hitler, while Jessica would counter that she was going
to run away and become a communist. (Their youngest sister,
Deborah, would complete the perfect predictive sequence by saying
she would become a duchess.) Unity and Jessica, their fights over,
would snuggle up and discuss how they would feel if one was
ordered to execute the other.

Scene four: 9 February 1935, the Osteria Bavaria, in Munich.
Unity Mitford finds her hand is shaking so much she cannot drink
her hot chocolate. After weeks of waiting and staring as he passes,
Hitler has finally noticed her and, his curiosity aroused, has invited
her to join him at his table. She introduces herself, and they talk
about how their two Nordic countries must never again fight each
other, about the global Jewish conspiracy, about films and London's
architecture. Earlier Unity's sage assessment of the Night of the Long
Knives, in a letter to her older sister Diana, is that she is terribly
sorry for Hitler: 'It must have been so dreadful for Hitler when he
arrested Roehm himself and tore off his decorations . . . Poor Hitler.'
As she starts to meet Hitler she writes to her father, that same child-
hunting peer, 'I am so happy that I wouldn't mind a bit dying. I

suppose I am the luckiest girl in the world.' She will go on to meet
Hitler privately a total of 140 times in the next four years, becoming
such a close member of his inner circle that there are widespread
rumours the two of them are lovers. Though she sits at his feet
while he strokes her hair, and though he is clearly intoxicated by her
presence, this is probably not so. Unity introduces her parents,
brother and some sisters to Hitler, attends the Nazi rallies, wears a
swastika given to her by the Führer and writes a foamingly anti-
Semitic letter to *Der Sturmer*, Julius Streicher's notorious paper,
declaring herself a proud 'Jew-hater'. Later she accepts the present of
a luxurious flat in Munich, recently evacuated by some Jews who,
the Nazis say, have 'gone abroad'.

Scene five: It is 6 October 1936. Diana, the beautiful older sister
we have not met since she was running from the bloodhound as a
small girl, is now divorced and standing in a spacious drawing room
beside the man she idolizes and will support all her life – Oswald
Mosley. They are looking out of the window of the apartment of
Diana's great friend Magda. Outside in the park-like garden the
autumn sunshine plays on trees just turning yellow as the guest
of honour arrives. Diana and Mosley are to be married, in secret
to spare the blushes of their families, particularly those of Mosley's
first wife Cimmie. The apartment is in Berlin, Magda is the wife of
Joseph Goebbels and the guest of honour is Hitler. Unity is there
too, as are Mosley's witnesses, one of whom is an MI5 agent. Hitler's wedding present is a silver-framed, eagle-surmounted picture
of himself. Mosley and Diana had been pressing him to allow them
to set up a radio transmitter in northern Germany from which they
could run a commercial station, broadcasting popular music the
stuffy BBC ignored, which would in turn make such a profit from
advertisements they could fund the British Union of Fascists out of
it. Hitler is not sure about this, and there is no time for a proper
discussion at the wedding feast. Later, the project will go ahead and
fails only because war comes, ruining Mosley's finances. That night
he and Diana retire to their grand hotel but their perfect day is
spoiled by a marital tiff.

Scene six: April 1937. Bilbao, northern Spain: a war zone.
Refugees are streaming into the Basque town as Franco's forces push
the Republicans back. Bilbao itself will fall in just six weeks' time. In

a hotel we find Jessica, who had the communist half of the room and aged nineteen has now run off with Esmond Romilly, a cousin and also Winston Churchill's nephew. Since the age of twelve Jessica had been accumulating money from birthday presents and other sources and placing it in an account at Drummonds Bank in London, labelled clearly as her 'running-away fund'. When she had enough, she duly ran away. She did so having long admired Esmond from a distance. Known to the popular papers as 'Winston's Red Nephew', Romilly had started a left-wing pacifist magazine, *Out of Bounds*, at his public school, Wellington, and circulated it round almost all the main private schools. He was expelled and sent to a remand home before setting himself up in a left-wing bookshop in London and continuing to produce his magazine. Aged seventeen, he set out for Spain to join the International Brigade and was involved in the Battle of Boadilla del Monte before being sent home with dysentery. There, at a house party near Marlborough, the romantic rebel met Jessica and she almost immediately asked whether he was returning to Spain and if so, whether she could go with him. After some subterfuge the two teenagers decamped and, in love, finally arrived at Bilbao, where Esmond was determined to make his way as a war reporter. But then the British papers, already fascinated by the fascists in the family, got hold of the story and, with the parents distraught, the foreign secretary Anthony Eden intervened. Jessica and Esmond were tracked down, blackmailed into getting onto a Royal Naval destroyer at a nearby port and taken to southern France. The story was reported across Europe. Hitler was much amused and, according to Unity, solicitous for Jessica's well-being. She married Esmond and they eventually returned to Britain to live in the East End of London, carrying out vigorous anti-fascist activities directed mainly at Jessica's brother-in-law Oswald Mosley.[31]

It is hardly surprising that the story of the Mitfords, the six sisters and their brother Tom, has lasted. It still seems impossible to quite believe. This is partly because the family itself spun its own myths. The oldest daughter, Nancy, lightly fictionalized their childhoods and parents in a sequence of novels which were almost as engaging as those of her friend Evelyn Waugh. She made their father Lord Redesdale, who appears in her books as 'Uncle Matthew', into such a grand comic figure that it is hard now to properly disentangle the admittedly wild-eyed but kindly peer from the caricature. Jessica Mitford's autobiographical books are as good. The press picked up the stories early and followed the girls from the early-twenties parties to the disasters and dramas of the late thirties, simplifying and distorting and glamorizing all the way. Yet the kernel of the story is true. The girls did divide into a novelist, a duchess, a farmer, two fascists and a left-wing muckraker. Unity, the Hitler-lover, really was conceived in a small Canadian town called Swastika, where her parents were prospecting unsuccessfully for gold: her middle name really was Valkyrie. Lord Redesdale, who fought in the First World War as well as the Boer War, really did loathe foreigners, just like his fictional alter ego, and fell into violent rages, during which he would pick people up and shake them. Life at his country homes was just as uncomfortable and disconcerting as it seemed.

But does their story tell us anything beyond its symmetries and lurid humour? First, this is a story of the right-wing gentry. Jessica, who became a socialist and eventually settled in America, was very much the odd one out. After she married Mosley, Diana served time in prison during the Second World War. Unity became a fanatical Nazi and anti-Semite. The novelist Nancy, though she sometimes claimed to be on the left, and worked for a while in a refugee camp, also briefly joined the Blackshirts and was a notorious snob. Both Lord Redesdale and their mother, Sydney, were enthused by Hitler. Redesdale was initially anti-Nazi, telling Diana after an early visit to Germany that he was 'absolutely horrified' that she had accepted the hospitality of 'people we regard as a gang of murderous pests'. But when he was brought to see Hitler by Unity, he changed his mind. Lady Redesdale underwent the same conversion. During the war she continued to speak out loudly and inconveniently in support of Nazi ideas, though her husband broke with all that, and consequently with her too. Another of the sisters, Pamela, had attended British Union of Fascist meetings and later married a brilliant scientist called Derek Jackson. He too strongly admired Mosley's brand of fascism. Tom, the brother, met Hitler under Unity's influence, went to Nazi rallies and, though not overtly political, told friends that, had he been German, he would have been a Nazi. The scene with the girls' floor equally divided between red and black, a basic of Mitford story-telling, is hardly a full account of the balance of the family politics. It is a little too twee, making a joke of extremism that was all too real.

The Mitfords were not typical, but their interest in far-right politics was not at all unusual for the upper classes of the thirties. As we have already seen, the landed gentry were in fast retreat in these years. Mosley had to sell his family estates, like hundreds of other once-landed families. After Lord Redesdale inherited his first large country house he soon found he had not the cash to keep it up, and the family was trading down throughout the inter-war years. When the family moved to Old Mill Cottage in High Wycombe again, the younger children would chant their downward curve in the property market: 'From Batsford *Mansion*, to Asthall *Manor*, to Swinbrook *House*, to Old Mill *Cottage*.' The unthinking support for Conservative politics was shaken, and not just in the Mitford home, by the steady squeeze on the old rural order. Brought up to fear the unknown but surely seething urban masses and the possibility of communism, many people began to talk of 'that Hitler feller' as being not all bad. During the General Strike, Jessica had even taken her pet lamb indoors in case the Bolsheviks came to shoot it. When war with Nazi Germany eventually came, almost all of the British followers of fascism would drop their previous attachments and serve their country. Only a tiny number became traitors and the official line of the BUF was to serve. But most of the wealthier British who fell out of love with the National Government were looking further to the right. Communism was their real enemy, not fascism.

This produced strange friendships across political boundaries, as well as breaking up relationships inside families. Again, the Mitford story is instructive. As we have seen, Jessica ran off with Churchill's nephew, Esmond; earlier he had been one of the leftists who caused the trouble at Mosley's Olympia rally. When he was killed, during a bombing run against Germany, Churchill was much distressed. But the entanglements only start there. One of Diana's closest friends was Churchill's daughter and Diana stayed with the family at Chartwell as well as later, when Churchill was Chancellor of the Exchequer, at 11 Downing Street. Diana remained a bewitching and welcome guest after she had given her life to Mosley and when she was regularly visiting Nazi Germany. This meant that she was in the extraordinary position of knowing both Churchill and Hitler well throughout the key years of pre-war crisis. She tried in vain to persuade Churchill that Hitler had his good points. None of this is to suggest that British high society was riddled with pro-Nazis to the point where a German takeover would have been easy. Churchill remained immune: the so-called 'Cliveden set' of upper-class appeasers was relatively small and, when the moment of crisis came, uninfluential. But the people who led the far right in Britain were well known to the people who remained in the political mainstream. Had the economic crisis been worse, or had there not been a modest recovery in the south of England and the Midlands well before the war, British politics might have been grimmer.

All of which is starting to become heavy-handed, perhaps. Are the Mitfords not also a confection to be enjoyed? That too is part of the story, and one which reflects better on much of the family. Their eccentricities emerged from a world in which more people were cut off from the mainstream, in relatively isolated family groups, more ready to shock, and to create private languages, than the more homogenized mass-media British of today. Some of them at least were great mockers, and a very large part of Mosley's problem was that he became easy to mock. In his jackboots, peaked cap, riding breeches and semi-military tunic, strutting and shouting, he was simply unEnglish. Even Hitler thought he would have done better to stop copying Germans and Italians. Nancy Mitford's least-known novel, *Wigs on the Green*, published in 1935, is a satire on the Blackshirts featuring a very funny caricature of her sister Unity. As Eugenia Malmains she is a young and ardent supporter of the 'Social Unionists' or 'Union Jackshirts' and first appears in a grey woollen skirt, plimsolls, a Union Jack jumper and a leather belt, with a large dagger, standing on an upturned washtub, haranguing the yokels of Chalford, a Cotswold village. Her nanny tries to haul her down but is arrested by Union Jackshirts as a filthy pacifist. Eugenia goes on about the dangers of putrescent democracy: 'In England today, society is rotten with vice, selfishness and indolence. The rich have betrayed their trust, preferring the fetid atmosphere of cocktail bars and nightclubs to the sanity of a useful country life. The great houses

of England, one of her most envied attributes, stand empty – why?
Because the great families of England herd together in luxury flats
and spend their patrimony in the divorce courts.'

The answer is the leadership of the Captain, wise, stern, 'a man
and not a tortoise'.[32] This is quite gentle satire, and the book's story
is a comic romance, but it clearly drove both Diana and Unity mad
with anger. Mosley banned Nancy Mitford from his house for the
next four years and Unity said she would never speak to her oldest
sister again. The book, though funny in a sub-P. G. Wodehouse way,
was never republished, probably because of the sisters' reaction.
They could take outright communist opposition – Jessica and Unity
remained friends throughout – but they could not stand being
laughed at. Wodehouse himself, who naively ended up broadcasting
from Berlin during the war, nonetheless also mocked the BUF. In
his *Code of the Woosters*, perhaps mimicking Nancy Mitford's book
of two years earlier, Wodehouse creates Roderick Spode, leader of
the Saviours of Britain or the Black Shorts, a 'big chap with a small
moustache and the sort of eye that can open an oyster at sixty paces'.
Bertie Wooster and Jeeves, needless to say, see him off. A national
sense of the ridiculous has helped Britain keep her balance more than
once.

Yet the final message of the Mitford saga was that it was tragic
as well as comic. For a final scene one could choose the broken man
that Lord Redesdale later became, driven to despair by his daughters'
extremism; or the miserable existence of the society beauty Diana in
Holloway Prison as Hitler's bombs fell on London; or the separation
of Jessica from most of the rest of the family. But the obvious scene
took place in the 'English Garden', a park by the River Isar in Munich
on 3 September 1939 when Unity Mitford stood outside an art
gallery, pulled out her pearl-handled pistol and shot herself in the
head. Her equally beloved Nazi Germany and Britain were at war
and she could not bear it. As she lay brain-injured and possibly dying,
Hitler visited her once more. She survived, however, and was taken
to Switzerland and thence to Britain. Her mother looked after her
through the war, in High Wycombe, London and their Scottish
island, Inch Kenneth, until she died of meningitis in 1948. But though
she could talk, walk and visit friends, she was left with the mind of a
twelve-year-old child, and incontinent. It was a terrible end but a

devilishly accurate commentary on those pre-war lives of infantile politics. The private language of sisterly jokes, the collusive sense that Britain could play-act as upper-class farce, what lesser breeds took seriously . . . that too was shredded by the story of the Mitfords.

The Lion in Winter

When you don't know what to do, write a book. In the summer of 1932, by now an old-looking man at fifty-seven, Churchill was touring the battlefields where his great ancestor Marlborough had conquered, doing research for a multi-volume biography. He had fallen out with the Conservative leadership. When the National Government was formed, he was pointedly not invited back. Thus he could be found in Munich staying at a hotel with his family. Here he was introduced to the same man who had helped the Mitford girls meet Hitler, the Harvard graduate, art dealer and passionate Nazi Ernst 'Putzi' Hanfstaengel. Putzi was very keen to introduce the two great men – Mr Churchill and Herr Hitler – and brought good news: Hitler came to this very hotel most afternoons. Interestingly, Churchill agreed to have a quiet chat with Hitler, though complaining about the would-be Führer's anti-Jewish views. It was Hitler who decided not to come. Churchill was out of office, wasn't he? Nobody listened to him, he told Putzi. Hanfstaengel rather boldly retorted that the same could be said of Hitler. He later said he thought Hitler was nervous of meeting Churchill, whose party left the hotel a couple of days later.

It would have been some after-dinner chat. Churchill had been avidly watching the rise of the Nazi movement well before Hitler finally achieved power, and warning that his victory would threaten European peace. It would take a heroically blinkered Churchill-worshipper to claim that his career had been a triumph of clear thinking since he left the Liberals. We have noted his backing until the late twenties for the ten-year rule, which pushed British defence spending to its lowest as a proportion of national wealth until very modern times. We have observed his wrong-headed, tedious obstruction of the Government of India Bill, a moderate and temporizing measure which seemed to derange his romantic mind. And a little

earlier there was his paranoia about Bolshevik insurrection in Britain
– though to be fair he was always right about the Soviet Union itself.
All of this led Baldwin by 1936 to muse to the Number Ten official
and diarist Tom Jones that one day he would say 'a few words in
passing' about Churchill – not a speech, but he had it ready: 'I am
going to say that when Winston was born lots of fairies swooped
down on his cradle with gifts – imagination, eloquence, industry,
ability, and then came a fairy who said, "No one person has a right
to so many gifts," picked him up, and gave him such a shake and a
twist that with all these gifts he was denied judgement and wisdom.
And that is why while we delight to listen to him in this House we
do not take his advice.' Words replayed by Denis Healey many years
later, talking of David Owen, though with a rather cruder finale,
they expressed a general view of Churchill at this time. He was
frankly laughed at by Oxford students when he lectured them on
disarmament. He was mocked into near-silence at a gathering of the
Conservative Central Council, and routinely abused in the Commons
by Tory and opposition MPs who thought him rude, over the top
and windy. Most newspapers applauded MacDonald and Baldwin for
keeping him out of office. The Labour Party constantly attacked him
as a reactionary warmonger. Many of his old friends, like Lords
Londonderry and Rothermere, sympathized with German diplomats
who complained about Churchill's rudeness towards Hitler. He was
genuinely isolated.

   Yet when it came to Germany, Churchill was early and Churchill
was right and Churchill was utterly dogged. Once Hitler was in
power, Churchill's demands for faster rearmament never flagged.
He was passionate but tried hard to keep to facts and to accurate
numbers. In Edwardian times the arms race had focused on Dreadnought battleships; in the thirties it was all about air power. Much
of the argument between Churchill and the ministers was therefore
about numbers of planes, the preparedness of Germany's aircraft
industry, pilot training, and so on. Again and again he told the
Commons that the Germans were further ahead than the government admitted, and that the RAF was further behind. Again and
again he was proved right. Churchill based his political assault on the
National Government from a clear vantage point, looking down at
Nazi Germany as a land full of 'war spirit', 'the pitiless ill-treatment

of minorities' and sloughing off civilized values 'solely on the grounds of race'. It cannot be said that he misunderstood in any way what was happening. He may not have met Hitler, but he seems to have understood him. In the early thirties this led to him being abused as a man obsessed, pursuing some kind of strange vendetta, even plotting for power.

Armed with inside information supplied to him by a series of patriotic but rule-breaking civil servants, he began to unsettle ministers, then very slowly to turn them round. Desmond Morton, the head of industrial intelligence for the Imperial Defence Staff, was a key Churchill source, visiting him frequently and passing on huge amounts of classified documents. Then there was Ralph Wigram, a Foreign Office official, working with his wife Ava and also with the private knowledge of his boss, Sir Robert Vansittart. Wigram went down to Chartwell and had Churchill round to his house, breaking every rule in the civil-service book; he died in mysterious circumstances, either because of a heart attack or by suicide, at the age of forty-six, greatly to Churchill's distress. There was Vansittart too: Churchill took to striding into 'Van's' rooms at the Foreign Office and haranguing him, rather disconcerting the man who was, after all, chief servant of the very people Churchill was opposing. There was Reginald Leeper, the head of news at the same department. But there were many others, up to twenty sources, including serving RAF, naval and army officers, who began to use Churchill as their only public weapon against a slow, appeasing and unimaginative government. Thanks to them he became extraordinarily well informed – about the exact condition of Britain's feeble tank technology and night-flying training, the number of anti-aircraft guns in Malta and the poor training of RAF technicians, the de-icing of aircraft wings and the latest issues in propeller technology. He knew a phenomenal amount, thanks to leaky diplomats and businessmen, about the German aircraft industry and the order books in Britain. Again and again, when he attacked publicly, he was better informed than ministers themselves.

Some of what was revealed was shocking. When it was agreed that German observers be given a sight of the latest RAF aircraft, they were so unready that fake gun-turrets and hurriedly trained special pilots had to be used to pretend things were better than they were. By 1937 even the cabinet knew that the Luftwaffe was stretching ahead in aircraft numbers and pilot training, and that Churchill had been right all along. There was always an ambiguity in the Baldwin–Chamberlain cabinet about the infuriating old man's campaign; from early on, though they hoped he was wrong, they accepted at some level that he might be right. In rejecting him as a cabinet minister after his triumphant 1935 election, Baldwin wrote to the Conservative chief whip that Churchill 'should be kept fresh to be our wartime prime minister', and he was not being merely wry. Meanwhile, Churchill used every method he could think of to keep the pressure up. He wrote a torrent of articles and soon had at least some of the press, notably the *Daily Mail*, on his side. He spoke endlessly in the Commons. He wrote privately to ministers. He accumulated a growing group of outriders, MPs like Harold Macmillan and Brendan Bracken, mavericks like the 'Red' Countess of Atholl, and increasingly press supporters too, along with Labour figures and even the odd trade unionist. He would hold court in the Savoy Hotel, and slowly but surely part of public opinion began to swing his way.

Behind the scenes, after 1935, British rearmament was underway, if progressing slowly. Sir Henry Tizard, one of the many conscientious public servants who found Churchill's attacks almost intolerable, had driven through the development and installation across the south of England of radio direction-finding (RDF) stations, later known by the American acronym radar (*r*adio *d*etection *a*nd *r*anging). The credit went both to the Scottish scientist who invented the system, Robert Watson-Watt, and to Tizard for understanding its implications; without these men, the Battle of Britain would have been lost. As to the aircraft themselves, a large system of shadow armaments factories, which could be turned to full armaments production, was being prepared. In February 1936 the first prototype Hawker Hurricane was tested. Correctly forecasting the government's changing attitude, the plane's privately owned manufacturers began planning for mass production of the fighter that would be the staple of the 1940 struggle; their foresight paid off in July 1936, when 600 aircraft were ordered. Even so, after years of downplaying military needs for civilian, it took a long time to prepare the factories and refine the designs, and by September 1939, against the RAF orders for 3,500 Hurricanes, fewer than 500 had actually been delivered. Reginald Mitchell's famous Spitfire Mark 1 began test flights at Southampton a few months after the Hurricane. Mitchell, who thought it had 'a bloody silly name', died in 1937 from cancer, leaving the aircraft to be refined by others. The first were delivered to the RAF by August 1938 but Supermarine struggled to build enough and the job was sub-contracted to a car maker, Nuffield, who built a new factory at Castle Bromwich. Nuffield's efforts proved no more successful than Supermarine's and by the beginning of 1939 only forty-six airworthy Spitfires had been delivered to the RAF.

In other ways, the numbers game being played by Churchill and the ministers had unhappy consequences. In an attempt to match the Luftwaffe's superior strength, every semi-modern design was ordered for the RAF during the late thirties, including aircraft that would prove obsolete by 1940, such as the ill-starred Fairey Battle light bomber and the Bristol Blenheim. In general, believing the old mantra that the bomber would always get through, both Churchill and most RAF commanders overestimated the effectiveness of bombing. By the time the war started, only a relatively small proportion of British bombers could actually reach Berlin, and their payloads were light. Churchill, like Baldwin and most other politicians, believed ten or twenty times as many people would be killed in bombing raids as actually were, and assumed gas would be used by all sides. It is this combination of hard-edged, unflinching warnings about the coming war and the fear of overwhelming air attack, against which there would be no defence, that explains the ambiguous popular attitude to Churchill. He was bravely speaking out, but his message seemed horrible and hopeless. Virginia Woolf's diary in 1938 reports the local postman saying that the country might be cheering Chamberlain now, 'but in five years time we may be saying we ought to have put him, Hitler, down now. These dictators & their lust for power – they can't stop. He'll get stronger & stronger.' Yet then the postal philosopher adds, 'But now we can't help being glad of peace. It's human nature.'

A Funny Kind of Crisis

The hardest thing to understand about the abdication crisis of 1936 is why it has been remembered as a moment of national trauma. After all, there were plenty of other things to worry about at the time. Mass unemployment remained at a monstrous level. The dictators were on the march. The Spanish Civil War was raging. Yet when the foreign secretary Anthony Eden arrived to tell the prime minister about his latest moves, Baldwin rebuked him: 'I hope you will not trouble me too much with foreign affairs just now.' He was, he explained, far more worried about the consequences of Edward VIII's love affair with American divorcee Wallis Simpson. Baldwin spent day after day wrestling with other ministers, his friends and the leaders of rival parties over what to do. For months, normal political life seems almost to have come to a standstill while archbishops, press lords, MPs, eminent lawyers and royal advisers argued with the forty-one-year-old monarch and with each other. In this age before international broadcasting or the internet, most of the public were ignorant of the story. Rumours leaked into Britain, of course. American and other newspapers were covering the great romance between the King and the sexy (though not beautiful) Mrs Simpson at lavish length. In the Commons it was asked why news magazines from overseas were on sale with certain pages torn out. Knowing fingers tapped knowing noses. Everybody who was any-body knew. One example of the kind of letters pouring in from British citizens overseas came from the US to the editor of *The Times* and protested that Britain's reputation abroad was being covered in a perfect avalanche of muck and slime: the doings of the King had 'in the course of a few months transformed Great Britain, as envisaged by the average American, from a sober and dignified realm into a dizzy Balkan musical comedy attuned to the rhythm of Jazz'.[33]

Yet until the episode was almost over, and the King on the road to abdication and exile, none of this was mentioned in the British press, never mind broadcast by the BBC. Lord Beaverbrook had been summoned by King Edward to Buckingham Palace and asked to help impose a news blackout on Mrs Simpson's second divorce, which would clear the way for their marriage. She was, said the monarch, 'ill, unhappy and distressed by the thought of notoriety'.[34] Beaver-brook promptly agreed. With Esmond Rothermere of the rival Associated Newspapers group, he set about creating a conspiracy of silence among the press barons. When the news finally broke, and it was clear that Britain was going to lose her new monarch, Beaverbrook's *Daily Express* would join forces with the *Daily Mail* to try to create a 'King's Party' to get him to fight on. They would be joined by Winston Churchill. It was another example of the romantic swashbuckling outsiders (as they saw themselves) confront-ing the timid, orthodox political and religious establishment still led by Baldwin. Baldwin saw it differently. Confronted by Harmsworth about the idea of a 'morganatic marriage' which would have allowed the two to marry but without Mrs Simpson becoming Queen of England, Baldwin told him that 'he and his filthy paper did not really *know* the mind of the English people, whereas I *did*'. And in a remark which perhaps explains as well as any other why the marriage plans of the King convulsed the country's leadership, Baldwin added, 'You are right: the ideal of morality and duty and self-sacrifice and decency certainly *has* gone down since the War: but the ideal of Kingship has gone *up* . . . And I tell you the English people will never accept the thing that you suggest.'[35]

We cannot tell what the British people really thought. Before scientific opinion polling, and with no vote that put it to the test, all we have are the impressionistic accounts from diarists and reports of the size of crowds on the streets. For what all that is worth, Baldwin seems nearer the truth than the 'King's Party'. Churchill found himself mocked and then shouted down in the Commons. In private he cried and raged at the way his King was being treated, one of the most humiliating episodes of his life at a time when he needed all his political credibility for the rearmament struggle. Churchill was widely thought to have miscalculated so badly that his reputation could not recover. This was still a country scandalized by divorce, particularly double divorce (Mrs Simpson's position), and which expected better behaviour from its leaders than from the rest of society. Later, in his famous broadcast, the Duke of Windsor, as he had suddenly become, cast his choice as a near-impossible one between love and duty. We have been acclimatized long since to assume that love should always win through – and that was how, even in 1936, Americans and many other people saw it. At the time in Britain, however, there was deep resentment about Edward's dereliction of duty. When the story finally broke, the vast majority of newspapers were brutally critical and there were reports of respectable middle-class people refusing to stand for 'God Save the King'.

Baldwin, the Archbishop of Canterbury and the heads of the Commonwealth countries had hoped that the King would give up Mrs Simpson. But what really scared them was the idea that he might not, and also try to stay on as monarch. Because he chose the other path, the full consequences have rarely been spelled out. But Baldwin and many others thought it would have destroyed the British Empire, since the monarchy was the keystone that held it together. The prime ministers of Australia and Canada thought so too. The story of 1939–45 would have been different had Canada, Australia and South Africa, which took a similar view, broken their formal links with the United Kingdom a couple of years earlier. Inside Britain there would have been a bitter stand-off between the King and the government. Baldwin would have resigned. There would have been a general election, in which neither of the opposition parties would have supported the King. After it, senior Commonwealth officials predicted, drastic cuts in the Civil List supporting the monarchy and an upsurge of popular feeling would have forced him out. Britain would perhaps have been nearer to ditching the entire institution than at any time since the return of Charles II. All this is speculation, though it helps explain Baldwin's dismissal of Eden's questions about overseas affairs.

Monarchy lives by symbols. On 28 January 1936, when King George V's body was being taken in a small procession from King's Cross to Westminster to lie in state, Edward had already tried a few symbolic gestures of his own. George and his father, Edward VII, had kept the clocks at Sandringham half an hour fast. It was eccentric, but meant to ensure punctuality. The new king went straight from his father's cooling body to order them put onto ordinary time: a clockmaker was summoned in the early hours of the night to do this. He meant it, perhaps, as a symbol of a new kind of monarchy. But you cannot always choose your symbols. That morning, as Edward walked behind the coffin, hatless, he could see the royal crown fixed to the lid of the old man's coffin. As the gun-carriage turned into Palace Yard, two watching Conservative MPs saw the Maltese Cross on the top of the crown suddenly topple and fall into the road. A sergeant-major picked it up and popped it into his pocket. The MPs heard the new king exclaim: 'Christ! What will happen next?' One turned to the other and suggested it was a fitting motto for the coming reign. Later in the short story of that reign, on 1 December 1936 when the story was finally breaking in the British newspapers, Crystal Palace burned down in a vast conflagration. As one of those papers remarked, it was fitting that a bishop's strictures against the monarch's behaviour were uttered 'on the day when a great monument of Victorian tradition lies shattered in a smoking ruin'.[36]

Yet in so many ways, Edward (who was always, confusingly, known as David to his friends and family) had brimmed with promise. He was short but strikingly good-looking. He spoke not in the upper-class voice of today's monarchy but in a more demotic tone variously described as 'a stable boy's' and 'off-cockney'. He dressed beautifully and much of the time was an excellent listener. For millions of Britons he was a brilliant symbol of modernization, a glamorous, informal super-celebrity when Britain was short on home-grown glamour. Though his love affair with Wallis Simpson would destroy his reign and reputation, it is perfectly possible to see it as another attempt to be modern at the time when all those writers and intellectuals were calling for honest relationships between the sexes. His grandfather had had mistresses and everyone had known, but that was acceptable so long as it was never publicly discussed. For Edward this was archaic hypocrisy, and dishonourable too. He would be told again and again that he could keep his mistress behind closed doors, just so long as he did not insist on 'flaunting' her in public. But he was from early on determined to be completely public and to marry her and to accord her proper status. He was deeply in love with this apparently shrewd, funny, assertive American woman. Later conspiracy theorists, noting how plain she could look in photographs, suggested she had some unique sexual power over him – or even that she was a man in drag. This seems to be nonsense. Those who knew her found her charming, even charismatic, and believed this was what it seemed, a simple case of romantic love.

Edward himself, however, was no kind of simple case. He had been brought up in an austere family. His mother found it hard to express her feelings. As for George V, there is a story which is of dubious authenticity but which seems to convey some kind of truth about his attitude to his children. The Earl of Derby, the King's oldest friend, thought he bullied them too much and raised the subject one day while they were walking. There was a long silence. Then George replied: 'My father was frightened of his mother: I was frightened of my father; and I am damned well going to see to it that my children are frightened of me.' As we have seen, George V was a shrewd monarch, who belied his reputation as a simpleton only interested in the details of dress codes and his stamp collection. During his reign, it has been pointed out, five emperors, eight kings and eighteen other dynasties disappeared; it was a measure of his success that he was still a popular figure by the late thirties. Yet it was a dour, deeply philistine environment in which he raised his children. Edward had survived it all, and a very harsh time at the Royal Naval College at Dartmouth, to emerge as an energetic and mildly rebellious young man. He was a talented and courageous horseman and tried desperately hard to get to the trenches during the Great War. He became a byword for risk-taking: even Kitchener found it impossible to keep him away from danger. As Prince of Wales in the early twenties, his trips to the Commonwealth had been staggeringly successful, even in India when the aftermath of the Amritsar massacre had made the royal tour a serious risk.

Yet he was also petulant, pleasure loving and in search of a mother substitute. His first one was a woman called Mrs Dudley Ward, whom he had met in March 1918 when she had run into a Mayfair house to avoid an air raid and found herself with a party made up of the Prince and some friends. It was hardly a brief affair. For fifteen years, during which time she separated from and then divorced her husband, he saw her almost every day he was in London and became very close to her children, who called him 'Little Prince'. Yet when he met Wallis Simpson, he ditched Mrs Ward in the most brutal way. He simply stopped turning up, and when she phoned as usual to speak to him at St James's Palace, a sobbing telephonist told her she had something so terrible to tell her she didn't know how to say it: 'I have orders not to put you through.' Later Edward would ruthlessly dump old friends, such as the wonderfully named 'Fruity' Metcalfe, when they became inconvenient. He ran with a flash set in twenties London, rich and fun-loving people, often Americans, christened by the novelist Compton Mackenzie the 'Invaders': 'the most heartless and dissolute of the pleasure-loving ultra-rich, the hardest and most hated people in England'. He was, in short, not only modern and dashing but thoroughly spoiled.

When Edward first started making love to the once-divorced, now remarried Mrs Wallis Simpson in Biarritz, she was honest enough to admit that his status was part of the attraction. It was, she said later, 'open sesame' to a new and glittering world which excited her as nothing had done before. He had 'an unmistakable aura of power and authority. His slightest wish seemed always to be translated instantly into the most impressive kind of reality. Trains were held; yachts materialized; the best suites in the finest hotels were flung open; aeroplanes stood waiting. What impressed me most of all was how this could be brought to pass without apparent effort.'[37] Indeed. As Prince of Wales, he also had his own toy castle, Fort Belvedere, near Windsor, and access to a life of stupendous self-indulgence, though he was neither a drunk nor sexually promiscuous. Still, George V was worried. 'After I am dead,' he once said, 'the boy will ruin himself in twelve months.' When Edward did become king he made economies which hit staff and retainers hard, while spending lavishly on jewels and other gifts for Mrs Simpson. As his biographer put it, there was a lot of public sympathy for the Buckingham Palace servants, 'who resented having their beer money cut down at a time when they were often employed loading cases of champagne, or furniture or plate, destined for Mrs Simpson's flat'.[38]

This all sits uneasily with the well-remembered image of Edward VIII as a natural social reformer, at odds with the stuffy conservatism of Baldwin's Britain. It is true that he had a lively conscience when directly confronted with poverty or other forms of misery. Before becoming king, as patron of the National Council for Social Service, he travelled widely through the most depressed parts of Britain, raising funds and recruiting volunteers to help. Unemployed families were given land in Wales to grow their food and try to become self-sufficient. He was also good at visiting maimed ex-servicemen. Yet the most famous of his industrial visits, when he went as king to south Wales to tour the depressed coalfields and a closed steel works and declared, with much feeling, that 'something must be done to find them work', was almost entirely meaningless. He promised he would do all he could for the men, and that unemployment would be dealt with. He did so knowing not only that he had no power, but also that he would soon be out of the country for ever: he had already told his family and Baldwin that he was abdicating.

More significant than these brief excursions into social policy, though, was Edward's apparent enthusiasm for Nazi Germany. Was it real? Berlin certainly thought so. Leopold von Hoesch, the German ambassador to London in the mid-thirties, not himself a Nazi, nonetheless assured his employers that Edward felt 'warm sympathy for Germany' and that, at the very least, 'we should be able to rely on having on the British throne a ruler who is not lacking in understanding for Germany'. As Prince of Wales, Edward had much disliked the anti-Nazi line of the Foreign Office. (Meanwhile, partly because it was worried about the way official papers were left lying about at Fort Belvedere, the Foreign Office screened, and thus censored, the red boxes of official documents they sent to him as King, the first and last time this has ever happened.) The Duke of Saxe-Coburg-Gotha went further than Hoesch. He was a first cousin once removed of Edward's who had been sent in Victoria's time to Germany from Eton when there was a princeling shortage and who had become an extreme right-winger after the Great War. He met the King in 1936 and sent Hitler a memorandum about conversations with him, including Edward's enthusiasm for a British–German alliance and the following assertion: 'To my question whether a discussion between Baldwin and Hitler would be desirable, he replied in the following words: "Who is King here? Baldwin or I? I myself wish to talk to Hitler and will do so either here or in Germany. Tell him that, please." '[39] These could be dismissed as the oily prot- estations of diplomats to a dictator, though there are other similar reports from the Italian ambassador and Hitler's foreign minister. But even some of the King's supporters such as the socialite Tory MP and diarist Sir Henry ('Chips') Channon thought Edward 'is going the dictator way and is pro-German . . . against too much slipshod democracy. I shouldn't be surprised if he aimed at making himself a mild dictator.' And later, shortly after he had abdicated, he visited Nazi Germany as Duke of Windsor with his new wife, meeting all the Nazi dignitaries, including Herr Hitler.

Many believed, and they included the Nazi hierarchy, that Edward had been forced to abdicate by Baldwin and an anti-German cabal because of his political views. It is true that in the summer of 1940, as Hitler planned his invasion of Britain, his agents were working in Portugal to lure, or snatch, the Duke of Windsor and keep him as a potential figurehead ruler. Churchill was clearly concerned and eventually had the couple hustled off to the Bahamas, where Edward sat out the war as governor-general. But there is no reason to think he had been forced to abdicate for being an appeaser or semi-Nazi himself. Every stage of the move to abdication was described at the time or later by the key participants. Baldwin struggled hard to persuade the King to give up Mrs Simpson and remain on the throne: he regarded the alternative as a profoundly sad and damaging outcome. Others tried to persuade Edward to send Wallis away for a year abroad, while he was crowned and the country grew used to him, after which time they might be reunited. As already described, many of his friends argued for a morganatic marriage settlement. So Edward had plenty of opportunities to find a way of remaining on the throne. It was his determination to marry as soon as Mrs Simpson's second divorce made it possible that made abdication inevitable.

Far from being a bully, Baldwin was slow and patient with the younger man. The most obvious reason for discounting an establishment plot to oust Edward for pro-Nazi sympathies is that so many of the strongest enemies of Nazi Germany were on the King's side – Churchill himself, of course, but also the Tory minister and diarist Duff Cooper, and the press magnate Beaverbrook. The appeasers were, in general, rather hostile to Edward, though it must be emphasized again that even his enemies acted as if they hoped that he would remain King – old habits of deference and custom die hard. The abdication was Britain's good fortune. Edward went and his dutiful younger brother became King in his place, another George (whose young daughter Elizabeth initially loathed the transition from a quiet, comfortable family life to the chill formality of Buckingham Palace). Baldwin stayed on as prime minister just long enough to see

George VI crowned and then resigned, passing power to his chancellor and long-term colleague Neville Chamberlain. George would be a good king. The abdication crisis, by removing a politically naïve, vain and petulant man from the British throne in the late thirties was, far from being a blow, the most fantastic stroke of national luck. Roosevelt was not the only American to do Britain a favour.

The Appeasers

The editor of the *Field*, that glossy bible of the fox-hunting and estate-buying classes, rarely features on the national stage. But in October 1937 he had a walk-on role. He picked up a pen and wrote to Lord Halifax, the number two minister at the Foreign Office, inviting him to an international hunting exhibition. There was nothing terribly surprising about that. Halifax, the former Lord Irwin who had negotiated with Gandhi when he was Viceroy of India, was also a keen and expert master of foxhounds. But this invitation came on behalf of Prince Lowenstein, who ran the German hunting organization, and was to Berlin. It was the first quiet move in the game of diplomatic chess which Britain played during 1937–9, known ever since simply as 'appeasement', a word which once had the gentle meaning of bring peace and now is loaded with shame and embarrassment. It was a game played out by British politicians and diplomats, and sometimes others, with skill, determination and even nerve. The only problem was that Hitler was not playing the game in the first place.

Because of what followed, where political leaders stood in relation to appeasement affected British politics well into the fifties and even sixties – a Tory prime minister in 1964 was still tainted by his marginal role in the policy. Conveniently, we now scapegoat a few politicians as being 'guilty men' who encouraged Hitler by their cowardice and foolishness. We forget that appeasement was hugely popular. It brought hundreds of thousands of enthusiastic people onto the streets of London to cheer Chamberlain. It was lauded in the City, in the newspapers, in private letters and diaries. Chamberlain enjoyed an almost unanimous standing ovation in the Commons for it. He was showered with letters and personal gifts – of fishing rods, gold watches, tweed for suits – by deliriously grateful voters. It is one of the stories of the thirties that is hardest to achieve perspective about, but which cannot be left as a dirty national secret.

Halifax, who, along with Chamberlain, is most often blamed for appeasing Hitler, was no lover of Germany. He came from a wealthy High Anglican family. Isolated by the death of his elder brothers and born with only one hand, he had been to Eton and Oxford, become an MP and served in the Great War, after which he expressed disappointment that it was not possible to burn down German towns to teach them a lesson, but at all events said they must be properly humiliated. Immensely tall, dry and grand, on first arriving at Berchtesgaden he mistook Hitler for a footman and tried to hand him his overcoat. Yet Halifax was not a man of inflexible views. As we have seen, he was far more open to the appeal of Gandhi than was Churchill, and by the mid-thirties he had completely rethought his 1918 enthusiasm for keeping Germany down and humiliated. He thought the Versailles settlement had proved unfair and that the League of Nations system of trying to keep peace by international diplomacy was clearly failing. If the Germans left inside the spatchcocked state of Czechoslovakia, remnants of the old Austro-Hungarian Empire, wanted to join Hitler's Reich, why not? If the Germans of Danzig felt the same, why not? If Germany wanted the return of some of her old colonies, again – why not?

An imperialist, Halifax was unenthusiastic about interfering in the internal affairs of other European countries. Once it was known that he was going to Germany to see the Nazi leadership, for the cover of the hunting exhibition was soon blown, Halifax was urged by friends to raise the subject of the repression that was already well underway in Germany. He barely bothered. In a chilling throwaway sentence he said only that there was much in the system which offended British opinion – 'treatment of the Church; to perhaps a lesser extent, the treatment of the Jews; treatment of the Trade Unions'.[40] Among his other views was that racialism, while 'power-ful', was not immoral, and that the Nazis were at least 'genuine haters of Communism', something he and Chamberlain both regarded as the greater threat. He was, in short, a catastrophic messenger to send to Hitler. He was also armed with a memor-andum of May 1937 from the diplomat Sir Nevile Henderson arguing that it was not against British interests to allow Hitler his way over Czechoslovakia, union with Austria, expansion into eastern Europe and the return of the colonies. This would all restrain Russia and, anyway, the choice of war would be far worse. Calm Hitler, said Henderson; don't treat him like a mad dog or you will turn him into one. In a twist worthy of Shakespeare it should be added that it was Henderson who, as ambassador to Berlin in 1939, formally issued Britain's declaration of war, acknowledging the utter failure of his policy.

The Halifax visit, which set the tone for so much else that followed, faithfully carried these messages directly to Hitler. It was Halifax himself who raised the issues of the German-speaking Czechs, Danzig and Austria, giving the German dictator the clear impression that if these could be resolved without full-scale war, Britain would be content. It meant the end of the Versailles era. Hitler and Halifax then had a gloomy lunch, after which the Führer told the former Viceroy of India that *Lives of a Bengal Lancer* was shown to the SS because it demonstrated how a superior race should behave, and suggested that Gandhi should be shot. Halifax was appalled. But why should he have been? He was the representative of an empire which had not long before practised the barbarity of air-bombardment against defenceless tribesmen, and which still officially regarded Indians and Africans as incapable of self-government. He defended racialism. He was, like Chamberlain, not keen on Jews. It seems that the real gap between Halifax (and men like him) and Hitler (and men like him) was not that the former thought racialist theories and the rule of the higher race were wrong, or unnatural, or that he had a more advanced view of universal human rights. It was rather that the Germans overdid things, and were too rough – and perhaps that, in British thinking among the racial hierarchies, Jews and Slavs stood higher than Indians or Africans. Thus it was one thing to bomb tribesmen, another to seize Jewish shops. The Germans were a little crude. That seems to have been the impression left on Halifax by Goering when he finally met him at the hunting exhibition after his visit to Hitler. Goering, in leather breeches and jerkin, wearing a green hat and a dagger in a red sheath, all geniality and reassurance, struck Halifax as entertaining and, though a killer, 'frankly attractive, like a great schoolboy . . . a composite personality – film star, great landowner interested in his estate, prime minister, party manager, head gamekeeper at Chatsworth'.[41]

It is impossible now to reach back and fully understand this thinking. What followed was too horrible, too big. Some have argued that appeasement was all along a clever and sensible strategy, forced on Chamberlain by the long years of under-investment in defence. Did it not allow Britain from 1935 (under Chamberlain's rule in the Treasury) to start to build the planes and recreate the army she would need to fight Germany? Was it not Chamberlain and Halifax who, by buying time, really enabled Britain to survive in 1940? It is an ingenious argument which contains some truth and attractively overturns a settled consensus. But it depends upon appeasement being a sly tactic, trying to delay Hitler's war on the West by throwing him pieces of middle Europe, while understanding all along that war was coming. This is simply unhistorical. Chamberlain was not lying when he said later he thought he had bought peace in his time, or that Hitler was honourable. Halifax was not dissimulating when he suggested that Hitler's behaviour towards the Jews and internal dissent was not really Britain's concern. Both men realized that war might not be avoidable and that, if so, Britain needed to be better prepared, particularly against air attack. But they also thought Hitler's Germany had legitimate grievances and that Hitler might be permanently bought off; and this is what they were trying to achieve, though Halifax realized the truth about Nazi ambitions long before Chamberlain. Certainly, Britain did not go to war to help European Jewry or to defend the Versailles settlement, or even to save Poland.

Another argument used to explain appeasement is that the prime minister forever associated with it, Neville Chamberlain, was a provincial ignoramus who had not the first clue about international affairs. This too is wrong. Chamberlain, by almost all the accounts of his colleagues, was not an appealing man. He was sarcastic, cold and profoundly partisan in politics. He was, however, not ignorant. As a son of the great imperialist Joe Chamberlain he had a very clear notion of the importance of the Empire and tariffs. As chancellor under both Ramsay MacDonald and Baldwin he had a finger in almost every international issue from the early thirties onwards, overseeing both the early austerity measures and then the beginning of rearmament as well as various talks and pacts involving European and imperial colleagues. His problem was not lack of knowledge but conceit. A comparatively old man of sixty-eight by the time he finally became prime minister, he had spent the second half of his life in national politics, working hideously long hours and feeling himself the real worker who underpinned the lazy habits of prime ministers. He was not, properly, a Tory but an old-style Liberal whose reform measures on rent control, housing and unemployment assistance partly mitigated his iron-hard economic views. He knew he was right. So when he reached Number Ten, as neither his father nor his half-brother Austen had managed, he preened: 'It has come to me without my raising a finger . . . because there is no-one else.' Only his wisdom had kept Britain out of the Spanish Civil War, only he had been able to soothe Mussolini. As chancellor, he wrote, he could hardly move a pebble: 'now I have only to raise a finger and the whole face of Europe is changed'. Yes, he was a vain old man.

But in his views, as we have seen, he was hardly alone. There were millions of ordinary voters thoroughly hostile to rearmament, who regarded war with just as much incredulity and horror as Chamberlain did. Yet again we push the blame onto an easy scapegoat, this just nation, always wise and moral with hindsight. We infantilize the final choice – Adolf Hitler, deal or no deal? – forgetting that appeasement was a slow, five-year process, rarely clear or simple but popular at every stage. It had started in 1934–5 with Mussolini's menaces against Abyssinia, at a time when Britain still admired the Italian dictator and hoped to use him as a counter-weight or ally against Germany. Various deals and secret plots were hatched to hand over parts of Abyssinia to the Italians, resulting in the resignation of one foreign secretary, much useless hand-wringing at the League of Nations, and threats of an embargo. Baldwin knew that threats were useless against dictators unless backed up by a credible threat of force, yet declined to begin the massive rearmament that would be needed. Two years before, at the Fulham East by-election of 1933, with Hitler in power and the European menace clear, the National Government candidate had been trounced by a Labour candidate with pacifist views. It was not a one-issue by-election, but it put the wind up Baldwin sufficiently for him to quote it later as a reason for not pushing ahead with rearmament.

The Fulham East by-election was not a one-off warning. Both the

1933 Oxford Union debate when students resolved not to fight for King and Country and the Scottish Nationalists' anti-conscription views have already been mentioned. More important was the Peace Pledge Union, formed in 1934 after a letter to the *Manchester Guardian* by a canon of St Paul's Cathedral, Richard Sheppard: by 1937 it had over 100,000 members. Anti-war groups proliferated. In 1934, too, the Labour Party had opposed strengthening the RAF because it would encourage war, and the following year it opposed the Defence White Paper for higher spending on the same grounds. In that year, outside Parliament, there was a 'peace ballot' organized by a pro-League-of-Nations group, in which 11.6 million people had voted, with a heavy majority saying they backed sanctions and diplomacy at first if one country invaded another, and only a smaller majority favouring war even as a last resort. Baldwin had drawn a lesson, if hardly a moral, from this: he went into the 1935 election hiding plans to sharply increase arms spending. As he explained: 'Supposing that I had gone to the country saying that Germany was rearming and we must rearm . . . I cannot think of anything that would have made the loss of the election from my point of view more certain.' The loudest people, if not always the cleverest, were deeply hostile to war preparations. On the left the communists were following the Moscow line and on the right the BUF were campaigning against war with Germany or Italy.

This was reinforced for the less political majority by the fear that, as Stanley Baldwin had put it, the bomber would always get through. Terror of aircraft attack was widespread in the mid-thirties. Both appeasers and anti-appeasers thought the Luftwaffe was much stronger than it really was: both the military chiefs and Churchill thought the first bombing attack would kill around 150,000 people – more than actually died from German raids in the whole Second World War. Later these fears would be fanned by film of the ruthless raid by German bombers on Guernica during the Spanish Civil War. When Hitler marched his troops back into the Rhineland, Britain did not want to go to war. When Franco's insurgency tore apart Republican Spain there was no appetite for intervention, except on the left. So by the time Halifax went to see Hitler, a clear pattern was established. The British people were against rearmament and favoured appeasement. The British government, which perhaps ought to have tried to lead the country in a different direction, was sufficiently cautious of public opinion to speak softly. To present this as the guilt of a few flabby mandarins is far too easy, a comforting democratic myth. It lets off the hook Labour, the Communist Party, the pacifist movements, those many business leaders who did not want to fund rearmament, and the many millions who thought Chamberlain had behaved superbly.

By the time Chamberlain had conceived his 'Plan Z', the theatrical notion that by flying in person to Munich to meet Hitler he could stop the invasion of Czechoslovakia and thus prevent a coming war, appeasement was a habit. Hitler was gambling, but he was gambling having seen his opponent's cards. He did not want war with Britain in 1938 – Germany was not ready for that – but he did want war with Czechoslovakia. In theory that would bring in France, and thus Britain, just as the Great War had swept in countries linked by alliances. In practice, he knew the British people were fearful of war. Chamberlain, it is important to repeat, was not simply buying time. He saw his flight to Germany as part of wider vision to end the 'mad armaments race' and bring in general appeasement. He did not tell his cabinet what he was doing, and he only revealed his flight the day before he took off, on 14 September 1938. It was regarded as sensational news around the world, with ecstatic tributes to the boldness of this new form of diplomacy. With his famous rolled umbrella, but accompanied by nobody who actually spoke German, Chamberlain took off the following morning from Heston aerodrome north of London in a small hired Lockheed passenger plane. It was the first substantial flight the old man had ever taken. Hitler had been initially taken aback by the proposal and suspected that Chamberlain was arriving to declare war in person. When the prime minister arrived in Munich he was greeted by Nazi salutes and 'Heil Hitlers' and responded by waving his Homburg hat. After a three-hour train journey to Berchtesgaden, and unimpressed by his first sight of Hitler, he settled down face to face.

This, the very first modern 'summit' meeting, was almost all British offer and German take. Despite the formal expressions of mutual respect, and Hitler's long protestations about Czech brutality, at its core was Chamberlain's offer to accept that the 3 million German-speaking Czech citizens wished to join the Reich; and his promise to bully the Czechs into agreeing. All he got was a pause, and a pledge that this would be done without German military invasion, so long as there were no frontier or 'terrorist' incidents, and that it would be carried out in an orderly fashion. In effect, Britain was selling off part of a country it had recently helped to create. Yet when Chamberlain returned home, the disgrace was greeted with enthusiasm because it put off war. Hitler drew the obvious conclusion. At a second summit, on the Rhine two weeks later, he upped his demands. Now German troops had to march into the Czech Sudetenland immediately. The Czech army must retire within two days. Chamberlain, aghast, protested. But with the Czechs now mobilizing, he made little progress beyond winning another short delay. This time when he came back to London he found the mood changing. Chamberlain proposed that in return for Britain and France guaranteeing that the Czechs would not resist by force, and guaranteeing the handover of the territory to Germany, Hitler would in turn promise not to use force either. By now the Foreign Office diplomats who had always worried about Chamberlain were in a state of grief and anger. Sir Alexander Cadogan, the senior official, wrote in his diary that he knew Britain was in no condition to fight, but 'I'd rather be beat than dishonoured. How can we look any foreigner in the face after this? How can we hold Egypt, India and the rest?'[42] He so stirred the conscience of Halifax, his boss, that the foreign secretary could not sleep and at cabinet the following day he began to turn against Chamberlain.

Winston and the Grasshopper

It was not only Halifax. The mood of the country seemed to be shifting, too, as the full implications of the betrayal of Czechoslovakia sank in. Chamberlain had heard some boos among the cheers as he set off for the second time from Heston. On the one hand the preparations for war, including the digging of trenches and underground shelters, the distribution of 30 million gas masks (though there were none for small children or babies) and amateurish advice about how to protect your home from bombs, was sending a cold shiver across the country. On the other hand Chamberlain's diplomacy seemed to be failing, bringing war, but on shameful terms. In

1938 the country was not ready. There were only five squadrons of modern Hurricane fighter planes available, and nothing like the necessary amount of anti-aircraft guns or barrage-balloon protection. Chamberlain capitalized on the sense that all this preparation was surreal by broadcasting: 'How horrible, how fantastical it is that we should be digging trenches and trying on gas masks here because of a quarrel in a far-away country between people of whom we know little.' This is remembered because, wittingly or not, its sense of half-embarrassed, frantic hand washing perfectly encapsulated what had become Chamberlain's policy.

Historians now speculate that, had Hitler gone ahead with the invasion of Czechoslovakia, dissident politicians and military officers were ready to mount a coup: ironically, he may have been saved by the last-minute diplomatic manoeuvrings. For Hitler blinked. Instead of invading he called a four-power summit, inviting Chamberlain, along with Mussolini and the French leader Daladier, back to Munich. When Chamberlain got the news, in a scribbled note during the final minutes of his report to the Commons, and read it out, to many MPs it seemed almost like divine intervention. Chamberlain himself called it 'the last desperate snatch at the last tuft on the very verge of the precipice'. The summit was not good for the Czechs, though the area of their land to be grabbed was slightly reduced and the timetable slightly extended. Knowing he needed to bring back more, Chamberlain had had a short yet waffle-filled note typed out and, after a further general talk with Hitler, persuaded him to countersign it. It spoke of the importance of Anglo-German relations, including an earlier deal concerning the two countries' navies, as 'symbolic of the desire of our two peoples never to go to war with one another again ... the method of consultation shall be the method adopted to deal with any other questions'. Hardly rousing stuff, but when he returned to Heston to be met by a large crowd, waiting in the rain, Chamberlain waved and read out his 'piece of paper' before driving to London, where the King thanked him at Buckingham Palace, and they waved to the crowds outside. Back at Downing Street there was another crowd and, leaning out of a window, Chamberlain let himself go. Referring to the reception that had greeted Disraeli returning from the Congress of Berlin, he told the people that it was the second time 'there has come back from

Germany peace with honour. I believe it is peace for our time.'
In the circumstances, it was a remarkably stupid thing to say, and
Chamberlain quickly realized it. Too late; but we should never forget
that the story of appeasement is the story of the people standing in
the street looking up and not just of the man talking down.

Soon the newspapers and much of the country had performed a
U-turn on the Churchill question. In the run-up to the final declaration of war, following Hitler's invasion of Poland, there was a
steady crescendo of demands for his return to government, at the
Admiralty or the War Office. Chamberlain sniffed. It would be
inconvenient for him, he said, to have such a difficult ego rampaging
about. The cries grew louder, including from many of those who
had ridiculed Churchill so recently. In the press, right across the
spectrum from the Communist Party's *Daily Worker*, the *Manchester
Guardian* and the *News Chronicle*, to the *Daily Mail* and *Daily Telegraph*
on the right, they all called for Churchill back. In Germany a member
of Hitler's cabinet privately said he should be brought back, as the
last Englishman Hitler feared. Eminent generals visited him. He
was shown round Biggin Hill to watch fighter exercises and heard
rumours that soon there would be some kind of new atomic weapon.
He was being treated already as a war leader in waiting. Still
Chamberlain refused to unbend. He and Churchill rowed in the
private members' lobby of the Commons. Anonymous posters, in
fact paid for by an advertising agent called Mr Beable, appeared
across London asking 'What Price Churchill?', and when Chamberlain went to the Commons for a crisis debate, he passed half a dozen
people carrying sandwich boards reading simply 'Churchill'. Once
war was declared, Chamberlain bowed to the inevitable and asked
him to join his War Cabinet and return to the Admiralty, where
Churchill had last set foot in 1915. One of his maps with the British
fleet dispositions on it was still hanging in a cupboard. The Admiralty
signalled to the fleet: 'Winston is Back'. But the man who perhaps
spoke for more Britons than any other was called Colin Thornton-
Kemsley. A member of Churchill's constituency party, he had tried
to have him thrown out of the Commons for disloyalty to the
Conservatives earlier in the year. Now in an army camp, he sent a
letter of abject apology: 'A grasshopper under a fern is not so proud
now that he made the field ring with his importunate chink.'[43]

Part Four

THROUGH FIRE,
A NEW COUNTRY

1939–1945

Courage is going from failure to failure,
without losing enthusiasm.

Winston S. Churchill, 1940

Defeats shape countries more than their victories do. Though Britain ended the Second World War on the winning side, during the first few years she was overall a loser, experiencing mostly defeat. It was what happened between the winter of 1939–40 and the spring of 1942 that provoked the great changes in the British. These islands were in the position of a besieged city. Through the years of hunger, boredom and fear the besieged displayed great ingenuity and found themselves knitted together in a new national comradeship. It excluded some whose political instincts, social background or foreign origins made them immune. And after a few years it began to fray. Privation, sleeplessness and fear chewed away. But the majority, for a hinge period of perhaps twenty months or so, were fused together in ways that changed the country permanently. It was the real end of Britannia, the imperial, now befuddled conqueror-island, and the real beginning of modern Britain. People saw defeat in the news-papers and the faces of beaten soldiers. They tasted it in rations and smelt the burned buildings. They asked how they had got into their plight. They looked hard at their old rulers and they identified with possible liberators coming over the hills – with Russians and Ameri-cans. They dreamed of a new start, a fairer, more modern and efficient nation. This change in national mood, which shaped us all, was established well before D-Day.

The Second World War has so many similarities with the First that some historians treat them as two episodes in the same long conflict. For Britain there was the obvious fact that they were fought against the same main enemy, Germany. Britain stood, once again, alongside France, Russia, America. There were other echoes. As in 1914, in 1940 the war proper began with a ruthlessly efficient German scythe through Belgium and northern France, at a time when the British Expeditionary Force (the same archaic-sounding name was used) was small and badly equipped. Both wars reshaped the British state, bringing higher taxes, endless new regulations, big changes in the role of women and earnest promises of a better future. In 1917 Britain had been brought almost to defeat by U-boat attacks on Atlantic shipping. In 1942 the same thing happened. The earlier war threw up a dynamic and controversial leader, Lloyd George, who enjoyed near dictatorial authority, though he bitterly rowed with generals. The next one similarly elevated his old friend and follower Churchill, who also enjoyed huge personal authority and also fought with his generals. And, of course, in both wars, the United States arrived late in the day as an ally and greatly changed the balance.

Yet the two wars were more different than alike. The First World War was essentially a land war, fought in France by professional, volunteer and then conscript soldiers, who suffered terrible losses. Despite raids by warships, Zeppelins and German Gotha bombers, the British civilian population was affected mainly by greyness, shortage and bereavement. In the Second World War, because of the defeat of the British and French armies early on, the most important fighting was in the air and at sea until the invasion of Europe in 1944. British armies fought in North Africa and in the Far East. But most British were cooped up at home, waiting. Churchill himself reflected, during the grimmest period of 1940, that 'this was the sort of war which would suit the English people once they were used to it. They would prefer all to be in the front line, taking part in the Battle of London, than to look on helplessly at mass slaughters like Passchendaele.'[1] Meanwhile the civilian population found that if there was any longer a 'front line' it ran through Coventry and Southampton, London and Glasgow. Some 60,000 civilians were killed. For the first three years of the war more women and children were killed by German action than were British soldiers. Add the hundreds of thousands injured, and the millions who lost their homes, and the butcher's bill is qualitatively different.

In the First World War millions of people found their lives changed as they became munitions workers or helped on the land. But in the Second virtually the entire country was mobilized. Britain put more of her people and more of her wealth into fighting the war than any other nation. Unlike the Germans or the Russians, she conscripted her women. Many of her cities were devastated and, in response, Britain carried out massacres of German civilians in air attacks which remain hugely controversial. Politically, too, the wars were very different. When the Americans came the second time it was not as late-in-the-day helpers but as saviours. The earlier conflict began, as we have seen, when Britain was in a ferment of radicalism. Its effect, as we have also seen, was eventually conservative. At the start of the Second World War, Britain was under a Tory, formally National, government. Radicalism was scattered. Labour looked very far from power. Its effect, however, was to drive the country fast and quite far to the left. By the end Churchill found himself leading a big-state, high-taxing and interventionist government, most of whose famous figures were socialists. He was a colourful twist of old Britannia decorating a new reality.

All this has led to the 1939–45 war being dubbed the 'People's War', and so it was. Heroism was distributed widely, embracing pensioners and firefighters, air-raid wardens and nursing mothers. Yet the people running the British war were still overwhelmingly male, white and upper class. No woman had a key position in directing the British war effort. Most of the intellectuals who shaped policy, including John Maynard Keynes and William Beveridge, as well as the important Whitehall officials, the leading military commanders and most MPs, were public school and Oxbridge men. Only in the increasingly important world of scientific 'boffins' and the handful of working-class Labour ministers, most obviously Ernie Bevin, do we find rougher voices. The rise of the grammar-school boy, so important in the Britain of the fifties, was still largely invisible. It was beginning, in the armed forces and in factories, but below the level of national leadership. The 'people' of the People's War were followers who were beginning to resent being followers and who would eventually shrug off their wartime leaders. Though in 1939 none of that seemed conceivable, never mind possible.

Adolf Hitler lost his war. One of his many miscalculations was to think the British would not fight or, if they did, would not fight for long. But Hitler left a changed Britain. He changed us more than any of our leaders. By directing at the British the full force of his far better-organized war-state with its unifying ideology, he forced Britain to become more organized and more united too. Though this was a war fought for liberty at home (if empire abroad), the British citizen ended it weighted down with rules, taxes and restrictions as never before. Though it was a war that can be blamed on incompetent leadership by politicians beforehand, during and after its fighting, it left the political class at a historic high point. The first great historian of the war was Churchill himself. His books are well worth reading for their glorious prose, vivid detail and grand sweep, but he gave a bowdlerized and sentimental account of what had happened. After and around him broke never-ending waves of military memoirs, war films, diaries, popular war histories and, at the sandy bottom of the salty turbulence, boys' war comics. They too glossed over the British defeats and failures and idealized the war in Churchillian terms – the darkest day, the finest hour, the turning of the tide. Spitfire pilots were nonchalant public-schoolboy heroes, Tommies were tough and dogged, the Germans bone-headed sadists and the British public were joke-cracking stoics who could take it. The Yanks . . . well, the Yanks came late. In the Cold War years, the Soviet 'Ivans' began, if not to drop out of our popular memory of the war – that would have been too ludicrous – then to slide away to one side.

All this was natural. The war had been traumatic enough. There was no repetition of the anti-war writing of the Great War survivors. Hitler allows for few second thoughts. Only in the 1960s did some historians begin to revisit the politics of wartime, and disinter some of the follies, arguments and failures buried in the mesmeric Churchillian account. By the 1980s this revisionism had reached the grand figure of Churchill himself, though criticism of the war leader has never impressed the British public, who voted him Greatest (ever) Briton in a BBC poll and still buy his books in large numbers. In recent years a few writers, mainly American, have suggested the previously unthinkable – that it would actually have been better for the world had Britain not fought on, but had sought a peace treaty with Nazi Germany. Then, they say, Hitler would merely have transported the Jews, perhaps to Africa, and there would have been no global conflict – no Stalingrad, no Dresden, no Hiroshima. Hitler would have mellowed, or been overthrown, at far lesser cost. This depends on heroic speculation about a parallel or 'counterfactual' twentieth century. The more historians dig into Nazi Germany, the less likely it seems. In Britain the very idea produced infuriated

He never expected or wanted the Crown, but George VI proved a sensible and popular wartime monarch.

The original Little Hitler; but Oswald Mosley was more sniggered at by the British than followed or feared.

Members of the International Brigade returning to London after fighting alongside the Republicans in the Spanish Civil War.

Not a novel way of trying to breed aircraft, but a strange coupling from the golden age of air travel: an Imperial Airways 'Mayo Composite', 1938.

'Say Appease': Chamberlain and Hitler smiling for the camera during their
September 1938 summit, when Britain gave all the ground.

Unity Mitford being returned to England after her attempted suicide
when war was declared on Germany.

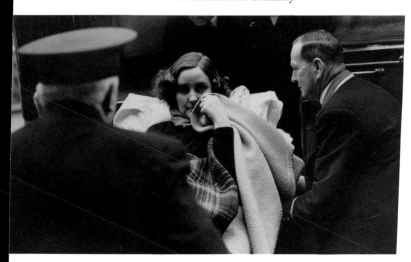

Hitler will send no warning –
so always carry
your gas mask

ISSUED BY THE MINISTRY OF HOME SECURITY

The horror we never faced: in 1939 gas attacks were particularly feared
and carefully prepared for.

One of the biggest social experiments in British history: children being
evacuated in January 1940.

Not 'the Blitz' but our many Blitzes. A family visits what remains of their house in Plymouth, May 1941.

Ruby Loftus Screwing a Breech Ring by Laura Knight. A new country, forged in fire.

Waiting for the invasion: a soldier at prayer in Westminster Abbey shortly after Dunkirk.

Spitfires flying high: down below them, for once, the British were better organized than the Germans.

Spin-masters behind him,
Nazis ahead: Monty in
North Africa in 1943.
He was a celebrity
general for a media age,
but was mocked as
well as lauded.

Bodies in the street after
the allied firebombing
of Dresden,
February 1945.

War leader on the line: Churchill had a schoolboyish enthusiasm for gadgets. Here he tries an American walkie-talkie.

Rainbow Corner, Piccadilly, 1945, where American popular culture really first invaded Britain. Eat your hearts out, Pilgrim Fathers.

reactions. This war, and how we remember it, still matters very much. The latest waves of books about it have been dominated by oral histories, diaries, letters and the Mass Observation archive of diaries and interviews, telling the story of the war from below – the people's history as opposed to Churchill's. These are gripping accounts but not 'the whole story', any more than the earlier history of the war seen only through the eyes of politicians, generals or pilots.

A book of this range cannot hope to tell that whole story. But we can try to weave together the most important facts and ask the obvious questions. How well did we do? How did we change? In general, we have the military books and the home-front books. The former seem to be for male readers, written by armchair strategists, full of detail about guns and kit and aircraft and contemporary first-person battle narratives. The latter embrace political histories and the 'people's history'. But if the term 'People's War' means anything it means a war that shaped and was fought by the population. So the military story cannot be pushed to one side. Norway, the battle for France, Dunkirk, the Battle of the Atlantic, Libya and the rest provide the essential context and force. Without them, the changes in British life cannot be understood. Britons fought bravely, as did other peoples. But for the first half of the war British forces were poorly organized and equipped and suffered defeat after defeat. Simply to remember the bravery and the humour is to miss half the point. We were never invaded. Actually, we were. But we were invaded by our friends, the Americans. And that invasion has never quite ended.

Neville's War

For eight surprisingly quiet months Britain had a popular war leader. His approval rating in the new-fangled opinion polls reached 70 per cent. Through the autumn, freezing winter and early spring of 1939–40, despite early fears of mass bombing attacks, Chamberlain's war seemed almost as staid as the man himself. As war was declared, the first air-raid siren went off and almost immediately a mass evacuation of children from the cities began. The British army arrived in France and had taken up positions in chilly dugouts, barns and houses alongside the French and Belgians. They were woefully ill equipped, but this was not yet apparent. There, endlessly, nothing happened. British troops impolite enough to fire at Germans on patrol were rebuked by their French allies. But no bombs fell. At sea there were early embarrassments: a U-boat managed to get right inside the main naval anchorage at Scapa Flow and sink an elderly battleship. There were successes too, notably the sinking of the *Graf Spee*, a German battleship, and Churchill made the most of his return to the Admiralty in boosting those. Yet the main use of the navy was for a blockade of Germany, on which ludicrous hopes rested. That country was living better than Britain, was well supplied for its immediate industrial needs and was far better prepared for war. Yet Chamberlain, vain as ever, wrote that he had a hunch the war would be over by spring because the Germans would realize 'it isn't worth their while to go on getting thinner and poorer'. The RAF set out to bomb Germany . . . with leaflets. After the initial fear when war had been sombrely declared, the country became puzzled, caught between suspicion and optimism.

Many thought it would end quickly after all. And then people grew bored. With that national talent for obvious puns so doggedly pursued by newspaper sub-editors, they called it the Bore War. (Only later did the Americanism 'phoney war' become current.) Churchill campaigned against boredom. He addressed the country on the wireless, by now in most middle-class homes, and spoke as if he was in charge of a great deal more than the Royal Navy. His grand historical sweeps and sideswipes at numerous neutral nations infuriated Chamberlain but began to reshape Churchill's reputation far beyond Whitehall. Chamberlain's own cabinet reshuffles were barely noticed. The sole exception was the sacking of Leslie Hore-Belisha, an energetic minister who had introduced pedestrian crossings and begun to reorganize the army but had antagonized generals and ministers. Chamberlain had been going to make him minister for information – he had a talent for publicity – but was persuaded not to. Why? Because Hore-Belisha was Jewish and it was thought the Germans would sneer. He was offered another post but turned it down. The newspapers were rightly outraged.

Meanwhile, the expensive restaurants stayed open, the parties went on and new models of car were produced by an industry that was still far from dedicated to tanks or warplanes. Yet Britain was already a different country. However lackadaisical or confused the Chamberlain cabinet might have been about prosecuting the war, it was relatively vigorous in reorganizing things at home. Before the war had begun it had been responsible for the shadow-factory system, which allowed the dispersal and acceleration of the war-making industry, as well as for the increased aircraft production already described. Reviving DORA, the 1914 Defence of the Realm Act, as the Emergency Powers (Wartime) Act, the government gave itself virtually dictatorial control over most of public life, allowing it to eavesdrop on, follow, intern, censor, direct and arrest citizens on the basis of decrees or orders. Phones were bugged. The propaganda-driven Ministry of Information began its work, though not very convincingly. New ministries, including those for Supply and Food, took new powers, controlling many imports and allocations. All together 1.5 million people had been enrolled and trained for the various forms of civil defence. A national registry of all citizens was compiled and everyone issued with a brownish coloured ID card and number. Rationing, based on lessons learned in 1917–18, did not actually begin for three months after war broke out; but as soon as the register was ready, everyone was given a ration book too. The first halting efforts were made to bring trade-union as well as business leaders into the direction of war industry. Neville Chamberlain may have been something of a ninny, but he was a hard-working and methodical ninny.

Socially, the single biggest immediate change was the official evacuation, in just three days in September 1939, of nearly 1.5 million people from cities to small towns and villages. These evacuees were the minority of those moving. By some estimates almost a third of the population shifted, most of them people moving privately, the better off buying places in boarding houses or hotels or staying with friends to escape the coming massacre from the air. Those who stayed spoke disparagingly of 'funk holes'. But the evacuation which really counted was the official one, of poorer people to 'reception areas' thought unlikely to be attacked. Here, though volunteers were sought, compulsion was available. Most of the official evacuees, some 830,000, were school children, but mothers and infants, pregnant mothers and 7,000 disabled people were sent too. They left

London and almost all the major industrial, port and capital towns, from Southampton and Portsmouth on the south coast, up through the Midlands to Manchester, Liverpool and Newcastle and all the major Scottish cities too. Most people were evacuated by Britain's then still-extensive railway system, though some went by bus or even by boat. School populations were deported en masse. Yet fewer than half those eligible to be evacuated actually went. Many refused to believe the imminence of the threat. Other families decided that, if they were to be killed, they preferred to die together.

Almost as soon as the evacuees set off, clutching bags with spare socks and pants, toothbrushes (if they had them) and food, the transport plan broke down. Not many anxious rural communities received the numbers they expected. In some towns and villages it was all fairly orderly. Officials were waiting to take the tired and confused children to church halls or schools, from where they would be allocated a family. In others the locals simply pitched up and took whichever evacuees they fancied. Hulking boys would be appropriated by farmers looking for cheap labour, while picky housewives selected the smartest, cleanest or simply most appealing children. The dirtier, poorer specimens were often left like rejected vegetables, hoping someone would finally pick them. So began one of the most dramatic social experiments to hit Britain. And, as the premier historian of the home front put it: 'Because they had bottled themselves up in the train, or because they were upset at being parted from their parents or because they thought the country darkness must harbour ghosts ... from Aberdeenshire to Devon, countless numbers of children wet the bed.'[2]

They did more than that. Very many, from the poorest districts of Glasgow, Liverpool, Manchester and east London, had fleas or head lice, skin diseases such as impetigo and little education in cleanliness. They were not used to bathing, brushing their teeth or using a modern lavatory. Some simply defecated inside, or weed in the corner of the bedroom. Others had never sat down at a table to eat before, and had never slept in a bed. Their language, by the standards of polite Britain, was foul. So was that of many evacuated mothers, who, with their cigarettes, liking for drink and relaxed attitude to parental discipline, seemed sluts or slovens to the vicars' wives, shopkeepers or teachers on whom they might be billeted.

Many children had only thin plimsolls as shoes, others had been sewn into their clothes for the winter; many had no changes of clothes, and no underclothes, nor ever had had. Thus, with a mixture of horror, revulsion and compassion, middle-class Britain had its powdered nose rubbed in the stinking reality of slum life for the first time. Some families reacted with Christian kindness and coped so well that the evacuated children did not want to go home. They grew fatter, saw with awe their first sheep, cow or apple tree and tasted food so creamy and fresh it might have come from another world. Other families blamed ignorant, immoral parents in the cities, and demanded that their evacuees be taken away again. A minority, undoubtedly, were cruel and abusive.

Though the extent of the most extreme squalor of evacuees was exaggerated, and the folk-tales spread by village gossip, the truths uncovered by evacuation shocked many conservative, perhaps rather smug parts of Britain. Anglican Englishwomen met their first Jew, Scottish Presbyterian farmers their first Roman Catholic. As we saw earlier, Britain in the thirties had become radically divided, with some areas becoming prosperous while others rotted. With evacuation, the two touched. It was a physical touch, involving smells and sounds, that was far more powerful than mere words. We cannot measure such things. But the vivid memories half a century on, and the ferment of press comment at the time, never mind anguished debates among politicians, suggest that evacuation was a nationwide social shock. No matter what an eloquent, chain-smoking intellectual hammering away at a *New Statesman* typewriter could say – even George Orwell himself – it was better said by the sight of scabies at bath time, or puzzlement at the sight of fresh eggs. Within months, when the bombers failed to arrive over the cities and factories, hundreds of thousands of families returned home again. By Christmas more than half had gone back. Many would have to flee again, and by then the arrangements would be better. Meanwhile, quietly but throughout the land, evacuation had already begun to shift the politics of the British.

Evacuation, however, was only part of it. Millions of sandbags, woven in Dundee and filled with sand from beaches and open-cast diggings, were piled up in front of official buildings, hospitals and at railway stations. Over the capital, and some other cities, portly silver barrage balloons wobbled in the sky. Trenches were dug in parks and prefabricated air-raid shelters, named Anderson shelters after the minister in charge, were widely distributed. Among the many war preparations that never turned out to be useful, luckily, was the provision of gas masks. Well before the outbreak of war, some 38 million of them had been issued, accurately described as 'a grotesque combination of pig-snout and death's head', and elaborate preparations had been made to cope with a macabre range of possible toxic attacks. A year into the war, many people had stopped bothering to carry the gas masks, though children were offered novelty versions, and there was even a gas-bag system for babies. Well tutored by terrifying newspaper predictions of hundreds of thousands of casualties, and popular memories of the use of gas in the earlier war, local councils had ordered in shrouds and cardboard coffins for the expected slaughter.

The 'blackout' was another early and dramatic innovation that would last for most of the war. Nobody was allowed to let any light stream from their windows after dark in case it alerted German pilots. Householders had to pin or nail thick curtains to windows. Street lights were turned off. Cars were allowed only a thin strip of illumination for headlamps. The anti-light mania was taken to ludicrous lengths, so that even glowing cigarettes or weak domestic torches (hardly visible from a Dornier) might lead to a bellow of 'put that bloody light out'. One result was that the number of people killed in road accidents doubled. Another was an increase in al fresco sex. But beware: on the streets new officials were striding, armed with new powers. A hierarchy of air-raid protection (ARP) wardens had been planned as early as 1937 and by the Blitz they would prove both useful and heroic. But in the early stages of the war, 200,000 strong, they seemed to many to be paid busybodies, striding around 'their' areas as if they owned them while ticking off or reporting neighbours. The semi-military organization of the civilian population would prove one of the most dramatic aspects of Britain's war effort. Not only the ARPs but the volunteer firemen and the women of the WVS – the Women's Voluntary Service, formed in 1938 – and before long the Home Guard filled Britain with a new officialdom. They were visible signs that Chamberlain's state, run by old liberal-minded

Conservatives brought up to view the state with suspicion, was growing fast. Already, Hitler was having an effect.

What, though, of the job of fighting him? Before the dreadful spring surprise of 1940, by which time Chamberlain was leaving Number Ten, the official attitude to Hitler's war machine was smug. His troops were reported to be keen, but raw. Even the shattering defeat of Poland had not made generals in the West understand the power of blitzkrieg, using armour, aircraft and infantry as one. It was assumed that if the Germans did attack France directly, a long and brutal war of attrition would follow which – in the worst case – the British government believed could go on in Flanders for three years. Britain had a smaller army than Germany, far smaller, but the French had a huge army and boasted some of the most advanced tanks in the world. The British Imperial General Staff placed great weight on the fighting ability of France, organized in and around its world-famous Maginot Line of bunkers, fortresses and heavy artillery. Churchill seemed to agree, going by his public utterances. But he was getting other advice too. The National Gallery director Kenneth Clark went to Paris before the German advance and found everyone, including the propaganda ministry, inexplicably upbeat: 'I suddenly realized why everyone in Paris was so jolly. The French were not going to fight. They had borne the brunt of the first war, both in losses of men and in occupied territory, and they did not intend to go through it again.' Back in London he reported this to Churchill: 'He sat hunched up, and occasionally nodded and grunted. He did not speak. He knew it already.'[3]

Meanwhile, searching for somewhere else to fight, Paris and London both alighted on Scandinavia. While this may seem odd now, it had some sound sense behind it. A famous German steel maker, Fritz Thyssen, who was anti-Nazi, had sent London a memo arguing that whoever controlled the huge iron deposits in northern Sweden and Norway would win the war. After the Soviet Union had used its new friendship treaty with Germany to allow it to attack Finland, and was suffering unexpected reverses, there was an excellent-looking reason for intervention in the region. Britain and France had stood back during the Spanish Civil War. But this was the invasion of a neutral country by the Red Army, which was still regarded as the 'real enemy' by many in both countries. Perhaps an operation could both help the Finns and cut off Germany from a crucial steel supply?

RAF planes were sent to help the noble Finns. An office was opened in London in January 1940 to encourage volunteers to go and fight for Finland – 300 men did so – while the cabinet asked the chiefs of staff to debate the pros and cons of declaring war on Russia as well as Germany. Before this hare-brained idea took hold, the Finns were suing for peace. In Whitehall, the debate went on. Should Norway and even Sweden have their neutrality violated? Churchill was an ardent advocate, not surprisingly. His critics winked at one another and muttered 'Gallipoli', not surprisingly. It was eventually agreed that the navy would mine Norwegian waters to stop the Germans getting their steel and that, meanwhile, British and French forces would 'secure' Narvik in the north of Norway and then move into Sweden, despite the horrified protests of the Norwegian and Swedish governments. (So much for Allied protestations when the Germans did the same to Denmark, Holland and Belgium.) All this took much time in Whitehall and in conversations between the French and British. Meanwhile, choosing the same date as his enemies, Hitler pounced. Taking personal control of the operation, he overruled military commanders. Using subterfuge and air power, the German army seized the major Norwegian ports and airports and within six weeks had taken over the country. British and French forces carried on fighting for a while before being evacuated and the German navy suffered losses, but it was a humiliatingly easy victory for Hitler. British troops had arrived without the snowshoes necessary to move overland. French alpine forces had their skis, but had brought the wrong bindings. The Royal Navy, egged on by Churchill, had followed German ships in the wrong direction. It was not all disastrous. The warship losses suffered by Germany ensured that, later on, her navy would be unfit for its part in an invasion of Britain.

Even so, the Norway campaign was a major defeat with huge implications. It showed that a dictator with courage and opportunism could flat-foot the dithering of democracies. Berlin was crowing, and rightly. It demonstrated that the British–French alliance was inefficient. It provided shocking evidence of the poor organization and

Through Fire, A New Country

equipment of the British army and reminded everyone that the Royal Navy, however vital to the survival of Britain, was of limited use in winning a continental land war. Other lessons were more ambiguous. From a Churchillian perspective, Norway showed the fallacy of the optimistic belief that, left alone, Hitler would sit still and become steadily less dangerous. Others, though, pointed out that he had seized Norway because and before Britain was about to do the same. Churchill drew the lesson that a bigger, earlier attack would have been successful and that Whitehall's dithering had been disastrous. Before the campaign started he had exploded privately to an admiral that 'the squandering of our strength proceeds in every direction . . . Do you realize that perhaps we are heading for defeat?'[4] His critics pointed to his interference in military matters, his public boasting and his lust for romantic adventures.

Churchill was certainly unpopular in Whitehall. He infuriated service chiefs with his meddling and colleagues with his long interventions in cabinet discussions. He campaigned vigorously to be allowed to chair the Military Coordination Committee, and to chair the Chiefs of Staff Committee, which would make him the effective controller of the war. Half of official London seems to have banded together against the latter idea. One of the inside observers was Jock Colville, a young diplomat seconded to Chamberlain's Downing Street, who was keeping a gossipy, politically detailed diary. He would soon become Churchill's private secretary and devoted to him, but at this stage he was hostile. Colville had a conversation with the permanent secretary at the War Office in which they spoke of Churchill and his crony, the commander of the Imperial General Staff, Lord Ironside (who, being very tall, was known as Tiny): 'We must get the P.M. to take a hand in this before Winston and Tiny go and bugger up the whole war.' A little later, when the Norwegian campaign had collapsed, Colville records Churchill saying mordantly on a wet May Day in 1940: 'If I were the first of May I should be ashamed of myself,' and adds, 'Personally, I think he should be ashamed of himself in any case.' And a little later still, just after Chamberlain had resigned as prime minister, Colville records arch Tory intriguer R. A. Butler saying that 'the good clean tradition of English politics, that of Pitt as opposed to Fox, had just been sold to the greatest adventurer of modern politics'. The victory of Churchill and his rabble was a serious disaster, Butler continued, and the Tory leadership had 'weakly surrendered to a half-breed American'.[5]

These may seem extreme words. They were not uncommon thoughts. Before he became prime minister, Tory whips were putting it about that Churchill was responsible for Norway and wondering out loud whether he should be sacked. For months after he entered Number Ten, Churchill was greeted in icy silence by most Conservative MPs while Chamberlain was cheered every time he appeared in the Commons chamber. Earlier the polls had shown others, notably the dashing Anthony Eden, as more popular replacements should Chamberlain be forced to resign. Despite his age and recent flattery of Hitler, Lloyd George was popular too. But inside Tory circles by far the most popular candidate was Lord Halifax, the fox-hunting churchman described earlier. Chamberlain expected Halifax to succeed and so did the King, who regarded Churchill with deep suspicion – perhaps not surprisingly, given Churchill's championing of Edward VIII during the abdication crisis. Among other Halifax supporters were the socialist politicians Hugh Dalton, Herbert Morrison and Stafford Cripps, along with Lloyd George. So Churchill's ascent to power, which now seems so obvious, was quite remarkable. He had comparatively little support in Parliament. He had less inside the ruling Conservative Party. Most of the Labour movement loathed him as a caricature class enemy who had ordered troops to move against workers and helped crush the General Strike. He was distrusted in Whitehall and by many service chiefs. He had some press support, but this was hardly overwhelming and was concentrated in the 'cheap' papers most disregarded by Westminster. And however one divides responsibility, he was one of those responsible for the Norway fiasco. So how did it happen?

The story of the Norway debate of 7–8 May 1940 has been told many times. It was one of the greatest parliamentary moments ever, and little about it was inevitable. The government had an overwhelming majority. Though small groups of MPs were plotting against Chamberlain, they were deprived of their natural leader by Churchill's presence – and publicly loyal presence – in the cabinet. It mattered that Chamberlain spoke badly, and with grating sarcasm.

It mattered that an angry admiral, in full fig, castigated him for the failures of the campaign and said he was speaking for the officers and men of the fighting, sea-going navy, 'who are very unhappy'. It certainly mattered that a fire-breathing Tory MP who had once been a great supporter of Chamberlain's father bothered to re-read some comments of Oliver Cromwell, so that he finished his speech by looking directly at the prime minister: 'You have sat too long here for any good you have been doing. Depart, I say, and let us have done with you. In the name of God, go.' It might be thought ironic that the words Leo Amery chose were directed by Cromwell at Parliament itself, as he established a ruthless military dictatorship, just what Britain was now fighting. At the time no one seems to have noticed and the words did their job, electrifying the Commons. Many more speeches followed, including a fine one by the elderly Lloyd George, and Labour decided to force a division. Attlee had been worried about uniting the Tories and cementing Chamberlain's position, but the atmosphere was changing. In a crescendo of emotion, forty-one Tories voted against the government, many of them younger MPs in uniform and, with abstentions, Chamberlain's majority crashed from 213 to 81.

It was a brutal rebuke. But was it the end? Chamberlain thought not. Churchill's real appeal had been outside Parliament, as a national figure who seemed to embody the fighting spirit the government lacked. If Chamberlain could put together a government of national unity, bringing in his Labour and Liberal critics, then he could remain as prime minister, no doubt with Churchill playing a larger role. Churchill himself agreed and urged Chamberlain to continue. Why? He cannot have seriously thought him fit to lead the war effort. Perhaps he believed Chamberlain was finished anyway, so it did not matter. More likely, he realized that his own position in the Tory Party was still so weak that to plunge in the knife now might make it impossible for him to succeed. Chamberlain asked the Labour leaders whether they would now join a National Government led by himself. They thought the party, then meeting for its annual conference, would not accept this but agreed to go and ask two questions – would they join the government under Chamberlain? Would they join a government under someone else? As they motored down to the Highcliff Hotel in Bournemouth, the question in London then became: if not Chamberlain, who would the 'somebody else' be – Halifax or Churchill?

With the Tory chief whip, the three men faced one another in Number Ten to decide. Though there are different and contradictory accounts of exactly what was said, it is clear that Chamberlain spoke first, and said he would serve under either man. The chief whip, speaking for the party, said Conservatives, or possibly 'some' Conservatives, would prefer Halifax. Then the issue arose of whether Halifax being in the Lords disqualified him from being prime minister? Churchill scented a trap and decided to say nothing. He simply turned his back and stared out of the window for what seemed a very long time – more than two minutes. Halifax then said he felt that his being a peer disqualified him – and Churchill was left in command of this small but important battlefield. This was a crisis in which parliamentary revolt had spoken in the language of anti-parliamentary Cromwellian dictatorship, and now the country's most eloquent speaker had won his victory by saying precisely nothing. It was concluded by the spectacle of the Labour leadership deciding to serve under a man most of them had reviled for years as the arch-reactionary hammer of the working classes; for Attlee called Chamberlain from Bournemouth to tell him Labour would join the government but not under him. On 10 May he went to the King to resign, followed that afternoon by Churchill's mission to kiss hands and change the fate of the world.

Melodramatic? Over the top? Churchill has that effect. He came back, according to his driver, close to tears and saying, 'I hope it is not too late.' These events have been pored over endlessly, and rightly.[6] They comprise the most important political crisis Britain has ever experienced. Some historians believe Halifax had proved a kind of Christian hero in the end: he knew he was not fit to be war leader and stood aside. Others think Churchill and Chamberlain had done a deal which tilted the balance: certainly, Churchill needed Chamberlain once he succeeded him in a way Halifax would not have done. Either way, Churchill was stubbornly determined to become the country's war leader if he possibly could. He was not put in power by popular acclamation, as the People's War myth might like us to believe. His morale-lifting, surging speeches had cheered the country up, and when he appeared on newsreels cinema audiences were already cheering him back. But public opinion, in the sense of informed, influential and media opinion, was at best divided about Churchill; and in the Commons, where his power would partly rest, he had been recently unpopular, even a figure of fun. He was put into power by other politicians, from the Tory dissidents who had plotted Chamberlain's fall with devastating effect in the Norway vote, to the Labour leader Clement Attlee, and those who now stood aside to let him pass, Chamberlain and Halifax.

They did this because they could see that none of the rest of them, no rival politician of the first rank in Britain at the time, could have dedicated himself to fighting and winning as Churchill did. Halifax wanted to talk peace with the Germans. There is some evidence that his under-secretary R. A. Butler was still conspiring to put out peace feelers even after Churchill became leader, telling the Swedes, possible intermediaries, that 'diehards' would not be allowed to stop a compromise between Britain and Germany and that 'common sense and not bravado' would dictate British policy. That was a rather different message from Churchill's to his new cabinet: 'We shall go on, and we shall fight it out, here or elsewhere, and if at the last the long story is to end, it were better it should end, not through surrender, but only when we are rolling senseless on the ground.'[7] Even those who accept the notion of a just war know that war is partly madness. Hitler had a vision, Wagnerian in colouring, that was mad. To combat him level-headed, coolly calculating people were not enough. Churchill was not mad in Hitler's way, but he had a simplistic, almost boyish and wholly romantic view of human history that was just as vivid. He looked down on lesser breeds and believed in his own 'race' and in his own destiny. In normal times this made him an embarrassment and a bore. But this was his hour; and it seems that a majority of the men who might have stopped him agreed. Chamberlain would soon die of cancer. Halifax found himself incapacitated at key moments of the crisis by stomach ache and toothache. The worse things got, the stronger Churchill felt. This is a mysterious tale too, of human will and life force. Meanwhile, the British political crisis was overshadowed by the enemy Churchill simply referred to as 'that man'.

Dunkirk Spirit: 80 proof?

The fall of France to the German blitzkrieg of May 1940 was not the failure of British policy, generalship or soldiers. By the time the attack happened, the quarter of a million British in France were only a small part of the forces colliding. The British Expeditionary Force had five regular divisions and five more made up of former part-timers. France by comparison had a huge army, 2.2 million strong, though including many reservists and conscripts in the eighty-eight divisions. The German army was 106 divisions strong. To put it another way, the BEF was not only less than a tenth of the size of the German force but smaller than the Dutch army and much smaller than the Belgian army. Numbers, notoriously, are not everything. Yet when equipment is compared, the BEF seemed even weaker than the numbers suggested. They had only a single tank division, which was not complete. British tanks essentially came in three varieties. There were tanks with strong armour but only machine guns – so useless against German Panzers. Then there were tanks with armour-piercing guns but whose own armour was dangerously weak. Finally, there were tanks with both useful guns and useful armour. There were very few of them – indeed, just twenty-three – and they arrived late. Transport comprised vans and lorries from post offices, butchers and other commercial companies, scattered across Britain, painted khaki and often in bad repair. General Montgomery, who commanded one division, said the army was not only unfit to fight a first-class war but was also unfit to take part in a realistic exercise. It did have anti-tank rifles, which rarely worked. It also had new French Hotchkiss machine-guns, but no British troops had been taught how to fire them by the time they landed in France. The RAF in France did have some of the new Hurricane fighters, but relied heavily on the unmenacingly named Fairey Battle light bomber, which must be one of the most dangerous and ineffective machines flown in combat. Almost all of them were quickly shot down; despite the courage of their pilots they were virtually useless.

Yet the appalling story of the 'battle for France' cannot be wholly excused or explained by equipment failures. The German army, after all, was using rifles just as elderly as the British and was less mechanized overall: it depended on horses for transport, for example. The French had more modern fighters than the Luftwaffe and tanks that were, at least on paper, better than the German Panzers, though British troops were quickly alarmed by what seemed to be poor morale and low discipline among their allies. In essence, the Germans had better, bolder tactics and a strategy which completely wrong-footed the British and French commanders. How did the Allies fight? Not very well. The German 'sickle' thrust depended on a feint, drawing the British and French up to respond to a thrust coming through Belgium, while the full attack was further south. It worked perfectly. They used transport aircraft to bring men forward quickly, while their air force kept hopping ahead from captured airfield to captured airfield. Above all, instead of using tanks in a scattered way to support slow-moving infantry, they used large formations of them to attack directly, backed up by infantry and aircraft.

None of this was new in principle. Such deployment had long been advocated by British tank theorists such as Basil Liddell-Hart, who had advised the sacked Hore-Belisha, and General Fuller, who later joined the British Union of Fascists. These British theorists were dismissed as self-publicists by the army at Aldershot, but were studied closely in Berlin. French theory was even more out of date. The great collapse was a French collapse, which followed a Dutch and a Belgian collapse. French generals broke down in tears. French politicians were openly defeatist. For none of this can British generals or soldiers be blamed. British politicians can be blamed, however, for the weight they placed on the great French army. They had inspected the Maginot Line fortresses and been wined and dined by affable French commanders, who told them of the latest French tanks and fighter planes. But they had not pondered the results of years of extremist and divided politics in France, the endless coalitions and the bitter rivalries between far right and far left. They had not observed the gap between French conscripts and the small pro-fessional army, mainly used in the colonies. They saw France through sunny, sparkling spectacles, perhaps to be expected of politicians who mostly went there for Mediterranean summer holidays.

Yet the BEF was a nervy shadow of the army which had beaten the Germans in 1918. It performed badly too. This is not to imply that British soldiers did not fight bravely. When modern British tanks, the Matilda Mark 2s, were used in a rare counter-attack, they alarmed even Rommel. Again and again, against impossible odds, British infantry armed with Bren guns, rifles and grenades made rearguard stands of spectacular valour. For their pains, when they eventually surrendered at villages such as Wormhout and Le Paradis they were massacred by Germans who felt humiliated and confused by the fight they had put up. Occasionally British troops fled in terror: one officer was shot by others when he tried to retreat. There were scenes of cowardice and selfishness when, towards the end, morale began to collapse and the British army streamed towards Dunkirk. But there were also heroic examples, and characters in the finest traditions of British eccentricity. One such was Brigadier Beckwith-Smith of the Coldstream Guards, who had to break the news that a battalion had been ordered to hold the perimeter and thus would not escape. He 'drove up in his car. "Marvellous news, Jimmy," he shouted. "The best ever! ... We have been given the supreme honour of being the rearguard at Dunkirk. Tell your platoon, Jimmy. Come on, tell them the good news."' Then, to his fellow officer's delight, Beckwith-Smith addressed the men on how to deal with the Stuka dive-bombers: 'Stand up to them. Shoot them with a Bren Gun from the shoulder. Take them like a high pheasant. Give them plenty of lead. Remember, five pounds to any man who takes one down.'[8]

Yet no number of last stands, good jokes or acts of individual bravery could disguise the fact of a stunning defeat. Twenty-two years on, the German army was relishing its revenge for 1918. Desperate last-ditch diplomacy by Churchill, including the extraordinary offer of joint citizenship between the British and French, could not halt the collapse. Now came an act of raw self-interest on the part of Britain that would poison relations with her nearest neighbour for a generation. For if the French were beaten, they did not all feel ready to give in quite yet. There were still courageous French generals and soldiers lined up alongside the BEF, and fighting further to the west. They believed that, by the terms of the alliance, the British would continue shoulder to shoulder until the end; or that, at any rate, an evacuation would be joint and agreed in advance. This did not happen. Once Field Marshal Gort, who commanded the

BEF, decided that the situation was hopeless, he broke his agreement with the French commander General Weygand in order to protect his embarkation point at Dunkirk. From then on, the sole British objective was to get out as many men as possible, whether or not the French felt deserted. Instead of making three battalions available for a counter-attack, Gort ordered them to defend a hole in the defences left by the surrender of the Belgian army; later, requests for more British divisions to stay in France, or to return, were refused. In the early stages of the evacuation French troops were more or less literally shouldered aside and it took desperate pleas from Weygand to Churchill before some kind of equity was established. The bombed and bloodied beach was a world away from Churchill's political fantasies of a united Franco-British spirit. Eventually, of the 338,000 men rescued at Dunkirk, 123,000 were French. Many of them went straight back to carry on fighting with the French forces still resisting in the west.

The story of Dunkirk remains a miniature epic. One can peel away the layers of misremembering for ever. It was not true that the soldiers simply lined up patiently on the beaches as the Stukas screamed down at them. Men did fight for places on the boats. Others became wildly drunk, or broke down. It is not true that the British army was saved by flotillas of little pleasure boats taken across the Channel by their plucky owners. Many fishermen, lifeboatmen and commercial boat owners refused point blank to help. Many of the boats which were assembled at Sheerness were then lost while being towed across the Channel. The Royal Navy was always in the lead, taking absurd risks and suffering severe casualties to get the troops away. Nor is it true that the BEF returned home full of contempt for Jerry and determined to get back to Europe and fight as soon as possible. There are many eyewitness and first-person accounts of demoralized, angry, near-mutinous men, shattered and humiliated, returning to the English ports. One entertainment officer, sent down to Bridport in Dorset, found a town crammed with seething soldiers expressing 'blasphemous resentment', including one in a bar making 'loud-mouthed criticism of the junior officers of his ack-ack unit in seizing the only available transport and making for the French coast, leaving their NCOs and men to fend for themselves ... These dismayed men, savagely wounded in their pride, were seeking relief in bitter criticism of those set over them. We promised each other that whilst the war lasted we would never speak of what we had seen and heard that night, and we never did.'[9] Though the RAF fought hard over the beach, the short range of their aircraft meant the Germans often got through. After Dunkirk, far from fighter pilots being heroes, they were the object of bitter and public derision by soldiers.

Yet when all this is admitted, and so is the skilful propaganda use to which the defeat and evacuation were put, there remains the kernel of something rare. The evacuation was a feat of improvisation and doggedness. When the BBC appealed for small boats of any kind to help save the army, they were never intended to bring troops back across the Channel. For that, larger vessels were required. But they were desperately needed to go in to the shoreline and ferry the soldiers to the waiting passenger ferries, destroyers and requisitioned Dutch motor boats. Those 'little boats' – yachts, cockle boats, fishing smacks, private motor and pleasure cruisers from the Thames – which were led across the Channel, were then cut adrift to reach the sand and the Dunkirk mole, and bring men back. Some were crewed by navy men and had been requisitioned. Others were crewed by retired watery potterers, Essex fishermen and amateur sailors who had never heard a shotgun fired at a rabbit, never mind seen a shooting war at first hand. There were groundings and much chaos. But without them, the evacuation would have been far, far smaller. Nor would it have happened had General von Rundstedt's German tanks not halted before a final assault. Later Hitler would claim that this was out of some kind of strategic tenderness: he had not wanted to destroy the British Empire, because Germany would not have been able to pick up the pieces; it was 'fair play'. More likely the halt order was given by Rundstedt himself, out of caution and because the Germans thought that with the British beaten and hemmed in, the priority was now to attack south, demolishing the remaining French resistance.

Back in London there was still optimism that the French would fight on. The politicians were out of touch and Churchill did not like the hard truths being relayed back to him by his commanders on the ground. He had, however, kept French requests for ever more squadrons of RAF fighters at arm's length, after the man in charge of the RAF, Sir Hugh 'Stuffy' Dowding, insisted he needed them at home to defend Britain. An idea of the foresight on that, at least, comes from Colville's Number Ten diary for 6 June: 'We should be insane to send them all our fighters, because if they were lost this country would be beaten in two days, whereas even if France surrenders we shall still win the war – provided our air defences are intact.' This presumably reflects the conversation in Downing Street. Even in the last hours before the surrender of France Churchill was making plans to go over himself to rally the French premier Paul Reynaud, and there were desperate hopes that President Roosevelt would offer active American support for France. The British general Sir Alan Brooke had been sent back to France to command a 'second BEF' consisting mainly of Scots and Canadians. Some, bizarrely, sailed in grand style, taking their dress kit and dining on the way over. Yet this was mere politics, Churchill's attempt to keep the French fighting. Brooke himself arrived on a Dutch steamer, soon concluded the position was utterly hopeless and, after an angry half-hour with Churchill on the phone, ordered another evacuation from further down the French coast. He himself only returned later by fishing boat, after the French war hero, now collaborationist leader, Marshal Pétain had ordered all French troops to lay down their arms: nobody had thought to warn the notional British commander first.

The hopelessness of the fight was underlined by the heroic rearguard action of the 51st Brigade, Camerons, Seaforths, Black Watch, Argylls and Borderers, who held St-Valéry under dreadful conditions, after running out of water and food, and often ammunition too, until their evacuation was made impossible by the arrival of German artillery on the cliffs. After the French around them had surrendered, they did too, and 8,000 men spent the war in captivity. They were luckier, however, than the majority of the soldiers, airmen, sailors, women and children who got aboard the Cunard liner *Lancastria* at St-Nazaire. After she was hit by bombs and sank, around 3,500 people died, many of them burned to death, some beheaded by their life jackets and a few by shooting each other in suicide pacts: this, not the *Titanic*, was probably the greatest British maritime disaster ever.[10] In London, Churchill made one final attempt to keep the French in the war. As Colville excitedly put it on Wednesday 19 June 1940: 'Apparently there is a stupendous idea of declaring the political unity of England and France.' Edward Bridges, the cabinet secretary, came out of the cabinet room and dictated a Declaration of Union: 'It sounded inspiring, something which will revive the flagging energies of the French and invigorate our own people. It is a historic document and its effects will be more far-reaching than anything that has occurred this century – and more permanent?' (Colville did at least put a question mark, though it is interesting that the French inspiration for this came from a young Jean Monnet, who later became a founder of the EU.) Meanwhile, nobody had told King George what was being done to his empire; a minister was despatched to see him that evening. He need not have worried, since the following day Reynaud resigned and Pétain surrendered.

In Britain, three famous pieces of instant propaganda were woven from the Dunkirk experience, and they have all lingered long. The most famous was, of course, Churchill's speech to the Commons on 4 June: 'We shall not flag or fail. We shall go on to the end. We shall fight in France, we shall fight on the seas and oceans, we shall fight with growing confidence and growing strength in the air, we shall defend our island, whatever the cost may be. We shall fight on the beaches, we shall fight on the landing grounds, we shall fight in the fields and in the streets, we shall fight in the hills; we shall never surrender.' He went on to promise that, in 'God's good time', America would come to rescue and liberate the Old World. Britain was about to stop fighting in France. Churchill's reference to 'growing strength' in the air refers to his thirties obsession with building up the RAF, the still-secret radar network, and perhaps encouraging reports about its performance over Dunkirk. Yet talk of fighting on beaches, landing grounds, fields and streets implies that he thought invasion would follow, despite the Spitfires. General Thorne, who had fought at Dunkirk and was now commanding troops south of London, told Churchill on 30 June 1940 to expect a landing of 80,000 German troops between Thanet and Pevensey. Churchill was less pessimistic, but not optimistic about Britain's ability to hold the whole expanse of beaches: Thorne warned him his troops were 'scarcely equipped at all . . . The German left wing could be held in Ashdown forest, but he did not see what could prevent the right wing advancing through Canterbury to London.'[11]

There was a rival belief that mass landings by gliders and parachute troops would be the next event of the war. Many English sports and cricket grounds were littered with pieces of derelict machinery, timber and agricultural equipment to stop gliders: golf courses were officially vandalized and iron barriers were spread over roads. The police were armed to shoot parachutists and once the Local Defence Volunteers, soon the Home Guard, were formed, the country was alive with rumours of white objects floating from the sky, to be pursued by locals with shotguns or clubs. On the same reasoning, road and railway signs were torn up and destroyed lest they tell invading Germans where they were. Factories and hotels had their names painted over. Even war memorials, with village names attached, were gouged. 'We shall – neva – suwendda' was hurled at the Commons and the microphone on the assumption that, after Dunkirk, the next land battles must take place across southern England. This seemed perfectly likely. Jitteriness should be seen in the light of the astonishing German progress across Belgium and France. That the Germans were not ready for such an invasion and could not get safely over the Channel was at the time unclear. The code-word 'Cromwell' was prepared for an imminent invasion and on 7 September 1940 it was actually issued, albeit prematurely. Churchill's novel technique was to rub the nation's nose in likely disasters ahead while promising a dramatic denouement at the end of the film – an epic imagination which Hitler would have understood but which was underpinned by 'the half-breed American's' realistic assessment of the real strengths of Britain and the US.

The second famous act of Dunkirk propaganda came a day later from the only broadcaster to rival Churchill in effectiveness and popularity at the time – the maverick socialist writer J. B. Priestley. His tone could hardly have been more different. He focused on the little boats: 'We've known and laughed at them, these fussy little steamers, all our lives. We have called them "the shilling sicks". We have watched them load and unload their crowds of holiday passengers – the gents full of high spirits and bottled beer, the ladies eating pork pies, the children sticky with peppermint rock.' The *Gracie Fields*, an Isle of Wight ferry, had been sunk: 'But now – look – this little steamer, like all her brave and battered sisters, is immortal. She'll go sailing proudly down the years in the epic of Dunkirk. And our great-grandchildren, when they learn how we began this war by snatching glory out of defeat and then swept on to victory, may also learn how the little holiday steamers made an excursion to hell and came back glorious.' Both men took for granted that they were living through historic days. (And do the great-grandchildren learn, by the way?) But where Churchill mingled defiance with dark warnings, Priestley was chirpily optimistic. Where Churchill swept the world with rhetoric, Priestley was local. Which was the more moving, the more effective? Churchill's 'we' and Priestley's 'we' are very different. The first really means 'I' – 'I shall never surrender' – and challenged worried listeners to identify themselves with that 'I'. The second was a real 'we', sentimental perhaps, but pointing more surely towards the democratization this war would bring.

The third act of post-Dunkirk propaganda was a yellow-covered tract by three young journalists who worked for Beaverbrook – Michael Foot, the later Labour leader; Frank Owen of the London *Evening Standard* and Peter Howard. Writing under the pseudonym Cato they called their book, written in the four days after Dunkirk, *Guilty Men*. They listed fifteen people, including Ramsay MacDonald, Baldwin and Chamberlain, plus another ten cabinet ministers and a couple of others as being responsible for Britain's failure to rearm or confront aggression, beginning with the Japanese assault on Manchuria in 1931. Published by Victor Gollancz, it was a crude, sarcastic and often unfair attack, written in the heat of anger and fear. It included some bizarre targets – Sir Thomas Inskip, for instance, who had directed Britain away from focusing on bombers to the fighters needed so badly later the same month that *Guilty Men* was published, and the entirely obscure Sir Reginald Dorman-Smith, blamed for poor food production. But it was a slashing attack at the right moment and hugely popular – some 200,000 copies were sold even though it was banned by W.H.Smith, which was then even more important in bookselling than it is today. Its prose now seems overblown and oddly grandiose for journalists of the centre and left. 'A great empire supreme in arms and secure in liberty' had been brought 'to the edge of national annihilation'.

Its technique of using the words of the condemned against them was effective and its conclusion savage, if badly written: 'One final and absolute guarantee is still imperatively demanded by a people determined to resist and conquer; namely that the men who are now repairing the breaches in our walls should not carry along with them those who let the walls fall into ruin ... Let the Guilty Men retire then ... and so make an essential contribution to the victory on which we are all implacably resolved.' The trio pinned on the pre-war appeasement generation, largely Conservatives, full blame for the disaster of Dunkirk and so laid the foundation for an analysis shared in due course by Churchill and which helped bring about the political revenge of 1945. Among those who lived to feel ostracized and humiliated by the *Guilty Men* analysis was Baldwin himself. This was, as it were, the serrated cutting edge coming days after the democratic sentimentality of Priestley's Dunkirk. It prefigured Churchill's great domestic dilemma – that he found himself as Conservative leader leading a 'People's War' defined in opposition to his own party. In July 1940, however, Churchill was not thinking of that. Like the rest of the country, he was raising his eyes to the skies.

Spitfire Magic?

The Battle of Britain, the single most important battle this country has fought, is part of the private furniture of most of our minds. It is settled there, our Thermopylae. What do we see when we close our eyes? The Spitfire, turning in a glint of sunshine, surely. Of all the weaponry and machinery that men have made to kill other men throughout history, the Mark 1 Supermarine Spitfire, balletic and simple, is probably the prettiest, and it was the one which won the battle. We see posh young men with tousled hair and moustaches, toying with a pipe or finishing a pint before scrambling for the waiting aircraft – perfect examples of plucky British amateurism, heading off to hunt the ruthlessly well-organized and overwhelmingly more powerful Luftwaffe. Against terrible odds they fight, return, snatch a quick sleep and fly again. For every one of ours brought down, we account for – what is it? – three or four of theirs. We hear, rather than see, those most famous Churchillian words: 'Never in the field of human conflict has so much been owed by so many to so few.' We perhaps have a vague sense of taciturn RAF leaders, shoulder to shoulder, in the background. But they were a few, and in this rare clash of modern chivalry, the rest of the country could only stand, stare upwards and wonder.

Most of that paragraph is untrue. This was the most important battle and the Spitfire is beautiful. But it was not the plane that won the Battle of Britain. Twice as many Hawker Hurricanes were involved, and though they were not quite a match for the best German fighter, the Messerschmitt 109, their pilots included as many of the top aces as Spitfire men. Hurricanes could be built faster and, furthermore, Spitfires were extremely difficult to repair, so that when damaged they were out of action for far longer. What about those public schoolboys? The RAF did have a 'chaps' ethos, with a tradition of favouring hunting-and-shooting types who it was thought would fly better. Flying generally was expensive and glamorous – the RAF pilots were sneered at by the other services as 'Brylcreem Boys' and its code was full of the stiff upper lip, its jargon nonchalantly off-hand. Yet around four in ten were working-class sergeants or flight sergeants. And a fifth of those who fought were not British at all – they were New Zealanders, South Africans, Poles, Czechs, Canadians and French. They may have smoked, but during the battle they rarely drank. They were too tired. It is not true that everyone behaved heroically. On 12 August, at an RAF airfield in Kent, repeated bombing sent airmen into shelters, and some refused to come up, despite pleas from their officers. On 15 September some Hurricane pilots saw Messerschmitts ahead and, instead of roaring 'tally-ho', turned smartly for home.[12] This was a battle, not a picture book.

Nor were the RAF pilots either amateur or ill-trained. As the battle continued and the losses mounted, training was slashed back. But the RAF which went into the fight was very well trained and highly professional; if anything the cult of knightly amateurism was found more in the Luftwaffe, with its obsessive interest in aces and decorations. The odds the RAF faced were not appalling, either. If you discount the cumbersome Stukas, which were essentially cannon-fodder for fighters, and the German bombers, which were targets too, the Luftwaffe had 963 fighters available, against 666 British fighters. Yet the German figure includes the unwieldy double-engined Me-110. Of aircraft directly equivalent to Britain's Fighter Command they had 702, roughly the same number. It is true that, at

any one time, the Spitfires and Hurricanes were likely to be outnumbered, since the Germans were attacking over a large area of
southern England. Against that, the Germans had little time in the
air before their fuel ran out, and they had to head home – oddly,
they did not use drop-tanks. So the fight was not so one-sided as is
usually assumed.

Above all, when it came to fighting an air war Britain was, for
once, better organized than Germany. Churchill often gets the credit
for this, thanks to his campaigning before the war, and, as we have
seen, he was generally spot-on. But it was actually Chamberlain who
in the late 1930s listened to Dowding when he insisted that, by
creating an excellent fighter force, annihilation by bombing could
be averted. As described earlier, radar was an essential component
of the new system. Its full effectiveness had been stumbled upon
during a fruitless search for a 'death-ray' and the famous chain of
radar stations along the coast had been built in great secrecy. The
Germans knew about them but never understood how important
they were – partly because of the command-and-control system
created by Dowding at the same time. Below Dowding in the RAF
was the great genius of the front line of the battle, the New
Zealander Keith Park, whose command of 11 Group, covering the
south-east of England, was inspirational. Dowding, who was personally rather dull, and Park were both constantly being conspired
against by another Air Vice Marshal, Leigh-Mallory, who believed in
grouping far more fighters together for a knock-out blow, the so-
called 'big wing'. His manoeuvring sidelined the later careers of both
Dowding and Park, neither of whom is even mentioned in the Air
Ministry's official history of the battle. Luckily, it did not seriously
impede the efficient command of the fight at the time.[13]

Getting the new Spitfires and Hurricanes to front-line squadrons
had been a slow business. The appallingly outdated state of Britain's
engineering industry meant that most of the machine tools used to
build them, and many of the components, had to be imported. But
one of Churchill's earliest appointments was to make the wicked
press baron Lord Beaverbrook his minister for aircraft production.
In a devilish whirlpool of activity, bullying, cajoling, stealing and
sabotaging Whitehall systems, Beaverbrook raised the monthly output of fighters from 256 in April 1940 to a peak of just under 500 in

July. He persuaded half the country, from towns to works canteens to coal mines, to raise money to 'buy a Spitfire'. The Germans, producing only two new fighters for every three British ones, had no idea how far away they were from destroying the RAF physically.

Even when it came to the famous fear of running out of pilots – and there were certainly anxious days – accelerated British training and the use of naval and other pilots more than filled the gap. Despite the deaths of 500 RAF pilots among the 3,000 or so who fought in the summer of 1940, the operational strength of fighter command actually rose between the beginning and end of the battle by around 40 per cent.[14] Outnumbered in individual fights, they also outfought the Luftwaffe, with a higher kill-rate across the battle. Far from this being a battle of 'the few', it was a military achievement of the many. Behind the 3,000 fighter pilots there were another 400,000 people in the RAF, including the mechanics, fitters, riggers and pilots (some of them women) ferrying new and damaged fighters. There were the Observer Corps, the searchlight crews, the gunners and the radar operators. Behind them were the frantically overworking factories, often in vulnerable parts of the south-east, and the repair crews who kept the few flying. This was a fight that involved industrial energy and organization, a sophisticated communications system, a high degree of professional training and the very latest technology. The RAF, whatever its own spin, was a disciplined and meritocratic outfit. In short, the Battle of Britain was not won because of amateur, public-schoolboy pluck but because for once, we fought with the same kind of focus and organization as the Germans.

None of which detracts an inch from the extraordinary courage of the young men who fought. And they were young – the oldest RAF squadron leader was twenty-four. Sitting behind eighty-five gallons of fuel, for a fighter pilot death by bullet was merciful compared with the horror of being burned alive, or at best burned out of recognition – the skin-graft technology of Archibald McIndoe's East Grinstead unit was much needed. Luck, excellent eyesight and reflexes and a killer instinct were essential, but often not sufficient. Though only one key airfield, Biggin Hill, was put out of action for a short time by German bombing, pilots regularly had to make emergency landings, bail out over the sea – where their chances of survival were low – and face being shot in the air as they tried to parachute to safety. What they achieved was deathless. Had the RAF lost control of the skies to Hitler's hitherto all-conquering war machine, invasion would have been far likelier. The army had left their tanks, artillery, machine guns, transport vehicles and most of their rifles behind in France. Had the Wehrmacht made it ashore at Dover or Brighton, there would have been little to stop them in Kent or Sussex. Hitler did not want to invade if he did not have to, and had indeed again offered what he regarded as reasonable peace terms to his defeated foe. (These were rejected not by Churchill or one of his ministers but, off his own bat, by a BBC announcer.) And the question of whether the German invasion of Britain, Operation Sealion, would ever have been successful cannot be answered. The German army was poorly equipped for a seaborne invasion, was still reliant on horse-drawn transport and was at that time not supported by warships which could have taken on the Royal Navy. It would have been another huge gamble. But Hitler at the time was a gambler on a winning streak.

The Battle of Britain was the first proper success the country had had since war broke out. It turned the RAF from being the least regarded of the British services to national heroes. It brought home to everyone living in the southern parts of England that this was a national war unlike any other, which was actually being fought on home territory. Rather like the 'halt order' which allowed the BEF to escape at Dunkirk, it is often said that Britain was saved by another German mistake, Goering's decision to shift the air attacks away from the RAF airfields to London. Yet the shift was not nearly as clear-cut as history remembers, and some of the hardest fights came after the Blitz was underway. Given the relative success of Britain's radar, aircraft production and kill ratios, it seems unlikely that the RAF would have been broken by a few more weeks of Luftwaffe assault. None of this was clear at the time. Exhaustion was taking its toll. Ahead lay an experience that showed just how democratically the carnage of war would be distributed: Britain might not be invaded on land but she remained open to bombing. Just as an evacuation is still a defeat, so a defensive success is not victory. The British have never been wildly enthusiastic about current affairs: nevertheless, it is remarkable that in the summer of 1940 a grand total of 3 per cent thought the country would lose the war.

All Our Blitzes

If 'the Blitz' refers to the bombing of London, first in 1940–41 by aircraft and then in 1944 by flying bombs and rockets, then we need a plural. Almost every major industrial city, and many smaller ones, were bombed. From Belfast to Exeter, Clydebank to Hull, high streets and city layouts today still bear witness to what happened. But the first Blitz was on London. There had been dramatic air attacks already, not only on Guernica during the Spanish Civil War but during the Polish campaign and against Rotterdam. Yet the first really serious attempt in the world to make a country surrender by bombing its civilians until the nation's morale broke began in September 1940. Up to a point, Britain was ready for this. A quarter of a million volunteers were organized as wardens, firemen, nurses and even amateur bomb-disposal teams. There was a national civil defence and air-raid protection structure in place. Public shelters had been prepared, though they would prove grossly inadequate. Anderson shelters and Morrison shelters – steel hide-unders for use inside the house – had been widely distributed. Many people had quietly left London – about a quarter of the city's population had gone by November 1940, and in some East End streets a majority had left their homes before the bombing started. Evacuation took place at the grander end too. King Charles I, having lost his head once, nearly lost it again: the vast painting of him on horseback by Van Dyck was part of the huge National Gallery collection moved out for the duration, eventually to the cave of a slate quarry in Wales. He got stuck under a railway bridge; rather than destroy the painting, the bridge was partially dismantled. All manner of valuables, public and private, were spirited out of the capital. A second evacuation of children and some women began, and by the end of 1941 1.25 million had been taken to the countryside or small towns. The air-raid warning system was working in every major population centre.

The bombing, when it came, was nothing like as lethal as the pre-war Cassandras had foretold. The Germans were using relatively light bombers originally designed to support their army, not to annihilate cities. Britain, not Germany, was the first country to invest seriously in heavy bombers. Yet the effect was indescribable. Literally: one can list horror stories for tens of thousands of sober words and still not scratch the surface of the full experience. Hundreds buried or crushed to death in Underground stations, either by direct hits or trampled in panic; people cut in half by falling plate glass; children's bodies lying in pieces in the streets; old people left wandering about, driven insane by the loss of their families; baskets of human flesh carried to morgues for jigsaw-puzzle identification; children buried alive for days beside their dead parents. Of the 60,000 people killed by German bombing and (later) rocket attacks, half were in London, and 43,000 were killed during 1940–41. About 230,000 people were injured. In the first six weeks alone a quarter of a million Londoners lost their homes. Below the statistics for death and destruction lay fear, squalor, humiliation and boredom. Ignoring official advice, people poured into the Underground, where at first they lived without sanitation, water, proper ventilation or privacy – a lice-ridden, stinking, undignified underworld which choked newcomers with its smell. Occasionally in the post-war years some idiot politician has promised to bomb this or that people 'back into the Stone Age'. Thousands of Londoners literally became cave-dwellers, bedding down in the ancient Chislehurst caves in Kent: special trains were laid on each night. Others lived under railway arches. The Tilbury arches at Stepney, crammed with people of all races living in appalling squalor, were so bad that sightseers came to gawp. At the other end of the social scale the most privileged could find shelter in the Turkish baths at the Dorchester Hotel. But class was not a waiver: even Buckingham Palace was hit three times and when the ritzy Café de Paris took a direct hit while crammed with revellers dancing to a swing band the carnage was frightful.

In the worst days of the London Blitz more than 175,000 people were sleeping in the Underground. Overhead, firefighters – of whom more than 700 died – and air-raid wardens, nurses, WVS women and ambulance crews, police and bomb-disposal teams acted with relentless courage, dousing, digging, bandaging, feeding, consoling and burying. Broken power lines and water pipes, sewers and cables were mended while the fires burned all round. Live bombs were dug out, despite booby-trap devices: St Paul's only survived because of two men who disobeyed instructions and dug deep to recover a huge bomb, which should have killed them. The first London Blitz ended after a particularly heavy and destructive raid on the centre of the city on 10 May 1941, when the Commons chamber was destroyed, along with hits on Westminster Abbey, the Tower of London and the British Museum, where there was an inferno of books. Irreplaceable artworks, records, sculptures and buildings went. Even a world-class collection of fossils was blown to pieces when the Royal College of Surgeons suffered three direct hits, leaving lumps of dinosaur and extinct mammal scattered through local gardens. More than 2,000 fires were started and 3,200 people were killed or injured. Many roads and most railway lines were blocked and the firefighters were struggling to put out fires for eleven days. After it was over, London was changed for ever; yet the city would go through a second wave of attacks in 1944 when first the 'Doodlebug' flying bombs and then the V2 rockets, harbingers of the post-war age, rained down, killing between them another 8,000 people. Croydon, once a beautiful market town, now a concrete metropolis, was particularly badly hit.

Though London took the worst, it is not clear whether it suffered more proportionally than other blitzed cities. The case of Coventry, which lost most of its ancient centre, a third of its houses, its cathedral and its railway connections on the night of 14 November 1940, after German bombers used intersecting radio beams and then incendiaries to guide them, is particularly poignant. A small town, comparatively, people there felt it had lost its soul and there was panic, hysteria and chaos. But what of Clydebank? It had 12,000 houses. After its attack, seven of them were left undamaged and the population able to sleep there dropped from 47,000 to 2,000. Plymouth suffered a two-night Blitz which gutted the place. So many houses were hit twice that the figures exceeded the total number of homes. It is thought that around 50,000 people trekked into the countryside to sleep in barns, fields or even on Dartmoor. But Merseyside, Birmingham and Bristol could claim to have suffered as badly and some believe that Hull was the worst-hit city of all. The point is that the Blitzes ranged right across Britain. The terror and uncertainty was spread from the north of Scotland to the English

West Country. It arrived in small and non-industrial centres, too, particularly after the bombing by Britain of the ancient port of Lübeck produced in response the 'Baedeker raids', when the Germans used the famous tourist guide to choose particularly historic or beautiful towns. This was when the 'People's War' was felt by the people.

A Warrior People?

Morale did not collapse. It may be that the myth of the cheery Londoner, 'taking it' and carrying on, was overblown propaganda. But the stories of shops staying in business with only three walls ('more open than usual' said the sign) and of workers struggling back to factories from demolished houses are true. The Blitz can be likened to a severe malady, affecting much of the population. It caused sleeplessness and exhaustion, fear for the future, anger and disorientation. It mingled people, as in hospital wards, who had nothing much in common but their misfortune. It provided a single topic of conversation and, as with some chronically sick, it actually gave many people a theme. Suicides fell in the war years; so far as it can be measured, there was less depression too. It certainly did not break Britain's will to fight, nor did it much impede the war economy. Even in the most shattered cities, such as Coventry, Bristol and Southampton, production was soon back to normal and the bombing spurred workers on. Yet by 1943 Britain was dropping on German cities fifteen or more times the explosive power used in the 1940–41 Luftwaffe raids, apparently under the illusion that, having not worked here, it would work there.

What was the political effect? It certainly bound the country together. Not all the country was alike, or affected in the same way. We should beware of thinking that the British were wholly united or unique in courage or perseverance. When the Channel Islands, far closer to France than to England, were abandoned in 1940 to the Germans, the islanders seem to have behaved very much as people did in occupied France, Belgium or Holland. Without an army, they did not try to resist and when a tiny occupation force arrived, they found most houses flying white flags. The authorities – councillors, postmen, teachers and police – collaborated with the Germans. The King's portrait remained hanging on walls and British currency continued to circulate for most of the war. A few of the tiny number of Jews on Jersey and Guernsey were sent to camps on the mainland. Both islands produced 'Jerrybags' – girls who slept with Germans and sometimes bore their children. There were examples of disobedience and a few heroes and a few outright traitors. Some islanders took great risks to help slave labourers drafted in to build Atlantic wall defences against invasion, but others worked the black market and enjoyed themselves. After the war there was much forgetting. All of this is exactly what would be expected, reading over from the behaviour of other Europeans: it showed how little different the British were.

It is worth remembering too that this was already a smaller United Kingdom. Southern Ireland had gone and would remain neutral. In 1938, against Churchill's strong protests, Britain surrendered her right to use the so-called Irish 'treaty ports' of Cobh, Berehaven and Lough Swilly, and when war came the newly named Eire refused to reopen the matter. The Irish partly depended on Atlantic convoys, whose journeys were made far more dangerous by this decision: Churchill even considered a retaliatory blockade. In the opening year of the war Coventry had been bombed – to start with not by the Luftwaffe but by the IRA, who killed five people in a shopping centre. That year there were other terrorist attacks by the IRA in London, Blackpool and Liverpool. As in the First World War, German agents were active in Ireland and in 1941 four divisions of British troops were sent to Northern Ireland in case of an invasion via the south.[15] In 1945, when Hitler finally killed himself in his bunker, the Dublin government presented its condolences via the German embassy. On the other side of the account, at least 160,000 Irish citizens went to do war work in Britain. Neither part of Ireland was affected by conscription into the British forces (because of the political impact of trying to conscript nationalists in the North). As it happens, rather more volunteers came from Eire, some 50,000, than from admittedly smaller Northern Ireland, which provided 42,000.

In Scotland and Wales, pre-war nationalism was much subdued. One leading Scottish Nationalist, Douglas Young, who believed that the Nazis would win the war, refused to serve and fought a lengthy legal battle. In Kirkcaldy in 1944 he came close to winning a by-election, and indeed the SNP did so in the following year. Once 'surplus women' were conscripted and sent around Britain for war work there was resentment and a small campaign in Scotland about the despatching of innocent Scottish lassies south. Germans thought it worth creating a Scotland-only propaganda station, Radio Caledonia, and dreamed of recruiting Welsh Nationalists to their cause too. Before the war Plaid Cymru activists had indeed attacked an RAF bombing site. Yet the binding-together impact of the siege of Britain, with constant patriotic propaganda, had a far stronger effect. The BBC was at the height of its authority. War films assiduously included Scots and Welsh characters; so, of course, did the war stories produced by the Dundee-based firm of D. C. Thomson. Scotland's greatest wartime politician, Tom Johnston, began to create the corporate, public-works country and used the threat of nationalism to get what he wanted from Churchill. A belief that 'we're all in it together' was only enhanced when servicemen returned home with common stories of France, Italy, North Africa and the Far East. Bombs fell alike on south Wales and southern England, the Clyde and the Thames. It was not coincidental that the years after the war saw the Unionist parties at their all-time peak: the Conservatives dominated Scottish politics during the fifties.

Yet the greatest political effect of the war was the impact on class distinctions. In the armed forces, in civil defence, in the long shifts in factories, where former debutantes struggled to help make shells alongside former maids, and in the fields and air-raid shelters, accents subtly accommodated one another and old differences mattered a little less. (Only a little: Diana Mitford was nearly thrown out of her air-raid role because the other women could not stand her voice any longer.) Taxes soared – income tax went up early in the war to the unheard-of rate of 50 per cent – while the incomes of the skilled working classes, putting in long hours in the key factories, rose too. With less to spend money on, and endless drives for patriotic saving schemes, disposable incomes became far less unequal. Apart from the few at the very top, mostly invisible to the masses, distinctions in clothing, diet and lifestyle were blurred. Above all, the Blitzes subtly undermined the old rulers, who had brought the country to this pass, while it bolstered the confidence of the ruled. As the bombing went on, official Britain became more organized. Bunks were put in tube stations; reception and rest centres were set up; bigger shelters were constructed (albeit too late to be useful); the work of demolition and clearance was carried out. Anti-aircraft batteries were sited in the key city areas where they greatly cheered the population – though more civilians were killed by shards of falling shells than were German aircrew overhead.

Yet the people at the sharp end were just the people; and the people who helped the people were overwhelmingly volunteers, folk like themselves, from their street, factory, office or club, now wearing a tin hat and an armband. More than any other organization, and thanks mainly to television comedy, we have remembered the Home Guard, first formed as the Local Defence Volunteers at the height of the Blitz. Within a few weeks of a radio appeal by Anthony Eden, the war secretary, 1.5 million men too old or too young to fight or prevented from full military service by their occupations had presented themselves to defend Britain from invasion. Every class of person from retired generals to village poachers, coal miners to schoolteachers, left-wing railwaymen to former rulers of the Indian Empire found themselves under rudimentary command. To start with, most had no kind of uniform other than an armband and paraded in bowler hats, caps and deer-stalkers rather than helmets. Their armaments were rudimentary, certainly while the evacuated regular army itself was lacking. In country districts there were shotguns to be had, but the Home Guard did indeed march around the country challenging the unwary with spears, golf clubs, pickaxes and 'guns' carved out of wood. One unit in Lancashire had rifles which dated back to mid-Victorian times – the Crimea and the Indian Mutiny – and even pikes.

The Home Guard were both lethal and useful, though rarely at the same time. They were useful because they guarded endless stretches of coastline, railway stations, bridges and factories which would otherwise have used up the regular soldiers. They were lethal because, particularly in the early days, they tended to fire on or attack all manner of objects, from dimly seen cows moving around at night to cars which failed to hear quavering calls to stop. Quite a few drivers were killed. So were quite a few innocent animals. During Blitzes, they helped with civil defence, fighting fires, digging people out and leading survivors to safety. Later on in the war, they had acquired battledress uniforms, boots and helmets. They had rifles and sometimes even machine guns and had learned to use them. They had effective transport and had become a younger organization, boosted by teenagers who were then semi-trained even before they were called up for the full-time army. They had cavalry, moorland specialists, river patrols and even marines. They had brass bands, served in anti-aircraft batteries and developed a great enthusiasm for challenging the full-time soldiers in exercises. There is no doubt that the Home Guard became a satisfying alternative lifestyle for many men, partly a club, partly a self-conscious schoolboyish escapade which relieved wartime boredom. But by jumbling the classes, so that bank managers and executives would find themselves being inspected by postmen or factory workers, the Home Guard also shook the class divisions a little. It too was part of the People's War. From the volunteer soldiers with pikes to the volunteer firefighters and bomb-disposal men, the women factory workers and nurses, this was a do-it-yourself response to a dictator's war. Even more than the Battle of Britain, the Blitz and the shake-up of society that accompanied it was a truly national experience. Official propaganda recognized it: in films and broadcasts the firefighters and the factory workers took central position, rather than generals or ministers.

Soil and Salt Water

Through 1940–41, when for most of the time Britain 'stood alone' – though with the Commonwealth and empire alongside her – life became rapidly drabber, harder, more equal. Rationing, which later became widely detested, was initially popular. Churchill warned Lord Woolton, the food minister, during the Battle of Britain that he should beware faddists: 'The way to lose the war is to try to force the British public into a diet of milk, oatmeal, potatoes, etc., washed down on gala occasions with a little lime juice.' This was a reaction to extreme plans for a 'basal diet' which would keep people healthy if the worst came to the worst. Woolton himself, who became very popular, knew rather more about these matters than Churchill did. He had been a department-store tycoon before the war, and a social worker before that. As Fred Marquis, he had become interested in diet when living in Liverpool's slums: his next-door neighbour had died of malnutrition. He set himself the task of ensuring that everyone would now have enough to eat, even if it was dull food. The 'Woolton Pie', invented by the Savoy Hotel's chef, was perhaps the most famous example. It consisted of mixed vegetables and oatmeal with a wholemeal crust. Yet Woolton's reputation survived even the pie. His technique was to combine education about food with strict fairness. Among the results would be a huge expansion of free school meals, free milk for children and free juice for under-twos. The poorer British grew stronger and healthier during this siege.

In the autumn of 1940 food was still reasonably easy to get, particularly meat. The fair and easily understood points system was first used for sugar, bacon, margarine and tea. The U-boat fleet was still small, and only just beginning to relocate to the French ports from where it would wreak its worst effects. By 1942 less than half the 55 million tons of food brought in each year before the war was getting through. Rationing had been steadily extended – tinned meats and vegetables, tinned salmon, dried fruit, condensed milk, canned peas, breakfast cereals, biscuits, syrup and oatflakes. This was popular because of the widespread and justified suspicion that the rich were avoiding their share of the pain, eating game and tinned luxuries out of reach for the common family. Non-profit 'British Restaurants', an idea which emerged from the Blitz and which were run by local authorities, offered cheap self-service meals in more than 2,000 locations. But normal restaurants, perhaps oddly, kept going too.

Diaries of the war years show that many of the better off did manage to drink and dine remarkably well for a long time. Churchill's private secretary Jock Colville, who certainly managed to, noted in a Censorship Report on 'home opinion' in February 1941 'a general expectation that this war must bring the end of class distinction and the abolition of great inequalities of wealth. There is no anti-democratic feeling. Obviously – and rightly – the fact that rationing and shortages affect the rich very little, since they can pay the extra price and feed in well-stocked restaurants, is causing some bitterness.' Beer, bread, potatoes and tobacco were never rationed during the war, but a grey diet of pies, hotpots, fake sweets and cakes made from stodge, cheerily advertised by Woolton and Cripps, atop a huge propaganda effort of pamphlets, leaflets, press adverts and broadcasts, eventually drove most people mad. Horse-meat, seabirds, whale meat and other nasty surprises could be found lurking in the kitchen. A vigorous black-market economy began to flourish.

Food was the most important rationed item, but soon petrol began to be unobtainable for private cars, and clothing was tightly controlled. As with furniture, china and cosmetics, the range being produced was radically cut down to make production more efficient. 'Utility' clothing from a narrow range of textiles, with a maximum number of buttonholes and pleats and a limited variety of underwear, arrived in 1942. Women found that most kinds of decoration were now banned and that skirts became shorter, jackets boxier. Men, already finding it hard to get razor blades, found they were allowed fewer pockets, no turn-ups on their trousers, no long socks and shirts which were so short they didn't tuck well into waistbands. Most forms of furniture stopped being manufactured and a limited stock of 'utility' designs was offered instead. Cups came in white only, often without handles. Pencils were reduced to only a few kinds; the same went for bedding and household goods. Any form of 'frippery' was officially condemned. Even toys went on to the list of banned products. All this was brought about and policed by a new state machine which operated with something of the same rigour and attention to detail later found in post-war Stalinist Russia.

This found acceptance not only because it seemed to reduce class divisions when the besieged country needed to feel united, but because it was self-evidently necessary. More than 40,000 merchant seamen were drowned, blown up or burned to death keeping the sea lanes to Britain open. The Battle of the Atlantic was fought out between U-boats and aircraft, convoys and mines, German raiders and tiny corvettes, with both sides inventing and then countering new technologies – a never-ending zig-zag of successes and failures. This was the real siege. Both Churchill and Hitler had envisaged a sea war still dominated by the old capital ships. Both were wrong. There were buccaneering fights, notably the sinking of the large, if outdated, battleship *Hood* by the newer German *Bismarck*, and the subsequent chasing down and sinking of that ship. In the Pacific war, the duels between the US and Japanese navies were very important, demonstrating how air power now trumped surface fleets. In the Atlantic, which mattered most to Britain, the capital surface ships became a sideshow. The life or death struggle was led from Brittany by Admiral Doenitz, the leader of the U-boat fleet, based in a sardine-merchant's château; and in Britain by a polio-stricken civilian lawyer, Rodger Winn, who, along with a chartered accountant, ran the Royal Navy's Submarine Tracking Room in an ugly concrete building near Downing Street. Their game of bluff, counter-bluff, changing tactics and secret intercepts was as important to keeping Britain in the fight as any other part of the war.

By the end of the war, the Germans lost more than half the 1,157 U-boats they had built. Across the world's oceans, submarines had sunk more than 2,280 ships, mostly U-boat sinkings of merchant vessels trying to reach Britain. Both sides had made serious mistakes. If Hitler had understood earlier the potential war-winning power of the U-boats and spent more on building up and improving his fleet, he could have starved Britain of food and fuel in the spring of 1941 before America was ready to join the war. Had Britain used more aircraft to fight the U-boats rather than bomb German cities, she might have seen off the U-boat threat and saved the lives of tens of thousands of seamen. But war is always a competition about mistakes as well as insights. Both sides developed new technologies, from 'snorkels' allowing U-boats to sail long distances underwater, and ever deadlier mines on the German side, to refined airborne radar, depth charges and code-breaking on the Allied side. Small shifts could lead to huge effects.

To give just one example: the breaking of the German Enigma code and the exploitation of secret traffic by the British academics, chess masters, mathematicians, linguists and military men at Bletchley Park was one of the war's most celebrated scientific success stories. (It should be remembered that Polish mathematicians and agents, French spies, British naval boarding parties and lackadaisical German intelligence officers were all part of the Enigma tale too.) Without Enigma intercepts the Submarine Tracking Room would have been half blind. The machines worked by scrambling information with three notched rotors, and in the summer of 1941, beginning to suspect that their codes may have been cracked, the Germans added a fourth rotor, greatly increasing the odds against code-breaking. Allied shipping losses rose four-fold.[16] In the end, new radar systems, new anti-submarine rockets, new depth charges and new British naval ciphers would defeat even the 'wolf-pack' tactics of Doenitz. During their most dangerous phase, in 1941–2, the U-boat commanders and seamen became celebrities in Germany. But then the U-boat losses mounted. With air cover spreading even into the 'Atlantic gap' their kill-rates fell dramatically until, in the final year of the war, most of the once war-winning submarines were tied-up targets at home.

This war of vast ocean wastes, appalling weather and applied science had a direct and almost immediate effect not only on what the British ate and how they dressed but on what Britain looked like, too. 'Dig for Victory', cried tens of millions of posters and leaflets. Parks, playing fields and verges were turned over to vegetables. Nearly 7,000 'pig clubs' sprang up to raise domestic porkers. By the middle of the war a quarter of all fresh eggs were coming from people who had put up hutches and chicken wire in their gardens. Some 600,000 extra allotment gardens were carved out of lawns, flower beds and waste ground. Rabbits had a hard war. So did rats: about 1,000 of the famous 80,000-strong Women's Land Army were employed as full-time rat hunters. But all this was as nothing compared to the expansion of mainstream agriculture. The amount of land under the plough rose by half. The land for potatoes doubled, and for wheat expanded by two-thirds, almost returning the look of rural Britain to mid-Victorian times. Downland, orchards and golf courses were all assaulted. It was not quite like the old days. British agriculture, like the German army, was still mostly horse-powered. Well over half a million horses were still working the fields by the end of the war. Yet meanwhile the number of tractors, mainly imported from America, had quadrupled. Excavators, new fertilizers and larger fields increased productivity. The voices down on the farm might be a mix of female cockney, broad Glasgow and foreign languages too: tens of thousands of Italian, and later German, prisoners were employed to harvest, milk, shear and sow.

So even the quietest and most backward parts of Britain felt the effects of war, and the long battle of the U-boats and convoys. In 1939 rural Britain had been depressed and poverty stricken. It was not much written about, except by novelists, who sold a sentimental, pickled-in-aspic story of Saxon villages and humorous yokels. Agricultural Britain was largely ignored, both by the new Britain of light engineering and consumerism and by protesting left-wingers. It was left to struggling farmers, fox hunters and holidaymakers. Yet most farms had no mains water supply and only a quarter had electricity. Low farm wages, earth-floored cottages, minimal education and ageing villages were common to most of the country. In 1940, looking for ways both to employ artists and to protect the skills of traditional watercolour painting and drawing, there had begun a far-sighted scheme to record Britain before the Luftwaffe destroyed it. The Ministry of Labour, using American charity money, employed painters such as John Piper, Kenneth Rowntree and Phyllis Dimond to do just that. Their work adds up to a glorious and romantic picture book, but scarcely of Britain. It is mostly England and mostly villagey, rural England. Sir Kenneth Clark, the director of the National Gallery, had set out categories of subjects including 'fine tracts of landscapes . . . old buildings about to be pulled down . . . Parish Churches . . . in a bad state of repair' and country houses and parks because 'these will be largely abandoned after the war and will either fall into disrepair or be converted into lunatic sanatoria'.[17] Which made for charming pictures but were hardly the Luftwaffe's central targets; the gap between how the people thought of rural Britain and how it really was both increased and then narrowed during the war. A wave of sentimentality about the old country, images of shire horses, swallows darting among the eaves and old churches, was used to stiffen morale. And then, to their surprise, city dwellers – volunteer farm workers, Land Army girls, amateur pig owners and evacuees – began to learn the truth of country living. Many even discovered that milk came from cows and potatoes did not grow on trees.

Deserts, Olive Groves and Bitters

The political challenges that shook Churchill were directly caused by military failures for which he himself was partly, though only partly, responsible. He was a great leader and a great politician. He was never a great general. Gallipoli had been a dreamer's thrust, Norway too. (It is possible to spend too long poring over maps.) During the final days of the battle for France, Churchill had allowed his over-optimistic hope of keeping France in the fight to overwhelm military realities, arguing with generals until beaten back. In Greece and in North Africa the pattern continued. Today, though 'Monty', the 'Desert Rats', Rommel and El-Alamein are part of our folklore, it is often vaguely thought that the campaigns in Libya and Egypt were sideshows. This was what the Americans and Russians often said, but it was not true. Had Britain utterly defeated the Italians' desert army early in the war, which came close to happening, then two years of fighting might have been avoided and the 'soft underbelly' of Nazi Europe would have been open to counter-attack by 1941. On the other hand, had British forces been ousted from Egypt by Rommel – and that seemed possible too – then a German vision of taking the oilfields of the Middle East in a pincer movement from the Caucasus and North Africa could have won the war for Hitler. The stakes were very high.

The first North African campaign under the poetry-loving imperial general Archibald Wavell, who had started his fighting career in the Boer War, went astonishingly well. Out-of-date Italian forces advanced towards out-of-date British ones in Egypt. Then, under General O'Connor, an audacious British (and Indian) blitz-krieg drove them all the way back again, and further. There were extraordinary heroics by British tank crews and Australian riflemen in a sixty-two-day campaign that had begun as a quick raid. By the time it was over in February 1941, the British Empire forces had advanced 500 miles, taking 133,000 men prisoner as well as capturing hundreds of tanks. Yet just when Wavell's army could have finally finished off the Italians in North Africa, Churchill ordered him to turn instead to help defend the Greeks. They were being attacked by Mussolini's army too, and had done a brutally effective job in repulsing them. Now, however, the Germans were intent on taking Greece, via Yugoslavia and with the help of their new Balkan allies. Trying to keep Greece in the war, as he had tried to keep France, Churchill told Wavell to send 60,000 men to repel the Germans. Supported by RAF aircraft, which were outnumbered about ten to one – far from the Battle of Britain odds – and equipped with tanks which broke down, the British, Australian and New Zealand troops had no chance. They were quickly and easily beaten and soon had to stage a Mediterranean Dunkirk, without the uplifting politics, retreating to Crete. That island, an important staging post for all sides, was then seized by German parachutists in a daring, bloody and (for Britain) humiliating campaign. Although successful, the losses by the attackers were so great that the Germans never attempted a mass parachute attack again; the point was obviously lost on the Allies, who started training to copy them.

Meanwhile, as the rest of the British and Commonwealth troops waited at Benghazi in Libya for orders to move forward again and finish off the Italians, a small hitch had occurred. Its name was Erwin Rommel. Rommel was already a German military celebrity and had been sent by Hitler to lead the newly formed Afrika Korps and help hold the Italian line. Wavell's top brass assumed that in desert conditions, with long supply lines for fuel and water, there was little chance of an early German attack. Within weeks Rommel had charged forward and thrown the depleted British forces into headlong retreat. In just three weeks he took back all the territory O'Connor had won from the Italians and soon had the Australian and other defenders of Tobruk surrounded, beginning a siege which would last for six months. A British counter-attack was smashed using the deadly German '88' anti-aircraft guns as anti-tank weapons. Churchill sacked Wavell and appointed a new commander, an Indian Army man, General Claude Auchinleck, whom he ordered to mount a fresh attack. Auchinleck, who, like Wavell, believed he had nothing like the necessary preparation, refused.

Rommel meanwhile prepared for another thrust that would throw the British out of Egypt and enable him to move into the oilfields. In theory it would have been a war-winning gambit: for Britain, Cairo was a key location for the whole conflict, linking the Mediterranean, India, oil and Africa. To lose there would have been disastrous. Had Rommel got the tanks and troops he wanted from Hitler, it is entirely possible that this is just what would have happened. However, when he visited the Nazi leader, of whom he was at this stage a devoted fan, Rommel found him strangely distracted and vague about the future of the desert campaign. This was not surprising. Hitler was planning something bigger. In June 1941 he launched 3 million men into his war-losing invasion of the Soviet Union, Operation Barbarossa. Four out of five German soldiers who died in the war would die on the Russian front. This gave Britain the first of her two major allies and it ensured that Rommel would never have the tanks, oil, men and equipment he needed to defeat British forces in the Mediterranean. Yet early in 1941 none of that was obvious or preordained. Meanwhile Rommel intended to start by taking Tobruk.

As is well known, he found this no easy task, and in November a long-awaited British counter-attack was launched that eventually rescued the isolated garrison from its long siege. By now, all around, the shape of the world was shifting. On the same day in December 1941 that Rommel ordered his pull-back, Japan attacked the United States Pacific Fleet at Pearl Harbor; four days later America entered the war, giving Britain her second and dominating ally. Meanwhile, refreshed and as daring as ever, Rommel launched a counter-attack of his own in May 1942 and captured Tobruk at last, taking 30,000 prisoners with a smaller force of his own. This was humiliating news, made more bitter still for Churchill because the message was passed to him by President Roosevelt while he was visiting him in America. Churchill partly responded by talking up the brilliance and mythical wisdom of Rommel – 'May I say, across the havoc of war, a great general.' Rommel became an odd kind of British hero too. Meanwhile, the great general was looking across the havoc of war and seeing the road to Cairo in front of him. All that stood in his way was the last key defensive area in the narrow fighting strip between the sea and the sand, El-Alamein. Auchinleck was standing there, building up his forces for the next battle. We have seen how politics and military strategy constantly clashed. They did again, with bloody results. Churchill now needed a quick victory. His new US allies were leading the joint Anglo-American 'Torch' landings further west in French-held North Africa and would eventually come behind Rommel. For Churchill's own position, British honour and the by now rather ragged reputation of British arms, it was important that Rommel lose to the Old World, not the New.

This was not the only way in which politics and war-making were entangled. If the Germans had an iconic military hero, so too must the British. Enter, in August 1942, the infuriatingly self-publicizing, rude and occasionally brilliant Bernard Montgomery. Churchill had lost faith in the cautious Auchinleck, as he had in the cautious Wavell. He sacked him and other key generals, men who had not only built up the Eighth Army but also drawn up many of the plans which would be adapted and claimed as his own by Montgomery. Churchill's second choice – his first was killed in a plane crash – Montgomery was, as a strategist, more cautious still. Protected by his commander, Sir Harold Alexander, 'Monty' used his personality and self-confidence to get Churchill's agreement to an attack even later than that planned by Auchinleck. Replacements have special rights. Other British generals tended to be clipped, traditionalist, formal men of few words. Flamboyant and inspirational, Monty was made for this new age of the celebrity general. He was perfect fodder for the hacks in battledress and the mass-circulation newspapers that would make him a star.

Rommel wore large British-made goggles on his cap and posed on Panzer tanks. Monty adopted a floppy beret – not his idea, but that of the head of the British army film unit, someone we would now call a spin-doctor – and was photographed with binoculars on a British tank.[18] He was brutal in his language, a master at blaming others for any problems while scooping the personal credit for successes. His commander-in-chief, Lord Alexander, is dryly hilarious about him in his restrained memoirs. But Monty became almost as great a hero to his men and the British public as Rommel was in Germany. He cajoled, inspired, mocked and buzzed noisily around in a way no previous British general had. Many of those who worked closely with him seem to have loathed him: General Patton certainly did and, personally, Churchill was no fan. But Monty had that go-and-kill-them spirit he called, obscurely, 'binge'. Again and again, in the desert and later after the D-Day landings, he would prove very slow in pursuit, and missed good opportunities because of it. He believed in assembling irresistible force and then destroying the enemy: despite the floppy hat and self-publicity, Monty was no cavalier.

Before El-Alamein he was both quiet and noisy. His noisiness was plain in his public pep-talking and tearing up of any plans for a further withdrawal. Quietly, however, he was taking and adapting Auchinleck's battle-plan while building up his forces to the point where British superiority in air power, tanks and men was all but overwhelming. He had nearly 200,000 men to Rommel's 104,000 and he had 950 tanks, many of them new American ones which had been snatched from the US army on Roosevelt's orders, compared to the 450-strong combined German and Italian tank forces. In terms of effectiveness, his superiority was even greater. Thanks to the Enigma code-breakers, he knew exactly what Rommel was saying to Hitler, often reading German reports before Hitler did. He could have lost the battle even so. He could have been lured into the open and allowed superior German tanks freedom to operate properly. But sheer British firepower made it a hard battle to lose.

On 23 October 1942 the Eighth Army opened up with a massive artillery barrage, beginning an eleven-day battle hailed afterwards as the turning-point in the war – though the real swivel was occurring at the same time 1,500 miles to the north-east at Stalingrad, a vastly bigger fight. The British made frontal and very bloody advances in a meat-grinder battle which simply shredded the Afrika Korps until Rommel, who had been ill and hurried back from Germany to direct the battle, was forced to disobey Hitler's 'victory or death' order and retreat while he still had an army intact. Montgomery could afford to lose two or three tanks to every Axis tank destroyed and simply keep going; and though the battle had many twists and turns, in essence that is what he did. Refused permission by Hitler to leave North Africa and regroup in Italy, most of the Afrika Korps would eventually be captured after a long pursuit and battles, now involving the Americans too. Churchill and Montgomery would have lost far fewer dead had they delayed the attack until the US army was advancing at Rommel from behind, but that would have been to lose face. (Montgomery's biographer and some historians counter-argue that El-Alamein was fought 'early' to demoralize the Pétain-supporting French forces in Tunisia and so aid the American landings; though motives are hard to prove so long afterwards, it seems a weaker case.)

The British attack had been launched two weeks before the US fleet and invasion force arrived in North Africa. It was won with all the odds for, not against them. It did not turn the British army into the equal of the German one in making bold tactical advances – German officers thought their opponents slow, pedestrian and easy to second-guess. But it did show that Britain had learned the importance of coordinating air power, strong supply lines and overwhelming force – not to mention the navy, which cut off many of Rommel's supplies. The victory came like a sudden ray of hope to the British. The BBC news announcer was so excited he forgot the traditional calm neutrality the Corporation expected: 'I'm going to read you the news, and there's some cracking good news coming in.' Though Alexander, as C-in-C, got most of the early credit, Montgomery had soon become a household name and a global celebrity. Churchill ordered church bells to be rung across Britain to celebrate the victory. Montgomery was knighted, and photographed in his becoming-famous beret and rumpled pullover. His vanity would become even greater but his celebrity gave self-belief and encouragement to the Eighth Army throughout the rest of the war, as they slogged after the Germans through North Africa, Sicily and up into Italy itself. With its own newspaper, eccentric clothing and self-mockery, it became a kind of citizens' army, led by a new kind of populist general. El-Alamein was a great British and Commonwealth victory and was the last of its kind in the main western theatre of war, since from now on the United States was fighting alongside as Britain's much larger, richer and better-equipped, if younger, brother. Among other things it saved Churchill's reputation after a low point in the war. As he himself put it, there were only defeats before, and only victories afterwards.

The worst of the defeats had not, in fact, been either Dunkirk – as we have seen, that was primarily a French defeat – or the surrender of Tobruk. The very worst had been the fall of Singapore, the main bastion of British imperial power in south-east Asia. The island was insufficiently defended to the landward side, where the Japanese armies arrived through Malaya in February 1942. Two great British warships had already been sunk by Japanese aircraft in an attack which owed much to pre-war British training. Moving fast with bicycles and attacking in small boats to cut off British and Australian units, the Japanese quickly took control of Singapore's water supplies, which meant that the garrison and the population were doomed. Even so, it was a force of 100,000 troops that surrendered to just 30,000 Japanese. Churchill told an old friend that he feared 'our soldiers are not as good fighters as their fathers were . . . We have so many men in Singapore, so many. They should have done better.' And Brooke, now commander of the Imperial General Staff, brusquely concluded that if the army could not learn to fight better, then Britain deserved to lose its empire. Montgomery's victory showed that when British troops had material superiority and inspirational leadership, they could fight just as well as in the Great War. Yet again and again they had been caught out in badly prepared positions, or outwitted by more audacious enemy commanders, and let down by poor equipment. They had also been the victims of politics, not just because of the years of appeasement and lack of investment in the military but because of decisions taken by Churchill himself after the war had begun. Amidst the propaganda and the talking up of victories and the general assumption that, in the end, 'England' could not lose, these obvious facts filtered back to the public at home.

A Soft Dictatorship

The politics of the war always depended on the fighting of the war. By the end, with Britain victorious, the state had reclaimed respect at home. But before that there was a long journey of grumbling, disappointment and protest. Politics did not stop. It simply twisted into strange shapes, unfamiliar then and forgotten now. Though the state became vastly more important, directing labour, controlling property and ordering the minutiae of everyday life, Parliament itself became less so. For most of 1940–45, so high was Churchill's public standing that the Commons effectively surrendered its great power of unmaking prime ministers. And though the war coalition, based on the Parliament of 1935, was dominated by Conservatives in raw numbers of MPs, by the end of the war the government was dominated by socialist or at least centre-left views. Somewhere along the way, domestic leadership was ceded by the elected chamber to unelected intellectuals, including Whitehall officials. The Tories had acquiesced in the ousting of Chamberlain and had slowly reconciled themselves to the bull-elephant Churchill. Then they had suffered the post-Dunkirk blow of the 'Guilty Men' thesis. Now they found the real government seemed to be barely Tory at all, but just

Churchill and a few cronies sitting atop an administration of pro-Soviet ministers, left-wing planners and Christian-commonwealth idealists. How had that happened?

We have to start with Churchill's own position. Rightly, he saw himself as a war leader rather than merely a prime minister. He spent far more of his time poring over military maps and closeted with generals than he did thinking about problems of education or health. He was no kind of domestic dictator: contrary to popular myth, he lost argument after argument. He was against clothes rationing but gave way because he was too interested in following the *Bismarck* chase. He was against the conscription of women in 1941 but was overruled. He was against singing 'The Internationale' at formal events when the Soviet Union had entered the war but was ignored. He wanted to ban material he regarded as defeatist, but others thought it fair comment. The famous film based on the cartoonist David Low's character Colonel Blimp survived an irate attempt by Churchill to have it withdrawn. He was against the appointment of William Temple, a famously leftish churchman, as Archbishop of Canterbury; he failed there too. These are just a few small examples, but they point to a bigger pattern. The plans for post-war reconstruction did involve Tories, mainly of the younger, reformist wing of the party. But they were shaped by a left-wing wind of opinion against which Churchill was almost powerless and which, when he noticed it, he allowed to blow him too.

This wind did not come from the lungs of political parties. Like the Commons, the party system was in a state of semi-stunned suspension. Labour was firmly part of the wartime coalition. Some of its local parties had opposed the war and called early on for a negotiated peace, but they quickly fell silent. In the Commons itself, Nye Bevan was a lonely if brilliant Labour opponent to Churchill. The communists set up a People's Convention calling for a popular government and attracted some fellow-travelling support, but switched to full-on patriotic backing of the war effort just as soon as the Soviet Union was invaded and the Moscow line changed. Later in the war, a Christian-leftish party called Common Wealth was created to fight (and to win) by-elections on a platform of public ownership and equality; but this was only a temporary measure until Labour was free to fight again under its own banner.

Instead, the wind blew from the battlefield defeats and an increasingly common view that Britain remained inefficient and badly organized. The Labour figures who came to dominate the home front were to a man believers in planning and a far bigger state. Clement Attlee gave Churchill loyal support while believing Britain must put forward a 'positive and revolutionary' programme for the post-war world, admitting that the 'old order' was over. Ernie Bevin, the great trade unionist, had with the direction of Labour a position of power over business, wages and hours no pre-war socialist could have dreamed of. Herbert Morrison, the former boss of London, described by Michael Foot as a 'soft-hearted suburban Stalin', had powers as home secretary that made him a national figure. Labour, which had started the coalition with sixteen ministers, ended it with twenty-seven, and completely dominated the cabinet sub-committees dealing with economics and social issues. Everywhere, from the clearing of blitzed cities to the more rational organization of farm-land, from the sending of women to factories where output rose to higher wages for aircraft workers and even miners, there was evidence of what a more assertive state could do. Churchill, needing to squeeze every ounce of extra effort from a fully mobilized nation, could hardly complain. Yet the same ministers helping to fight the war were sitting on committees looking forward to national recon-struction along socialist lines.

Outside Westminster, this seemed to be the new view of public opinion, as expressed by the leading newspapers, the churches and popular broadcasters. When the main church leaders signed a joint letter to *The Times* in 1940, top of their list of demands for a better future was that 'extreme inequality in wealth and possessions should be abolished'. A few months later a large gathering of clergy and Christian intellectuals at Malvern concluded that private ownership of industry might itself be wrong. Left-wing Penguin books sold spectacularly well. As soon as the Soviet Union was drawn into the war, Churchill elegantly pirouetting from his famous anti-communist beliefs to a gracious welcome for the new ally, the wind of change started to feel like a hurricane. The Asiatic monster Stalin was lauded as an efficient tough-guy who got things done. At Earls Court a celebration of the new alliance, organized by communists, featured the Bishop of Chelmsford and the band of the Coldstream Guards. A few months later, in February 1943, another event in the Albert Hall included music by composers such as William Walton, a poem by Louis MacNeice called 'Salute to the Red Army' and fanfares for Stalin by the Brigade of Guards. In an extraordinary about-face Beaverbrook, that champion of right-wing capital and imperialism, left the government to campaign for a second front to help the Soviets, telling an American audience the war could end in 1942: 'Communism under Stalin has produced the most valiant fighting army in Europe . . . the best generals in this war.' Tory ministers took to praising Stalin, workers chalked pro-communist greetings on tanks being sent to Russia, membership of the Communist Party rose five-fold and T. S. Eliot, that most conservative and cautious of poets, refused to publish George Orwell's *Animal Farm* because it would be offensive to Stalin. Strange days, indeed.

Churchill, uneasy about the turn in domestic politics, was obviously right to devote himself instead to the grand strategy of the war, although he would periodically fire off his own thoughts on post-war reconstruction. He hoped and assumed that he would survive as prime minister well into the peacetime years, leading the coalition forward. He never came close to losing his premiership, though had British forces lost in the Western Desert, many of those close to him thought he would be finished. At a low point in the war, with the Eighth Army retreating before Rommel, Sir Stafford Cripps, the Christian vegetarian and former revolutionary who had been ambassador in Moscow and was a popular possible alternative to the prime minister, used a radio broadcast to criticize the 'lack of urgency' in Britain, as if 'we were spectators rather than participants'. The Soviet Union was showing the way, Cripps suggested. His broadcast was very popular. Military humiliations followed. Two German battleships slipped up the Channel, evading the embarrassed Royal Navy. More significant was the shocking fall of Singapore to the Japanese – in Churchill's opinion the worst disaster in British history and a genuine disgrace. He brought Cripps into the War Cabinet as leader of the Commons, from where Cripps urged ever more austerity, self-sacrifice and efficiency . . . and yet, now on the inside, his allure as an alternative war leader faded.

After the fall of the Tobruk garrison in North Africa in 1942 there was a more serious backlash against what was beginning to look like an incompetent war leadership. Lord Beaverbrook considered himself a possible replacement, but the idea of a press baron becoming prime minister was a fantasy. A motion of no confidence in the direction of the war was laid in the Commons by a Tory MP who then badly muffed it by calling for the younger and obscure brother of the King, the Duke of Gloucester, to be put in charge of the armed forces. This was so silly that MPs responded with red faces and muffled laughter and any danger for Churchill evaporated in chuckles. Nye Bevan's attack was more dangerous, pointing out that Churchill 'wins debate after debate and loses battle after battle . . . The country is beginning to say that he fights debates like a war and the war like a debate.' Churchill survived that, too, but he was a little diminished. This was, however, the most threatening challenge to his authority and it emerged not from the Commons but from the barrels of Rommel's tanks. No wonder Churchill was forever berating generals for not attacking more effectively and, from time to time, sacking them.

Later in the war the National Government would lose a spectacular series of by-elections to independent or Common Wealth (but always left-wing) candidates who pinpointed Churchill's problem by lauding him personally but insisting the country needed a change of moral direction. Meanwhile the old Commons, a chamber which should have been cleansed by the vanished general election of 1940, became reduced from chamber to echo-chamber. Committees of officials and more junior ministers were hard at work on detailed post-war plans, of which Beveridge's blueprint for the welfare state is deservedly the most famous. Keynes, the other great public intellectual Britain produced, was far advanced in his quiet overthrow of Treasury orthodoxy, something in any case inevitable as Britain bankrupted herself to fight the war. As for the Commons, its most important role was as Churchill's personal theatre. In the semi-hysterical conditions of 1940 there had even been proposals to take things to their logical conclusion and shut down Parliament for the duration. A group of young Tories, including Harold Macmillan and Bob Boothby – key Tory politicians of the fifties – suggested a Committee of Public Safety, martial law and the standing down of Parliament, to be recalled only occasionally to hear statements and vote the necessary supplies. Churchill brusquely rejected that. It would have been strange for a country fighting for democracy to suspend its democracy. Yet in most respects, with government by ministerial diktat, this is effectively what had happened.

What did this sidelining of Parliament mean for liberty during the war? On paper, almost all civil liberties were suspended. The direction of labour meant people could be ordered where to work, and at what. Britain became a militarized and controlled society, bound by thousands of new laws, some vital and others petty. There were some notable acts of censorship, such as the closure of the communists' newspaper the *Daily Worker*. Many people were interned. They ranged from the far-right Tory MP and anti-Semite Captain Ramsay to Oswald Mosley and his wife and IRA men. Most were released later in the war and Churchill said he loathed locking people up, was saddened by the suspension of habeas corpus and in any case thought British fascists less dangerous than 'those filthy Communists'.

In the early hysteria about spies and fifth-columnists, unfortunate Germans, Austrians and Italians were rounded up and sent to internment camps in the north of England or on the Isle of Man. Of these, many were Jewish professional people who had fled Hitler – the Isle of Man camp became a bubbling centre of culture unmatched almost anywhere else in wartime Europe, with lectures, string quartets, theoretical science and art all flourishing. Other internees were Italians who had been living in Britain for most of their lives, doing nothing more dangerous than introducing the islanders to decent ice-cream, fish and chips, olive oil and coffee. In one terrible incident many internees were drowned at sea while being deported for the duration to Canada. There were shameful attacks on Italian restaurants and shops, but this too proved a passing hysteria, less serious than the window smashing and shop burning of the earlier war. By 1943 the vast majority of internees had been released to do war work.

Similarly, compared with the First World War, the treatment of conscientious objectors (and there were many more of them, no doubt reflecting the pacifist mood of the thirties) was humane. Some of the most courageous bomb-disposal teams and front-line medical staff were COs. Pacifists included Britain's most celebrated composer,

Benjamin Britten, who produced some of his finest work during the war, and the famous novelist and memoirist of the Great War Vera Brittain, one of whose pacifist works sold 10,000 copies when it was published in 1942. It was possible to protest against the war even as it continued. Bishop Bell of Chichester had campaigned for German refugees before the war and for internees when it started. Friendly with some of the most courageous Christian opponents of Hitler inside Germany, Bell publicly attacked the RAF bombing of enemy cities as a degradation of the spirit and called for it to be suspended. He attacked the practice in the Lords as 'threatening the roots of civilization' and, though much muttered against, was free to do so.

In 1940, when things were at their most dangerous, Peace Pledge Union activists were putting up posters urging people not to fight. They were put on trial at a police court. The magistrate dismissed the case with the words: 'This is a free country. We are fighting to keep it a free country, as I understand it.'[19] There were times when ministers panicked. One of them was in response to a cartoon by Philip Zec of the *Daily Mirror*. He had drawn a sailor on a raft, presumably a survivor of a U-boat attack, whose vessel had been bringing fuel. The caption, written by another *Mirror* journalist called William Connor, read, ' "The price of petrol has been increased by one penny" – Official'. This could be taken as almost banal; an injunction to remember the sacrifices being made, and not to whinge. The War Cabinet decided that it must be an attack on profiteering and threatened to close the paper down. Connor himself, who had been writing as 'Cassandra', a very popular columnist, went off and joined the army. Yet this was a relatively rare example. Censorship was not extreme. Criticism of the conduct of the war was widespread and at times loud. On paper, Parliament had acquiesced in the creation of a wartime dictatorship, with savage repressive powers. In practice it turned out to be a satisfactorily soft dictatorship.

The Americaning

We have seen how Churchill lost much of the initiative in domestic politics, and have seen too how he tried to interfere, not always successfully, in military decisions. But where he proved shrewdest as the war leader was in his ardent and wily wooing of the United States, followed by an even tougher campaign to influence where and when they would fight. Nothing like this had happened in the Great War, when Britain had been comparatively stronger. One of the key differences between Churchill and the leaders of the thirties was that MacDonald, Baldwin and Chamberlain were somewhat contemptuous of America. Churchill was an ardent, romantic admirer. His mother had been American, he had many American friends and, above all, from his early years he had made a lot of money by publishing and talking in America. It was fortunate for Britain, perhaps, that Churchill was a 'half-breed' hack writer on the scrounge and not the affluent English aristocrat he could be mistaken for. Later in life he would reflect that, given another chance, he would like to have been born American. Though an old-fashioned British imperialist, he was emotionally prepared for a world in which the United States would lead: his *History of the English-Speaking Peoples* had a title which both acknowledged reality and flattered his home island.

Churchill had understood from the first evidence of France's 1940 collapse that Germany could be beaten only if the United States came in. His defiant speeches nodded to the possibility of the fight being carried on from 'the New World', which of course included Canada. From the start of the war he had begun a secret correspondence with President Roosevelt, warning him that the US would face 'a United States of Europe under the Nazi command' better armed and stronger than the USA. Next, Churchill began badgering Roosevelt for obsolete US destroyers to help defend the Atlantic convoys in return for British bases – a deal done in August 1940. Finally, and against the advice of the bitterly anti-British US ambassador Joseph Kennedy, he slowly persuaded the sceptical president that he was, indeed, the voice of the British people. Even apparently excessive acts such as the sinking of the French Mediterranean fleet in case it fell into German hands (which poisoned French official views of the British for years) were intended to persuade Roosevelt of his ruthless determination to fight on. Roosevelt's emissaries Averell Harriman, Harry Hopkins and the new ambassador Gilbert Winant, who replaced Kennedy, were subjected to the full force of Churchill's charm and wooing. He spent remarkable amounts of time confiding in them, hosting flirtatious weekends at Chequers and flattering them while writing more than 2,000 letters throughout the war to Roosevelt himself. Churchill, the bricklayer and oil painter, could lay it on thick.

Perhaps the most extraordinary example of Churchillian wooing was the mission led by Sir Henry Tizard to Washington in September 1940, when he carried over in a single case most of the deepest scientific secrets of his country and – more or less – handed them over. There was rising hysteria about the possible new weapons to be delivered by science: Hitler himself was prone to warn about terrifying inventions on the way, and officialdom was bombarded by cranks promising death-rays. Tizard was a remarkable man. He was a real scientist. An aeronautics specialist who had tested his own theories by piloting Royal Flying Corps machines in the Great War, he had become one of the British government's key advisers by the outbreak of the next one. An early enthusiast for jet engines and radar, it was on his desk that the first detailed memo from Manchester University about a coming weapon, the nuclear bomb, arrived. Tizard's idea was to draw in American productive capacity to help Britain, by giving the Americans British secrets covering plastic explosives, rockets, gunsights, radar and much more. He told Churchill the mission should be 'to tell them what they want to know, to give them all the assistance I can ... to enable the armed forces of the USA to reach the highest level'.[20] There had been a brisk fight in Whitehall about this. It was, after all, long before America had entered the war. Could the Americans be trusted? Would they give anything back?

Churchill gave Tizard the go-ahead. He set off on a cold and dangerous journey by flying boat, sustained mainly by Bovril, while most of the rest of his group went by ship. In a clever stroke, he insisted he would be joined not by high-ranking RAF, naval and army staff but by serving officers who had themselves recently fought. Among the loot being carried was the cavity magnetron. This is a high-powered vacuum tube which generates microwaves (and is still used in microwave ovens today). Developed at Birmingham University, the 1940 British version increased the effective power of radar beams by a thousand-fold beyond anything the Americans had, and would soon allow radar in night fighters and bombers hunting U-boats. An example was brought to Washington, luckily being recovered after it was nearly lost at Euston station. The cavity magnetron, even apart from the other secrets, was a war-changing device, described by one US historian as 'the most valuable cargo ever brought to our shores'.

When Tizard finally arrived in the US after a stopover in Canada he was brought to see President Roosevelt, smuggled into the White House by a back door to avoid photographers in what was still a pro-neutrality Washington atmosphere. There followed, between the British mission and US military chiefs and scientists a kind of intellectual strip-poker, with both sides playing 'I'll show you mine, if you show me yours' until the British secrets had been handed over. Not all of them this time, however: the process of passing over the full breakthroughs by two exiled German scientists on the nuclear bomb, and then teams of British nuclear scientists, would come later. Tizard had been an early convert to the possibilities of nuclear power. His pre-war warnings to the Belgian owners of the world's only uranium mine, in the Congo, resulted in shipments going to America which would end up in the world's first atomic bomb. For now, he only passed on general details to scientists in the US, who were sceptical about the British approach. It was the same story with Frank Whittle's jet engine. This humbly born, risk-taking and anti-establishment RAF officer turned scientist had been working for years on jet propulsion. In the late 1930s he nearly lost everything thanks to official lack of interest: the delay would be part of the reason that the Germans were flying jets nine months ahead of the RAF. But in 1940–41 Whittle was far ahead of the Americans. Again, Tizard dropped hints.

The British got little useful information in return. Details of the latest US bomb-sight were withheld even after Pearl Harbor. But a full exchange of facts was not really Tizard's aim. He thought British industry, much of it outdated before the war and much of it being heavily bombed now, could not hope to produce the radar gear, never mind atomic bombs, that the larger and protected American industrial base could. Not, at least, if she was building tens of thousands of warplanes, tanks and guns at the same time. Like Churchill, he was sure that the US would be drawn into the war whether Britain was beaten or not: if so, they needed to be as strong as possible. Finally, only by convincing the Americans that Britain was ready to be a full ally and to share her secrets might the US be induced to assist in full. And in all those ways the Tizard mission, along with Churchill's wooing and the brute facts of the 1940 world, worked. First, there were large and increasing supplies of American aid, then Lend-Lease, and American protection of large tracts of its side of the Atlantic, long before the US formally entered the war.

In August 1941, when the Russians were allies but the Americans were not, Churchill and Roosevelt had their first meeting in two warships off the coast of Newfoundland and announced the 'Atlantic Charter' of joint aims for the post-war world. It was vague and skated over profound disagreements about the future of the British Empire. What was really remarkable about it was that Britain, fighting, and the US, apparently neutral, were agreeing war aims at all. At the end of that year, on 7 December 1941, came Pearl Harbor. Roosevelt, by now re-elected for a third term, led the US into what had become a world war – although, rather bizarrely, it was Nazi Germany that declared war against the US on 11 December, not the other way about. Churchill, who heard the news of the Japanese attack while closeted with Roosevelt's men Harriman and Winant, famously reflected: 'So, we had won after all!' It was a clear-headed judgement. After America's entry into the war Churchill devoted just as much time to Roosevelt and took considerable personal risks to visit him in Washington. The US president came almost to love him, and certainly treated him with a respect and affection that Stalin never showed.

If the first phase of Churchill's great diplomatic victory was wooing, the second was an endless dance of titillation, teasing and delay, which led to great American frustration. Roosevelt decided early on that, despite Pearl Harbor, the main enemy was Germany and that Japan would collapse if the Nazis were defeated. But where and when to defeat them? His military commanders wanted an early landing in France. So did Stalin, hard pressed. He certainly did not want to help shore up the British Empire. Churchill and his key military strategists, led by Sir Alan Brooke, thought differently. Shaken by the effectiveness of Hitler's soldiers, and never forgetting the slaughter of the Great War battles, they did not believe any landing in France in 1942, or perhaps even 1943, had much chance of success. Only overwhelming superiority, in troops, tanks and in the air, as at Alamein, would be worth chancing. Yet Churchill and his generals could not afford to say this openly. Had they done so, Roosevelt might have turned away and concentrated on the Pacific. Somehow the British had to lure the Americans into sending vast numbers of troops to the United Kingdom, committed to a 'Germany first' strategy, while not actually being prepared to invade France for a long time to come.

In tense summits in Washington and London Churchill effectively bamboozled his new and closest ally. He persuaded the president to agree to concentrate early US landings in North Africa, the Torch operation referred to earlier. Then he bound them into a strategy of striking north through Italy. Meanwhile, he managed to allow the US garrison to keep growing inside Britain while delaying all plans for an early assault on France. The details of this brilliant dance, with Churchill apparently agreeing to US ideas while always pushing them gently off, need not concern us here. Historians and armchair generals (plus some real ones) will argue for ever whether an earlier Allied invasion could have worked, and therefore ended the war in 1943. It seems highly unlikely. It would have meant the British army playing the dominant role. This was an army which had been recently beaten by the Wehrmacht and whose commanders had private doubts about its fighting ability, even after Alamein. It was poorly equipped in tanks and landing craft. A failed invasion and defeat, as Churchill constantly pointed out, would hardly help the Russians. It may have been embarrassing and difficult, but the strategy of delaying until victory was likely was surely the right one.

Yet it came close to lying. Churchill had constantly to spew out a cloud of oompa-oompa verbiage about the coming 'crescendo of activity' in Europe, which was designed to cajole but also to deceive. Some Americans realized this early on. Roosevelt seems not to have done. Later some of the British commanders who were party to the game expressed regret. General Ismay, another veteran of the trenches, said in his memoirs that 'I think we should have come clean, much cleaner than we did and said: "We are frankly horrified because of what we have been through in our lifetime . . . We are not going to go into this until it is a cast-iron certainty." '[21] Certainly, this long delay had consequences. It meant Americans as well as

Russians wondering whether Britain any longer had the courage and self-confidence for a full-scale land war. It chipped away at the reputation of the British Empire, and it would eventually mean that victory was more Russian – particularly Russian – and American than British. When the Overlord landings in Normandy were finally being prepared, it was Eisenhower, not Brooke, who was appointed supreme commander. Part of the shape of the post-war world was revealed in these meetings – Britain deferring to the US from a position of weakness while trying to wheedle and dodge towards a better result; and the Russians regarding both Western powers as liars. On the surface, Churchill was full of praise for the valour of the British fighting forces and brimming with pugnacity and confidence. Meanwhile, he was conducting a stubborn and exhausting operation to delay the big fight. Inglorious, in a way; yet this was also Churchill at his finest, and wisest. Ripeness is all.

Three thousand American soldiers, or GIs, arrived in Belfast in January 1942 almost immediately after the US entered the war. They were the pioneers for a vast build-up of men and materials which turned large corners of England into military camps and would alter for ever the mutual attitudes of the British and Americans. The GIs accounted for more than a million of the 1.4 million foreign troops crowding into Britain by spring 1944, joining Poles, Free French, Canadians, Australians, New Zealanders, South Africans, Dutch, Czechs and even a few Russians and Chinese. If Britain today is the 'world's island', it had a brief foretaste then. Yet from the first it was the Americans who stood out. They were taller, louder, better dressed and richer. They had chocolate bars and cigarettes and plenty of money to spend in pubs and clubs. With them they brought millions of condoms as well as razor blades, nylons and other hard-to-get commodities. Their jive and swing music had already taken Britain by storm in the thirties and their Hollywood stars were as well known in Leicester, Glasgow or Portsmouth as they were back home. Their imported forces radio stations soon drew local British listeners. Their comics were passed from hand to hand until ragged and their jargon spread like a fever.

While US camps the size of market towns sprang up, and unfamiliar, too-big-to-be-true trucks, tank transporters and cars pushed their way through the country lanes of Devon and Wales, and while vast tracts of East Anglia were given over to the United States Air Force, the Americaning was also about sex, sounds, tastes and friendship. If the US held the future leadership of the free world, the GIs just looked and sounded like the future. Not surprisingly, all this went down badly with British men, including soldiers with their baggier, dowdier uniforms and their sparse pay packets as wives and girlfriends ogled something better. 'Over-paid, over-sexed and over here,' went the British jibe. 'Under-sexed, under-paid and under Eisenhower,' the GIs replied. It is estimated that around 20,000 children were born from relationships between British women and American servicemen. More than 100,000 'GI brides' would emigrate to the US from Britain after the war.

There was one particular issue which became a public talking point and certainly provided a foretaste of post-war Britain. More than a tenth of the GIs, some 130,000 men, were black. To understand just what a shock this must have been, the total black population of Britain before the war was estimated at just 8,000. The US authorities tried to retain the 'color bar' or 'Jim Crow' regulations which at home kept black and white men from drinking or socializing together.[22] In Britain, some expressed horror. The War Cabinet decided that the Americans should not expect British civil or military authorities to help segregation: 'So far as concerned admission to canteens, public houses, theatres, cinemas and so forth, there would and must be no restriction of the facilities hitherto extended, to coloured persons.' A public opinion poll in 1943 showed strong British hostility to segregation. Yet Britain too was a racist society. It was markedly anti-Semitic, even in the middle of the Hitler war, and the Empire was underpinned by a residual belief in the hierarchy of races. So it is hardly surprising that there were references to 'jungle behaviour' in the papers after reports of black GIs and white women fraternizing, or that British men too found the idea of black Americans in nightclubs threatening. If they were to be treated equally, what about Indians and Africans from the Commonwealth? Here the 'new attitudes' of a more liberal and leftish country taking stock in the middle of war clashed with the old attitudes of an imperial power in which the white man was top dog – old attitudes that would take a terminal battering from the Japanese in Malaya.

The Americaning of Britain was intimate as well as political. It would last, as the pro-Soviet mania of 1942 did not. It meant that post-war Britain would be more conditioned to the American goods and attitudes which would soon begin to colonize the Western world. Many families kept in touch with Americans who returned home. Churchill became almost as much an American hero as a British one and his sentimental belief in the spiritual oneness of the two English-speaking peoples was widely accepted through the fifties and sixties. In turn, Roosevelt's death in 1945 was treated in Britain as the demise of a British leader. The mourning here was widespread and intense, as it would not be for any modern U.S. president. Just as important, with key Labour leaders now bound into the alliance, Attlee and Bevin would be co-creators of the post-war world of NATO. The wartime summits, rows, games and agreements had consequences which touch our lives still. They are barely history.

The War on Germany

The second phase of the war showed what the British could do if they were well supplied (by America) and sufficiently bossed about by a determined government. Britain became a country organized around a single aim. It was partly an armed camp but also partly a nationalized industrial giant. Of the 32 million Britons of working age, which then meant over fourteen, 22 million had been mobilized in one way or another. As the official Ministry of Information booklet put it after the war, with no exaggeration, 'Britain has been fanatical in stripping herself for war.' Government controls seemed to apply to everything except poetry, sex and dreaming. Under 5 per cent of spending was on goods that were not controlled, either by rationing or by price. State-set wages and conditions spread from Ernie Bevin's Ministry of Labour in all directions, covering farm labourers and tea-shop assistants, railwaymen and bricklayers. Country girls and older men in the cities could find themselves ordered scores or hundreds of miles away to work where they were needed. Around 100,000 men were compelled to become coal miners. From December 1943 onwards, a ballot picked out one in ten seventeen-year-olds to serve the country down the mines, rather than in the forces, causing great resentment, though in the end only 21,000 boys actually served in that manner.

Of all the industries partly rationalized and taken under Whitehall control, aircraft production was the most famous. By the middle of 1944 more than 1.7 million people were engaged, one way or another, in building bombers and fighters: British production rose from 3,000 planes a year before the war to 26,000 by 1944, and they were much more complicated aircraft, too. Engine production rose nearly five-fold. Production of aluminium, iron ore, timber and steel jumped. Overall, an astonishing 102,000 aircraft, from Spitfires and Mosquitos to the vast Lancaster and Halifax bombers and the new Meteor jet, were built in Britain during the war. Doing this meant extraordinary changes in British industry. At the top end, rivals had to cooperate. Rolls-Royce, producers of the vital Merlin engines, teamed up with the mass car maker Ford, who built a new factory in Manchester, staffed partly by women workers, where they stripped back the painstaking Rolls-Royce production process in Derby to make the engines faster and almost a third cheaper. It was one small example of the kind of jump in efficiency Britain had failed to show before the war, and would fail to show again soon afterwards. Indeed, the overall pattern was of desperate if ingenious extempore flexibility. Chains of sub-contractors were involved, ranging from housewives in back rooms and tiny woodworking firms right up to the main factories in Southampton or Castle Bromwich. To make the Mosquito, church-pew carvers and piano makers were roped in. Lancaster bombers were assembled on a Northampton airfield from parts made in shoe factories and bus garages. Firms that once made roll-down blinds for shops or printed cardboard boxes, or built fat-fryers for fish and chip shops, found themselves building fuselages and gun turrets. This was a mobilized country: but it was a mobilized country of craftsmen and small traders, not the Soviet Union or National Socialist Germany.

The effect on the millions working on wartime production was both exhausting and liberating. Women entering factories for the first time found friendships and pride in their achievements, as well as aching feet and boredom. Men who had been classed as unskilled before the war were hurriedly trained and found their pay packets fattening. Young trade union activists or shop stewards found the weight on them from their union officials higher up the chain suddenly lifted. Many of the latter had become government functionaries, leaving a power vacuum. Though striking had been made illegal at the start of the war, strikes continued, particularly in the coal mines and the very same engineering works producing aircraft, guns and tanks. There were more than 1,700 strikes in 1943 and nearly 2,200 the following year – small beer by pre- and post-war standards but enough to worry both Churchill and Bevin. They were the result of long hours, old-style managers irritating new workers and skilled workers trying to stay ahead of the new arrivals. Far from strikes being caused by communist agitators, the communists were in general keen to keep production thriving in order to help Moscow. To keep up industrial morale, canteens, resting places and entertainments were laid on, from radio's *Music While You Work* to the travelling singers and musicians of ENSA (the Entertainments National Service Association) and CEMA, a more highbrow version, which would eventually morph into the Arts Council. ENSA provided comedians and stars such as Vera Lynn and George Formby, who would tour factories and perform lunch-hour concerts, but also some rather lower-grade fare, much complained of. CEMA offered classical recitals, and even stripped-down operas.

This was not the start of a permanent industrial shake-up of Britain. It was temporary, perhaps even more temporary than it seemed at the time. The spiders' webs of industrial cooperation formed under war pressures would break in peace. Old rivalries reasserted themselves. The 1945 government's nationalizations brought some rationalization too, but never came near the heart of the new industries. Above all, the great focus on winning the war was bought at the price of bankrupting Britain as an international power. Her empire would fall away and previously vital overseas assets would have to be liquidated to pay the Americans for their help. Industrially, Britain's war was an exhausting one-off sprint by a scared creature in late middle age, not the appearance of a freshly trained athlete on the world arena. In some areas British industrial achievement was still world-class. The great Mulberry harbours, vast steel erections completed in secret on the Kent marshes and at Southampton by tens of thousands of welders and labourers, to be towed out to the Normandy beaches to provide instant D-Day ports, were perhaps the most spectacular examples. The jet aircraft, sophisticated radar systems, superb bombers, bouncing bombs and vastly more powerful engines produced during 1939–45 showed that Britain retained her ingenuity. What all this hid was a creaking industrial base and bleeding financial position, both of them revealed only too starkly when peace came.

For those directing the war, the great questions were about how the mighty but temporary national force should be used. It does not help to increase production of the wrong things. We have seen how Churchill fought to delay the invasion of France. He spewed out other ideas all the time for new ways to get at Germany – through the Balkans, via Rome, or Norway – but until D-Day his real options were limited. This led to the most controversial and least defensible of all the big choices Britain made: the concentration on heavy bombing of German cities. In the early phases of the war, bombing by the RAF was generally ineffective and low key. British bombers were too small and too few to do a lot of damage. Unlike Germany, Britain had concentrated on defensive radar, rather than offensive radio-beam tracking, so British accuracy was worse than the Luftwaffe's. Sending out the RAF's bombing squadrons was more a morale-booster than serious warfare – a defiant raspberry from a country on her back, not a punch from a standing man. But as the long waiting of the besieged went on, the notion that the war could be won by bombing grew stronger. It had been firmly held by military thinkers and scientists in the thirties. The RAF, developing as an imperial police force, was overexcited by the power of light bombers – handy to flatten Iraqi villages and terrify native horsemen, but of less use against a modern power. By 1941 it had a new generation of long-range bombers, but they did not have direction-finding equipment sufficiently accurate to hit military bases or factories from a high altitude. Nor were they well enough protected to fly low. During that year, Bomber Command was suffering horrendous losses for little impact in Germany. According to one of its historians, 'the entire front line of Bomber Command had been statistically wiped out in less than four months'.[23] How, then, should they be used – and where?

By the spring of 1942 the aircraft factories were delivering hundreds of new, four-engined bombers to the RAF equipped with better direction-finding radio systems. There was also a new policy: destroy German cities. It came from Frederick Lindemann, the German-born scientist who was now Lord Cherwell. He was one of Churchill's closest friends and advisers: Churchill used to muse that Cherwell's brain was 'a wonderful piece of mechanism'. The mechanism now turned to destruction. Based on what he said was careful analysis of the effect of raids on Hull and Birmingham, Cherwell wrote to Churchill forecasting that Britain's output of heavy bombers could make a third of the German population homeless in that country's fifty-eight main towns: 'There seems little doubt that this would break the spirit of the people.' The memo became known as the 'de-housing paper' since Cherwell spoke of Germans being 'turned out of house and home'. Of course, given the effects of incendiary and high-explosive bombing, de-housing would also mean mass killing of non-combatant men, women and children. Straightforward language was avoided. Anyway, would it work? Morale had not broken in Britain.

A feud began. Cherwell, an arrogant and opinionated man, had fallen out badly with that other favoured adviser Tizard, who had lost his job after returning from his Washington mission. The two were in many ways similar. Like Tizard, Cherwell had spent time in the Great War trying out his radical theories about aircraft with himself as test pilot, and both men were devoted to the idea that technology could win this war. Neither was soft on the 'Boche', though Cherwell was the more extreme – he was also a supporter of proposals to 'pastoralize' post-war Germany, returning it to a pre-industrial farming country. Tizard was more cautious, less arrogant, and now he hit back at the Cherwell paper, accusing him of being 'extremely misleading' and reaching 'entirely wrong decisions . . . with a consequent disastrous result on the war'. He did not say destroying German towns was immoral. He did say it would not have the decisive effect Cherwell thought, and he feared that to devote Britain's resources to carpet-bombing would leave the battle for the Atlantic dangerously close. Cherwell snorted. He could afford to snort. He had Churchill's ear. What Tizard did not know at the time was that Cherwell had deliberately misquoted the effects on Hull and Birmingham.[24] In fact the relevant document had found no

signs of panic in either city, nor any great effect from bombing on
their morale or health. It was a shabby piece of evidence-tweaking
that would have awesome consequences.

The man who directed Bomber Command was Sir Arthur Harris,
known to history as 'Bomber Harris' but known to his crews, so
many of whom died, as 'Butcher'. He had fought in the Great War
as a pilot and commanded imperial bombing squadrons after it
ended. Energetic, coarse and direct, other service chiefs feared he
had too strong an influence on Churchill – though Churchill seems
to have found Harris a little too much. Once he was stopped by a
police constable for racing his Bentley at breakneck speed between
his headquarters at High Wycombe and London. 'You might have
killed somebody, sir,' the policeman told him. 'Young man,' replied
Harris, 'I kill thousands of people every night.' He was a devoted
believer in the ability of bombing to end the war. It was the only
way of defeating 'the Boche', he said; an offensive of the right weight
for long enough would 'be something that no country in the world
could endure'. He added that it was anybody's guess what effort, and
how long, would be needed. One of the earliest raids under him was
on Lübeck, an ancient medieval port which was lightly defended
and, said Harris, built more 'like a fire-lighter than a human habita-
tion'. He had wanted his crews to be well 'blooded', as in fox
hunting, and was delighted at the carnage caused to a gentle and
unimportant place. This was not a subtle fighter.

By the end of the war he had a thunderous, awesome fleet of
four-engined bombers, some 1,600 of them, under his command. It
has been estimated that building, sustaining and using this giant fleet
took up to a third of the country's resources during the war, a vast
amount. This was aluminium and steel, factories and skill, machine-
tools and oil that might otherwise have gone into long-range aircraft
to protect the convoys, or into new British tanks and weaponry for
the coming invasion. A choice was made. More than 55,000 Bomber
Command aircrew were killed and nearly 10,000 shot down and
taken prisoner. This made serving on a British bomber more dangerous than any other job on either side except crewing a German
U-boat. Though Bomber Command had some glamorous and
famous figures, including Leonard Cheshire and Guy Gibson, most
of its people were lower-middle class and less glamorous than the

'Brylcreem Boys' of Fighter Command. They suffered terribly but their morale held.

For this expense – what? It is estimated that as many as 600,000 men, women and children were killed by Bomber Command and by the American bombers which began to arrive in East Anglia from 1942. Most were not soldiers or even vital industrial workers. Many were refugees or slave labourers from other parts of Nazi-occupied Europe. After Lübeck came Cologne, Hamburg, the Ruhr, Essen, Berlin and Dresden. The slaughter harrowed and shocked Germans and led to a flood of bitter anti-Goering and anti-Hitler jokes, but German citizens had no way to topple the regime. There were major diversions from the carpet-bombing of cities. At different times the RAF was ordered to concentrate on oil supplies, transport networks and pre-D-Day military targets. Yet, thanks to the German industrial leader Albert Speer's dispersal of industry and similar makeshifts to those used in Britain, the bombing is estimated to have cut German industrial production by only a tenth or less. Only once the land war was being lost did German industry collapse. The bombing diverted Luftwaffe forces and much artillery from the Russian front, which pleased Stalin, and therefore bought Churchill more time before D-Day. We cannot know what battles it saved, but it emphatically did not win the war. It did not break the spirit of Germany any more than the Blitz broke the spirit of the British.

The thing ended, in effect, with Dresden, on 14–15 February 1945. By now Germany was teetering on the edge of surrender, essentially defeated. Bomber Command and the Americans returned again and again with massive fleets, creating a firestorm in Germany's seventh largest town and burning or blowing to pieces up to 100,000 people. The purpose was to interrupt German communications to the east and to harm 'morale'. Dresden had been one of the loveliest cities of old Germany, a cultural and artistic centre known throughout the world, almost on the scale of Venice. Its destruction sent, if not a shudder, then a thin shiver of unease, even through the overlords of the Allied war effort. Churchill, who was as responsible for Dresden as anyone – he had spoken of east German cities as 'especially attractive targets' – now changed his tune. He wrote to the chief of the air staff that, 'The destruction of Dresden remains a serious query against the conduct of Allied bombing' and ordered 'more precise concentration upon military objectives ... rather than on mere acts of terror and wanton destruction, however impressive'. The military historian Max Hastings has justly commented: 'It is impossible to regard this memorandum as anything other than a calculated political attempt by the prime minister to distance himself from the bombing of Dresden and the rising controversy surrounding the area offensive.' Bomber Command was awarded no campaign medal. Harris was not given the kind of honour heaped on similarly senior military leaders – in protest at his men's treatment he refused a peerage. Churchill insisted on a baronetcy eight years later. In 1992 when a statue was unveiled to him by the Queen Mother, no member of the cabinet attended.

The End of the Affair

The period from the great build-up of American forces in Britain to the end of the Hitler war in Berlin was long and bloody. The Overlord landings on D-Day at five French beaches by American, British and Canadian forces from 6 June 1944 were an astonishing achievement, technically and in terms of courage and subterfuge. The secret had held. Phantom armies of inflatable tanks, ambitious misinformation and extraordinarily tight security meant that von Rundstedt, the German commander-in-chief, believed until the last minute that the invasion would come far to the east, between Calais and Dieppe, though Hitler always suspected it would be Normandy. Nevertheless, the Allies' armada, giant though it was, was limited by the landing craft and the size of the beaches so that only nine divisions could reach France in the first attack. This compares with fifty-eight defensive German divisions, of which ten were fast-moving Panzer commands. True, the Germans had a long line to defend and, by spring 1944, had been thoroughly beaten in the air. But had German commanders moved faster, and had their intelligence been better, it is perfectly possible that they could have flung back the invaders within the first few days. This was a horrendously dangerous operation, and no amount of planning could have made it anything else.

As in North Africa and Italy, there were rows between British and American commanders and much later argument about mistakes made. Montgomery had been placed under Eisenhower, the supreme commander, as the commander of all the Allied ground forces for Overlord. At St Paul's School in west London he had laid out a ninety-day plan to take the coast and break out, with the British forces drawing the main German attack to the east, leaving the Americans to wheel round further west and head for the heartland of France. Bad weather delayed the full plan, and there was much controversy about whether Montgomery's tanks, having achieved a major advance near Caen, then missed a great opportunity to break through. Certainly, British forces got stuck, and the near destruction of Caen by bombing has since been criticized as a war crime. American commanders, notably Montgomery's old enemy General Patton, argued that he had been too slow and could have smashed a weak German line.

Later on, with British forces reaching Antwerp in Belgium, less than a hundred miles from the Rhine, there was another British pause. In fact it turned out that there was only a paltry German defence prepared – including, in the words of one military historian, 'policemen, sailors, convalescent sick and wounded, as well as boys of sixteen'.[25] With an Allied majority of twenty to one in tanks and near complete air superiority, there was a golden chance to finish the war in September 1944. Had it been taken, a further half million British and American soldiers might not have died – certainly, the British First Airborne Division would not have been sacrificed in the failed Arnhem operation. Uncountable numbers would have been saved from concentration camps or immolation in bombed cities and the Russians would have ended the war far further east than they did. Arguments about why this chance was lost founder in mutual recrimination about intelligence, strategy, tactics and courage between British and American commanders.

All the British public knew at the time was that after the heroic news of the invasion itself, advances seemed to be frustratingly slow, as in Italy. Why? The truth seems complicated, a failure caused by divisions in the command, bad transport systems – including a mere 1,400 British-built lorries unusable because of faulty pistons – and a certain complacency about the inevitability of German collapse. This was based on a misunderstanding of Hitler's power and of the continuing devotion to him in the minds of millions. The German army, told they were fighting to protect their nation from annihilation, fought hard, cleverly and tenaciously. Nowhere, from the hedges of Normandy to the banks of the Rhine did the Allied armies have it easy. In December 1944, pursuing a wild 'Hitler Order', the German army hit back with a surprise counter-attack in just the same place as the 1940 blitzkrieg on France, and with the same intention of cutting off the British army and forcing a second Dunkirk. It took the Americans completely by surprise and, though it was contained, was a further bloody shock.

There had been a parallel shock for British forces in Asia. After the early and humiliating defeats by the Japanese, most of the advances had been made at great cost in the Pacific by American forces. In Burma, Orde Wingate's guerrilla force of Chindits – the name taken from a half-lion, half-eagle mythological Burmese beast – had restored some British pride and shown that it was possible to learn new ways of fighting. But in March 1944 the Japanese, who, like the Germans, were now heavily outnumbered and had lost command of the air, counter-attacked from Burma, a daring last-throw operation designed to lead to the invasion of India. They broke across the Indian border and desperate defences at Kohima and Imphal succeeded only thanks to air drops. Luckily the British imperial forces, which included Hindu, Sikh, Muslim, Gurkha and African troops, were superbly commanded by General William Slim. Slim, a burly and much-loved Indian Army officer, then doggedly pursued the broken Japanese across Burma, fighting in appalling conditions. It has been argued that this was all unnecessary, merely intended by Churchill to restore British pride after the imperial humiliations of the previous few years. Yet Slim's army, the 'Forgotten Fourteenth', who never felt they got the admiration they deserved after the war, greatly helped the US forces by drawing in tens of thousands of Japanese, who were therefore not available to defend the Pacific islands.

So the final acts of the war brought ambiguous messages for Britain. Outside the worlds of boys' comics and self-serving memoirs, it was hard to argue that the British were inherently better fighters than other nations. In France, Germany and Burma it seemed that tattered enemy armies, without air cover, without the huge industrial support of the US and without as many troops, could still give British forces nasty surprises. Who was 'superior' now? It is eloquent that, after the war, the dominant images from the Far Eastern campaigns were of the savagery of Japanese prisoner camps. There followed books, drawings and films in which the British depicted themselves almost masochistically as haggard, beaten and sometimes degraded survivors. These celebrated the triumph of the human spirit under atrocious conditions. They were hardly the martial epic of a living empire. Japan was defeated by the vast US war machine and finished off by atomic bombs. The memory of 'little yellow men' with bicycles shattering the defenders of the Raj would not be erased: Indian and Pakistani independence would have followed at any event, but it was made certain by the Japanese war.

Nor could the war be claimed to have ended in every way gloriously. The devastated cities of Germany and the horror of the camps cast a grey pall over things, apart from the eruption of joy and relief on VE Day itself. The Russians squatted over half of Europe and those who wanted to look at the record knew what that would mean. In October 1944, at a summit with Stalin in Moscow, Churchill had acquiesced in the first stage of the carve-up, asking the Soviet leader, 'How would it do for you to have ninety per cent predominance in Romania, for us to have ninety per cent of the say in Greece, and go fifty-fifty about Yugoslavia?'[26] He then drew up a handwritten paper listing the percentages of influence for these countries, plus Hungary and Bulgaria, which Stalin simply ticked with a blue pencil. Worse, perhaps – since Soviet control of most of those areas was a military fait accompli – Churchill joked with Stalin about the unspeakableness of the Poles. It was a far cry from his early anti-Bolshevik crusading and a far cry too from the day Britain had declared war in 1939 in response to the invasion of Poland. This would be a new world, torn down the middle, with little space for a British Empire, or even a strong independent British voice. At home, in a series of by-elections, independents and socialists had trounced Tory and National Government candidates. As early as 1944 Tom Harrisson, whose Mass Observation system had done so much to record the real feelings of the British in wartime, wrote that voters would distinguish between 'Winston the War Leader, Bulldog of Battle' and the prime minister who was 'no man of peace, of domestic policy or human detail'.[27]

We could call this the end of the Age of Churchill. At no time in history had the British played a more important role than during 1900 to 1945, when the world's worst wars were fought. It measured up to the age of Elizabethan England, the winning of empire, and the high noon of Victorian inventiveness, though the country's aggression and even vitality had waned. This was a time, barely more than half a modern lifetime, during which Britain changed from being an imperial island, with essentially aristocratic values, glaring outwards, to become the more inward-looking nation we still are. We had gone out into the world. Now, the world would come home to us. We had been the noisy, red-jacketed, grossly unequal Royal Navy-worshipping land of Young Winston. Now we were the crumpled, relieved and bolshie democracy of VE Day, frightened and freed to become the modern British. The crowds cheered 'Our Winnie' and gave him his V-for-victory sign but they were saying goodbye. He was already a picture from an old story. In researching this story, I found myself haunted by the references by Churchill and his military leaders to the lack of fighting spirit they found in British soldiers. These private comments were forgotten after the war was over, pushed out of sight. We moved on. Yet sometimes the most important truths come from the side of the mouth. The truth is that after the First World War the British had become less willing to fight. Far from being shameful, as Churchill thought, this was a reasonable, modern response. Only nations traumatized by humiliating defeats and perverted by ideological mania were still keen fighters. By the beginning of the Second World War, the British were not among them.

By the time it ended, Britannia had become Britain. It had taken the worst wars in human history to shake away the illusions of superiority over lesser breeds and give 'the common man' a slightly better break. Britannia had been grand. Her servants had been high-minded, decent people more often than they were bullies or sadists. But she had not shown the vigour of the evil empires, Nazi and Soviet, nor the swirling energy of America. At home she was homely. Abroad her people had lost their appetite for territorial expansion or for keeping other peoples down. So, at last, one of the largest and least likely empires in all human history was dying. Yet Britannia's finest hour really had come as she expired. In 1940 the British under Churchill had not done the obvious thing and walked away from the fight. They had drawn together, and together they had stupidly, unimaginatively and unreasonably fought on. This was ridiculous. Modern Britain is our share of the reward.

Notes

Part One: Living in the Future, 1900–1914

1. See Christopher Hibbert, *Queen Victoria: A Personal History*, HarperCollins, 2000.
2. See R. C. K. Ensor, *England, 1870–1914*, Oxford University Press, 1936.
3. Winefride Elwes, *The Feilding Album*, Geoffrey Bles, 1950, extracted in *The Faber Book of Reportage*, ed. John Carey, Faber & Faber, 1987.
4. *Illustrated London News*, 26 January 1901.
5. Fred Kaplan, *Henry James*, quoted in Roy Hattersley, *The Edwardians*, Abacus, 2004.
6. Randolph S. Churchill, *Winston S. Churchill*, vol. I, *Youth, 1874–1900*, Heinemann, 1966.
7. *The Times*, 1 September 1902, quoted in Asa Briggs, *Seebohm Rowntree*, Longmans, 1961.
8. Quoted in Randolph S. Churchill, *Winston S. Churchill*, vol. II, *Young Statesman, 1901–1914*, Heinemann, 1967.
9. All quotations from *Nature*, October 1901, which reproduced Galton's lecture, with diagrams, in full.
10. Ibid.
11. See Nicholas Wright Gilliam, *A Life of Sir Francis Galton*, Oxford University Press, 2001.
12. David Smith, *H. G. Wells: Desperately Mortal*, Yale University Press, 1986.
13. Gilliam, *A Life of Sir Francis Galton*.
14. See Robert Lloyd George, *David and Winston*, John Murray, 2005, and Peter Brent, *The Edwardians*, BBC Books, 1972.
15. Margot Asquith, *Autobiography*, Eyre & Spottiswoode, 1962.
16. Quoted in Randolph S. Churchill, *Winston S. Churchill*, II.
17. Ibid.
18. John Grigg, *Lloyd George: The People's Champion*, HarperCollins, 1997.
19. Roy Jenkins, *Asquith*, Collins, 1964.
20. See Richard Anthony Baker, *British Music Hall: An Illustrated History*, Sutton Publishing, 2005.
21. Ibid.

22. Colin MacInnes, *Sweet Saturday Night*, MacGibbon & Kee, 1967.

23. Winston Churchill, *My Early Life: A Roving Commission*, Thornton Butterworth, 1930, and Randolph S. Churchill, *Winston S. Churchill*, I.

24. J. B. Priestley, *The Edwardians*, Heinemann, 1970.

25. Asquith, *Autobiography*.

26. All this is taken from Ruth Hall, *Marie Stopes, A Biography*, André Deutsch, 1977.

27. Quoted from the Shaw papers, for instance in Julia Briggs, *A Woman of Passion*, Hutchinson, 1987.

28. Different accounts can be found in David Smith, *H. G. Wells – Desperately Mortal*, Yale University Press, 1986; Victoria Glendinning, *Rebecca West*, Weidenfeld & Nicolson, 1987; and John Sutherland, *Mrs Humphry Ward*, Clarendon Press, 1990.

29. See Fran Abrams, *Freedom's Cause*, Profile Books, 2003.

30. Jill Liddington, *Rebel Girls*, Virago Press, 2006.

31. Hannah Mitchell, *The Hard Way Up*, Faber & Faber, 1968.

32. Jill Liddington's *Rebel Girls* was the groundbreaking study that has done most to set this right.

33. Rebecca West's real name was Cissie Fairfield, but I have used her pseudonym for convenience. Her story can be found in Glendinning, *Rebecca West*.

34. Donald McCormick, *The Mask of Merlin*, Macdonald, 1963.

35. Grigg, *Lloyd George*.

36. Quoted in Roy Jenkins, *Churchill*, Macmillan, 2001.

37. E. P. Hennock in W. J. Mommsen, ed., *The Emergence of the Welfare State in Britain and Germany*, Croom Helm/German Historical Institute, 1981.

38. William George, 'My Brother and I', London, 1958.

39. R. F. Foster, *Lord Randolph Churchill*, Oxford University Press, 1988.

40. Randolph Churchill, *Winston S. Churchill*, II.

41. Lord Willoughby de Broke, *The Passing Years*, Houghton Mifflin, 1924.

42. See David Cannadine, *The Decline and Fall of the British Aristocracy*, Yale University Press, 1990.

43. George Dangerfield, *The Strange Death of Liberal England*, Harrison Smith/Robert Haas, 1935.

44. See S. J. Taylor, *The Great Outsiders*, Weidenfeld & Nicolson, 1996, and I. F. Clarke, *Voices Prophesying War*, Oxford University Press, 1966.

45. Quoted in Clarke, *Voices Prophesying War*.

46. Caroline Benn, *Keir Hardie*, Hutchinson, 1992.

47. See Jonathan Schneer, *Ben Tillett*, Croom Helm, 1982.

48. See Juliet Nicolson, *The Perfect Summer*, John Murray, 2006.

49. Pat Thane, 'Labour and Welfare', in D. Tanner, P. Thane and N. Tiratsoo, eds., *Labour's First Century*, Cambridge University Press, 2000.

50. Grigg, *Lloyd George*.
51. Max Pemberton, *The Life of Sir Henry Royce*, Selwyn & Blount, 1936.
52. Ibid.
53. See Peter Thorold, *The Motoring Age*, Profile Books, 2003.
54. All quotes from *Motor Cars and Driving* by Lord Northcliffe and others, Longmans Green & Co., 1904 edition.
55. Lord Montagu of Beaulieu, *Rolls of Rolls-Royce*, Cassell, 1966.
56. H. Rider Haggard, *Child of Storm*, quoted in Tom Pocock, *Rider Haggard and the Lost Empire*, Weidenfeld & Nicolson, 1993.
57. See David Gilmour, *The Long Recessional*, Pimlico, 2003.
58. Ibid.
59. See A. T. Q. Stewart, *The Ulster Crisis*, Faber & Faber, 1967.
60. Sir Edward Grey, *Twenty-Five Years*, London, 1925.
61. Quoted in Michael and Eleanor Brock, eds., *H. H. Asquith: Letters to Venetia Stanley*, Oxford University Press, 1982.

Part Two: The Meaning of Hell, 1914–1918

1. Quoted in Brian MacArthur, ed., *For King and Country*, Little, Brown, 2008.
2. For these statistics see J. M. Winter, *The Great War and the British People*, Harvard University Press, 1986.
3. See Dan Todman, *The Great War*, Continuum, 2005, working on figures from Winter, *The Great War and the British People*.
4. Gordon Corrigan, *Mud, Blood and Poppycock*, Cassell, 2003.
5. Quoted in Peter Parker, *The Old Lie*, Constable, 1986.
6. See ibid.
7. Quoted in the facsimile edition of the *Wipers Times*, introduced by Patrick Beaver, Peter Davies, 1973.
8. All letters quoted from Michael and Eleanor Brock, eds., *H. H. Asquith: Letters to Venetia Stanley*, Oxford University Press, 1982.
9. *The Duff Cooper Diaries*, ed. John Julius Norwich, Phoenix, 2005.
10. Corrigan, *Mud, Blood and Poppycock*.
11. Martin Gilbert, *Winston S. Churchill*, vol. III, *The Challenge of War, 1914–1916*, Heinemann, 1971.
12. For Fisher generally, see Jan Morris, *Fisher's Face*, Penguin, 1996.
13. See Robert K. Massie, *Castles of Steel*, Cape, 2004.
14. Philip Gibbs, *The War Dispatches*, Anthony Gibbs & Philips Ltd, 1964.
15. The story is told fully in Adam Hochschild's *King Leopold's Ghost*, Macmillan, 1999.
16. Sean Keating, 'William Orpen, A Tribute', in *Ireland Today*, quoted in Bruce Arnold, *Orpen, Mirror to an Age*, Hamish Hamilton, 1983.

17. William Orpen, *An Onlooker in France, 1917–1919*, BiblioBazaar LLC, 2008.
18. Frank Moraes, *Jawaharlal Nehru*, Macmillan, 1956.
19. See John Grigg, *Lloyd George: The People's Champion*, HarperCollins, 1997, for all this.
20. Robert K. Massie, *Castles of Steel*, Pimlico, 2005.
21. See ibid.
22. See notes to John Grigg, *Lloyd George: War Leader*, Allen Lane, 2002.
23. See Arthur Marwick, *The Deluge*, Bodley Head, 1975.
24. Sir Robert Bruce Lockhart, cited ibid.
25. Corrigan, *Mud, Blood and Poppycock*.
26. See Ian Passingham, *All the Kaiser's Men*, Sutton Publishing, 2003.
27. *Diaries of Siegfried Sassoon*, ed. Rupert Hart-Davies, Faber & Faber, 1983.
28. Marvin Swartz, *The Union of Democratic Control*, Oxford University Press, 1971.

Part Three: Keeping Our Balance, 1919–1939

1. Charles Loch Mowat, *Britain Between the Wars*, Methuen, 1955.
2. Jon Savage, *Teenage: The Creation of Youth*, Chatto & Windus, 2007.
3. K. E. Meyrick, *Secrets of the 43*, John Long, 1933.
4. H. A. Taylor, *The Life of Viscount Brentford*, Stanley Paul, 1933.
5. Tom Cullen, *Maundy Gregory, Purveyor of Honours*, Bodley Head, 1974.
6. David Clark, *Victor Grayson: Labour's Lost Leader*, Quartet, 1985; Donald McCormick, *Murder by Perfection*, John Long, 1970.
7. Roy Jenkins, *Baldwin*, Collins, 1987.
8. See John Worthen, *D. H. Lawrence: The Life of an Outsider*, Allen Lane, 2005.
9. See Miranda Seymour, *Ottoline Morrell: Life on the Grand Scale*, Hodder & Stoughton, 1992.
10. See David Kynaston, *The City of London*, vol. III, *Illusions of Gold*, Chatto & Windus, 1999.
11. See Martin Gilbert, *Winston S. Churchill*, vol. V, *Prophet of Truth, 1922–1939*, Heinemann, 1976.
12. I am heavily indebted for these passages to Matthew Sweet's 2006 BBC4 documentary *Silent Britain*, available on DVD from the British Film Institute.
13. Rachael Low, *The History of the British Film*, George Allen & Unwin, 1950.
14. Alan Crisp, 'The Working-Class Owner-Occupied Home of the 1930s', Oxford University M.Litt thesis, 1998, available on the internet at www.thesis.clara.net.
15. Finn Jensen, *The English Semi-Detached House*, Ovolo Books, 2007; much of the material in the preceding two paragraphs comes from this work.

16. Robert Finch, *The World's Airways*, University of London Press, 1938.

17. Robin Higham, *Britain's Imperial Air Routes, 1918–1939*, G. T. Foulis & Co., 1960.

18. Wyndham Lewis, *Hitler*, Chatto & Windus, 1933.

19. All quotes here and in the previous paragraph come from David Marquand, *Ramsay MacDonald*, Cape, 1977.

20. Professor Keith Laybourn in Greg Rosen, ed., *Dictionary of Labour Biography*, Politicos, 2001.

21. Thomas Jones's diary, quoted in Jenkins, *Baldwin*.

22. R. R. James, ed., *Memoirs of a Conservative: J. C. C. Davidson's Memoirs and Papers*, Weidenfeld & Nicolson, 1969.

23. Quoted in Ian McIntyre, *The Expense of Glory: A Life of John Reith*, HarperCollins, 1993.

24. See Asa Briggs, *The BBC: The First Fifty Years*, Oxford University Press, 1985.

25. See Rolf Gardiner's entry in the *Oxford Dictionary of National Biography*.

26. See Richard Thurlow, *Fascism in Britain*, Blackwell, 1987.

27. Kynaston, *The City of London*, III.

28. Stephen Dorril, *Blackshirt: Sir Oswald Mosley and British Fascism*, Viking, 2007.

29. See Jan Morris, *Farewell the Trumpets*, Faber & Faber, 1978.

30. Jessica Mitford, *Hons and Rebels*, Gollancz, 1960.

31. See, among an extensive literature, Jonathan and Catherine Guinness, *The House of Mitford*, Hutchinson, 1984; Mary S. Lovell, *The Mitford Girls*, Little, Brown, 2001; Mitford, *Hons and Rebels*.

32. Nancy Mitford, *Wigs on the Green*, Thornton Butterworth, 1935.

33. Quoted in Frances Donaldson, *Edward VIII*, Weidenfeld & Nicolson, 1974.

34. Lord Beaverbrook, *The Abdication of King Edward VIII*, Hamish Hamilton, 1966.

35. As quoted by Monica Baldwin in Donaldson, *Edward VIII*.

36. The *Nottingham Journal*, quoted ibid.

37. The Duchess of Windsor, *The Heart Has Its Reasons*, Michael Joseph, 1956.

38. Donaldson, *Edward VIII*.

39. All quotations ibid.

40. Quoted from Halifax papers in Andrew Roberts, *The Holy Fox*, Weidenfeld & Nicolson, 1991.

41. Ibid.

42. See David Reynolds, *Summits: Six Meetings that Shaped the Twentieth Century*, Allen Lane, 2007.

43. This paragraph, like earlier ones on Churchill, leans very heavily on volume V of the official Churchill biography by Sir Martin Gilbert, an utterly invaluable source.

Part Four: Through Fire, a New Country, 1939–1945

1. John Colville, *The Fringes of Power*, Hodder & Stoughton, 1985.
2. Angus Calder, *The People's War: Britain, 1939–1945*, Cape, 1969/Pimlico, 1992.
3. Kenneth Clark, *The Other Half*, John Murray, 1977.
4. Martin Gilbert, *Winston S. Churchill*, vol. V, *Prophet of Truth, 1922–1939*, Heinemann, 1976.
5. All quotes from Colville, *The Fringes of Power*.
6. I have relied on accounts by Churchill himself, in his history of the war; on John Lukacs in his splendid *Five Days in London*, Yale University Press, 1999; Paul Addison's *The Road to 1945*, Cape, 1975; Angus Calder's *The Myth of the Blitz* and *The People's War*, Cape, 1991 and 1969; Gilbert's *Winston S. Churchill*, 8 vols., Heinemann, 1966–82; and Roy Jenkins, *Churchill*, Macmillan, 2001.
7. Ben Pimlott, ed., *The Second World War Diaries of Hugh Dalton*, Cape, 1986.
8. From Hugh Sebag-Montefiore, *Dunkirk: Fight to the Last Man*, Viking, 2006.
9. Quoted in Calder, *The People's War*.
10. See Sebag-Montefiore, *Dunkirk*.
11. Colville, *The Fringes of Power*.
12. See Calder, *The Myth of the Blitz*.
13. See Len Deighton, *Blood, Tears and Folly*, Vintage, 2007.
14. For this and other information in this section I have scanned a large amount of literature, but particularly recommend Stephen Bungay, *The Most Dangerous Enemy: A History of the Battle of Britain*, Aurum Press, 2000.
15. Calder, *The Myth of the Blitz*.
16. See Deighton, *Blood, Tears and Folly*.
17. David Mellor, Gill Saunders and Patrick Wright, *Recording Britain*, David & Charles/V&A, 1990.
18. Nigel Hamilton, *Monty, Master of the Battlefield, 1942–44*, Hamish Hamilton, 1983.
19. For all this, see Calder, *The People's War*.
20. Ronald W. Clark, *Tizard*, Methuen, 1965.
21. Andrew Roberts, *Masters and Commanders*, Allen Lane, 2008.
22. David Reynolds, *Rich Relations*, HarperCollins, 1995.
23. Max Hastings, *Bomber Command*, Michael Joseph, 1979.
24. See ibid.
25. Basil Liddell-Hart, *History of the Second World War*, Putnam, 1971.
26. Winston Churchill, *The Second World War*, vol. VI, *Triumph and Tragedy*, Cassell, 1954.
27. See Kevin Jeffreys, *Finest and Darkest Hours*, Atlantic Books, 2002.

Acknowledgements

Writing is a lonely process that requires keeping your bottom stuck to a chair for ridiculous amounts of time. As with other books, I could not have endured writing this one without the help and cheerful encouragement of others, beginning with my wife, Jackie, and our children. Most of it was written in a small garden shed, surrounded by the noise of feral parakeets, which have taken over my part of London. But it would have been impossible without the wonderful London Library and its lovely staff. At a time when so many institutions seem corrupt, or to have failed in their primary job, this private members' library has been for me both a beacon and a refuge. (Which makes it sound like a hot cave; which isn't far off.)

The book would not have been written at all without my mordantly funny agent, Ed Victor, who fed me fish and prodded me at all the right times. Philippa Harrison hacked, shaped and re-ordered my last book; she sculpted, smoothed and sandpapered this one. The team at Macmillan, initially including Andrew Kidd, and latterly Jon Butler, the top man Anthony Forbes-Watson, and the amazing Jacqueline Graham and Lorraine Green, have been kind beyond reason. We have been through some tough times together recently and I cannot imagine a better bunch to have on your side. They make publishing seem huge fun; I hope it really is.

But my final thanks go to another team, who turned the lonely process of writing into the garrulous moveable feast that is documentary film-making. Roly Keating and Janice Hadlow at BBC2 commissioned the series. My great colleague and now, I hope, good friend Chris Granlund was the series producer. The individual films were made by the directors Robin Dashwood, Fatima Salaria, Francis Whately and Roger Parsons, each of them slightly nuts in the best possible way; with the camera genius of Neil Harvey and Lawrence Gardner, the attentive ear of Simon Parmenter and the research efforts of Edmund Moriarty, Lulu Valentine and Kemi Majekodunmi, all of us herded and corralled by Michelle Clinton and Alison Connor in the office. Stuart Robertson was the spectacularly successful and relentless archive researcher; Libby Hand organized us all; and in the creative hothouse of the edit suites, Mike Duly, Jo Wade and Ged Murphy were the editors. We worked very hard and, because life is short, just occasionally we played fairly hard too. I am a lucky man and raise a wobbly glass to them all.

Index

Picture Acknowledgements

Section One

Page 1 – top: © Bettmann / Corbis. 2 – top: © Private collection / The Stapleton Collection / Bridgeman Art Library; bottom: image courtesy of the estate of Graham Laidler / *Punch*. 3 – all: © Getty Images. 4 – top: © Mary Evans Picture Library; bottom: © Press Association Images. 5 – all: © Getty Images. 6 – top: © National Portrait Gallery, London; bottom: © Blue Lantern Studio / Corbis. 7 – top: © National Portrait Gallery, London; bottom: © Mary Evans Picture Library. 8 – all: © Mary Evans Picture Library.

Section Two

Page 1 – all: © Getty Images. 2 – top: © Getty Images; bottom: © Private Collection / The Stapleton Collection / Bridgeman Art Library. 3 – top: © Getty Images; bottom: © Bettmann / Corbis. 4 – top: © Getty Images; bottom: © Mary Evans Picture Library. 5 – © Mary Evans Picture Library. 6 – both: © Getty Images. 7 – top: © Getty Images; bottom: © Mary Evans Picture Library. 8 – top: © Mary Evans Picture Library; bottom, both: © Getty Images.

Section Three

Page 1 – both: © Kibbo Kift Foundation / Museum of London. 2 – top, both: © National Portrait Gallery, London; bottom: © Mary Evans Picture Library / Illustrated London News. 3 – all: © Getty Images. 4 – top: courtesy of the British Cartoon Archive, University of Kent © Mirrorpix; bottom, both: © Getty Images. 5 – all: © Getty Images. 6 – image courtesy of The Advertising Archives. 7 – top: image courtesy of NRM – Pictorial Collection / Science & Society Picture Library; bottom: © Mary Evans Picture Library. 8 – top: © Mary Evans Picture Library; bottom: © Getty Images.

Section Four

Page 1 – both: © Getty Images. 2 – top: © Bettmann / Corbis; bottom: © Getty Images. 3 – both: © Getty Images. 4 – top, both: © Imperial War Museum, London; bottom: © Getty Images. 5 – top: © Getty Images; bottom: © Imperial War Museum, London. 6 – both: © Getty Images. 7 – both: © Getty Images. 8 – top: Bettmann / Corbis; bottom: © Getty Images.

Text Acknowledgments

The author and publisher would also like to thank the following for their kind permission to reproduce copyright material:

Angus Calder for *The People's War* (Jonathan Cape, 1969). The Estate of Winston Churchill for excerpts from his letters, reproduced by kind permission of Curtis Brown Group Ltd. The Estate of Duff Cooper for Diaries, ed. John Julius Norwich (Weidenfeld & Nicolson, 2005). Gordon Corrigan for *Mud, Blood and Poppycock* (Cassell, an imprint of The Orion Publishing Group, 2003). The Estate of T. S. Eliot for *Collected Poems 1909–1962* (© T. S. Eliot), reproduced by kind permission of Faber and Faber Ltd. Ford Madox Ford for *A History of Our Own Time* (Carcanet, 1988). John Griggs for *Lloyd George: The People's Champion* (Harper-Collins, 1997). *Max Hastings for Bomber Command* (Michael Joseph, 1979). The Estate of Frieda Lawrence Ravagli for *Women in Love* by D. H. Lawrence. The Estate of Colin MacInnes for *Sweet Saturday Night* (© Colin MacInnes, 1967), reproduced by kind permission of Curtis Brown Group Ltd. Robert K. Massie for *Castles of Steel* (Jonathan Cape, 2004), reproduced by kind permission of The Random House Group Ltd. The Estate of Hannah Mitchell for *The Hard Way Up* (© Hannah Mitchell), reproduced by kind permission of Faber and Faber Ltd. The Estate of Jessica Mitford for *Hons and Rebels* (© Jessica Treuhaft, 1960, 1989). The Estate of George Orwell for *The Road to Wigan Pier* (© George Orwell, 1937), reproduced by kind permission of Bill Hamilton as the Literary Executor of the Estate of the Late Sonia Brownell Orwell and Secker & Warburg Ltd. The Estate of J. B. Priestley for *The Edwardians* (© J. B. Priestley, 1970), reproduced by kind permission of PFD (www.pfd.co.uk). Andrew Roberts for *Holy Fox: Biography of Lord Halifax* (Weidenfeld & Nicolson, 1991). The Estate of George Sassoon for 'Blighters' and *Diaries of Siegfried Sassoon* (© Siegfried Sassoon). The Estate of Benjamin Seebohm Rowntree for *Poverty: A Study of Town Life* (Policy Press, 2000). Sony / ATV Music Publishing for 'Livin' in the Future' lyrics (© Bruce Springsteen Music, 2007). The Estate of H. G. Wells for *Anticipations, Mankind in the Making and Ann Veronica*, reproduced by kind permission of A. P. Watt Ltd. The Estate of Wallis, Duchess of Windsor for *The Heart Has Its Reasons* (Michael Joseph, 1956). The Estate of Virginia Woolf for *The Diaries of Virginia Woolf* (Hogarth Press), reproduced by kind permission of the executors of the Virginia Woolf Estate and The Random House Group Ltd.

'Engaging, readable, vivid . . . An entertaining and thought-provoking survey of the half-century that destroyed one world and brought another into being'
Scotsman

Between the death of Queen Victoria and the end of the Second World War, Britain was a nation shaken by war and peace. Recovering from the grand wreckage of the old Empire, the people of Britain struggled to answer the question 'How should we live?' Socialism? Feminism? Fascism? In *The Making of Modern Britain*, Andrew Marr looks beyond trench warfare, mass strikes and Spitfires in search of the stories of Britons whose lives are often thrilling like our own. From organic food to drugs, nightclubs to package holidays, crooked bankers to sleazy politicians, the echoes of today's Britain ring from every page.

'The most exciting book of history I can remember reading . . . Exhilarating'
Spectator

'Vivid character studies and colourful vignettes, some of cinematic brilliance . . . Marr has an enviable ability to unravel complex issues and expound them in simple terms'
Guardian

NON-FICTION
Cover design by Two Associates
Union Jack supplied by Jeff Overs / BBC

www.panmacmillan.com

ISBN 978-0-330-51099-8

9 780330 510998

90100

UK £8.99   CDN $14.99